31753

320 BEN
2ⁿᵈ cop

SOCIAL PRINCIPLES AND
THE DEMOCRATIC STATE

D0279476

WITHDRAWN

0 6 JUN 2022

York St John
Library and Information Services
Normal Loan

Please see self service receipt for return date.

RETURNED		
1 5 NOV 2011		

Fines are payable for late return

ohn

3 8025 00166886 5

COLLEGE OF EDUCATION, RIPON

LIBRARY

SOCIAL PRINCIPLES AND
THE DEMOCRATIC STATE

S. I. BENN
B.SC.(ECON.)
Lecturer in Government
University of Southampton

R. S. PETERS
B.A., PH.D.
Reader in Philosophy, Birkbeck College
University of London

London
GEORGE ALLEN & UNWIN LTD
RUSKIN HOUSE   MUSEUM STREET

FIRST PUBLISHED IN 1959
SECOND IMPRESSION 1961
THIRD IMPRESSION 1963
FOURTH IMPRESSION 1965
FIFTH IMPRESSION 1966
SIXTH IMPRESSION 1968
SEVENTH IMPRESSION 1969
EIGHTH IMPRESSION 1971
NINTH IMPRESSION 1973

This book is copyright under the Berne Convention. All rights reserved. Apart from any fair dealing for the purpose of private study, research, criticism or review, as permitted under the Copyright Act, 1956, no part of this publication may be reproduced, stored in retrieval system, or transmitted, in any form or by any means, electronic, electrical, chemical, mechanical, optical, photocopying, recording or otherwise, without the prior permission of the copyright owner. Enquiries should be addressed to the Publishers.

© *George Allen & Unwin Ltd*, 1959
ISBN 0 04 300100 1 *cased*
0 04 300028 2 *paper*

PRINTED IN GREAT BRITAIN
BY COMPTON PRINTING LIMITED
LONDON AND AYLESBURY

PREFACE

There are a great number of students who take Social Philosophy as part either of an Honours Degree or of a Diploma in Social Studies, Sociology, or Public Administration. The authors, in teaching such students, have been constantly embarrassed by the absence of a text-book which takes account of recent developments in philosophy without being too remote from the institutions of the modern welfare state. They therefore set to work with the limited intention of providing a text-book in this field, Richard Peters tackling the ethics and Stanley Benn the politics and institutional analysis. The hope was that there would be a kind of intellectual osmosis in the middle region of social principles.

But this was not how the plan eventually worked out. The chapters on Moral Theory and Justice and Equality were the first to be written and discussed, and they showed that the authors were thinking on remarkably similar lines. These chapters became a growing point for the rest of the book, which thus grew from the centre outwards. This has two results. Firstly, instead of merely 'covering the syllabus' in the mundane manner originally planned, the authors found themselves developing, in a concrete institutional setting, a few central social principles. Secondly, it became increasingly difficult, especially in the central part of the book, to disentangle the ideas of one of the authors from those of the other. They are both to blame, therefore, for whatever defects the book has. And if it be a defect for a modern book on Social Philosophy to have a definite point of view—a cautious Utilitarianism which takes full account of the principle of impartiality—they are equally responsible for that too. They do attempt, however, to give reasons for it. Indeed, this is in a way the theme of the book: the close relationship between what is implied in 'being reasonable' and the principles and institutions of the democratic state.

Thanks are due to Maurice Cranston for his comments on Ch. 15, to A. Phillips Griffiths for his comments on Ch. 11, to Dr Peter Richards and Professor W. E. Armstrong for their comments on Chs. 5, 6, and 7, and to Professor H. L. Hart for his comments on some of the material of Ch. 8 (a substantial part of which was published in an article in *Philosophy*, October 1958) and to Anthony Manser, on whom Stanley Benn tried out many ideas before ever they reached paper, and who helped to point a way out of many difficulties. The authors are especially grateful to Professor W. Harrison who made detailed comments on the completed MS. Thanks are due, too, to Mrs Dunn and Miss Rouse for typing the MS and to Miss Marshallsay for compiling the index. Miriam Benn did much to clarify the ideas, and laboured to simplify the style of the book, in the face of every possible objection and obstruction from its authors. To her they owe their very special thanks, for this and for much besides.

STANLEY BENN

RICHARD PETERS

London and Southampton
1958

CONTENTS

PART THREE

PRINCIPLES OF ASSOCIATION AND THE DEMOCRATIC STATE

PART ONE

SOCIETY: ITS RULES
AND THEIR VALIDITY

CHAPTER 1

SOCIETY AND TYPES OF SOCIAL REGULATION

I. SOCIAL WHOLES

Man, said Aristotle, is a political animal. He lives in society and is thereby able to survive, to talk, and to develop a culture. This is no doubt true, but the initial difficulty in theorizing about society is to be clear what we are talking about. If an ornithologist says that woodpeckers live in trees there is little to puzzle us. For trees and birds are easily picked out; they have definite contours; they move about; they have parts which mutually influence one another so as to make them both recognizable wholes. But when a social theorist tells us that men live in society, the matter is more puzzling. We are not inclined to dispute what he says, but it is not quite clear what he is saying. For though men are recognizable wholes like birds, societies are not wholes of the same order at all. The way in which a man lives in a society is quite different from the way in which a woodpecker lives in a tree. For membership of a society does not necessarily imply residence in some larger spatial whole. What then does it imply?

The first and obvious observation to make is that there is no such thing as society. By this is meant, firstly, that men are members of various societies rather than of society, and, secondly, that societies are not things in the ordinary sense of 'thing'. The most obvious characteristic of a thing is that it is spatially extended with recognizable contours. Yet quite obviously such a criterion does not fit the Society for the Propagation of Christian Knowledge. Indeed, very few societies conform to this criterion. For all members would have to be present at a given place—a rare occurrence at even the annual general meeting of any society. The fact, however, that societies are not things in the obvious sense of the word 'thing' need not worry us unduly; for neither are minds, and yet we all think that we have got them—except, perhaps, behaviourists. People palpably are things—though, of course, things of a special sort—and when we speak of societies we are using language to pick out types of order which make an intelligible pattern of the activities which people share with one another. As a matter of fact we have to be taught to recognize forms of order which seem obviously given to us, as the psychologists have shown. Language itself makes possible a new level of life; by initiation into it we are also introduced to the contours of our environment. We learn words for cats, cars and clouds. And the process of learning the word is part of the process of learning the type of order intimated by it.

The trouble, however, about societies is that they are *not* given for us to recognize in the obvious way in which trees, toads, and turnips are. What we call a social whole is largely a matter of our construction; for the conventions of our language mirror the social forms which we develop. Of course, our selectivity and constructiveness enter into all our classifications, but in the case of social wholes much less is given and much more is constructed.

Consider, for instance, the case of social classes about which so much has been written since Marx popularized this way of grouping people together. His notion of class presupposed a highly sophisticated theory about the relation of people to the means of production. The proletarian class, for example, where those who sold their labour but owned none of the means of production. Yet others, who did not share Marx's theory about the significance for social life of people's relationship to the means of production, held that it was more fruitful to define a social class in terms, perhaps, of people's education or occupation. The point is that such ways of grouping people together presuppose all sorts of assumptions which are highly disputable.[1] If there are such wholes, they obviously are not palpable wholes.

It is, as a matter of fact, a cardinal mistake to assume that just because we have terms like 'nations', 'state', and 'social class', there need be any one type of order that is properly referred to by the word. People still hotly dispute about whether any recognizable type of order is referred to by the term 'nation' at all.* Words are only tools for communication. Provided that we understand what other people mean when they use words, it is idle, unless we are writing a dictionary, to insist that one way of using the words is alone correct. For students of society an interest in terminology should take the form of asking what theory about society the terms are being used to state. This, as a matter of fact, is a very difficult attitude to maintain. For our hopes and fears, our desires and dreads, are much more easily aroused by theories about man than by theories about Nature. It is significant that the sciences which were the first to develop were those which dealt with the stars— the bodies most remote from man. And even astronomy itself developed

* See discussion in Ch. 11.

in the face of strong opposition because of the emotional and religious significance of the behaviour of the heavenly bodies. It was not until the nineteenth century that men achieved the degree of detachment necessary to study themselves scientifically. So when we talk about states, nations, social classes, and other such postulated types of order, it is very difficult to detach our emotions from our analysis; for holding on to a definition of 'social class' or 'nation' is too often a way of defending our valuations rather than of getting clearer about the facts.

II. NATURE AND CONVENTION

So far it has been shown how much human constructiveness helps to form the contours which we recognize in our social environment, and it has been intimated how difficult it is to separate our valuations from an analysis of society. These two difficulties in achieving a detached description of society may both be in part due to one of the outstanding differences between our social and physical environments. The order discernible in the natural world—the constitution of a crystal or a sponge, the rotation of the earth round the sun, the way in which lead melts at a certain temperature—is universal and not dependent on human desire or decision. Human decision enters, of course, in the choice of an order, in the way in which we select and group what is given. The laws of nature, after all, are human utterances or human marks on paper. Nature is what is the case—concrete particular facts; it does not consist in generalizations made about such occurrences. But whether or not these laws are true depends upon facts which are independent of human decision. No Act of Parliament can alter the constitution of a crystal or the laws of planetary motion. The order of society, on the other hand, is only maintained because of certain rules or norms which are very variable and which depend upon human desire and decision. This is not to say that all such rules have been consciously thought out and instituted; for what we call customs quite obviously have not. It is to say, rather, that such rules are expressive of human desires and aversions and that they are the sorts of things which can be altered by human decision. If men cease to think that divorce is always wrong, then marriage laws, which introduce a form of order into a certain area of human behaviour, can be changed. The vital difference between these forms of order is concealed by the fact that in English we use the word 'law' for both. We speak of marriage laws and of the laws of planetary motion. This often obscures the crucial point that whereas laws, in the legal sense, *prescribe* what ought to be, laws of Nature only *describe* what is invariably the case.

This distinction is a trifle over-simplified, but, perhaps a consideration of one or two complications will make it clearer. It will be said that the distinction is not clear because we can, on the one hand, alter the course of Nature, and on the other hand, we can develop laws about social orders. Both these assertions are true but they do not affect the crux of the distinction. Of course, we can tinker with Nature and introduce alterations. We do this every time we make a table, build a bridge or dam a river. But in making these alterations what we can do is limited by the properties and modes of change of the objects which the laws of Nature describe and explain. We cannot suddenly introduce large quantities of arsenic into an organism and expect the organism to live unless, because of our further knowledge of the properties of arsenic and organisms, we also introduce an antidote. When we adopt the interventionist attitude to Nature we are only successful if we have a thorough knowledge of the things with which we are dealing. Scientific laws tell us what we cannot do. Now psychologists and social scientists attempt to discover similar properties of human nature—the limitations imposed on our decisions by the material with which we have to work. Every system of social order grows up on a foundation of human nature. The problem is to discover which properties of human nature are universal and unalterable. Similarly, we can try, like the sociologists, to develop descriptive laws about the conditions under which normative orders of a certain sort develop, just as psychologists can make generalizations about the conditions under which people tend to conform to rules, or to deviate from them, about the different ways in which rules can be handed on from parents to children, and about the various 'needs' which rule-following satisfies. These laws resemble those in any natural science; but they just happen to be laws *about* rule-following. In the same way the sociologist can try to develop laws about the conditions under which scientific laws tend to emerge. But the admissions do not affect the basic distinction between natural laws which hold because of facts independent of human decision and normative laws which can cease to hold if human beings so decide.

This distinction between normative rules and scientific laws, which is here regarded as basic in our understanding of society, was made explicit comparatively late in the history of thought—probably in Europe in the eighteenth century. In primitive thought not only are these forms of order lumped together, but the sort of order discernible in our social environment is taken as the universal type. The regularities of Nature are laid down or ordained in the same kind of way as social codes. We still hear relics of this more primitive way of thinking when people speak of the laws of motion *governing* the movement of the planets. To the primitive mind Nature is peopled with gods and spirits who are responsible for different departments. If there is a storm at sea, Poseidon is angry. If the crops fail, Ceres must be placated. Elaborate rituals are performed to ensure that the customary order of Nature is maintained. When, with the development of abstract thought, all-pervasive forms of order are discerned, then men tend to suppose that this is instituted by some all-powerful agent. Plato, for instance, conjectured that in everything some kind of geometrical order was manifest, and added that God everywhere does geometry. The implicit assumption of this mode of thought is that any form of order presupposes an orderer. Hume's *Dialogues Concerning Natural Religion*, published in 1779, were a landmark in the history of thought in that Hume emphasized that there were different forms of order—that of a vegetable, of a house, of a commonwealth, of a mind—and showed conclusively that just because some forms of order presuppose an orderer, it cannot be inferred that all forms of order do. The order of the world, he suggested satirically, is just as likely to have developed spontaneously like that of a vegetable as to have been consciously instituted like that of a house.

In the light of this distinction,[2] which took so long to develop, between what is natural and what is normative, we can become clearer about what constitutes a human society. Men, of course, like the rest of Nature, have certain natural ways of behaving. Psychological theories about universal, unalterable and, perhaps innate, tendencies (e.g. doctrines of human instincts) are attempts to sketch what these ways of behaving are. But imposed on these tendencies and providing the social conditions under which they operate are all kinds of normative rules which introduce order of a different kind. This order can only persist if it does not violate the unalterable properties of human nature. Indeed a frequent criticism of revolutionary reforms is that they take no account of human nature. What we call a human society is a number of individuals bound together by such an order of normative rules. They behave predictably in relations to one another because of this normative system. These rules define the rights and duties which they have towards one another, the ends which they may pursue, and the ways in which it is legitimate to pursue them.*

Men, then, are rule-following animals; they perform predictably in relation to one another and form what is called a social system to a large extent because they accept systems of rules which are variable and alterable by human decision. Indeed we cannot really bring out what we mean by a human action without recourse to standards laying down what are accepted as ends and what are efficient and socially appropriate

* For fuller discussion of various types of social whole, see Ch. 11.

ways of attaining them. Actions like buying a watch or signing a contract are not just movements of the body; they are movements which we make to bring about ends which are defined largely in terms of man-made standards. They can be performed more or less intelligently as well as more or less correctly, which implies standards of social appropriateness.[3] They are not just things that happen like the blowing of the wind or the falling of the snow.

III. AUTHORITY AND OTHER FORMS OF SOCIAL REGULATION

Rules and standards are passed on and originated to a large extent by means of speech, which has a most important regulatory function in the life of men, and which makes possible a quite distinctive form of life. The artifice of speech introduces systems of order into human life which make no sense in the forest or the farm-yard. For what human beings do can be described as 'right' or 'correct', and things are done just because they are right or correct. And together with the notion of 'rightness' develops the necessity of *procedures* for deciding what these standards are and whether or not they are being conformed to. And this is very closely linked with the idea of 'authority'. For such standards being man-made, alterable, and, to a certain extent, arbitrary, procedures are necessary in some spheres at least, for deciding what standards are to be maintained, who is to originate them, who is to decide about their application to particular cases, and who is entitled to introduce changes. Where we find such an arrangement for originators or umpires in the realm of rules, we are in the sphere of 'authority'. For the concept of 'authority' is obviously derived from the old concepts of 'auctor' and 'auctoritas', which referred to a producing, inventing or cause in the sphere of opinion, counsel or command.[4]

Now in some spheres of social life it is imperative to have such 'auctores' who are producers or originators of orders, pronouncements, and decisions. It is also the case that in social life, whether we like it or not, there are such 'auctores' to whom commands, decisions and pronouncements are to be traced back in any factual survey of how social regulation is brought about. The authority structure is very much part of what we mean by terms like 'a social system', and, to a large extent, accounts for its continuance as a whole while its members pass away. It would be difficult to understand what is meant by an army, a state, or the Roman Catholic Church without an understanding of the concept of 'authority'. Indeed Hobbes relied on the notion of 'authority' to give an analysis of how it comes about that there is a social system rather than a multitude of men,[5] and recently de Jouvenel has seen in 'authority' in all-pervasive bond that integrates men into purposeful groups.[6]

But in spite of the pervasiveness of authority and of the indispensability of the concept in the analysis of social systems, we think it important to stress that the concept is itself rather a complex one. Hobbes and de Jouvenel, for instance, were using it in different ways. It is also important to guard against making the sphere of authority co-extensive with that of social regulation, as is done by de Jouvenel amongst others. In our view the use of authority should be clearly distinguished from other techniques of social regulation like the use of moral guidance on the one hand and the use of various forms of power on the other. Let us briefly consider each of these points in turn.

(a) Types of authority

We must first of all note that 'authority' is used both as a *de jure* and as a *de facto* concept. (Hobbes illustrates the first use, de Jouvenel the second.) In its *de jure* sense it implies a set of procedural rules which determine who shall be the 'auctor' and about what—as when we speak of those 'in authority', 'the authorities', or 'an authority'. In its *de facto* sense it involves reference to a man whose word in fact goes in some sphere—as when we say 'he exercised authority over his men'.

One of the great services done by the sociologist Max Weber has been to stress the *different* types of normative systems which are connected with different types of authority *de jure*. For legitimacy may be bestowed in different ways on the commands or decisions or pronouncements issuing from an 'auctor'. In what Weber called a legal-rational system the claim to legitimacy rests on 'a belief in the "legality" of patterns of normative rules and the right of those elevated to authority under such rules to issue commands'.[7] There is also traditional authority 'resting on an established belief in the sanctity of immemorial traditions and the legitimacy of the status of those exercising authority under them'. There are most important and interesting differences between these types of authority—but in both cases to speak of 'the authorities' or 'those in authority' is to proclaim that on certain matters certain people are entitled, licensed, commissioned or have a right to be 'auctores'. And the right is bestowed by a set pattern of rules.

This type of authority is to be distinguished carefully from other types of authority where the right derives from personal history, personal credentials, and personal achievements, an extreme form of which Weber took account of when he dealt with 'charismatic authority' —'resting on devotion to the specific and exceptional sanctity, heroism or exemplary character of an individual person, and of the normative patterns or order revealed or ordained by him'.[8] Weber, of course, was thinking primarily of the outstanding religious and military leaders like Jesus and Napoleon. He therefore pitched his account rather high and personal authority was decked with the trappings of vocation, miracles, and revelation. Nevertheless there is something distinctive about the charismatic leader which he shares in an exaggerated form with other natural leaders who exercise authority in virtue of personal claims and personal characteristics. For the reference to personal characteristics is a way of establishing that a man has a right to make pronouncements and issue commands because he is a special sort of person. And, although in some societies a man who sees visions and goes into trance states is in danger of electric shock treatment, in other societies pointing to such peculiarities of personal biography are ways of establishing man as *an* authority in certain spheres.

We usually speak of a man being 'an authority' in the sphere of pronouncements rather than that of commands and decisions where reference to 'the authorities' or 'those in authority' is more natural. Thus we speak of a man being 'an authority' on art, music, nuclear physics, or the Bible. Such a man has not been put in authority; he does not hold authority according to any system of rules. But because of his training, competence, and success in this sphere, he comes to be regarded as an authority. He has a right to make pronouncements. And his right derives from his *personal* history and achievements in a specific sphere. These more mundane cases of where we speak of a man being 'an authority' are similar, in this respect, to Weber's charismatic authority, where the legitimacy also is regarded as grounded in personal characteristics.

(b) *Authority and Power*

So far we have distinguished the different grounds of entitlement which are involved in speaking of a man being 'in authority' or 'an authority'. But we also speak of a man exercising authority over another man in a purely *de facto* sense. And although as a matter of fact he usually does this because he is in authority over him or because he is regarded as an authority, this is not necessarily the case. There is the Admirable Crichton situation, for instance. Or we might say that a man exercised authority over others if, during a crisis like a fire in a cinema, he rose to his feet and told everyone to file out quietly, and everybody in fact obeyed him, even though he was not the cinema manager or a fireman and was a complete stranger to all present. In such a case a man would exercise authority even though he was not in authority.

We are inclined to say that this would be an exercise of authority because the basic features of the concept fit even this situation. The audience files out just because he says so. Equal weight must here be given to the 'he' and the 'says'. To exercise authority over another is to get him to do things by giving orders to him, or by making pronouncements and decisions. It is inseparable from the use of *speech*. Hens, it is said, have a pecking order; but there is no hen *in* authority over other hens, neither does one hen *exercise* authority over other hens. Their system looks like a pure power system. They give no orders, make no pronouncements, and have no rules bestowing legitimacy. The main function of the term 'authority', when it is used in its *de facto* sense of 'exercising authority', is therefore to stress the regulation of behaviour by means of speech and symbolic gesture as distinct from the use of power. In other words it has its meaning by contrast with other ways of regulating behaviour that do make sense in the forest or farmyard.

This is to reject the more usual attempts to analyse 'authority' in terms of power as exemplified, for instance, by Weldon, who claimed that 'authority' means power exercised with the general approval of those concerned.[9] For often, what we want to bring out when we say that men are 'in authority' or 'exercise authority' over other men is that they get their way or ought to get their way by means other than those of force, threats, propaganda, and other ways of exercising power. It is only when a system of authority breaks down or a given individual loses his authority that there must be recourse to power if conformity is to be ensured.[10] The ability to exercise power may, of course, be a necessary condition for the exercise of authority under certain circumstances. It may also be a ground of entitlement as in the old saying 'no legitimacy without power'. But a necessary condition for the exercise of authority or a ground of entitlement to it should not be confused with what 'authority' *means*.

(b) Authority, science, and morality

We have claimed that the implication of saying that a man is 'in authority' or 'exercises authority' is that others do what he says just because he says so. The stress so far in our elucidation of this has been on 'says'. But in other contexts it is equally important to stress the 'he', the existence of an 'auctor' or originator in the sphere of decision, pronouncement or command. For in some such spheres the notion of there being an 'auctor' is anathema; not all decisions or pronouncements are authoritative. Perhaps commands must always be authoritative, the very concept of 'command' or 'order' implying this. For commands, roughly speaking, are the sorts of regulatory utterances for which no reasons need be given. Questions of course can be raised about a man's right to issue commands; but granted that he is entitled to give them and is not straying from his field of competence, there is no further question of justifying them. Indeed the tone of voice in which they are given bears witness to this.

Commands, however, are not the only sort of authoritative utterance. There are also decisions and pronouncements. And, as we have pointed out, not all these are authoritative. Indeed there is a long tradition which stresses the incompatability between authority and certain specific human enterprises like science and morality. For it would be held that in science the importance of the 'auctor' or originator is at a minimum, it never being justifiable in scientific institutions to set up an individual or body who will either be the originator of pronouncements or who will decide finally on the truth of pronouncements made. The procedural rules of science lay it down, roughly speaking, that hypotheses must be decided on by looking at the evidence, not by appealing to a man. There are also, and can be, no rules to decide who will be the originators of scientific theories.

In a similar way, as we shall maintain later, a rule cannot be a moral one if it is to be accepted just because someone has laid it down or made a decision between competing alternatives. Reasons must be given for it, not originators or umpires produced. Of course, in both enterprises provisional authorities can be consulted. But there are usually good reasons for this choice and their pronouncements are never to be regarded as final just because they have made them. In science and morality there are no appointed judges or policemen. This is one of the ways in which life in the laboratory differs from life in the army and law courts.

IV. THE DEVELOPMENT OF TYPES OF SOCIAL REGULATION

So far we have distinguished between natural laws and normative rules and have suggested that what we call societies are individuals bound together by varying patterns of normative rules. We have also suggested that the concept of 'authority' is intimately connected with the regulation of behaviour by means of such rules in a social system. For in certain spheres of social life it is imperative to have originators or umpires, men whose pronouncements and decisions determine what rule is to be followed or what interpretation of a rule adopted. In considering the different rules of *procedure* from which men derive their right to be 'auctores' in different spheres we had occasion to mention Weber's distinction between legal and traditional rules; we also made a contrast between the fields where authorities are appropriate and the fields of scientific pronouncements and moral decisions, where there can be no authorities. More must now be said about the distinctions implicit in our account of these different types of social regulation.

In some simple and cohesive types of social system a man's behaviour is regulated almost entirely by the roles deriving from his status in society—as a father, a husband, a warrior, or a hunter. But in our modern type of social system our duties are not all so derivable from our station in life. There are, in addition, rules of an all-pervasive character like those relating to non-injury, respect for property, veracity, gratitude to benefactors, unselfishness, and fair play. These very general rules which are binding on all who live in a given area are usually referred to as social codes.

But we do not regard such social codes as being all of a piece; for we distinguish between customs and traditions, laws, moral rules, and religious rules. We would say, for instance, that it is traditional or customary for a man to walk on the outside of a woman on a pavement; but this is not a law, neither is it a moral duty. Primitive people make no such distinctions, as social regulation in pre-literate societies is comparatively undifferentiated. Indeed, if an anthropologist were to ask one of his subjects whether the prohibition on incest were a moral, legal, religious, or customary rule, he would be greeted with blank incomprehension.

How then do we make these distinctions? Surely, they presuppose, on the part of the people who make them, a certain degree of consciousness of *procedures*, of differences in formal rules by means of which substantive rules like 'contracts ought to be kept' or 'debts ought to be paid' are decided upon. It is, surely, such differences in procedures that lie behind the distinctions, which obviously are not simply in terms of the content of the rule. The prohibition on incest, for example, is a moral, legal, religious, and customary rule, and the fact that we can say that it exemplifies all these different types of rule shows that it is not the content alone which decides its status.[11] What, then, is the criterion of distinction?

(a) The emergence of law

Perhaps the best way of arriving at a general understanding of these distinctions is to say very briefly how they probably arose. In small, preliterate or semi-literate, self-contained societies norms tend to be quite undifferentiated. The lives of the people are regulated by a system of rules which are thought to have been handed down from time immemorial. The question of justifying the rules does not arise. They are part of the order of the world like the movement of the sun or the properties of fire. When, however, social change or social expansion develops—perhaps in a society by the sea that trades with other societies, or in a society that conquers or is conquered by others—the system of local rules proves inadequate either because new contingencies have arisen or because some over-all system of rules is necessary for societies to fuse with one another. At such times a system of what we call law tends to arise. This differs from custom in that it is usually written down, it issues from a determinate source like a king, and it is supported by determinate sanctions. Literate societies often hold in reverence someone who is assumed to have been their first great lawgiver—Lycurgus of Sparta, Solon of Athens, and so on. Custom, of course, is not abrogated. Sections of it—usually those which are of most far-reaching social importance—are merely clarified and codified. But the life of the individual continues to be determined by countless customs which have not been converted into laws.

In our society right up to the seventeenth century custom was the predominant form of social control together with the Common Law which was intermediary between custom and law. A man's status and the roles which he had to play in the various departments of life were prescribed by rules handed down from time immemorial. Economic life was static and secure, regulated by the guild system which blocked undue competition and self-assertion. There was little social mobility, and the world view propagated by the Church assigned a proper place to everything in the divine order of things. But with the growth of international commerce in the fourteenth and fifteenth centuries, with the invention of printing and the improvement of communications, a new individualistic order gradually began to take shape. Social life became more and more characterized by acquisitiveness, the pursuit of power, and the striving for honour.[12] Life, indeed, became rather like a race, as the great seventeenth century philosopher, Thomas Hobbes, pictured it. Thrift, efficiency, and hard work became virtues of the rising middle class. Individual effort and initiative, as well as traditional status, came to determine a man's place. In the religion of Protestantism much was made of the priesthood of all believers; the individual was confronted with God without the intermediaries of the Church hierarchy; he had to make his lonely way in quest of salvation by his own individual effort.

The rise of individualism brought about great gains in the field of liberty, self-discipline, and personal responsibility. But these were achieved, to a certain extent, by the loss of the sense of security that goes with a small close-knit traditional society. The need for a new kind of security was almost universally met by the development of a new form of social control—the strengthening and extension of the powers of the king. The nation state emerged with the increase in statute law as the method of social control appropriate to it. And in most countries acute controversy developed about the proper relationship between the individual and this new form of social control which Hobbes aptly dubbed 'Leviathan'.[13] What rights had the king over his subjects or the subjects against the king? What made his authority legitimate? On what grounds were they justified in resisting his decrees? How could the insistent demands for the liberty of the subject be reconciled with the obvious need for security? These are the crucial questions of social philosophy. They tend to arise acutely only at a time of social change and intellectual bewilderment; for philosophy is intellectual unrest made explicit. In periods like that of the seventeenth century in England men were confused and undecided about how they stood in relation to this new form of social control that was developing. And it was at this period that the distinctions between the major forms of social control began to be hammered out.

Law, in the order that was passing, was closely related to custom in that it was thought to be a *declaration* of existing custom. *The law* was there to discover—a kind of appurtenance of the people—as it applied to particular circumstances. With the development in England of Common Law or the King's law this view still persisted. The king and his courts never *made* laws; they declared what the law was. Common Law was intermediary between custom and law in that the judges, in declaring the law, did so by attempting to make explicit the customs of the realm. Parliament itself was regarded as only a kind of court rather than as a law-making body. But when James I claimed that law was simply his command and that customary law was only valid because his silence denoted his assent, and when later on in the seventeenth century the Long Parliament indulged in an unprecedented amount of legislation, it became increasingly clear that laws were not simply declarations of existing custom. For where was the precedent for a Parliament prolonging its own life by statute? Was law then, as Hobbes suggested, 'the word of him that by right hath command over others'? Our analysis of 'authority' helps to explain this suggested connection between 'authority' and 'command'. For commands, roughly speaking, are the sorts of regulatory utterances for which no reasons need to be given. A man can only give a command if, like a king, he is in a position of authority or if he exerts authority in a *de facto* sense. For as an occupant of an office or as a status holder he has a right to make decisions which are binding and to issue orders. Authority, however, is not exercised *only* in the giving of commands. There are also the spheres of making pronouncements and decisions. Behaviour or opinion in these spheres is regulated by the utterance of a man which carries with it the obligation for others to accept, follow, or obey. The claim put forward by Hobbes that law is command is right in stressing the connection between law and authority but wrong in conceiving of commands as the only form of authoritative utterance. A law is obviously an *authoritative* utterance; but it does not follow that it is a command. Further clarifications of such problems about the status of law must, however, await our third chapter.

(b) The emergence of morality

The rise of individualism was also manifest in another distinction which was as old as Socrates and those others who had been the mouthpieces of the individualist movement in Greece in the fifth and fourth centuries BC. This was the difference between a moral rule on the one hand and a custom or law on the other. Socrates and his followers insisted that the individual should accept only those rules which he himself could justify. It was not enough to adopt traditional standards secondhand because they were sanctified by immemorial custom or laid down by some authority. After all, times change, and authorities disagree. Even the law might be unjust and, although in general the individual should obey the laws of his state, these laws might conflict with his conscience, his own reasoned conviction about what was right and wrong.

This critical rejection or acceptance of custom or law is what is distinctive of morality, just as the critical attitude to theories about Nature is what is distinctive about science. The germ of both morality and science emerged at about the same time; they were manifestations of the emergence of individualism. For, with the development of trade and the interchange of ideas between societies, it came to be realized (and made explicit by writers like Herodotus) that men lived under a bewilderingly different number of laws and customs just as they accepted quite different theories of Nature. The individual like Socrates or Protagoras who reflected on this diversity was thrown back on himself; authorities had to be challenged and the truth arrived at. Men began to proclaim that, whatever their civic allegiances, there was a bond between them as reasonable beings. The concept of the individual and respect for the individual as an individual developed. In the dispute about Nature and convention, which can be found in the writings of Plato and Protagoras, this distinction was implicit;[14] for it was held by some that all men shared in a certain common 'nature' whatever conventions they happened to live under. Later on, with the breakdown of the autonomous city states and the consequent decline in the importance of man's duty as a citizen, the notion developed of a universal system of rules binding on all men in virtue of their nature as rational beings. This universal system of rules or law of nature[15] as it was called was contrasted with the laws and customs of particular states. The Stoics, who were the first to formulate this conception of natural law with explicitness, spoke of man as a citizen of the world as well as of a particular state. As rational beings men occupied a cosmic status and were equal, whatever their civic status; and as rational beings they could not doubt that contracts ought to be kept, life and property respected, and that justice should prevail between men. These were the sorts of rules that could be justified in any society whatsoever. Thus the Stoics, who flourished after the conquests of Alexander and the cosmopolitan tendencies which he fostered, developed with greater explicitness the implications of the Socratic tradition. They began to systematize what we now call a moral code. For the characteristic of a moral rule is that it should be regarded as universally applicable and rationally acceptable to the individual.

The notion of such an ideal universal code persisted in Rome through the influence of the Stoics. It exerted a simplifying and humanizing influence on the Roman law of nations—a practical system of law developed to regulate dealings with those foreign cities with which Rome was brought into contact through her commercial and military expansion. With the coming of Christianity, cosmopolitanism and egalitarianism found a more dynamic and emotional form of expression. Later, with the development of theology, the system of natural law came to be regarded by Aquinas as a selection from God's rules which could be rationally discerned and which did not need to be supernaturally revealed. It was appealed to by the more philosophically minded of the clergy to humanize, and often to condemn, current laws and customs.

The heyday of natural law, however, was the post-Renaissance growth of individualism.[16] The Renaissance, as has often been said, focused interest on man as an individual. The law of Nature was thought to be rooted in man as an individual rather than derivative from his ecclesiastical or civic status. Hence its appeal at this time. Also, at a time of acute religious controversy it appealed to reasonable men, like Grotius in Holland, who wanted peace and toleration; for it suggested a set of rules which were rationally acceptable and unaffected by the revelations and authoritative claims of rival religious sects. The law of Nature was also a godsend to those rising representatives of the middle class who feared the absolutist ambitions of the rulers of the developing nation states; for the law of Nature provided a system of universal principles binding on king and subject alike to which appeal could be made in calling in question the justice of laws.

It was in this kind of context that moral philosophy grew and flourished. For moral philosophy is the attempt to find criteria in virtue of which rules can be rationally justified.[17] It presupposes a critical attitude to rules and the refusal to equate what is right with what is laid down by custom, law or any other authoritative source. This attitude is only possible in an individualist era where the distinction is made between man as a citizen of a state and man as an individual belonging to other societies and able to criticize the laws and customs in which he has been nurtured. In our second chapter we shall give a brief outline of the criteria suggested for distinguishing a moral rule from a custom. So far we have claimed only that a moral rule differs from a custom in that it has been critically examined in accordance with some criterion other than the degree to which it is generally accepted or the competence of the authority prescribing it. In the same way scientific laws become differentiated from a mass of heterogeneous assumptions about the world. They emerged as those assumptions which stood up to observational tests. The task of moral philosophy is to make explicit the test in the sphere of normative rules which corresponds to that of the observational test in the sphere of descriptions of Nature. For what we call moral rules are those that have emerged from an undifferentiated mass of normative rules after a certain kind of test has been applied to them.

(c) Morality and religion

Of course, the distinction between man as an individual and man as a member of a state was enormously helped by Christianity with its stress on the brotherhood of man and the distinction between man as a subject of temporal authorities and man as a child of God. Indeed, the very existence of the Church institutionalized this distinction. Protestantism especially emphasized the conscience of the individual in his endeavour to find out what was right by searching the Scriptures and his own heart. Catholicism inhibited the development of morality by its stress on the authority of the church hierarchy in matters of right and wrong. This raises the question of how moral rules are to be distinguished from religious ones—a very difficult question in view of their similarity of content. Probably the answer would be that a rule is specifically religious if it is thought to have been laid down by some divinely inspired individual or group of individuals or if the individual himself regards the rule as revealed to him personally by God, and if the divine nature of its origin is thought to be the justification for obeying it. A religious rule does not have the same connection with man's reason as is usually claimed for moral rules; it depends much more on the authority of a man. This suggested criterion raises the fundamental question of the existence of God and of the criteria possible for claiming that God's will has been revealed. As this book makes no attempt to enter the field of the philosophy of religion, the problems connected with this suggested criterion of distinction will not be further explored.

We have, in this introductory chapter, suggested that the important respect in which society differs from Nature is that its order is largely the product of systems of normative rules. We then showed how the concept of 'authority' is intimately connected with the regulation of behaviour within such a social system. We claimed, however, that the sphere of authority is to be distinguished from the sphere of power on the one hand and the sphere of moral regulation on the other. We then embarked on a brief description of the contexts in which the distinction between law, custom, and morality arose. We can now proceed to examine in more detail the criteria assumed in making these distinctions.

CHAPTER 2

MORAL THEORY

I. MORALITY AND RATIONAL JUSTIFICATION

When we speak of 'morality' we can be using the term in a very general way to speak of a system of rules that are not legal rules but which nevertheless have a widespread application in our conduct. Indeed, some moral philosophers speak of 'customary morality'. Or we can be using the term in a more specific sense to indicate that these rules are not merely customs but rules which have had certain special criteria applied to them. In this second and more specific sense of 'moral' we would not say that a child was a moral being who simply did what he was told without thinking about the rightness of the general principle implicit in his behaviour. The Swiss psychologist, Piaget, maintained that children as a matter of fact remain in this 'transcendental' stage for some time.[1] They never question the rightness or wrongness of rules like 'Thou shall not steal' any more than they question the rules of games like marbles. Of course, they may follow their inclinations or their selfish interests, just as people under an authoritarian Catholic regime often followed their inclinations rather than the authoritative commands of the Church. But they do not challenge the rightness or wrongness of the rules. Standards are regarded as authoritatively ordained by some external agency. It is only later, at about the age of seven or eight, that they begin to see that rules of games and rules of social life have some *point* to them and that they can therefore be changed by common consent if they no longer have any point. In this way, if Piaget is right, the development of a child in an open society mirrors the development of man's consciousness from the authoritative ties of a traditional society.

We are here concerned with morality only in the second and more specific sense of the term in which morality is distinct from custom. Our problem is to suggest criteria in the light of which a rule becomes a moral rule. This sort of enquiry is usually known as ethics or moral philosophy. Historically speaking moral philosophers have often been the mouthpieces of a social movement in which this distinction between custom and law on the one hand and morality on the other hand was of cardinal importance. They have attempted to state clearly and explicitly criteria which were implicit in judgments made on social practices. Immanuel Kant, for instance, excited by the spectacle of the French Revolution, claimed that he was making clear what was presupposed in the judgments of ordinary men who were standing on their own feet and condemning existing social regulations as being unjust. Others, like David Hume, whilst deploring violent departures from tradition, have tried to show the grounds on which it can be held that what is traditional is also moral.

In our view moral philosophers, in so far as they have sought seriously to make explicit the criteria implicit in calling a rule a moral rule, have already in an embryonic form committed themselves to two of the basic criteria for which they have sought. For, as was indicated in our first chapter, morality arises when custom or law is subjected to critical examination. Now if a person like Socrates asks *seriously* whether a particular rule is right, whatever the traditional authority for it, or attempts *seriously* to decide between the demands of different authorities, then he must, as a rational critical individual accept certain normative standards or procedure. He must respect truth at all costs. Now respecting truth, as Socrates held, involves being prepared to admit that we are mistaken. Just because it is *our* opinion, or anyone else's for that matter, it need not necessarily be correct. Issues, in other words, must be decided in the light of *arguments*, and not because of the authority or personality or religion or social class of the person who propounds them. Socrates held that he could reason with a slave. And surely he was right. For what has a man's social position to do with the truth or falsity of what he says? It may be that because he is a slave he is also ignorant and is therefore likely to put forward false statements. But this connection is purely contingent. He may be ignorant in general and yet be quite correct in what he says about a particular matter. Logically speaking, the fact that he is a slave is quite irrelevant to the truth or falsity of what he says. For this is decided in terms of *evidence*, and the fact that he is a slave is usually quite irrelevant. The very idea of searching for truth takes for granted, then, a norm of *impartiality* which holds that issues should be decided according to the *relevant* criteria and that exceptions should not be made on irrelevant grounds. Of course, the difficulty often is to decide, in particular contexts, what *are* relevant grounds. But in this context, when the question at issue is the truth of an assertion, it is manifestly irrelevant to decide it by reference to the personal or social characteristics of the person who puts forward the assertion. In the context of the search for truth impartiality amounts to being prepared to admit one's own fallibility and being prepared to admit that the other person may be right although one may dislike him personally or object to his religion, colour, social class, voice, or any other such irrelevant attributes. This criterion can be put more strongly in terms of *respect for persons*. For if we are prepared to attend seriously to what another person has to say, whatever his personal or social attributes, we must have at least a minimal respect for him as the source of an argument.*

But, it might well be argued, respect for people as sources of arguments is a far cry from the sort of criteria that are needed to justify a rule as a moral rule. Science deals only with the truth of assumptions; morality is concerned with the rightness or wrongness of rules. A man might be quite reasonable in a scientific discussion yet eminently unreasonable when any question of duty arose. He might be reasonable enough in deciding between the claims of different 'authorities' on scientific matters, but refuse to discuss rationally the suggestions of anyone whom he regarded as an 'authority' on moral matters. He might reason when in a laboratory; but his life outside might be directed by authorities and by irrational taboos.

This is quite a possible situation; indeed it may well be a common one in countries where conduct is predominantly regulated by custom and political or religious authorities. But we are conceiving of a situation where a man is really doing moral philosophy, where he is really seriously worried about the justification of rules. He is demanding *reasons* for rules. Now to say that he is demanding reasons for rules is to say that he has rejected the appeal to the authority of a man or of a custom. And, surely, the only sorts of reasons that count when such a demand is made are those that refer to the effect of the rule on someone or other's interests. Discussions about the rightness of rules do not take place in a social vacuum. They occur when people are worried about rules because somebody's claims are being neglected or somebody's interests damaged or disregarded. Notions like 'harm', 'injury', 'advantage', 'benefit', and so on are surely not accidentally associated with the discussion of the rightness of rules. For what other sorts of reasons could there be that would count?

Given, then, that the context of the justification of rules is one where people's interests are adversely or beneficially affected by their change or continuance, it is surely illogical for a man who is seriously interested in giving reasons for rules to consider any particular person's interests as being any more important than anyone else's unless good reasons can be shown for making such a distinction. There may well be a gap between considering another man merely as a source of arguments and

---

* The substance of this argument derives from Prof. K. R. Popper who once developed it in a series of seminars.

as a source of interests and claims. But surely both are cases of impartiality, and we would call a man unreasonable if he disregarded other people (or himself) in either of these respects.

It might be said that often questions about what ought to be done are prudential questions. A person can give reasons for what ought to be done purely in terms of what is likely to be advantageous to himself. But we understand, surely, the difference between this sort of 'ought' and a moral 'ought'. As Hume put it, if the question 'Is this right?' were the same question as 'What is this to me?' It would seem very odd that this quite distinct way of speaking has emerged. A man who is seriously producing reasons to support the view that a rule is *right* may give reasons in terms of his own interest, but not *only* his own interest. He has to show *reasons* why his interests rather than anyone else's have priority; and it is not a reason to say that they have priority just because they are *his* or anyone else's. For this is like an irrational appeal to authority. He has to give reasons for placing himself or anyone else in such a special category. The presumption, surely, of the reasonable man, in the discussion both of the truth of assumptions and the rightness of rules, is that people shall be treated impartially as sources of arguments or of interests. In other words reasons must be given for treating anyone as being more or less important than any other.

In our view the impartial consideration of the interests affected by rules is basic to morality. This is a purely procedural criterion; for it does not dictate which rules are right or wrong, only how to set about deciding whether a rule is right or wrong. What counts as a good reason for putting a person into a special category will vary from circumstance to circumstance; and there are all sorts of disagreements about what is detrimental or beneficial to people whose interests are affected by rules. Nevertheless, as a procedural criterion it distinguishes morality from reliance on custom and from the acceptance of authority in the fields of law and religion. And in so far as men are philosophers they are implicitly committed to some such procedural rule; for philosophy itself is pre-eminently an exhibition of reason in action. In so far as men are serious in their search for justification and for making explicit the criteria of such justification, they must be committed to a minimal degree of impartiality. For without this, rational discussion could not proceed. Ethics, or moral philosophy, is the attempt to make explicit how moral rules are justified. Our contention, therefore, is that moral philosophers, in so far as they think and demand that reasons can be given for rules, and discuss rationally what sorts of reasons count, have already assumed in a minimal degree the criteria which they are looking for when they do moral philosophy—provided, that is, that they do it

B

seriously, and not merely as an intellectual exercise. The crucial distinction is between those who are prepared to discuss rules rationally and those who are content to rely on the external authority of custom, leader, Pope or book. In comparison with this cleavage the differences in the criteria suggested by moral philosophers are differences of emphasis within a fortress of agreement. Kant was fundamentally right in holding that the criteria of morality are implicit in the concept of a rational being—provided, that is, that 'rational' is used in the sense of 'reasonable', and not in the stricter sense of 'unable to accept logical contradictions'.

An exposition of the different ethical theories in so short a space as one chapter must necessarily be from a point of view. For how else could a selection be made from the mass of details connected with each of the theories? But in adopting our particular point of view we feel that we are not only bringing out those features of morality which distinguish it from custom and law, but we are also stressing the kernel of morality in so far as it affects questions of rights, justice, equality, and other such concepts which we are to discuss later in this book. Our point of view explains certain omissions—those thinkers in the Christian tradition, for instance, who have suggested a specifically Christian foundation for conduct. This implies no adverse judgment on the historical importance of these theories; for obviously the way of life preached by Catholics, Puritans, Calvinists, and other such Christian sects, were of very great historical importance. But in so far as such systems of conduct had a specifically Christian foundation, they were based on some kind of divine authority or revelation. They must therefore be regarded as religious codes rather than as moral ones. Of course, a code of behaviour, like that of the Sermon on the Mount, could be accepted because there seemed to be good reasons for it. But such rational acceptance must be distinguished from acceptance on the grounds that the code issued from a man who was God, or divinely inspired. There is a distinction between accepting what Jesus said because he said it, and accepting what he said because there are good reasons for it. If religious codes are to be distinguished from ethical ones, they must surely be regarded as having as their basis faith in a particular man or in other sources of revelation rather than the acceptance of rules for reasons that any rational being might suggest.

II. INTUITIONISM

We have already explained in our first chapter how moral philosophy began to gather momentum after the Renaissance when reflective people were casting round for a basis of conduct which any rational man could accept whatever his religion or country. The Dutch thinker, Grotius, was particularly interested in finding a rational basis for international law by means of which trade could be facilitated. He fell back, naturally enough, on the old tradition of the law of nature which had been passed down from the Stoics.[2]

In Stoic thought there had always been a close connection between the concept of a rational being and that of the law of nature. All men, it was said, had reason or the divine spark within them. The possession of this would lead them to accept the law of nature and, in so far as men had reason, all men were equal and should be treated with respect. There was no place for slavery in a life 'according to nature'. This connection between man's reason and natural law was present in all attempts to formulate it, as, for instance, in the Catholic conception of natural law. Grotius' importance consisted not so much in the content of the rules which he suggested, but in his conception of 'rationality' in virtue of which men must accept them. For, in this respect, he may be regarded as one of the earliest exponents of the ethical theory known as 'intuitionism'.

The period at which Grotius wrote was one of revolt against the prevailing Aristotelian tradition. Men were impressed by the advances made in the mathematical sciences of astronomy, mechanics, and optics, which were being pioneered by Copernicus, Kepler and Galileo.[3] It was thought that their success had been obtained because they had made a fresh start. They had cleared their minds of Aristotelian clutter and had used a different method of thought. Instead of beginning with careful observations and working gradually up to a knowledge of essences by reference to which they could explain the behaviour of things, they had followed the methods of Euclid. The works of Archimedes, for instance, had become available in translation in the sixteenth century, and exerted a great influence on the school of Padua where Galileo worked. In this geometrical method a situation had to be analysed or resolved into components which seemed intuitively simple, which permitted no further analysis. The ball rolling down an inclined surface, for instance, was resolved into its simple elements of extension, figure and motion, which were quantifiable. If these simple concepts were held together in the mind certain relations could be intuitively grasped as holding between them. These could be formulated as axioms and a deductive system developed by means of which the behaviour of the ball could be explained. The 'intuition' of these primitive elements and their inter-relations, together with the deductions or 'demonstrations' that could be derived from them, were regarded as the work of reason. Descartes held that all men possessed reason and, as rational beings, they were all on an equal footing. They had only to learn the method of geometry and they could not fail to understand the structure of the world. For God, according to the Pythagorean-Platonic tradition which these early physical scientists inherited, was a great geometer and had constructed the world according to geometrical principles. Descartes generalized the method of geometry and held that *all* knowledge must be of this type. The truth of physical theories depended, on his view, on the self-evidence of the clear and distinct ideas from which reasoning started.

It was not, therefore, surprising that this picture of the acquisition of knowledge was transferred to the sphere of rules. And Grotius was one of the first to make this move. He tried to do for international law and morality what Galileo was alleged to have done for physics—to provide an axiomatic basis from which all subordinate principles could be derived. Grotius conceived of the law of nature as a set of moral axioms which any rational being must accept, like 'contracts ought to be kept'. Given these basic axioms, all the duties of man could be regarded as applications of them to particular social conditions which varied from state to state. On Grotius' view man's rationality was a necessary but not a sufficient condition for acceptance of these axioms. For man was also a social animal 'by nature', as Aristotle and Plato had taught, and it was because of his unalterable regard for his fellows and his need for some kind of social order, that his rationality led him to accept such principles as self-evident.

This rejuvenated conception of the law of nature was employed in a political context by John Locke, the apologist of the Bloodless Revolution of 1688, who followed Grotius closely.[4] The Stuarts, in the view of those whose demands he made explicit, had violate the Common Law tradition of England by extending their prerogative into its sphere. They had, for example, raised a tax on property without the consent of Englishmen through their appointed representatives in Parliament. But Locke, instead of quoting precedents from the Common Law and the traditional sphere of the king's prerogative, claimed that this invasion of property was against the law of Nature. For according to this universal law all men had a natural right to life, liberty, and estate. King and subjects alike were bound by this law of Nature which consisted of a self-evident set of rules which any rational, social being must accept. Moral knowledge, said Locke, was demonstrable knowledge like mathematics.

There were others who used the law of nature somewhat differently, but they all followed Grotius in connecting it with man's reason. Thomas Hobbes[5] for instance, denied that men were by nature sociable.

But he nevertheless maintained that the law of nature was the foundation of civil society. For men, driven solely by their desire for power and their fear of death, were pictured as being led by their fear of death to rational acceptance of rules like 'that men perform their covenants made'. The law of nature was a set of 'conclusions or theorems, concerning what conduceth to self-conservation and defence'. The fundamental law of nature was that 'every man ought to endeavour peace as far as he has hope of attaining it'.

In the eighteenth and nineteenth centuries many onslaughts were launched on this conception of the law of Nature—for instance by Hume and Bentham. But in moral philosophy its major claims survived—that there was a universal set of rules binding on all men and that these rules were self-evident truths like mathematical axioms. Richard Price defended this view with great ingenuity and ability in the eighteenth century and anticipated many of the arguments of the twentieth century intuitionists like G. E. Moore and W. D. Ross. The Utilitarian systems of Bentham and Mill, although hostile to the natural law tradition, were nevertheless explicitly based on the self-evident axiom that happiness ought to be promoted.

This ethical theory, which is often called 'rationalism' rather than 'intuitionism', is defensible, in our view, only up to a point. It is acceptable in so far as it distinguishes between custom and morality and in so far as it holds that moral rules are singled out in some way by what is popularly called the use of reason. But, in our view, the picture it presents of rational justification is quite unacceptable; for saying that a whole set of rules are self-evident or intuitively known to be true is another way of saying that no further justification of them is possible. Reference to some alleged power of the mind called 'intuition' is a way of making the *logical* point that no further reasons can be given for the rules in question.

Of course, it is true that many rules can be exhibited as deductions from simpler and more universal rules. Hence the interest of natural law theorists in the contractual theory of the state; for they could then exhibit the duty of allegiance to government as derivative from the self-evident rule that contracts ought to be kept. But once it has been established—if it ever could be established—that, in some sense, men have contracted to obey government, how does this self-evidence theory help? For a man might be convinced that he had contracted to obey the government but might still doubt whether, on this occasion, he ought to keep his contract. And it is just this sort of situation of doubt about a principle that leads people to seek for a justification of a principle. In such a situation it is absurd to say that the general principle that contracts ought to be kept is self-evident. For his own doubt on this occasion is a standing refutation of the view that the general principle that 'contracts ought to be kept' is a self-evident principle. For how can it be self-evident if on one of the occasions to which the principle applies he can doubt its truth? For not only is it no *justification* of a principle to say that it is self-evident; it is also palpably false that it *is* self-evident if a person finds himself doubting it and looking for a justification. And, although a case can be made for saying that a very general principle like 'happiness ought to be promoted' is self-evident in the sense that no further justification of it can be given, this seems quite untrue about lower-order principles like 'contracts ought to be kept'. For all sorts of reasons can surely be produced to support such principles. Dogmatic intuition, as Sidgwick called it,[6] which holds that lower order principles are self-evident, is thus a much less plausible theory than what he called philosophical intuitionism, which holds that only very high-order principles 'like pleasure alone is good' are self-evident.

In our view, the root of the mistake in this theory is the assumption, descending from Descartes and the early rationalists, that the self-evidence of an assumption guarantees its truth. This view developed at a time when there was only Euclidean geometry and when it was thought that space was Euclidean and that the intuitively grasped relations which form the basis of geometry were the underlying formal structure of the world. Thus, the view that the axioms of geometry were self-evident had a degree of plausibility because they worked well for extended objects having figure and moving about, which we meet with at the level of ordinary unsophisticated perception. But later, with the development of non-Euclidean systems of geometry, it came to be realized that deductive systems need not start from self-evident axioms, the choice of axioms being mainly a matter of convenience. Also, the work of Locke, Hume, Kant and others emphasized the difference between formal sciences like geometry and the empirical sciences—a difference which had formerly been obscured. Mathematical systems may generate statements that are necessarily true, simply because they are derivable from definitions of terms like 'triangle' and 'straight'. But they need not apply to the world at all. The postulates of the empirical sciences, on the other hand, are established by comparing their deduced consequences with observations. As a matter of fact, Galileo differed in this respect from Descartes; for he insisted on observational confirmation of his rationally conceived expectations. In the empirical sciences the self-evidence of postulates has little to do with their truth. Indeed, the history of science is littered with self-evident assumptions that had later to be discarded. It may be the case, however, that many true assumptions come to seem self-evident because they are so obviously true. A metallurgist may come to regard the statement that 'metals expand when they are heated' as self-evident because its truth has been so often confirmed. But it has become self-evident because it is so obviously true and he is so used to assuming its truth. It is not true *because* it is self-evident. Indeed, self-evidence is more an index of our habituation to an assumption than of its truth.

Thus, those who held that certain lower-order principles like 'contracts ought to be kept' were self-evident may just have been registering their psychological inability to doubt them. After all, people like Locke were so imbued with the Common Law tradition that it must have been psychologically very difficult for them to doubt that property ought to be respected. Or it might have been the case that there were such good reasons for these simple rules that they came to seem self-evident to them because the point of them was too obvious to mention. Our suggestion is that a readiness to accept simple social rules like 'contracts ought to be kept' and 'property ought to be respected' seemed almost part of what was meant by being 'rational' —i.e. being the sort of man who was presumed to reflect on such rules. For, as we have indicated, Grotius and Locke were the mouthpieces of those who wanted a rational justification of rules rather than an appeal to their traditional or supernatural authority. Such rational justification presupposes a minimum degree of impartiality and respect for persons. A man who is prepared to admit his own fallibility and to respect another person as a source of argument is likely to extend his respect to his life and, under certain historical conditions, to his property. For disputes about rules can perfectly easily be settled by violence. It is not everyone who demands rational justification. The model of the acceptance of mathematical axioms was thus a historically conditioned vehicle of expression for making explicit the demands of a reasonable being who is dissatisfied with the appeal to tradition or supernatural authority and who demands that social claims as well as theories about the world should be settled by reasonable discussion. The norms of natural law which they held to be self-evident axioms on which civil society must be based were really implied in a loose manner by their quest for a rational basis. They were the sort of rules that anyone concerned to settle disputes by reasonable discussion would more or less take for granted at that period.

III. THE MORAL SENSE OR EMOTIVE THEORY

The likening of moral rules to the axioms of geometry was unfortunate not only because of the self-evidence theory of truth which it presupposed, but also because it ignored a crucial difference between mathematical and moral reasoning. Mathematics, said David Hume,[7] is concerned only with truth or falsity, not with preferences. If, as mathematicians, we intuit relations between our ideas, there is no implication that anything should be done. Yet there does seem to be some sort of necessary connection between assenting to a moral proportion and our will . . . 'morals excite passions, and produce or prevent actions. Reason of itself is utterly impotent in this particular.' . . . 'Tis not contrary to reason to prefer the destruction of the whole world to the scratching of my finger.' Reasoning, according to Hume, was concerned only with relations between ideas and deductions from them (as in mathematics), or with inferences about matters of fact (as in the empirical sciences). By the use of reason alone, in the above senses, we could arrive at no normative judgments. Indeed the only sense in which our normative judgments could be said to be unreasonable would be if they presupposed faulty inferences about matters of fact. The gap between what is and what ought to be could only be bridged if we were to turn our reflection into our breasts and there find a sentiment of approbation or disapprobation which might arise towards the object. 'So that when you pronounce any action or character to be vicious, you mean nothing but that from the constitution of your nature you have a feeling or sentiment of blame from the contemplation of it.'

On Hume's view this sentiment of approbation or disapprobation is often mistaken for reasoning because of its calmness. It is what he called a 'disinterested passion'. It presupposes sympathy for others and only arises if we adopt an impartial point of view. Indeed sympathy is the generalizing agency which imparts to the pleasure of approval that reflective aspect which many moralists have mistaken for reason. Moral sentiments are aroused by the contemplation of certain classes of actions—conscious voluntary actions which bring harm or benefit to those for whom we feel sympathy. And, of course, we can adopt this disinterested point of view towards our own actions or towards the actions of others that affect us. Very often this moral way of looking at a situation conflicts with our impulsive reactions to it or with our own interests. We may, for instance, start thinking about a proposal to ration food from the point of view of the public interest and fair shares for all, and find ourselves distracted by momentary irritation or by the thought that we may be able to make a bit of profit by black-market dealing. Indeed Hume believed that impulsive reactions and selfish passions, together with the cumulative irrational influence of habit and tradition, were usually much stronger than our moral sentiments. But he insisted on the difference between the questions 'What is this to me?'

and 'Is this right?' Language develops in no haphazard manner; the distinctions of ordinary language reflect important differences of substance. If prudence were the same as morality, why should we have the different expessions? The distinguishing mark of our moral judgments is that they are expressions of our disinterested passions.

This view of Hume's is surely basically correct. He probably did not mean, as he is often interpreted as meaning, that a moral judgment is a judgment *about* our feelings, that we are in some sense *describing* what is going on in our breasts. For it is obviously untrue that when we make a moral judgment we are engaging in any sort of introspection. And, if we were doing this, moral disagreements would be impossible.[8] For we would each be describing what was going on in our own breasts and would therefore be talking about ourselves instead of the situation. We could not therefore be said to be disagreeing about any situation external to both of us. Yet people who make contrary moral judgments quite obviously are disagreeing about a situation external to both of them. If they were not it would not make sense to say that there was a moral disagreement. They would just be comparing introspective notes, not disagreeing. Hume meant, surely, that when people make moral judgments they are *expressing* approval or disapproval, not describing how they feel. Whether he meant that they must be *feeling* an emotion at the time when they said 'right' or 'wrong' is not clear. All that this view has to maintain is that at some time such an emotion must have been experienced at the contemplation of situations of a certain sort. It need not maintain that we have to experience that emotion every time we make the judgment, any more than a scientist has to look at observational evidence every time he declares that a hypothesis is true. To approve or disapprove of a situation, whatever its status as the expression of an emotion, is certainly to commend it or the reverse to those who hear the expression of approval or disapproval. And in stressing this aspect of moral judgments. Hume did a great service in bringing out their normative or prescriptive force. There is, he held, a necessary connection between a moral judgment and the will. To say that something is wrong implies that something ought to be *done* about it. This explains the gap between reasoning and moral judgments, which, on his view, so many thinkers had illegitimately jumped in their transition from 'is' to 'ought'.

But, maintained Hume, we do not approve or disapprove of *any* sort of actions. Commendation and its reverse always presuppose some sort of descriptive criteria in virtue of which we commend. Hume held that, if we are thinking about particular actions, it is only conscious voluntary actions that are so favoured and that because of their tendency to benefit or harm their author or society generally. Social conventions, too, are morally approved of solely because of their utility to society. And, when confronted with the question which the later Utilitarians had to face: 'Why bother about social utility?' Hume gave not so much a justification as a psychological explanation: 'Some particle of the dove is kneaded into our frame together with the elements of the wolf and the serpent.' We all have a degree of sympathy for others which enables us to take this disinterested standpoint. We cannot view the sufferings of others with equanimity. But, it might be objected, why should we not try to harden our hearts? Why should we not condition our children so that they no longer feel sympathy for others? Hume did not face this logical objection to his theory, because he was ostensibly concerned with explanation rather than with justification. Posing as the Newton of the social sciences he wanted merely to distinguish moral judgments from other sorts of judgment and to suggest psychological and sociological explanations of them.

It is arguable, however, that Hume, while claiming to give psychological explanations of moral judgments, was in fact including logical points about justification in his psychological descriptions. This thesis is particularly relevant to his claim that moral distinctions do not derive from reason but from moral sense or the disinterested passions. It will therefore be profitable to look a little more closely at Hume's account of moral sense; for this is a cardinal point in our exposition of moral criteria.

Hume emphasized that virtue for most people means doing the done thing. Men act justly and feel that they ought to obey the government mainly because they have acquired the habit. Their sense of duty is the product of their education and of the propaganda to which they are submitted. But, he insisted, 'no action can be virtuous, or morally good, unless there be in human nature some motive to produce it distinct from the sense of its morality'. It may be our duty to act justly and we may do so because we feel that it is our duty. But we may just have been told this, have accepted it on trust. In virtue of what characteristics should our sense of duty be annexed to some sorts of actions rather than others? What bestows *morality* on certain classes of actions? For it is a vicious circle to argue that morality is bestowed by the sense of morality. Hume's answer is that actions which spring from natural dispositions like benevolence and which are socially useful, are approved of by the disinterested spectator who takes the 'general view', whereas those that spring from socially injurious tendencies are disapproved of. It is idle to look deeper than this. We are so made that a benevolent action done to someone for whom we have sympathy pleases us in a certain way and a malevolent one displeases us. Thus the natural virtues like benevolence awaken immediate approval in us whilst conventional virtues like justice, which have no one natural motive underlying them, awaken our approval indirectly because of our reflection on their use to society on the whole and in the long run.

Now this purports to be a psychological explanation. Indeed Hume developed an elaborate theory of the passions in which the disinterested passions are distinguished from natural appetites, direct and indirect passions, and so on. But surely it looks much more like an example of the well-worn philosophical device of dressing up logical points in psychological guise. We have already suggested that philosophers who have spoken of self-evident axioms being known by 'intuition' have been making in the guise of psychology the *logical* point that no further reasons can be given for certain assumptions or rules. Similarly when Hume held that moral sense exhibits itself in contemplating conscious voluntary actions from the standpoint of the disinterested spectator who takes the 'general view', he was suggesting that the criterion of impartiality is what distinguishes moral judgments from other sorts of judgments. We must distinguish reasons in terms of self-interest from reasons in terms of the general interest in which our own interest is included but no special weight given to it simply because it is ours. Of course this criterion can only be applied by a person who has sympathy or respect for others. Some sort of imaginative sympathy with the condition of another may be a necessary condition for making a *moral* judgment. Criteria cannot be applied in a psychological vacuum. Hume's psychological story about sympathy and the disinterested passions may well indicate something of the psychological make-up of the rational being who alone is capable of making *moral* distinctions. But such necessary conditions of making a certain type of judgment should not be confused with what the judgment *means*. To say that a judgment is impartial is to say that certain types of reasons for it are excluded. It is not to say anything about the psychological make-up of the man who makes it. Men cannot make moral judgments without brains; but the necessary condition of having a brain is not part of the meaning of the judgment. Our view therefore is that Hume made a great contribution to moral theory in showing that moral distinctions do not derive from reasoning in the sense in which this is used to describe scientific or mathematical calculations. There is a logical gap between statements about facts and normative judgments, and moral rules are quite unlike mathematical axioms in many respects. But in sketching the moral sense from which he thought that our moral distinctions are derived he introduced the normative criterion of impartiality which we have claimed to be necessary for explaining what is meant by a rational being. For on our account a rational being is one who abides by the norm of impartiality in assessing arguments and claims.

IV. AUTONOMY, IMPARTIALITY AND RESPECT FOR PERSONS

Hume made much of the distinction between natural virtues like benevolence and conventional virtues like justice. The former were qualities of mind useful to society and to the agent himself which universally aroused the immediate approval of moral sense; the latter could only be justified on utilitarian grounds under certain economic and psychological conditions—e.g. the co-existence of economic scarcity with limited benevolence in man which made rules essential for the preservation of property. This distinction, Hume insisted, was a matter of fact. He was merely recording differences in the judgments of men; he was attempting no justification. Indeed, his celebrated remarks on the distinction between 'is' and 'ought' were directed in part against those who thought that a justification of virtuous behaviour could be provided by describing the nature of man. One of the most famous of such theorists was Bishop Butler,[9] who aimed to commend the Christian way of life on the ground that it was natural to man.

From our point of view Butler's main argument is not of great interest; for he relied on the Greek doctrine of function, and his account of nature therefore included norms. Man's 'proper nature' he said, was to rely on calm reflection to canalize his instinctive energy into paths acceptable to cool self-love and benevolence, and to be guided by his conscience when these principles conflicted. This hierarchical account of the soul of man in which conscience, like a bishop, presided over the principles of self-love and benevolence (the vicars) who had to calm and organize the turbulent passions (the laity) was, by admission, not merely a psychological description. For conscience had not necessarily the psychological *power* to enforce its manifest *authority*. And it was the normative structure of authority in the soul that made it a hierarchy, not the actual constitution of human nature which too often lost this structure. So Butler's appeal to 'nature' as a justification for virtuous behaviour included a norm in the form of conscience's authority. But in spite of this logical defect in his main argument, some of his remarks about conscience are important to our thesis.

First of all he held that what distinguishes man from animals is that they possess conscience, that they are a law unto themselves. Whatever the facts of this comparison—and surely one of the most important differences between man and animals *is* their ability to follow rules of their own making—the emphasis on the individual conscience was important in so far as it stressed the connection between morality and critical reflection by the individual. For conscience was 'a principle of reflection in men, by which they distinguish between, approve and disapprove their own actions'. Following conscience was thus different from doing the done thing, or simply following custom.

Secondly, though Butler believed that conscience was more or less an infallible guide, he did say that if conscience errs, this is due either to superstition (i.e. unreflective and uncritical assumptions) or to partiality to ourselves. Here we find the same connection between impartiality and morality which we have already noted in Hume and which we shall find so prominent a feature of Kant's theory.

Thus, from our point of view, Butler's theory is important in so far as it stresses the autonomy of the individual as a lawgiver and in so far as it postulates a connection between conscience and impartiality. These notions were most explicitly stated by Kant whose theory we must now state in more detail.

Kant's critical philosophy[10] was stimulated, to a large extent, by two contemporary developments—Newtonian physics and the French Revolution. His self-appointed task was to make explicit what these two movements presupposed. In the practical sphere he claimed to start from the moral consciousness of ordinary men who, under the influence of the Enlightenment, were challenging the traditional order and making up their own minds about what was right and wrong. The first and basic presupposition of morality was, therefore, the autonomy of the individual. Man, unlike the kingdom of nature, is a law-giver. Not only, as in Newtownian physics, is he capable of understanding the laws which explain his behaviour as part of the natural order—e.g. when he falls off a cliff; but also, in the sphere of normative order, the laws which he obeys are his own creation. The categories of the sciences like substance and cause may be creations of his rationality, of his demand to understand the natural order; but the truth or falsity of the laws which he is able to formulate by means of these categories does not depend on him. In the moral sphere, however, man is a law-giver, and the truth or falsity of laws depends entirely on his rational insight. Such laws, Kant held, are true or false, but they are not found to be so by observing facts, nor are they deductions from descriptions of facts.

Autonomy implies adopting standards of conduct that the individual has seen for himself to be right; but, of course, he will do most of the duties expected of him by conventional morality. His conformity, however, will not merely be the product of psychological conditioning; for he will have seen the point of the rule. On Kant's view a man's psychological make-up or conditioning has nothing to do with his moral goodness. For these are examples of what he called the heteronomy of the will, the clearest cast of which is acting under orders from another. Moral goodness is the product only of rational choice, of acting on principles that the individual has accepted for himself, of what Kant called the good will. And a good will is the only thing in the world that is good without qualification. For whatever the individual does—whether it be scientific research, statesmanship, or commercial activity—may be marred by being done with undesirable intentions or aims in view. Integrity of character is the sole unconditioned good.

Now integrity of character or having a good will is quite different from acting from certain sorts of inclinations. A man may be innately sympathetic or brought up to be kind. What moral worth has his action if it is prompted by such inclinations for the possession of which the individual can be neither praised nor blamed? Similarly individuals very often act out of self-interest. This is a matter of prudence and there are rational counsels of prudence just as there are rules of skill for attaining particular ends. But a man who is rational enough to adopt the means which are in fact necessary to reach a given end has done nothing of moral worth. After all a man may adopt the means necessary to make money or to promote his own happiness; but in itself there is nothing either moral or immoral in this. Acts are only moral, on Kant's view, if they are done on principle (subjective maxims) and if these principles conform to certain criteria so as to be acceptable as what he called objective principles. When Jesus said 'Love your neighbour as yourself' he cannot have been issuing commands to feel certain emotions. For either we feel them or we don't, and, if we don't, we cannot summon them at will. This must be an injunction to act on a certain principle, to have certain *intentions* whatever our feelings; otherwise it is an absurd injunction. For it is a matter of either preaching to the converted or of demanding the impossible. Of course, we may *also* be inclined to do what a principle dictates; it may also be in our interest. But what we are inclined to do and what it is prudent to do must be distinguished from our moral duty. It is our intentions that make actions right or wrong—what we aim to bring about; and these intentions are particular examples of general principles or maxims, other than those of prudence.

Acting on principles, then, is a necessary condition of morality; but it is not a sufficient condition. For there are all sorts of principles which we might as a matter of fact apply in our conduct which would be manifestly wrong. What then makes a principle morally right or wrong? What converts what Kant called a subjective maxim into an objective principle? Kant held that moral principles were those which could stand up to the test of the supreme higher-order or procedural principle which he called the 'categorical imperative'. This was a principle for deciding between principles of a lower order just as the verification principle in science is a principle for deciding between hypotheses which any scientist may as a matter of fact think up. He formulated this procedural principle in three different ways which he thought to be equivalent:

i. 'Act only on that maxim through which you can at the same time will that it should become a universal law.'
ii. 'So act as to use humanity, both in your own person and the person of every other, always at the same time as an end, never as a means.'
iii. 'So act as if you were through your maxims a law-making member of a kingdom of ends.'

Kant thought that acceptance of these principles was entailed by man's rationality. As he held that the rightness of actions had nothing to do with the ends which man's psychological make-up might lead him to pursue, there was no test to which his subjective maxims must conform save one which was deducible from his rational nature. For Kant held that men's behaviour as rational beings could not be accounted for in terms of the cause-effect concepts of the natural sciences.* Their rationality was not therefore part of their *psychological* make-up. As rational beings the only laws which were relevant to them were the laws of logic. So Kant held that *qua* rational beings men could only will actions the principles of which did not land them in some kind of logical contradiction. They could, therefore, only accept laws which were properly speaking laws—i.e. universal statements applying every-where to all men in similar conditions and not to a particular man in a particular condition. In so far as there was any 'end' which a man could will *qua* rational being, this could only be other rational beings who were 'ends in themselves'—as he stated in his second formulation. By this strange phrase he meant that the only unconditional good which any rational being could will to produce would be the development of a good will or integrity of character in any rational being. Rational beings could be induced to act on such principles because, as rational beings, they had reverence for law and for other rational beings as the source of law. But such reverence was not regarded by Kant as being part of man's psychological make-up.

Now Kant, we hold, was substantially right in connecting the moral criterion with man's rationality, though not in the limited sense of 'self-

* For a further discussion of the rational and causal accounts of human behaviour see Ch. 9.

consistency' which Kant's concept of 'rationality' implied. Scholars, however, have argued ever since about the sort of test that this limited types of rationality required. He took very different examples to illustrate his formulation of the categorical imperative, examples which many consider singularly ill-chosen: suicide, in which the maxim was 'from self-love to shorten life if . . . it threatens more evil than it promises pleasantness'; borrowing money and promising to pay it back without any intention of doing so; neglecting the cultivation of one's gifts for the sake of pleasure; and the maxim of neither helping others in distress nor requiring any help when one is oneself in distress. He claimed that no one could consistently will that any of these maxims should become universal laws of Nature; so they are immoral.

But why could they not be acceptable as universal laws? One interpretation, which is favourable to contractual and semi-contractual duties, (what Kant called 'perfect duties'), that if everybody made promises with the intention of breaking them, or if everybody always told lies, the concepts of 'breaking a promise' and 'telling a lie' would no longer have any *meaning*. For such deviations are parasitic on the standard cases of people keeping their promises and telling the truth. Universalization of the exceptions or deviations from the norm would bring about the logical collapse of the norm by contrast with which the deviations obtained their meaning. Another interpretation (favourable to what Kant called 'imperfect duties') stresses not the logical collapse of the concept in question but the impossibility of willing a law that is incompatible with laws of nature—especially human nature. Suicide, for instance, as a universal rule, would be absurd in the light of man's universal tendency to preserve himself; not helping others in distress nor requiring help when in distress oneself would, as universal rules, conflict with the known predictable inclinations of man. It would be impossible seriously to will universal legislation which would introduce a form of behaviour which was psychologically impossible. There is, too, the further point that, whichever interpretation is favoured, it is difficult to dissociate applying the test 'how would it be if everybody acted on this principle?' from repugnance at the large-scale consequences of things like the breakdown of the contractual system, large-scale suicide and indifference to distress. Many would therefore see Kant's universalization tests as utilitarianism in rational disguise.

Whichever interpretation of Kant is favoured, his main contribution was surely of a more limited and negative sort which he tied too closely to the notion of logical inconsistency. He was here stating the impartiality principle which is basic to morality. This is that if we maintain that a principle is a *moral* principle, then part of what we *mean* is that it is a principle which holds for *anyone* in a similar situation. This is what distinguishes morality from various forms of privilege. The best way of bringing home to a person whether or not his principle is a moral one is to get him to consider it from a point of view other than *merely* his own. This is what we do with children when we say to them 'How would you like it if somebody did this to you?' or 'How would it be if we all acted like this?' Of course, people may not be moved by looking at a situation in a moral way. They may still follow their own interests. But Kant's principle brings out what the *moral* way of looking at the situation is. The fact that *I* am acting on the principle is morally irrelevant unless a case can be made for my claims which would apply to anyone in my shoes. This implies a judgment of relevance; for many who try to justify privileged actions conceal the privilege by giving a description of themselves which puts their claims on an impersonal level. The man who seeks to justify breaking a promise in this way might say, for instance, that he held a responsible position in the community which put him in a very special category. Kant's universalization test would then make him face the question of whether this constituted a relevant consideration. Would he say that anyone else in such a position was justified in breaking the promise? If he would not, then his plea is obviously the plea of privilege. He has failed to justify it as a moral principle which requires impartiality, or that exceptions should only be made on relevant grounds. And surely the minimum requirement of 'being reasonable' is that *reasons* must always be given for making distinctions.

Kant's second formulation was that of respect for persons. This is very closely connected with impartiality as we argued at the beginning of the chapter. For refusing to be swayed by irrelevant considerations —e.g. a person's race, religion or social class in scientific discussions— suggests a minimum of respect for him as a source of claims, whatever his claims may be. Kant, of course, realized quite well that we have to treat other people, in their capacity as functionaries, as means to our ends. What else do we do when we buy a ticket at a railway station? But he insisted that we must not treat them *only* as functionaries. As rational beings they deserve our respect; for they, too, like ourselves, have ends to pursue and maxims to apply. To recognize other people as moral beings means that we must allow them to make their own decisions about principles. Being a moral being implies a certain degree of imaginative insight into the condition of others. We cannot *make* other people good; for that is denying autonomy to them, the necessary condition for anyone to develop a good will. This principle of Kant's is a good negative guide; for it tells us the sort of principles that are obviously immoral—those that involve using other people purely as means to our own ends. And this is another way of stating the rule of impartiality; for treating others merely as conveniences is surely an example of being unduly partial to our own claims.

The third formulation stresses man's activity as a law-giver and is really Kant's reply to Rousseau's conception of the General Will. Rousseau's problem was how to conceive of a community in which men could both be free and members of a civil society. His answer was that law, which binds men in a civil society, is an expression of the General Will of that society, as formulated by some wise law-giver, and accepted by them all at a public assembly of all citizens. Individuals are 'free' in proportion as they let this General Will work through them and free them from the irrational promptings of their inclinations. Men may thus have to be 'forced to be free'. Kant held that the individual is free in so far as his *individual* will makes a difference to what he does. This will finds expression in his law-making activities as a rational being, in acting on rational principles. The laws of an ideal community or 'kingdom of ends' are the product of agreement between rational beings, not the edicts of some wise and mythical law-giver. They are rules limiting the pursuit of individual good which any rational being would accept as necessary conditions for the possibility of a kingdom of rational beings. Thus Kant's third formulation of the categorical imperative provides, in a very abstract form, a kind of schema for what is often called the democratic way of life. A just constitution, he held, is one 'that achieves the greatest possible freedom of human individuals by framing the laws in such a way that the freedom of each can co-exist with that of all others'. The relevance of Kant's formal principles of impartiality and respect for persons to social justice, liberty and equality, which are intimately bound up with the democratic way of life, will be treated in separate chapters.

Our conclusion on Kant, therefore, is that he was fundamentally right in stressing the connection between rationality and morality and in isolating the norms of impartiality and respect for persons as the basic criteria to supplement the necessary condition of individual autonomy. It is often objected that these principles are too formal and give no guide to action. The answer is obvious. Kant meant them to be formal and never envisaged them as *guides* to action. Moral rules are those subjective maxims which stand up to the tests formulated in the categorical imperative and can thus be accepted as objective principles. They are not intended as *deductions* from these procedural principles any more than scientific laws are deductions from the verification principle. Their virtue is that they are formal. Kant never intended to provide guides to action any more than a methodologist of science could provide recipes for making discoveries. To compile a list of principles would be to deny the necessary condition of morality—man's autonomy. All he hoped to make explicit were the criteria used by autonomous moral beings in deciding what principles they ought to adopt. Such criteria in our view, indicate the sort of principles that would be obviously immoral. But they perform little more than this rather negative function. To ask much more of moral criteria would be to demand that the necessary condition of man's autonomy should be abandoned.

It is often said, too, that Kant's categorical imperative is of little use in a situation when a man has a *conflict* of duties. Existentialists, in recent times, have made much of the necessity for individual choice and the uselessness of general principles in such predicaments. But *of course*, in such situations, the individual himself must choose. Any moral philosopher worth his salt has said so from Aristotle onwards, who claimed that in such circumstances 'the decision lies with perception'. Kant only attempted to formulate criteria for showing what rules are in *general* right or wrong. He did not set himself up as a moral guidance bureau.

There is, however, a more fundamental objection to Kant's criteria that we have already stated. He claimed that the rightness of actions depends not upon their consequences but on the principles on which they are performed. By this he meant to exclude consideration of the happiness promoted by an action. This is fair enough; for in judging the moral worth of a particular action we take account of the happiness it promotes only in so far as it forms part of the result deliberately intended. But the rightness of the intention depends upon the general principle of which it is an application. And when we ask 'How could it be if everybody acted on this principle?' how can we exclude from consideration the interests of the persons affected? People have interests or needs which they put forward as claims. The criteria of impartiality and respect for persons are satisfied when these claims are assessed on relevant grounds, and privilege excluded as a basis for allowing a claim. In so far as we consider people's claims we consider their interests, and therefore we are making decisions which affect their welfare; for part at least of what is meant by 'welfare' is the satisfaction (or at least the non-frustration) of people's interests and needs.

V. UTILITARIANISM

Kant's neglect of welfare affected by rules was certainly remedied by his successors, the Utilitarians. For they claimed that what makes social practices right or wrong is the happiness or misery promoted by them. As J. S. Mill put it in his *Utilitarianism*, 'pleasure and freedom from pain are the only things desirable as ends' and 'actions are right in proportion as they tend to promote happiness, wrong as they tend to promote the reverse of happiness'. Bentham held that the equalitarian axiom of 'each to count as one and none for more than one' should govern the distribution of happiness and Mill stressed that impartiality was essential in deciding between our own happiness and that of others. 'In the Golden Rule of Jesus of Nazareth we read the complete spirit of the ethics of Utility. To do as you would be done by and love your neighbour as yourself constitute the ideal perfection of utilitarian morality.' In other words the Utilitarians insisted on the criterion of impartiality, though they laid much more stress on happiness or misery promoted by actions. Indeed the later and more careful Utilitarian, Henry Sidgwick,[12] inserted a special axiom of justice in his system to include Kant's contribution to ethical theory within the more general framework of Utilitarianism. He also inserted the axioms of egoism and benevolence. The first was that a man should consider his own pleasure on the whole, mere position in time of the pleasure being irrelevant. For why should a man who is out for his own pleasure be prudent, instead of indulging himself in the pleasures of the moment? The second was introduced because Sidgwick saw that Utilitarianism is only defensible if it is assumed that men ought to bother about the interests of others. Mill spoke of being impartial about the distribution of happiness; but such impartiality presupposes that we care about the happiness of someone other than ourselves, that we do not regard this merely as a means to our own happiness. If a man says 'But why should I consider anyone else's happiness, unless as a means to my own?' we can say that he is refusing to consider the matter morally. But if he replies that he only *understands* prudential duties, there is little more to be said. That is why Utilitarianism requires a basic principle of benevolence, as Sidgwick clearly understood. So does *any* system which holds that there are duties distinct from prudential ones.[13]

In our view both the Kantian and the Utilitarian contributions to ethical theory need to be included in an adequate formulation of the moral criterion. But before pressing this point, a little more must be said about some of the details of Utilitarian theory. We must first deny that 'right' *means* productive of happiness. It is very doubtful whether the Utilitarians were in fact concerned to defend such a view. Sidgwick, for instance, held that 'right' was an undefinable term and Mill was concerned only to set out what made right actions right rather than to analyse what the term 'right' means. 'Right' surely defies analysis in terms of 'production of happiness' largely because it is a *normative* term, the primary function of which is to commend or prescribe a course of action. Thus though normative terms imply descriptions (for we commend in virtue of explicit or implicit criteria), and though one of the main grounds for condemning by the use of the term 'wrong' is that a social practice promotes 'misery', it does not follow that 'right' *means* 'productive of happiness' and that 'wrong' means 'productive of misery'. For that would be to disregard the normative force of the term.[14]

Secondly, a distinction must be made between the terms 'right' and 'wrong' as applied to particular actions and to types of action in so far as they are defined by general rules. For very often we say that a particular action is right or wrong and mean simply that it is an application of a general rule.[15] We do not have to think carefully about the consequences of each particular action. Mill understood this perfectly well. He stressed the necessity for secondary principles in morality (the equivalent of Kant's maxims). We usually need to appeal to the consequences in terms of happiness promoted only when such secondary principles conflict. Experience has established, on Utilitarian grounds, that such secondary principles are in general right; but we do not have to sit down in each particular case and ponder about consequences any more than a Christian has to read through the New Testament before every action. The Utilitarian principle, like the Kantian one, provides a criterion for deciding upon the rightness or wrongness of general rules; it would be absurd to apply it rigorously to every occasion on which we have to act.[16] But this does not mean that we must treat past experience as absolutely authoritative either. For we may decide that the rule needs revising in the light of new circumstances, or that it needs modifying slightly to be defensible in a particular case. The Utilitarian, like anyone else, must have established principles; but he believes in following them intelligently, in adapting them to concrete circumstances. And the relevant criterion is always their conduciveness to the 'ultimate end' of happiness.

This distinction between particular actions and general rules helps, too, to clarify the problem of motive in relation to morality. Mill made the celebrated remark that 'The motive has nothing to do with the morality of the action, though much with the worth of the agent', and his doctrine has therefore seemed to be quite inconsistent with that of Kant, who held that the morality of an action has *only* to do with its motives. Utilitarianism is often represented as holding by contrast that it is the *actual* consequences of actions that render them right or wrong. And this is surely an absurd view, because we could then do right actions by luck or commit immoral acts while sleep-walking. Mill, however, held no such absurd view. He made clear that by 'motive' he meant the feelings and other psychological causes which prompt us to act. And he was right in saying that these are irrelevant to the morality of an action. For, as Kant said when making the same point, 'ought' implies 'can', and it is ridiculous to judge people for emotions which they cannot help feeling or to expect them to have emotions which they cannot summon at will. But Kant used the term which is sometimes translated 'motive' to refer to people's intentions, to the reasons which a person has for an action which fall under a general principle. Mill agreed with this; for he said that the morality of people's actions is a matter of their intentions.

Mill contrasted the motive of an action (in the psychological sense of 'motive') with the rule which is being applied, the agent being presumed to have certain deliberate intentions. The Utilitarian criterion, he said, applies to the rule of the action. Feeling of concern for others is not a necessary condition of a right action, though we think highly of kind-hearted people, and, in the long run, people with such kindly feelings are more likely to do right actions than people without them. If we apply the Utilitarian criterion to general rules for action, or what he called secondary principles, the importance of the stress on actual consequences becomes understandable. For many such rules, when put into practice, have consequences which are socially injurious but which are neither foreseen nor intended by the agent who applies the rule. For instance, we might hold that everyone ought to be allowed to accept any wage which he can manage to get for a job. But if it could be shown that the widespread application of this rule *actually* led to considerable exploitation and misery, a case could be made, on moral grounds, for modifying the rule. Utilitarianism is the inveterate enemy of traditionalism, of doing the done thing because it is an established practice, without considering carefully the actual consequences of the practice in terms of human misery. The connection between Utilitarianism and the development of social science is not fortuitous. For social science is largely the attempt to develop laws about the unintended consequences of types of action. These may be phenomena like slumps and wars which come under the general formula of misery promoted by the application of general principles. It is not therefore surprising that Utilitarians stress actual consequences in the context of general rules; for by the conscientious following of ill-considered rules unfortunate consequences are often produced. Utilitarians put a premium on foresight, on the constant questioning of established practices and condemn culpable ignorance and complacency.

There are, however, some subtle moral dangers inherent in too much stress on consequences and 'ends' produced. For it is often concluded that what makes actions right is solely the end produced rather than the manner in which it is produced. This, of course is morally outrageous. For we would condemn putting mental defectives and criminals to death even if it could be shown that this was the most efficient means of promoting the welfare of the bulk of the community. In stressing the welfare of the bulk of the community, we should lose sight of the principle of impartiality; for the claims and interests of the victims would in this case receive scanty consideration. Bentham himself was aware of the danger; for he laid down that 'each was to count for one, and for no more than one'. In considering punishment, for example, he insisted that the criminal's suffering was a 'mischief' to count against the benefits to the rest of the community. Perhaps, therefore, it would be better to stress the consequences to people or classes of people who are obviously affected by a social practice, rather than to refer loosely to 'the general welfare'; for some are manifestly more affected by a certain social practice than others. People cannot be treated on a level as pint pots waiting to be topped up with the waters of welfare. Rules about trade, adoption, or homosexuality, for instance, affect some members of the community much more than others according to all sorts of social economic and personal differences. People's differing claims should be considered in the light of relevant differences between them.

Furthermore, happiness or welfare is not an 'end' in the usual sense of 'end' in which going to sleep or passing an examination can be regarded as ends. Happiness is no extra state of affairs supervenient on activities. It is a term for describing ways of life where needs are not grossly frustrated, where there is absorption in interests, and where the interests are mutually compossible. Activities, as Mill himself admitted, are better regarded as *parts* of happiness rather than as means to it. This admission involves abandoning the linear conception of means to an end. It also helps us to see that activities may be undesirable because they are in themselves manifestations of misery and not merely because they are means to it. The promotion of happiness is therefore largely a matter of removing or altering conditions that obviously frustrate the satisfaction of people's needs and which prevent them developing interests which may absorb them. Some therefore prefer to state the Utilitarian criterion in terms of the minimization of misery rather than in terms of the promotion of happiness. For pain and the frustration of needs are more palpable to an outside observer than the more idiosyncratic conditions necessary for individual happiness. Also concern for promoting happiness too often leads to attempts to impose high-level personal preferences on people whose temperaments, interests, and social habits are quite different—a practice which it is difficult to reconcile with respect for persons. It is difficult enough to make those whom we love happy; with people outside our immediate circle it is wiser and less dangerous to concentrate on the obvious causes of pain and frustration when we are considering the social effects of social practices. The individual, as Mill said, is much more likely than any external agent to know what will make him happy; morality is only concerned with removing conditions which palpably prevent him from finding out.

VI. CONCLUSION

Our view about morality, therefore, which we have expounded by considering the contributions of the main schools of moral theory can be summed up as follows:

i. A moral rule differs from a customary one in that it implies the autonomy of the individual. A rule becomes moral by being critically accepted by the individual in the light of certain criteria.
ii. The criteria can be summarized by saying that the rule should be considered in the light of the needs and interests of people likely to be affected by it with no partiality towards the claims of any of those whose needs and interests are at stake.
iii. The acceptance of such criteria is implied, albeit in a minimal degree, by the notion of rationality in the sense of reasonableness.

Our contention is, therefore, that there is a sense in which moral philosophy or ethics, which is the attempt to make explicit the criteria in terms of which rules are morally justified, itself exemplies, in a minimal degree, the acceptance of the criteria which it attempts to make explicit. For philosophy, like science, is a clear example of rational discussion, and is conducted in accordance with the norms of impartiality and respect for truth. Philosophers flourish only in societies where the rational tradition has taken root. And though, as philosophers, they are not committed to any particular maxims like 'debts ought always to be paid', they are, as philosophers, committed to the very abstract procedural criteria implied in being reasonable. We have, however, been careful to stress the point that there is a gap between the bare impartial consideration of people as sources of arguments, which is strictly implied by being reasonable, and the richer impartial consideration of people as sources of claims and interests, the procedure implicit in being moral. Being moral is a species under the genus of being reasonable; it is not a synonym for being reasonable.

CHAPTER 3

LEGAL THEORY

I. INTRODUCTORY: QUESTIONS ABOUT LAW

It might seem appropriate to open a chapter on legal theory with the question 'What is law?' To ask that, however, would be to invite an embarrassing variety of answers. Law, we should be told is,

> *i.* the formal expression of conventional morality, or of that part of it which the state should enforce;
> or *ii.* a system of rules by which the interests of a dominant class are safeguarded;
> or *iii.* a system of rules held to be 'binding' or 'obligatory';
> or again *iv.* a system of rules aimed at realizing justice;
> or *v.* a system of rules discoverable by reason;
> or again *vi.* the commands of the sovereign;
> or *vii.* what judges decide in the courts;
> or *viii.* a system of rules backed by coercive sanctions.

There might even be other answers. How can so many diverse replies be given to what seems such a simple question?

The question is not so simple; on the contrary, it can be interpreted so variously that only confusion can arise from asking it. For the answers listed above are not possible answers to one and the same question, but to quite different ones (though couched in the same words), and they do not necessarily compete, merely because they all begin 'Law is . . .' To grasp this point is to realize the futility of so many acrimonious controversies in the history of legal theory; for to adopt one of the views cited need not entail rejecting the rest.

'What is law?' has often been taken to be a request for a definition of 'law', and answers like the above have all been suggested, at one time or another. Now to ask for a 'definition' is to ask how a *word* is or ought to be used; and the proper way to discover how to use a word is to consult a reliable dictionary. Many philosophers since Aristotle, however, have thought that when we know the correct definition of a word we know something essential about the thing named; and further, that it is this one essential property which entitles it to that name. In arriving at a definition then, we should arrive also at an insight into this essential feature. We believe this view to be mistaken. The meaning of a word is inseparable from the variety of contexts in which it is used. To treat any one property as 'essential', in the sense implied, would be to make one context a standard for all contexts. Things possess many properties, none in itself more essential than another. The 'essential properties' of a thing are generally those we think important for the questions that immediately interest us. But other questions could be asked, for which other properties might be 'essential'.

But 'What is law?' rarely raises questions in practice about the use of the word 'law'. More usually it is a disguised way of asking any of a number of more elaborate and more interesting questions about law itself. These may be of many different types. Here are eight such questions, and the statements about law at the beginning of this chapter are matched to the ones to which they supply possible answers:

(a) How does the content of law relate to that of other rules? (i)
(b) What functions does law perform in a society? (ii)
(c) Why do people in fact obey the law? (iii)
(d) Why ought people to obey the law? (iii, iv, and v)
(e) What moral criteria should laws satisfy? (iv and v)
(f) What criteria must a rule satisfy to be a valid law? (vi)
(g) How are legal rules related to particular decisions? (vii)
(h) How does law differ from other types of rule? (viii)

Of these questions, only the last is concerned with the use of the word 'law', since it seeks to classify and label rules by reference to their characteristics. Of the rest, (a) to (c) are questions about facts, (a) and (b) being concerned with the actual role and the social determinants of law (sociological questions), while (c) is psychological. Questions (d) and (e) are moral questions. (f) and (g) involve analysis of the formal structure of a legal system, and of the relation between norms of different levels of generality; they might be termed *meta-legal* questions. Statement (iii) is listed twice, in answer to questions of different types, psychological and moral; that, we shall show, is because it is itself ambiguous.

In Section II of this chapter we shall deal with theories that are predominantly sociological or psychological, though misconceived attempts have been made to deduce from them moral conclusions. In Section III we deal with genuine moral questions. In Section IV we treat meta-legal questions. We shall try to show that answers to questions of any one type do not, and cannot, preclude or entail any particular answers to questions of other types.

II. LAW AND CONVENTIONAL MORALITY—QUESTIONS ABOUT LAW AS A FACT

In the last chapter we distinguished two senses of the word 'moral'; it is used in one sense of rules to which certain rational tests have been applied; in another, of rules conventionally accepted in a society, guiding the behaviour and forming the basis of judgment for most of its members. A rule of conventional morality has two aspects. It may seem 'external' or imposed to someone who sees it as the standard by which other people judge his conduct; yet for most people it is an accepted rule, by which they themselves judge, and so is not for them imposed.

Rules of law and rules of conventional morality may have similar content, but are not identical, nor is there any necessary relation between them. Thus there is in England no *legal* obligation corresponding to the conventional moral obligation to attend to the sufferings of one's aged parents. Legal duties are usually more precisely formulated than those of convention, and neglect of them entails sanctions formally enunciated by the rule.

Conventional morality and obedience to law

Impressed by the similarity of content, however, some writers have argued that it is this that gives law its 'binding' quality; they remark not only that men in general obey the law, but that they commonly feel they *ought* to obey it. A. L. Goodhart, for example, attaches so much importance to this feeling that he defines 'law' in terms of it: 'I should therefore define law as any rule of human conduct which is recognized as being obligatory,'[1] where 'recognized' refers not to particular individual recognition, but to recognition by the bulk of the community.[2] This of course gives a very wide sense to the word 'law', and Prof. Goodhart later distinguishes between State (or civil) law, the 'moral law', religious law, etc. What he means by 'the moral law' is not wholly clear: sometimes it seems to be conventional morality, sometimes a 'natural law' of which convention is a particular manifestation.[3] For the moment, however, we need not pursue the point; his argument is of present interest as an attempt to show that the close correspondence between generally accepted morality and legal rules is, at least in part, the reason why we *feel* the latter to be obligatory. The fear of punishment alone would not account for widespread obedience and respect for law; there could never be enough policemen to maintain a legal order were that the sole motive; it is, he says, because most men feel the law to be right that we have to coerce only a minority.

Sir Ernest Barker[4] offers a similar view. For him, law expresses the 'common conviction' of a community concerning what is just. Moral attitudes evolving in a society by experience and discussion find formal expression in its legal order. T. H. Green[5] thought in similar terms of a society of men engaged, throughout many generations, in a corporate experimental search for the external conditions for a good life and the fulfilment of personality. Conventional morality and law together represent the collective and institutionalized wisdom of the nation. Not indeed that existing institutions, or even conventional morality, are perfect; but in Green's view they necessarily tend to the ideal.

A widespread feeling in favour of obedience to the law is not, however, in itself sufficient proof that law reflects conventional morality. Hägerström speaks of a 'general law conviction', a feeling that law is obligatory.[6] He seems to mean that, in any society, the moral rule 'The law ought to be obeyed' is one that is widely acceptable. We might call this attitude simply 'respect for law'. It is this, he says, which explains the fact of obedience, or alternatively why coercion is available to support the rule where necessary. This is what makes the law 'binding' or 'positive'.

If such an attitude to law exists, it is easy to see why. For a society to survive at all, its members must generally favour obedience to rules (and not only legal rules); we learn to live as members of a society precisely by learning to respect rules. Each of us builds up a rule-conforming habit, grounded in early training and family relations, confirmed by education, and sustained by the pressures of public opinion. Unless there is some special reason for doing otherwise, we conform to the rule, simply because it is a rule.[7] Outside academic discussions, we do not ask why people keep rules, but why they break them. It is the exceptional and unexpected, not the usual, that requires explanation.

Goodhart maintains, however, that the 'obligatoriness' of law rests on stronger ground than this alone. The 'general law conviction' is reinforced by the widespread approval of particular rules of law which coincide with the 'moral law'.[8] Only an extensive sociological investigation could show whether there is really such a correspondence; we should probably find that it varied from one society to another. (It is arguable, indeed, that close correspondence would be assumed as a matter of course only in a liberal democracy, where law and opinion are brought into contact by institutional arrangements designed for that purpose.) But certain limitations of the theory may be noted even without special sociological research:

(a) On some matters regulated by law, conventional morality is silent; for instance, whether the charterers or the owners of ships should be liable for losses through a dock strike. In many matters, what the rule is, is of less importance than that there should be a rule: law apart, there is no special virtue in driving on the left. Even if conventional morality supports the general intention of an enactment or policy, e.g. economic planning, it may not support its details, e.g. a legal obligation to make returns of statistical information.

(b) So far from merely reflecting conventional morality, the law may lead it and modify it. An 'advanced' minority might bring about a reform with which a majority was out of sympathy, particularly if the majority did not feel very strongly about it, or was inarticulate or lacked organization. The passing of the minority morality into law might attract to it some of the dignity and respect associated with law in general. For some, the new rule in operation might come to justify itself by its results; for others, respect for its legal authority might in the end be transmuted, by mere habit, into a favourable attitude towards its content. Because conservative opponents of law reform frequently insist that law must *reflect* conventional morality,* reformers make the point that it can sometimes *lead* it.

(c) In some cases, there may be clear contraditions between law and conventional morality. In English criminal law, a principal may be liable for certain offences committed by his agent, irrespective of *any* precautions he may have taken to prevent the offence being committed, a rule which would receive doubtful support from conventional morality. Why should we expect such a rule ever to be amended, if it demands nothing from most people, and if those not affected feel no particular sympathy for those who are? On the other hand, the lack of moral support for the anti-liquor laws in the USA led to widespread disobedience, the breakdown of the enforcing machinery, and ultimate repeal. Similarly, the penal law had to be reformed in early nineteenth century England when juries began to refuse convictions because of the monstrous penalties.

(d) We must not assume that there are always standards of morality that are *general*. In a stratified society there may be different moral standards at different social levels. The police can easily prevent street betting in Tunbridge Wells, but in Whitechapel, where public sympathy is with the bookmaker, they admit defeat. If a society is divided by culture or religion, there may be no 'common conviction' on issues

* For instance, the government refused to implement the recommendations of the Wolfenden Report on homosexuality on the grounds that they ran counter to the weight of public opinion.

like divorce, capital punishment, and homosexuality. Laws may reflect the morality of a group or class which is dominant, but not necessarily a majority. Traditionalists like Edmund Burke maintain that the very survival of an order is evidence that it can satisfy the moral needs of a nation. The Marxist retorts that it is evidence only that it satisfies a dominant class. This might get its own standards accepted throughout a society for a time, but eventually changing conditions produce new, self-conscious, and rebellious classes, determined to re-shape the legal order in the light of their own needs and experience. This is what happened in pre-revolutionary France. In such conditions the 'common conviction' theory is simply irrelevant.

(e) Finally, the theory takes for granted a liberal society, in which opinion is formed by free and public discussion. It presents law as a formal, authoritative structure, reflecting moral rules, which develop independently of authority, in a social forum where all ideas and experiences are canvassed. By using modern techniques of censorship and propaganda, however, rulers may make not only the law, but also the opinion to support it. If law and accepted moral standards coincide, this may only be because there is an efficient ministry of propaganda.

III. THE OBLIGATION TO OBEY THE LAW—MORAL QUESTIONS ABOUT LAW

(a) Moral and sociological questions distinguished

According to the view we have been discussing, men generally obey the law because it requires of them what they would themselves consider right conduct, even without the law. This is often true; nevertheless, a complete answer to the question 'Why do men generally obey the law?' would need concepts and techniques not commonly used by social or legal philosophers. For this is a psychological or a sociological question, not a philosophical one. It has seemed important, however, to some philosophers, because they have thought it provided an answer to another question, namely, 'Why *ought* people to obey the law?' Now this is surely a mistake, for this a *moral* question, and a factual account of other people's motives cannot provide anyone with a *moral* reason for obedience. Prescriptions cannot be derived from simple statements of fact. If most other people approve of the law, that may be a reason for not condemning it without serious thought; it cannot be reason enough for either approving it or obeying it. We argued in Chapter 2 that an appeal to authority is not a moral argument; this is as true of the authority of the multitude as of a despot or a priest.

Sir Ernest Barker maintains, however, that the law ought to be obeyed because it generally conforms to the commonly accepted standards of justice; and this, he holds, is *equivalent* to saying that it is just.[9] But it is surely wrong to equate 'justice' and 'what is commonly held to be just'. A public opinion survey will establish whether the law is generally approved, for this is a question of fact. But it cannot establish whether a rule is just. That depends on whether it bears impartially on those affected by it, which is a matter not of fact but of moral judgment. Professor Goodhart's view, referred to earlier, is more complicated. He believes that English law approximates to 'the moral law', by which he understands not simply a commonly accepted set of standards, but also a sort of natural law, objectively valid as the law of reason, to which accepted standards are supposed to conform. The moral law is held to validate positive law, so far as the latter corresponds to it. This idea that natural law provides criteria of moral validity for positive law is important, and must be treated fully.

(b) Natural law
(i) *The eighteenth century view of natural law as quasi-geometry*. We have shown in Chapter 2 how, in its seventeenth and eighteenth century form, natural law was understood as a quasi-geometrical or deductive system, resting on self-evident axioms about man's nature and place in the universe, and prescribing general rules for the dealings of man with man. Resting on 'the nature of man', it was held to be universal, valid without respect to time and place; and because it was said to be the law of reason, it was thought to provide irrefutable justification for any act or judgment that accorded with it. The legislator's duty was to enact natural law; the subject's, to obey because (or to the extent that) it was so enacted.

A quasi-mathematical view would treat natural law as a body of theorems, any one of which would be deducible from higher order theorems and ultimately from self-evident axioms. But a system of rules for conduct, unlike a geometrical system, has to be interpreted. And though we can give reasons for particular prescriptions by referring to general rules, such rules do not determine their own application. When deciding on action according to rules, we have to decide into which category the given circumstances fit, or what amounts to the same thing, which of several competing rules is the one to apply here. In using proverbs, we often meet contradictions; for instance, 'Too many cooks spoil the broth' and 'Many hands make light work' are veiled prescriptions, which might be applied in appropriate circumstances—but we have to decide what these are. Anyone deciding according to rules, whether moral or legal, has to make choices of this sort.

A judge faced with contending counsel, each seeking to construe a statute in his own way, or to bring the case under one precedent rather than another, must decide whether the provisions of the statute are to extend to this case or not, or which precedent to treat as the appropriate analogy. His decision may well be influenced by the thought of the uses to which it might be put in later cases, or by the general trend of legal interpretation. Consequently, while he may be able to say *afterwards* that his decision is a deduction from a general rule applied to the particular facts, he cannot in fact arrive at it by deductive reasoning, since the critical step is that which places the facts in one legal category rather than another.[10] In some instances, it is true, ordinary usage or lawyers' rules for construing legal language will clearly show what the decision ought to be: magistrates are rarely in doubt in a case of driving without lights, for everyone agrees about what constitutes a light on a vehicle; but opinions on 'dangerous driving' may vary considerably. If therefore some rules *seem* to determine their own application, it is because there is wide agreement not only about what the words mean in general terms, but about the particular circumstances to which they properly apply.

Now the geometrical method involves strict definitions, leading to conclusions from which *logically* there can be no dissent. We do not have to *decide* whether to accept Euclid's conclusions; the decision is made for us as soon as we have accepted his definitions and rules of inference. But to accept them is only to commit ourselves to doing geometry—to using words in a certain way, and to abiding by the rules of inference of the system. It does not commit us to any assumptions about the world. A deductive system of law or morals, on the other hand, like a deductive system in empirical science, presents the problem of the minor premiss, of applying rules or laws to particular cases, as well as the problem of the truth or falsity of the major premiss.

Natural law was thought to be a system in which the reason moved progressively from higher order to lower order general rules, and thence to particular prescriptions. But the more general the rule, the vaguer it will be, and the greater the possibility of disagreement when it is applied to a particular case. Standard cases could always be found, to which such a rule could be applied with the full consent of those who accepted it. But there will be some cases where some consider that the rule applies and others do not. We may all agree that we should love our neighbours; but what is love, and who are our neighbours?

Natural law theory sought an ultimate standard by which to test the justice of positive legal rules and decisions, a law behind the law; but in adopting geometry as its model, it misconceived the logical structure of systems where decisions are taken according to rules, and confused the conclusion of a chain of reasoning with a decision taken after weighing evidence and argument.

Nevertheless, there is an important difference between a decision according to a rule and one not governed by rules. Unless one is on a diet, deciding to have steak and onions for lunch is not a decision according to rules; for it is not an answer to the question 'What is the right thing to do?' To answer this question necessarily involves applying rules or standards which, for the man making the decision, supply its grounds. Another man, of course, might apply the rules differently. The pacifist might justify refusing to do military service by the rule 'Killing is wrong'; the minister for war would limit this rule to exclude killing his country's enemies, justifying himself by another rule, like 'It is right to defend one's country'. They can discuss all this; for instance, one might show that if the other had his way, another rule that both accepted would be broken. Agreement depends, however, not only on their willingness to discuss the matter reasonably, but also on their both accepting at least one relevant rule, which neither is prepared to see limited or infringed. There can be no guarantee that, even with the best will in the world, moral differences (unlike mathematical differences) can be resolved by argument; but equally there is no guarantee that they cannot, and to continue arguing implies the belief that common ground might still be found.

(*ii*) '*Natural law with variable content.*' Legal theorists no longer think of natural law as a body of theorems eliminating decision, but rather as a body of flexible general rules, discoverable by rational reflection on man's nature, *within* which decisions are taken, and which operate variously under different conditions. This point of view is sometimes described as 'a theory of natural law with variable content'. It has affinities with the older views of Aristotle and Aquinas, which permitted flexibility of application.

The phrase 'man's nature', however, presents difficulties. For Aristotle and Aquinas, the 'nature' of a thing is what it would be if it realized its potentialities, its end which is the 'good' for that thing. Furthermore, they would say it has a tendency towards its good. Thus Aquinas argued that man has natural inclinations towards self-preservation, propagation of the species, the pursuit of truth, and social living. He appealed to these tendencies not merely as descriptions of what men are likely to do in appropriate situations, but also as grounds for prescriptions of what they ought to do. From such basic prescriptions can be derived less general, though still universal, maxims like 'Murder is

C

wrong' or 'Debts must be repaid'. Admittedly these alone do not yield particular prescriptions beyond dispute, for not every case of homicide is murder, and as Aristotle pointed out, the law of nature does not specify *how soon* or *in what form* a debt must be repaid. Reason can pronounced on details only in particular contexts.

We may agree with Aristotle that man, as a living thing, differs from the inanimate world in that his movements are self-originated, to be explained in terms of his particular 'ends' or 'goals', and that most men differ from other living things by imposing a plan or rule (the use of reason) on the pursuit of such goals. But to say that man has an over-all 'end' *as a man* is to use the term 'end' in a different and extended sense. Being a rational and social animal is not an 'end' in the sense in which having a meal and going to sleep are ends. Furthermore, though all men have certain ends like eating and drinking, they vary enormously in the extent to which they develop or mature towards the norm of rational self-control which Aristotle envisaged as the 'end' for man, let alone towards that of the search for truth, which he also included in the concept 'rationality'. To take this as the 'end' for man is to conceal a norm in a description of development. And the type of conduct prescribed by that norm has been rejected by many romantics, who have held, with Rousseau, that a thinking man is a depraved animal.

The older theory of natural law received some support from the Roman conception of a *jus gentium*, or law of nations. This was not international law in the modern sense, but a body of rules consistent with the law of every nation, which was therefore acceptable for regulating relations between individuals of different nations. This seemed to argue a substratum of natural law upon which all positive systems were founded, which derived necessarily from the nature of man, and of which maxims like 'Murder is wrong' and 'Debts must be repaid' were parts.

'Murder is wrong' is self-evident or 'natural', however, not because of any characteristic of human nature, but because the term 'murder' is one we use to condemn. We should not call a killing 'murder' unless we deemed it wrong, so that 'murder' is necessarily 'wrongful killing'.*[11] Similarly, 'Debts ought to be repaid' is incontrovertible, since we normally use the word 'debts' only inconnection with transactions where an obligation to repay would be generally understood. (In some circumstances, of course, a debtor may honestly ask: 'Ought I repay *this* debt?' But in doing so, he recognizes that transactions of this type *normally* demand repayment; the question arises only because the conditions are

---

* We are not saying that 'murder' *means* 'wrongful killing', for there are other sorts of wrongful killing which are not murder.

not normal, i.e. they differ in relevant particulars from the usual pattern.) Similarly, there must be very few societies that do not prohibit incest —but sexual relations which are legitimate in some would be prohibited in others. 'All societies prohibit incest' entails that all prohibit *some* sort of sexual relations, not that they all prohibit the *same* sorts. We cannot therefore conclude that any particular relations are 'unnatural'.

(*iii*) *Science as a basis for natural law.* Some recent expositions of natural law theory have been based on psychological, sociological, or biological accounts of man's nature. According to Prof. Montrose, for instance, 'the biologists and anthropologists are apparently now prepared to state that the characteristics of man's health can be determined by empirical science, and that man's values can thus be objectively determined'.[12] He quotes Ashley Montagu: ' "The basic test of a value is the extent to which it contributes to the survival of the organism as a healthy and harmonically functioning interdependent whole ... A soundly functioning organism is something which has a real existence and whose critical requirements can be investigated." (*The Direction of Human Development* p. 156.)'

A biologist's account of the conditions for survival of an organism cannot, however, determine a 'value', unless we postulate that it is valuable for the organism to survive. In any case, human life is never simply a matter of just surviving, but of surviving in a certain manner. And included in 'the manner' are standards and conventions laying down what is valuable. Mere survival is not the only moral principle, or necessarily the most important one. Biological, psychological, and social sciences may have important contributions to make to the study of morals and law—but they cannot answer moral questions, because their propositions are descriptive or predictive, whereas answers to moral questions must be prescriptive. If they *appear* to provide such answers, it is because at some stage a moral prescription has crept in unnoticed.

Similarly, a biological notion like 'health' is far too narrow to be a universal criterion of moral behaviour (for there are times when we feel it right to sacrifice health for other things*)—and to extend it beyond the biological field, to include notions like 'healthy relations with other human beings', 'a healthy social atmosphere', etc., is to give up even the appearance of an objectively verifiable condition. The much-worked

---

* If it could be shown that great works of art could be produced only by the maladjusted, should we be willing to accept the psychologist's criterion of 'adjustment' as a value to be realized in all human beings? Some people, at least, might rate a masterpiece more highly than 'mental health'.

term 'mental health', for instance, is either a way of referring to something purely negative like the absence of unconscious conflicts, or it is a way of stating social and personal preferences that are highly disputable. It is not that the findings of the empirical sciences are irrelevant to moral questions, but rather that, when all the information is assembled, decisions must still be made on principles that science simply cannot provide. To substitute scientific research for quasi-mathematical deductive reasoning places natural law on no firmer a footing of objective truth.

(d) *Natural law and moral judgments.* There can be no objection to natural law theory if it says only that rules of law must be tested against moral rules, like 'It is wrong to tell lies', 'Love thy neighbour', 'Pay your debts'. Criticisms of positive law, or judicial decisions that claim to rest on natural law, inevitably refer to maxims like these. They are the common currency of moral discourse; and if the natural law theory implies only that judges ought to interpret, and individuals to evaluate law in the light of moral principles, these maxims will clearly have their place. But natural law theory seems to claim more than this; in using words like 'natural' and 'reasonable' it seems to claim a validity for its maxims independent of the attitudes adopted by the persons applying them, as if, indeed, they could themselves be validated by reference to some still higher law. In Aquinas' case this point of view was explicit— natural law was valid as a manifestation of the rational will of God—as an insight into the eternal law governing the whole universe.* Such a position, however, leads only to an infinite regress—for if we seek the validity of a law of any given order always in terms of a law of a higher order, there can be no end.

It is surely a mistake to search for ultimate, absolute, or objective values to provide tests of validity for the actual moral rules used in judgment, decision, and action. The existence of objective standards— in the sense of 'standards existing independently of anyone's knowing or adopting them'—would simply make no difference to us unless there were some mark by which they could be recognized as different from 'subjective' and 'false' standards. Now individuals adopting different

---

* Similarly, any view which rests natural law on a scientific demonstration of the characteristics of man's health appeals implicitly to a higher law, science, as a validating principle for moral maxims. But science is not a prescriptive but a descriptive or explanatory activity, and cannot be a 'law' in this sense. The same criticism applies to Duguit's attempt to construct a theory of law on the basis of social and economic science, where the conditions for 'social solidarity' are represented as the objectively validating principles. This is natural law theory in disguise. (See H. J. Laski on Duguit, in *Modern Theories of Law* (ed. W. I. Jennings), 1933.)

standards are often equally confident of being right; there is plainly no mark of the 'true' standard such that, when recognized, it settles all arguments. Moral differences are not all based on ignorance of fact, or on wrong-headed refusals to 'see reason'; and so long as genuine differences continue, the most we can do is to seek agreement based on some mutually accepted standard, if it is to be found. We shall make no progress by alleging that somewhere, somehow, there is one *right* answer to the problem, established as part of the universal order independent of anyone's acceptance. Anyone adopting that view will be inclined to assume that the one right attitude is his own (for it would be odd to adopt a moral position without believing it to be the true one), and may be reluctant to accept any reconciliation that requires him to yield any ground at all.

If the theory of natural law—'the law of reason'—asks only that we consider rationally and impartially how others will be affected by a law, it is just another way of stating the procedural norms for making moral judgments (see Chapter 2). The only sense in which such judgments could be said to be absolute would be the sense in which a moral being, like a scientist, might be said to be committed to certain norms of procedure that he is not prepared to give up. But there is nothing absolute about rules or assumptions justified by such procedures. If natural law theory means more than this, if it looks beyond the particular judgment to an independently existing moral order, it is either barren, declaring the existence of unknowable, and therefore useless standards, or it leads to a rigid dogmatism which, so far from settling arguments, can only embitter them.

(*e*) *Natural law and the duty to obey the law.* Our discussion of natural law stemmed from the question 'Why ought people to obey the law?' The natural law theorist would answer: 'There is a duty to obey positive law if it corresponds with natural law, or is consistent with its general prescriptions, since natural law is an expression of the moral order of the universe (or derives from man's "end" or "good").' Unsatisfactory as this formulation may be, it has the virtue that it seeks to answer the question in moral terms, rather than in sociological or strictly legal terms. It admits that on occasion there may be no moral duty to obey, and even a duty to disobey. Thus law can be rationally criticized; the authority of a legislature or of public opinion cannot in itself constitute a moral ground of obligation. Natural law theory is right to focus attention on the content of law rather than its source: whether we ought to obey the law must surely depend, in some measure at least, on what the law demands of us.

(c) 'Why ought people to obey the law?'—The question analysed

Some modern writers[13] object to natural law theory because they interpret it as asking for necessary and sufficient conditions for obedience. If any law fulfilled such conditions regardless of attendant circumstances there would be a duty to obey it. If it did not, there would be no such duty. Now we have already remarked that we cannot lay down any detailed prescription for all circumstances precisely because circumstances will affect its results and thus its desirability; and further, that the more general the prescription, the less clear we are when to apply it. If natural law theory does seek to establish necessary and sufficient conditions for obedience, it must fail, either because its *detailed* criteria cannot be applied universally without outraging our sense of what is fitting, or because they are too *general* to be a useful test. (Whether the prohibition of murder in natural law justifies conscientious objection depends on the precise scope of 'murder' in a given situation—yet the prescriptions of natural law are admitted to be incapable of that degree of particularization. Anything short of that, however, will make a statement of 'necessary and sufficient conditions for obedience' at best a rule of procedure to be adopted in dealing with such questions, not a crucial test for answering them.)

The critics argue that the search for 'necessary and sufficient conditions for obedience' is prompted by a confusion. We can answer 'Why should I obey the Road Traffic Act?' and 'Why should I obey the Incitement to Disaffection Act?', because they presume a particular situation. We can refer to their aims, to their chances of achieving them in that situation, to possible alternatives, etc. But to ask 'Why should I obey *any* law?' is to divorce the question of obligation from *all* circumstances. It is tempting to look for some general principle in the answers to all the particular questions, from which we could later derive answers to similar questions. But if the particular situation is deliberately excluded, a generalized answer, in respect of *any* law, would be too broad to indicate the necessary and sufficient conditions for obedience in any new particular instance. This is only another way of saying that particular prescriptions are not *deducible* from general rules; that the application of a rule requires, not the method of deductive reasoning, but decision.

Similar objections have been raised to theories which offer a general formula characterizing every just law (such as 'the greatest happiness of the greatest number' or Barker's 'maximum development of individual personality'); for at that level the maxims are so vague that *any* rule could be shown to be consistent with them. If we said that a rule of law was so consistent, we should not be using the formula as a test; we should be interpreting the formula to include the rule, having already approved it in the light of lower order moral rules applied to the particular circumstances. The formula is only a way of summarizing the particular approvals we have made, each new addition having been considered as a separate problem. Consequently we can derive from the formula only those particulars we have deliberately decided to include.

In so far as any theory purports to offer necessary and sufficient conditions for obedience, it is open to these criticisms; and to that extent, it is true that the question 'Why should I obey *any* law?' is unanswerable. There remains, however, another possible interpretation of the question and of the theories designed to answer it. While no formula could provide necessary and sufficient conditions for obedience for every situation, the maxims offered may still act as guides for reflection. The principle 'Murder is wrong' will not *settle* the moral problems of military service but it suggests one aspect of them that must be considered. The maxims of natural law theory indicate, as it were, the sort of things that will be relevant to the discussion of the rightness of a given law, or the sort of procedure that the discussion ought to follow. Similarly, the Utilitarian formula suggests that to test the rightness of a law we must consider the probable consequences for everyone closely affected by it, not the years it has been in force, or the influential people who support it. For as we have shown in Chapter 2, while the first are moral considerations, the second are not; and if the question 'Why must I obey *any* law?' be taken to mean 'What sort of considerations would be relevant to a decision whether I ought to obey a given law?' the theories under discussion are not without significance. It is worth noting, in this connection, that modernized natural law theory emerged in England in the seventeenth century, and in France in the eighteenth century, in opposition to doctrines looking, not to the content of law, but to its source or to religious authority as sufficient grounds for obedience. And Utilitarian doctrines were enunciated in England by Benthamite reformers challenging a doctrinaire and traditionalist acceptance of the principles and procedures of the Common Law. In an age preoccupied with reform, one would expect the predominant political and legal theories to hinge on the criteria of *moral* criticism, which reformist activity necessarily presupposes; in an age of consolidation and retrenchment, the emphasis is likely to shift towards principles that lend authority to rules of law, whether religious (e.g. Divine Right doctrines in Tudor England) or traditionalist (e.g. Burke's appeal to the 'prescriptive' constitution, against the critical attitudes engendered by the French Revolution).[14]

IV. THE STRUCTURE OF LEGAL
SYSTEMS—META-LEGAL QUESTIONS

(a) Validity of a rule within a system

The question 'Why ought people to obey the law?' is sometimes confused with 'What makes a law valid?' The former asks what moral criteria a rule must satisfy if there is to be a duty to obey it. The latter asks 'What are the criteria for determining whether a rule is a rule of *law*?' It is not a moral but a legal question.

This new question requires that we examine the notion 'a legal system', and especially what determines whether a rule is part of such a system, and how rules of law are related to one another. This investigation is important to anyone with the function of administering law, or, like a solicitor, of advising clients on their legal rights and duties.

Classification distinguished from Systematization of Rules. In Chapter 1 we observed that the word 'society' implied rules governing the behaviour of its members. We are accustomed to distinguishing between rules of different types—between, for example, conventional rules and legal rules, between the rules of football and those of cricket, between fashion and etiquette, etc. To make distinctions of this sort is to classify. Nothing, however, classifies itself: what categories or pigeon-holes we employ for 'sorting' phenomena, or what common characteristics we choose to regard as reasons for putting otherwise dissimilar things into the same category, will depend on the purpose of the classification. Thus cricket caps and scoreboards might be classified together, and distinguished from the class that includes football boots and goalposts, if we are interested in what is needed for a well-ordered game; but a sports outfitter would classify caps and boots together as his proper stock-in-trade, leaving scoreboards and goalposts to those equipping sports' grounds. Rules, too, are variously classified, and no one way is inherently superior to another. We can classify, e.g. (*i*) according to the type of activity regulated (thus the rules of cricket are distinguished from those of football, and maritime law from industrial law); (*ii*) according to source (thus Acts of Parliament are distinguished from the rules of cricket laid down by the MCC); (*iii*) according to whether they are procedural or substantive (as we distinguish constitutional rules, like the Parliament Act of 1911 or the constitution of the Transport and General Workers' Union, from rules like the law protecting wild life or Beau Nash's code of etiquette and dress for eighteenth century Bath); (*iv*) according to the degree of formality (as we distinguish Acts of Parliament, or the MCC rules, from constitutional conventions or cricket etiquette). The scheme of classification will depend on our purpose—for classification is a means to an end, not an end in itself.*

A criterion for classifying rules indicates a property common to all rules of the class so constituted, distinguishing them from others. It is therefore concerned with similarity and difference. A criterion for systematizing rules, however, is a criterion of validity. A society which has officials acting in its name and enforcing its rules must provide tests of their authority, and ways of recognizing the rules that it is their duty to enforce. When social relations reach a certain degree of complexity, disputes must be settled by an authoritative arbiter. For the sake of convenience and security, his judgments must be as far as possible predictable, and therefore according to known rules, rather than standards peculiar to himself. Since there may well be rules governing behaviour in that society which are nevertheless not meant to be used by such authoritative arbiters, there will have to be understood criteria for determining what is, for his purpose, a valid rule. These criteria are basic rules, from which others derive validity, the whole being 'a

---

* Arguments about 'the definition of law', or 'the essence or nature of law', are therefore often misconceived, for there is no one 'right' scheme by which rules *ought* to be classified, such that those possessing some 'essential' property must alone be called 'laws'. It would be pointless to argue, for instance, about Goodhart's use of 'law' in the term 'the moral law'. Similarly, the perennial question 'is international law "law"?' is mainly about how words are to be used, not about law. (Cf. Glanville Williams: *The Controversy concerning the Word 'Law'* in P. Laslett (ed.): *Philosophy, Politics, and Society* (1956); and R. Wollheim: *The Nature of Law*, in Political Studies, Vol. II, 1954, p. 128.) In ordinary usage, 'law' may denote rules, and systems of rules, ranging from 'the laws of football' to 'Talmudic law'. Necessary and sufficient conditions for the correct use of words can be given only for artificial languages, like the scientists'. The Oxford Dictionary has several pages on meanings of 'law' sanctioned by ordinary usage.

However, a writer may *stipulate* a definition of 'law', and so deliberately limit discussion to the rules that fit it. This is often useful, and is unobjectionable in principle. It would be a mistake to object that what he says about laws in the stipulated sense is inapplicable to other rules usually called 'laws'; or that he has chosen the 'wrong' definition, if he does not imply that it corresponds with ordinary usage.

Nevertheless, some definitions may be more useful than others. A legal historian who defined 'law' in terms of statute would probably find himself inconveniently restricted by his conceptual framework. (Cf. H. Kantorowicz: *The Definition of Law* (ed. A. H. Campbell) 1958.) Again, a decision to call a set of rules 'law' may have emotive consequences. Many international lawyers object to definitions that exclude international law, because they believe, probably rightly, that to deny it the name 'law' would be to weaken the respect in which it is held.

system'. If conditions are changing fairly quickly, new rules have to be devised and old ones amended. So the system will have to define what conditions a rule, deliberately made rather than customarily evolved, must satisfy to be a valid part of the system. It will have to establish legislative organs, and criteria for identifying their members, and legislative procedures, to distinguish their official acts from their acts as private persons. Constitutional law consists of rules of this sort—but so too does the constitution of any organized association, from a trade union to a social club, each of which is a normative system in the same sense as law. What characterizes a normative system, then, is that it possesses a basic norm, or norms, providing criteria by which the validity, within that system, of other norms may be determined; or what amounts to the same thing, which give to other norms their authority.

The nineteenth century jurist John Austin was moving towards something like this view of the structure of a legal system, in his famous *Lectures on Jurisprudence*. From him sprang the school of analytical jurisprudence which until very recently dominated English legal studies.

Austin's object was to free the study of law from Natural Law theory, which in his view confused moral and legal issues, and blurred the distinction between the questions 'What test determines whether a law is valid within a given system?' and 'What are the tests of the moral value of a law?' The latter question belongs, he asserts, to the 'science of legislation'; jurisprudence is properly concerned only with the former. Austin himself did not see the issue altogether clearly: he declared that the purpose of his course of lectures (*The Province of Jurisprudence Determined*) was 'to distinguish positive laws (the appropriate matter of jurisprudence) from . . . the objects with which . . . they often are blended and confounded'. He proposed to do this by 'determining the essence or nature which is common to all laws that are laws properly so called'. [5] Now had this been all he meant to do, he would have achieved no more than a prolonged exercise in stipulative definition of the words 'law' and 'jurisprudence' and it is unlikely that he would have had so profound an influence on legal studies. For, as we have argued above, rules do not classify themselves, and one may stipulate any definition one pleases.

(b) Austin and the command theory of law

Laws properly so called, Austin declared, are a species of command. A command is a 'signification of desire . . . distinguished from other significations of desire by this peculiarity; that the party to whom it is directed is liable to evil from the other, in case he comply not with the desire.[16] This evil is termed the 'sanction'. Furthermore, 'a signification of desire' implies a determinate person or body of persons having the desire; while the definition of 'command' implies that these persons have the ability to inflict the sanction on the disobedient, this being what is meant in saying that laws are addressed by 'superiors' to 'inferiors'.[17] Since in an independent political society there cannot be an infinite hierarchy of superiors and inferiors, there must be within it 'a *determinate* human superior, *not* in a habit of obedience to a like superior, (receiving) *habitual* obedience from the *bulk*'[18] of the society. That superior is termed 'sovereign'. Laws are commands coming from the sovereign, directly or via subordinate authorities; they are distinguished from other commands by their generality. Austin called them 'positive laws', to distinguish them from other man-made rules which, like 'positive morality', lack a formal sanction, and from the laws of God.

Now were this only a system of stipulative definitions, it would be beyond criticism; Austin intended it, however, as an account of the actual legal systems operating in modern states. We are therefore entitled to ask, not indeed whether the scheme is 'true' but whether it enables us, without making arbitrary exclusions or distortions, to arrange in a significant pattern the rules and procedures that are the usual objects of legal studies.

Austin's view of law was naturally influenced by the particular characteristics of English law. *Prima facie*, Parliament looks like an Austinian sovereign, and an English criminal statute like the sovereign's command. Even English law, however, can present difficulties for the scheme. Not all statues fit so comfortably into the 'command' pattern. Austin recognized that some rules, usually included in 'law', are of 'incomplete obligation', in that as they stand they impose no specific obligation, and consequently (in Austinian terms) involve no sanction. An Act of Parliament requires that a will must have been witnessed if it is to be valid—but no one is *obliged* to make a will. If one ignored the prescribed procedure, one's wishes would be legally ignored after one's death, because the will would not be in law a will at all. This result is not however a sanction. Rules of this sort are often called 'permissive' or 'enabling'; they do not prescribe that a given act shall be done; they lay down a procedure to be followed if the act is to have legal consequences. Much of constitutional and administrative law is of this sort; a minister empowered by statute to issue such orders 'as he thinks fit' is not thereby *commanded* to make any order at all. To call an enabling rule a 'command', even 'of incomplete obligation', is to mistake its function; its effect is to give to rules made in accordance with it a legal status that they would otherwise lack. We distinguished earlier in this chapter between rules of substance and rules of procedure; permissive rules and most constitutional rules are of the latter sort. While Austin's scheme has a certain persuasiveness in respect of rules of substance, it will fit rules of procedure only at the cost of considerable distortion either of the facts or of the ordinary use of the word 'law'.

What lends colour to Austin's analysis is that all rules, whether legal or otherwise, can be expressed in the imperative mood, for this is what makes them rules and not statements. But the logical or grammatical form of a rule is not evidence of the existence of a determinate 'commander'. Legislation is not the only source of law; Common Law grows through judicial decisions, out of which may be distilled, as it were, the legal profession's view of the rules that judges ought to use in deciding cases; even local custom may provide rules having legal force. Austin dealt with laws of this sort by arguing (in Hobbes' words) that 'the legislator is he, not by whose authority the law was first made, but by whose authority it continues to be law'. To speak, however, of the current Parliament as the author of the entire law of England is curiously perverse, when what is meant is that Parliament is legally competent to alter or repeal any existing rule, of whatever origin.

The command theory as a pattern for criteria of validity.[19] Austin's account seems inadequate, if it is treated as an attempt to describe how laws are made, or why they are observed, or who in the last analysis initiates all social behaviour so far as it is governed by legal rules. But these were not really the issues that interested him. He was really asking, in this part of his work, 'What test is to be applied to a rule to determine whether it is a legal rule?' And this, as we suggested earlier, is an important question; it is not, however, one of definition or classification but of validation. In insisting on sanction and command as defining characteristics of a law Austin was confusing the issue; for what he wanted was not a classification of rules for its own sake, but a scheme or generalized pattern to which the criteria of validity of any legal system must conform to do the job that a judge asks of them. Sanction, as an attribute of particular rules, is irrelevant. If we can establish a general pattern for all criteria of validity, of the type 'A law is valid if it derives, directly or indirectly, from the sovereign', and if, in any *given* legal order, we can determine who is sovereign, we shall not need to examine every particular rule to discover from any attributes of its own whether it is a rule of law.

We have used the phrase 'general pattern for all criteria of validity' and this needs explanation. Every legal system will have its own criteria, related to its own institutions; in Great Britain the principle that

Parliament is sovereign provides such a criterion, in that no judge need inquire further once a rule is established as an Act of Parliament; in a country with a written constitution the criteria will be found there. Austin sought, however, not the criteria of any particular system, but the general form which any such criterion must display. We are therefore entitled to ask whether in all legal systems, at least of the type of the modern state with which Austin was concerned, a determinate sovereign can be found to whose authority, mediately or immediately, all rules of valid law can be referred. Early doubts were cast on Austin's scheme by the analysis of federal systems, and in particular of the United States, where the constitution divides legislative powers between federal and state bodies of co-ordinate status.[20] Some Austinians have located sovereignty in America in the Supreme Court; for as the body empowered to interpret the constitution, the source of all other legal powers, it can make the latter mean whatever it chooses. But it is not very convincing to treat a body, whose primary function is to elucidate, interpret, and apply known and established rules of law, as if it were the sovereign will, on whose pleasure their existence depended.

A more serious weakness in Austin's system is that the sovereign may be determinate only in legal terms. Austin glimpsed the difficulty when he suggested that to describe the 'generic characters of the persons who compose the British Parliament . . . minutely and accurately, were to render a complete description of the intricate and perplexed system which is styled the British Constitution'.[21] Yet it is by their 'generic characters' rather than by their individual and personal attributes that they are said to be determinate. What he seems to be saying is that while Parliament is sovereign, to know what body is Parliament, and which men are its members, we must consult the law of the constitution. But if law is the 'signification of desire' of the sovereign, we cannot then appeal to the law to determine whose desire shall be law, unless we first accept the validity of the constitution on other grounds; otherwise 'law' and 'sovereign desire' will appear like a dog chasing its tail. This is no mere theoretical issue; in 1952 the South African Supreme Court had to pronounce on the validity of an Act passed by the Parliament of the Union by procedures other than those prescribed by the constitution for that type of law. The court took the view that while the Parliament of the Union was a sovereign body and therefore competent to pass any law whatsoever, its members did not constitute a Parliament unless they acted according to procedures laid down by the constitution.[22] To know the conditions of sovereignty, it seems, we must look to the law; but Austin tells us that to know what is law we must look to the sovereign.

Austin attempted to break out of the circle by defining his sovereign as the person or body 'receiving habitual obedience from the bulk of a given society'. This would on the face of it enable us to identify the sovereign by a sociological rather than a legal test, and thus to argue from sovereign to law without circularity. The attempt fails, however, not only because this is not what judges do (whether the bulk of South Africans habitually obeyed their Parliament was never in question in the case cited), but also because the bulk of a society might habitually obey a given body, simply because it is empowered by law. Once again law precedes sovereignty.

(c) Kelsen and the 'Pure Theory of Law'

Hans Kelsen, in the so-called Pure Theory of Law, has produced an analysis of legal structure in many ways resembling Austin's, while avoiding most of its difficulties. In Kelsen's theory, the 'determinate person or body' is replaced by a norm. A legal system is a normative hierarchy, in which 'the creation of one norm—the lower one—is determined by another—the higher—the creation of which is determined by a still higher norm' and 'this regressus is terminated by a highest, the basic norm which, being the supreme reason of validity of the whole legal order, constitutes its unity'.[23] The basic norm 'is nothing but the fundamental rule according to which the various norms of the order are to be created'.[24] But whence, asks Kelsen, comes the validity of the basic norm itself? Now the difficulty with Austin's scheme is that the equivalent question 'Whence derives the authority of the sovereign?' is capable of an answer, namely, 'from the law'. Kelsen's strength lies precisely in the point which many of his critics have attacked, that the question is unanswerable.[25] The basic norm, he says, must be 'presupposed to be valid because without this presupposition no human act could be interpreted as a legal, especially a norm-creating act'.[26] It is a 'legal postulate'. What this means in fact is that to be an English judge one must accept the postulates, e.g. the sovereignty of Parliament, on which the English legal order rests; to be an American judge, one must accept the USA constitution; to act otherwise would be inconsistent with the office. Just as for Austin an independent political society is one in which there is a sovereign giving habitual obedience to no human superior, so for Kelsen a sovereign (or self-sufficient) legal order is one where the basic norm derives from no other norm.

But Kelsen is not content to leave the matter there. 'The basic norm of a national legal order is not the arbitrary product of juristic imagination. Its content is determined by facts . . . Legal norms are considered to be valid only if they belong to an order which is by and large efficacious . . . The validity of a legal order is thus dependent upon its agreement with reality, upon its efficacy.'[27] At this point the argument becomes obscure. To say that the validity of the basic norm must be presupposed is tantamount to saying that questions cannot be asked about its validity—and this is reasonable. Why then is it necessary to bring in the question of effectiveness? If Kelsen is seeking a general scheme for criteria of validity, it is unnecessary to deal with the question whether any particular body of rules constructed on this principle is in fact effective (i.e. generally obeyed and applied by courts, etc.). This is not a philosophical question, nor even strictly a legal question. What system of law it is the business of a judge to apply depends on the court he is sitting in. It is difficult to imagine a judge doubting the validity of a rule he was about to apply, on the grounds that no one took any notice of the system of which it formed a part. If the legal systems we analyse are on the whole effective ones, that is not because an ineffective one would not be a legal system, but because it is rarely worth while examining any other. There would be nothing odd, however, in calling a code prepared by a government in exile, in the hope of better days, a 'code of law'[28] and such a code would possess the hierarchical structure Kelsen attributes to legal systems.

In using the word 'validity' in relation to either the basic norm or to a legal order as a whole, Kelsen seems unaware of the very virtue that in our view distinguishes his scheme from Austin's. For if the word is used of rules within a total order to define their relationship to the whole or to the basic norm upon which it rests, it is clearly improper to ask if the whole itself is valid, unless it is thought of as itself subordinate, or dependent on some greater whole of which it forms a part. Thus, from the point of view of the national legal order, the Charter or basic norm of a University is a subordinate norm, and the university of which it forms the foundation is a partial order, so that it is not improper to speak of its being validated by the relation it bears to the whole. But in that case validation is purely a matter of normative structure, and 'effectiveness' is irrelevant. If however we regard any order as self-subsistent, it is meaningless to speak of its validity unless that word is given some meaning different from the one it bears when applied to subordinate rules. It is as if, having asked what is the physiological function of the liver, the heart, and the brain, we were to go on to ask the same question about the whole man.

The source of the confusion seems to lie first in the idea that law is a science, to be studied by strictly logical methods, yielding true propositions which like those of the natural sciences must be mutually compatible. Kelsen speaks of 'a world of law', as if the object of this science were an objectively existent order like the natural order, the 'facts' of which are valid norms forming a universal and coherent pattern. From this he concludes that there cannot be two mutually inconsistent norms valid for the same place and time.[29] If we accept the analogy of the natural sciences, this looks convincing: we could not logically allow that there might be two gravitational laws, applying equally to Newton's legendary apple tree, one implying the fall, the other the ascent of apples. But (as Kelsen fully appreciates) normative laws are prescriptive, not descriptive. There is no *logical* reason why two prescriptions should not conflict. If the conflict occurs within a single order there will no doubt be rules for the use of judges determining which shall take precedence in a given context (e.g. the English rule that statute takes precedence over Common Law). But there might be two conflicting statutes, valid within different orders, both prescribing for a disputed territory. There would then be no way of showing one to be 'objectively' valid unless the two orders were looked at as derivatives from a third, embracing them both. This is in fact how Kelsen looks at them. For the second source of confusion in his argument in his inclination, resting on moral rather than on legal or logical grounds, to exalt international law at the expense of national legal orders. The notion of an objectively all-embracing 'world of law' is thus identified with international law, which is then said to be the source of validity of the national legal orders, delimiting their fields of competence according to the rule that a legal order is valid where, and so long as, it is effective.

Now this is all very well from the standpoint of the international lawyer. He is operating within a system of rules that does in fact provide criteria for resolving conflicts between the rules of national orders deemed subordinate. But this is not the only possible way of thinking about law and, more important perhaps, of administering it. This is shown by the fact that English, French, or American judges will not admit incompatibility with international law as an argument against an otherwise valid statute of their respective orders. National orders recognize international law, by making it a subordinate part of themselves. An English judge will defer to international law only when it is not in conflict with other rules of English law, deemed, by English legal criteria, to be of over-riding authority. For that is what it means to be an English judge rather than an international judge. Similarly, since in English law certain issues originating outside England must be determined according to the law of the territory in question, English judges are sometimes required to interpret the law of another state. This involves recognizing another legal order as a subordinate part of the English order. 'Subordinate' does not here imply political subordination of one territory and its inhabitants to another. It means that a judge can logically give effect to the norms of other orders only if the basic norm of his own order, from which his competence derives, authorizes him to do so; or, what amounts to the same thing, if it *confers* validity on them. This is not a peculiarity of English law; it is a logically necessary implication of what is involved in treating a legal order as self-subsistent or sovereign.

If we translate this argument into Kelsen's terms, we find that there is a characteristic and different view of the 'world of law' from the standpoint of every norm we postulate as 'basic'. This may be politically unfortunate—a world state might be a more secure and peaceful order than the one we know; but Kelsen's account of the 'world of law' would be realistic only if judges of the various national legal orders treated international law not as subordinate but as superior to their own constitutions, i.e. if they deemed national legislation invalid if incompatible with international law. (Even then it would be *logically* possible to imagine non-effective basic norms each with its own view of the 'world of law'.)

The progressive concretization of norms. Like Austin, Kelsen insists that the *sanction* is the characteristic element distinguishing rules of law from other rules; but, unlike Austin, Kelsen treats it not as an actual evil that a political superior can inflict on a subject, but as a consequent, provided by the rule, of conduct of a given type. Kelsen insists that it is not the *effectiveness* of the sanction in respect of any given rule that makes it a rule of law (and here he differs from Austin) but simply that it is *prescribed*. This is not therefore a statement about why people obey laws, or even a prediction of what will happen to them if they do not; it merely asserts the general logical form or pattern which a legal proposition must take.

Like Austin, Kelsen recognizes that many rules commonly deemed law (e.g. constitutional laws) do not conform to this pattern, and he too treats these as 'incomplete'. But Kelsen carries the argument further: in a normative hierarchy, superior rules from which the lower derive their validity remain incomplete as rules of law until 'individualized' or 'concretized' by lower norms, and ultimately by the individual (i.e. nongeneral) norm created by a judge, when he says 'You must go to prison for six months.'[30] This analysis evades the difficulty implicit in Austin's treatment of 'permissive' or 'enabling' rules; for the Act requiring that, to be valid, a will must have been attested by two witnesses, remains incomplete until an actual will is given effect to by a court, with an implied sanction against anyone disregarding the court ruling. This seems to be no more than an ingenious terminological device to meet the objection that not all rules of law provide a sanction. From another point of view, however, it is illuminating, for it brings together within the broad structure of the legal system a diverse collection of legal forms that on Austin's analysis were divorced. Austin defined a legal rule in terms of 'generality', thereby excluding things like private acts of Parliament, administrative orders, contracts entered into by private individuals, wills, and so on. Since these are all legal instruments creating legal obligations, it is the virtue of Kelsen's analysis that he finds a place for them all within his hierarchy of norms. For each of them is a 'concretization' or 'individualization' of a higher and more general norm which is the source of its validity; thus law-making is not confined to what are usually called legislative organs but is undertaken by judges, ministers, and even private persons.

The traditional classification of modes of state action into legislative, executive, and judicial functions (the first being the making of general rules, the second and third the applying and interpreting of them), fitted the facts without too many discrepancies until about the middle of the nineteenth century. Collectivist political theories, however, led to the extension of executive powers, and the water-tight division has become increasingly misleading. Whatever value the classification possesses must now rest on some other basis, possibly on a distinction between procedures, rather than on that between making rules and applying them. Operating a complex modern statute inevitably involves making further rules, and the point at which ministerial legislation merges into the exercise of particular executive discretion is impossible to determine. The value of Kelsen's analysis is that it requires no such distinction; progressive individualization of law is a continuous process, in which the links between the various stages are provided by the notion of 'authorization'. This is consistent with a discretionary element at every level, wider or narrower according to the limits laid down by the norm above. The relevance of this to the relation between general rules and judicial decisions will become apparent when we consider the American Realist school of jurisprudence.

'Sanction' as a definitional characteristic of legal systems. A good deal of criticism has been directed at both Kelsen and Austin for the part played in their schemes by the idea of the sanction. We have shown that the result of stipulating that a rule must provide a sanction for it to be 'a legal rule' is that some rules normally regarded as laws, and having a proper place in the hierarchy of norms, have to be treated as in some way 'incomplete'. The purpose of the stipulation, in both these analyses, is to exclude from the class 'law' the rules of so-called natural law and

conventional morality, and to limit it to systems like those actually operated by the courts of modern states. This can be done, however, by stipulating defining characteristics, not of *every rule* in a legal system, but only of a legal system as a whole, for each system itself defines what rules are rules of law. Now if the 'sanction' were treated as a defining characteristic of '*a legal system*' rather than of a legal rule, it would be open to far few objections.[31] When we talk of a *legal system* we do usually imply one that provides penalties for the breach of some at least of its rules: and given the sort of social function expected of law as a system, it is difficult to see how it could be otherwise.*

(d) 'Realist' criticisms of Austinian analytical jurisprudence

Since the 1920s Austinian jurisprudence has come under heavy fire from the so-called 'Realist' school of American jurists, who claim that it rests on a myth. The movement drew its initial inspiration from Mr. Justice Holmes[32] and, in a lesser degree, from Mr. Justice Cardozo,[33] but in the extreme form in which the doctrine is expounded by Jerome Frank[34] it has far outstripped that inspiration.

The Realist criticizes Austinian jurisprudence for adopting a syllogistic or deductive view of the rule/decision relation (already discussed in the context of natural law), according to which the role of the judge would be like that of a mechanical computer into which problems are fed and from which right answers should emerge. It makes no allowance for the very considerable discretion that a judge enjoys in 'interpreting' the law. Even where, as in England, precedents are considered binding on courts of equal or inferior jurisdiction, and where even the supreme court, the House of Lords, is reluctant to ignore its own previous decisions, the judge must still decide which of competing precedents is the one applicable to the case before him. For no two cases are ever alike, and, as Mr. E. H. Levi has said, 'The problem for the law is: When will it be just to treat different cases as though they were the same?'[35] In answering that question the judge is not behaving like a mechanical computer. The relation between a given case and the prece-

---

* International law, which Austin excluded from 'law properly so-called' because it emanated from no determinate superior, and provided no effective 'sanction' in his sense, would not be excluded on this definition of a legal system, for all that is now needed is that some rules of the system prescribe a sanction as the legal consequent of a delict—not that the sanction shall always be effective. In the Corfu Channel case, the international court awarded the UK damages against Albania for the loss of a destroyer in an illegal minefield: the delict (the laying of the mines) entailed as a legal consequent the sanction (damages). It is irrelevant that the damages have not been paid, for the definition does not demand that sanctions be effective.

dent upon which its determination is modelled is not syllogistic but analogical. That is to say, the judge, in examining possible precedents, elects to follow the one in which the features he deems relevant in the present case seem most closely reproduced. But which he deems relevant will depend not on logic but on a value judgment. Though each case in its way creates a new rule for all other cases of exactly that type, there never are any other cases of *exactly* that type. Rules of precedent, and formal statutory rules, create categories to which they attach legal consequences; but it is for the judge to decide to which of these categories the present case belongs.

The Realist view of law flies to the opposite extreme; so far from being a general and certain determinant of particular disputes (were it certain, who would ever go to the expense of fighting a certainly unsuccessful action?), law exists only as a series of isolated particular judgments.[36] There is no law on any case until the moment when the judge pronounces upon it; and what passes as law, in the text-books and elsewhere, is no more than a guess at what a judge would say when presented with a case. Accordingly the Realist urges the lawyer to devote more study to the psychology of judges in general and of the present occupants of the bench in particular.

But, it might be replied to the Realist, the judge certainly *thinks* he uses general rules to determine cases; the point is, how does he use them? Not, certainly, syllogistically. Nevertheless, a decision according to rule is still different from one ungoverned by rules. Judges do ask what the law requires of them; they employ known and agreed techniques for determining the rules, and may well decide differently after the search, from the way they would have done without it. A judge has been known to express moral dissatisfaction with a decision that he feels the law requires of him and which he sees no way of escaping. It is difficult to see how, on a strictly Realist view, this could ever occur. Even where the categories are fairly flexible, there is a body of legal professional opinion, in which the judge himself has a voice, which not merely expects a particular application of a rule, but, in those instances where the law is imprecise and therefore capable of development, expects that it shall be developed in a particular direction.

The Realist view is, we might say, too narrowly focused on the courts. Cases that come to court are likely to be the ones where the law speaks equivocally; but how many would-be litigants settle out of court on counsel's advice that they have no case? That advice may be, in one sense, a guess at what a judge would decide, but it is based on a pre-existent rule of law, married to the expectation that judges would act upon it. The Realists tend to confuse the legal adviser's question:

'What is a judge likely to do?' with the judge's question: 'What does the law require me to do?' Psychology may be a relevant study for answering the first (though the rules and traditional methods of interpretation will necessarily figure as psychological determinants); it has no relevance for the second.

Kelsen's account of the relations between general and particular norms allows for the element of judicial discretion that has so impressed the Realists, without committing him to the divorce of the general and the particular which is so paradoxical a feature of their doctrine. On his analysis, the general norm not only empowers the judge to create a particular subordinate norm, it also places limits of substance upon his competence. The extent of his discretion depends in practice on the vagueness of the rule. The question 'What considerations do in fact affect the judge's decision within the limits set by the superior norm?', which seems so important to the Realists, is not one that Kelsen asks, but asking it is not ruled out by the terms of his analysis.

The Realist view, in the extreme form, would make nonsense of the experience of the ordinary man; for we know well enough that there are general rules requiring us to do X and refrain from Y, and that if we break them we shall be punished by a court. Judicial decisions are irrelevant to this experience for the most part, and a law consisting of isolated and particular dooms could not provide a system of social controls just because they are not general. The Realist view is meaningful and significant only if we accept arbitrary restrictions on the meaning of the word 'law', and confine discussion only to those aspects of the legal process which impress the legal adviser looking to courts of appeal where the uncertainties of law are necessarily more evident than the certainties.

V. CONCLUSION

The 'command theory' and the 'pure theory' have been frequently attacked; sometimes for misrepresenting, in their insistence on the role of the sanction, the motives that lead most people to obey law; sometimes for offering no sufficient reason for obeying it; sometimes for ignoring the ends of law; sometimes for ignoring the relation between law and social facts.[37] They are condemned as a sterile exercise in logic, unrelated to life (Laski). Behind these criticisms is the assumption that a satisfactory 'theory of law' ought to deal with some, if not all, of these matters.

Prof. Stone[38] has pointed out that Laski's comment 'need be only a statement of the proper limits (of the pure theory) and not a criticism at all'. For neither Austin nor Kelsen sets out to provide answers to any of the questions dealt with in the first two sections of this chapter.[39] They are concerned with the formal structure of the legal system. If they ask what makes a law 'binding',[40] they mean 'What are the conditions that it must satisfy, to be a valid part of a legal system?', not 'Whence derives the moral duty to obey?' If they assert that what characterizes the legal order is the 'sanction', or that it is 'a coercive order', they do not mean that the principle motive for obedience is the fear of coercion,[41] but that it differs from other normative orders in that its rules invoke coercive sanctions as the consequents of delicts.

This being so, neither theory *excludes* the asking of moral and sociological questions about law; Austin's refusals to treat 'natural law' as 'law properly so-called', and Kelsen's rejection of it, with other moral notions, as 'meta-jurisprudence' are symptoms of an impatience with theories that fail to distinguish questions of validity from questions of value: but neither writer denies altogether that moral questions about law can properly be asked. Austin devoted a considerable portion of his *Province of Jurisprudence Determined* to 'the principle of utility' as the key to 'the science of legislation'; Kelsen leaves sufficient room for a moral theory of law in admitting that a judge may be empowered by the basic norm to draw on conventional or 'natural' moral principles as grounds of judgment. He insists only that until such principles have been introduced into the formal legal structure, they have no legal standing. To this there can be no reasonable objection. If exception has been taken to it, it is largely because the critics treat the word 'law' as if it had some unique significance, so that questions like 'Is natural law, law?' must have a right answer, one way or the other. This, we have argued, is a mistake. 'Natural law' is certainly not positive law unless, and until, a judge or a legislature makes it so, and its positive validity derives from other norms of positive law, which authorize the decision that embodies it.

It is not therefore inconsistent with these doctrines to ask what norms a judge ought to employ (or what laws a legislature ought to enact) in exercising a discretionary competence; nor to ask how the rules which judges do in fact employ (or legislatures enact) relate to social needs, conventional morality, the class structure of society, and so on. Neither is it a defect in any writer's work that he does not address himself to all these matters. No single theory could deal systematically with questions of the logical structure, the moral obligatoriness, and the sociological relations of law; for each group of questions requires its own methods, and a legal theorist is no more bound to provide answers to them all than an anatomist is required to answer physiological or psychological questions.

We have sought in this chapter to distinguish the main types of questions that legal theorists have asked, and to show that answers to some will not necessarily provide guidance in answering others. In treating particular theories, therefore, we have endeavoured to make plain not only their scope, but also their limitations.

Law shares with other sorts of normative discourse a common vocabulary, which makes it easy to confuse statements about the formal structure of legal systems with assertions of moral duty. Words like 'rights', 'duty', or 'binding' occur in both moral and legal contexts. It is tempting to think that just as a man either is, or is not, bound by a rope, so he either is, or is not, bound by a rule. But to be bound by a rope is a matter of fact; to be bound by a law is not, at any rate, a fact of the same sort, if it is a fact at all. For to say, in a legal context, that a law is binding is to say that it satisfies the criteria of validity of a given legal system. But to use the same words in a moral context is to recommend that people obey it, and to suggest that there are other than purely legal reasons for doing so. The legal obligation is not the same as the moral obligation, neither is it a reflection of it. One of the weaknesses of natural law theory is that it tends to blur this distinction.

We shall have occasion, in the next chapter, to pursue the analysis further, applying it particularly to the word 'rights'.

CHAPTER 4

RIGHTS

I. ANALYSIS OF 'RIGHTS'

We drew attention in our first chapter to the importance of the distinction between normative and descriptive statements, and we have shown in connection with natural law theories how the failure to observe it can lead to confusion. Now words like 'rights', 'duties', 'ought', and 'obligation' belong primarily to normative discourse; they are used, that is, in prescribing conduct according to rules, and have a descriptive force only if we assume the rule to be in force, i.e. widely observed, when to know what the rules require of people is to know also what they are likely to do. But in any case to use words like these is to imply a rule of some sort from which the particular prescription derives. 'X has a right to R' is thus a sentence of a quite different type from 'X has a pen'. The latter can be verified by observation of facts; the former must be established by reference to rules.

(a) Rights and duties

Rules prescribe behaviour, and in so doing are said to impose 'duties' or 'obligations'. If we say that Y has a duty to act in a certain way, we mean that there is a rule that leaves him no choice in the matter, that 'requires' it of him. This is not the case with a right. If X has a right to R, he may have (or do) R, or not, as he prefers. In what sense then can it be said that rights derive from rules, if rules prescribe or require conduct of a particular type? The answer lies in the correlation of rights and duties, such that the right of X is the duty of Y. To say that X has a right to £5 is to imply that there is a rule which, when applied to the case of X and some other person Y, imposes on Y a duty to pay X £5 if X so chooses. Without the possibility of the correlative duty resting somewhere, the attribution of the right to X would be meaningless. In some cases, such as those arising from contracts, the duty will rest on one person, or a number of persons, in particular; in others, X's right will impose a duty on everyone else. X's right to personal freedom implies a duty on everyone else not to interfere with him. A right may thus entail, at the most, active performance on the part of someone else, at the least, non-interference on the part of other men generally.

The correlation that we have noted between rights and duties is a logical, not a moral or legal relation. A rule giving rise to a right does not give rise to a duty as a separate and different thing. Right and duty are different names for the same normative relation, according to the point of view from which it is regarded. One writer, indeed, has argued that the statement of a right is only another form of the statement of the duty: 'The two terms are as identical in what they seek to describe as the active and passive forms of indicating an act; "A was murdered by B"; or "B murdered A".'[1]

However, rights are often said to imply duties in another sense. The enjoyment of rights, it may be said, is conditional on the performance of duties; no one can reasonably expect that his interests will be safeguarded by the social order unless he recognizes and respects corresponding obligations towards others. If I claim a right to property, this requires, it might be argued, that I ought to refrain from dispossessing other people of their property. Now in this case the correlation of rights with duties is not a logical relation but a moral one.* The rights and duties in question are attributed to the same person, and are not merely different ways of looking at one normative relation. The claim that there is such a correlation consequently needs support by reasoned argument, and though it may be true in most cases, there are certainly some cases in which it is not. We attribute rights to infants, idiots, and even animals, to whom it would be absurd to attribute duties. To say that a person has a duty to do something presupposes that he is capable, as infants, idiots, and animals are not, of knowing the rule, and deciding to act in accordance with it. To attribute a right makes no such assumption, since the realization of the right depends on someone other than the subject conforming to the rule; the most it demands of the subject is that he shall do what he pleases. Thus there is no necessary connection (in a logical sense) between X's rights and X's duties, though it may be possible to show that his enjoyment of any given right (as in a contract) may depend upon his performing some duty towards someone else. There is one important qualification to be added to this—the case of a rule of such general application that everyone qualifies as a subject both of the right and the duty specified by the rule. Rights traditionally regarded as fundamental, like the right to free speech, or the right to security of the person, may derive from rules of this type. In such a case it would obviously be unreasonable to demand that others perform

* It might also be a matter of *prudence* to acknowledge one's duties, for otherwi one's rights might not be acknowledge by others.

their duties to oneself while refusing to perform the same duties towards them; for the definition of a rule logically entails that all who satisfy the conditions it lays down are equally bound to observe it. However it does not follow that if X fails to respect Y's rights, Y is thereby absolved from his duty to X. This may be true in the case of contractual rights; but if X steals from Y, Y is not thereby empowered to steal from X; and if X murders Y, the universality of the right to life is not a reason for putting X to death. While it is true, therefore, that the same rule that confers a right on X will also impose a duty upon him, if he satisfies the appropriate conditions, it does not follow that his enjoyment of the right is conditional upon performance of his duty.

(b) Positivist theories of rights

We have argued that the words 'rights' and 'duties' possess meaning only in the context of rules, and that sentences embodying them express a normative relationship, prescribing how one person shall behave in relation to another. The so-called 'positivist' theories of rights break down precisely because they ignore this point, and seek to treat sentences including 'rights' and 'duties' as though they were descriptive of facts.

A clear case of such a positivistic account of rights is that given by Spinoza:

> 'by natural right I understand the very laws or rules of nature, in accordance with which everything takes place, in other words, the power of nature itself. And so the natural right of universal nature, and consequently of every individual thing, extends as far as its power: and accordingly, whatever any man does after the laws of his nature he does by the highest natural right, and he has as much right over nature as he has power.'

When civil society is formed, and government established,

> 'the right of the supreme authorities is nothing else than simple natural right, limited, indeed, by the power, not of every individual, but of the multitude, which is guided, as it were, by one mind—that is, as each individual in the state of nature, so the body and mind of a dominion have as much right as they have power. And thus each single citizen or subject has the less right, the more the commonwealth exceeds him in power, and each citizen consequently does and has nothing, but what he may by the general decree of the commonwealth defend.'[2]

Hobbes also equated rights with powers, though his views about rights were more puzzling and less consistent than Spinoza's.[3]

The account of rights in terms of power reappears in Austin. 'Every right (divine, legal, or moral),' says Austin, 'rests on a relative duty; that is to say, a duty lying on a party or parties other than the party or parties in whom the right resides. And, manifestly, that relative duty would not be a duty substantially, if the law which affects to impose it were not sustained by might.'[4] Austin is ready to admit the possibility of rights other than strictly legal rights, for he concedes that there may be sanctions besides legal ones, e.g. public disapproval for a breach of conventional moral code, or Divine punishment. With this qualification, however, his position is that of Spinoza: there is no right where there is no power to secure the object of the right, the power arising from the exercise of a coercive sanction to enforce the correlative duty.

A variant form of this analysis is that of the Realists, who treat rights not as powers but as expectations. On this view, a man may be said to have a right when there is reasonable ground for the expectation that it will be upheld (e.g. by a court of law).

Prof. Hart has indicated some of the difficulties arising from the treatment of rights as if they described facts. 'A paralysed man watching the thief's hand close over his gold watch is properly said to have a right to retain it as against the thief, though he has neither expectation nor power in any ordinary sense of these words.'[5] He will probably never see his watch again, but this in no way invalidates his right; for the chance of enforcement of the right in any particular case is beside the point. In a country in which judges were corruptible, X might be quite properly said to have a right against Y, even if he had no hope of prevailing against Y's influence or wealth. There seems nothing odd in claiming a right in a case where there is simply no question of a sanction. A patient might say to his doctor: 'Tell me the worst; I have a right to know', without implying that if he refused, the law would impose a sanction or his other patients would desert him. Nor does he mean that there ought to be a law to this effect, or that that would be an appropriate response on the part of public opinion to the breach of a conventional rule.

Hägerström tries to meet these difficulties by treating rights and duties as 'mystical forces and bonds' that exist, like ghosts, only to the extent that people believe in them. 'Modern science in general,' he declares, 'and therefore, modern jurisprudence, seeks to use only such notions as correspond to facts. But as soon as one tries to determine the facts which correspond to these ideas one lands in difficulties.'[6] 'The notions in question cannot be reduced to anything in reality. The reason is that, in point of fact, they have their roots in traditional ideas of mystical forces and bonds.'[7] If rights cannot be expressed in words like 'command', 'power', or 'expectation', which describe facts, must we not therefore conclude that the facts that the word purports to describe do not really exist at all; that when we attribute a right to X and a duty to Y, we are saying that they believe themselves bound by some mystic bond, which can be said to be a fact only by virtue of their believing it to be so? On this view, any concrete legal consequences following from 'X has a right to R' are the effects of belief; in so far as a right corresponds to a power, it is because people are led by their beliefs to act in some particular way, which gives 'reality' to the right.

Hägerström is practically admitting that the attempt to elucidate 'X has a right to R' as if it described a set of facts, fails to explain its meaning at least in some of the contexts in which it is ordinarily used. But he is surely wrong to conclude on that account that it describes something magical, that enters the world of reality only when it induces people to act in particular ways because they subscribe to the illusion. Hägerström's search for alternative forms of expression that will *describe the same set of facts* as 'X has a right to R' is mistaken precisely because it does not describe facts at all; and the problem arises only because of a failure to distinguish normative and descriptive discourse.

There is, however, one way in which 'rights' might properly be used in the course of description. It is the business of the historian and the sociologist to describe how people live, and that involves giving an account of the rules that regulate their behaviour. A historian who said that the English agricultural labourer of 1810 had no right to organize in trade unions, would seem to be making a statement about actual conditions which could be judged true or false as it accorded with the facts. This presents no real difficulty, however. The word 'right' in this context is still prescriptive since it indicates what the law required; the proposition is descriptive only because one understands that the system of law was in fact broadly effective. It does not necessarily imply, however, that unions were not actually formed, nor that their members were always punished (though many were).

The fact that 'X has a right to R' has this quasi-descriptive force in some contexts lends colour to the positivist accounts, particularly in jurisprudence. Where the object of study is a legal system, supported by judges, policemen, and prison warders, it is broadly true that legal rights correspond with powers, and that to enjoy a right is to have a certain expectation that a judge would decide in a given way. But this is not what it *means* to have a right; these things follow because the right in question derives from a system of rules that policemen enforce and judges respect and apply. The rule, and therefore the right, are logically prior to the power and the expectation. And if this is the case, there is no reason why we should not speak of other sorts of rights, deriving from rules that are not so enforced.

The weakness in Austin's account of rights is that it excludes this possibility. He employs a system of definition in which 'right' derives from 'duty', 'duty' from 'law', and 'law' from 'command', 'sanction', and ultimately 'power'. The critical step is from 'duty' to 'law'; for if we accept the definition of 'law' in terms of power, we can no longer use 'duty' in relation to any rule that is not 'law'. This is to impose an arbitrary limitation on the use of the term 'rights', which pays too little attention to the variety of contexts in which the term is found.

II. LEGAL AND MORAL RIGHTS

We have argued in earlier chapters that rules may be classified according to the activities they regulate, how they originate, or their degree of formality. Some are enunciated and upheld through institutional arrangements like legislatures and courts, others exist wholly by custom or convention, others again are more or less consciously adopted by individuals as moral rules. Yet they all have this in common: being rules, they prescribe conduct and to that extent impose duties or obligations. If a duty is owed to a particular person, there is nothing peculiar in saying that he possesses rights under the rule. Thus by the rules of cricket, whoever wins the toss has the right to choose who bats first; the loser has a duty to field or bat as he is told. The question of a sanction does not arise, yet one can still talk about the right arising under the rules.

Rights may be classified, then, in ways corresponding to classifications of rules (see Chapter 3, Sec. IV (a)). We might classify, for example, according to the type of activity or interest that the right protects: thus we might distinguish economic rights, like the right to work, or the right to a living wage; civil rights, like the right to appeal to a court of justice, or to be represented by counsel; and political rights, like the right to vote, or to stand for election to public office. Or we might classify the right according to the way in which it is established and maintained. Thus we might distinguish, with Austin, between legal rights and 'moral' (in Austin's sense, of conventional) rights—the former established and upheld by state institutions, the latter by the force of majority opinion. There is nothing odd in saying that in England a healthy person has a conventional duty to give up his seat in a crowded bus to a cripple, nor in attributing to the latter a corresponding right, though neither the right nor the duty is recognized in English law (unlike French law).

Conventional acceptance, however, is not in itself sufficient moral justification for a rule or a right. As we said in the previous chapter, when it is a matter of choosing between right and wrong, Gallup polls are no substitute for reasoned argument. If we adopt moral canons by which we criticize convention, those canons themselves will give rise to rights. When Mary Wollstonecraft wrote the *Vindication of the Rights of Woman* (1792) she was criticizing the law of England and also the conventional moral attitudes of most men and women of her time. She was not wrong merely because she was in a tiny minority; she could have been proved wrong only by a reasoned attack on principles or their application. The reformer 'fighting for the rights' of an oppressed minority must be claiming, not that established rules of law or custom accord the rights in question, but that they *ought* to do so. This may be a strictly moral judgment. For the reformer at least it is justified by moral criteria; whether anyone else agrees with him in no way affects the moral validity of those rights.[8]

This point is of importance because it demonstrates the systematic ambiguity of the sentence 'X has a right to R', which positivist theories ignore at the cost of confusion and paradox. In the mouth of the lawyer, the sociologist, or the historian, it is quasi-descriptive, i.e. it means that there is an established rule, whether legal or conventional, which accords the right. But in the mouth of the reformer and moralist, it must necessarily mean: 'I believe (for reasons I am prepared to give) that X ought to have R if he wants it—whatever the rest of the world may think about it.' (Rights attributed in this way might properly be called 'moral rights', provided the word 'moral' is not also used, in Austin's sense, as a synonym for 'conventional'). Now any analysis which treats an attribution of rights as if it were a simple description of facts makes nonsense of this latter usage, which is, nevertheless, a very common and useful one, that ordinarily presents no difficulties in moral and political discussion.

It is no mere accident or perversity that has led philosophers to adopt positivistic definitions of 'rights'. Bentham, for instance, in employing the definition of rights developed later by Austin, was prompted by a reforming impatience with lawyers who assumed dogmatically that the Common Law of England enshrined the natural rights of man, and was therefore, sacrosanct.[9] For the theory of natural rights, in origin a critical weapon against authority, was by then being used to defend the established order as well as to attack it. By denying that 'rights' could mean anything but 'positive rights' Bentham was denying his opponents the advantage of a term that by long tradition was capable of arousing a favourable response. Austin's interest was more strictly methodological, being part of the attempt, already discussed in Chapter 3, to separate moral from juristic questions. We have argued, however, that this can be done quite satisfactorily without placing on words arbitrary limitations of meaning that too readily become perverted into substantial statements of principle.

If sentences attributing 'rights' are treated as stating rules or applying rules, we need no longer worry about questions like 'Is a right that is not recognized in law really a right?' For if there are extra-legal rules there can be extra-legal rights. And it follows that there is no contradiction in saying that while 'X has a right to R' is invalid in law, it is valid in morals.*

III. NATURAL RIGHTS

(a) The seventeenth and eighteenth century doctrine

Ascriptions of rights of different types may thus conflict, without creating logical difficulties; and the distinction between legal and moral rights corresponds exactly to the distinction between legal and moral rules. Since the seventeenth century, however, there has been a persistent and powerful body of opinion in the West attached to the idea that all men possess certain rights 'by nature', irrespective of particular social, legal, or political institutions, and that these can be demonstrated by reason. How far can this doctrine be accommodated within the present analysis?

We have already remarked that in the seventeenth century the doctrine of natural law was given a new twist, on the model of mathematics; but this was not its only new feature. 'The modern theory of natural law was not, properly speaking, a theory of law at all. It was a theory of rights.'[10] The distinction cannot be *strictly* drawn, for a theory of one must, in some degree, be a theory of the other. The question is one of emphasis; for whereas the mediaeval doctrine proclaimed the rationality of the established social order as part of the universal order, the modern theory made claims against the established authorities of church and state, when the social structure was becoming increasingly fluid. The idea that every man had his appointed status and function in a pre-established order was breaking down in the face of an advancing individualism expressing itself theologically in protestantism, economically in mercantile capitalism, and politically and philosophically in the theory of natural rights and the social contract. The new theory was intended not as a justification but as a criticism of the existing order; its tone was radical, and in its ultimate employment it was revolutionary.

* Compare our discussion (see p. 80) of Kelsen's contention that two conflicting norms cannot both be valid for the same place and time.

It was embedded in the doctrines of the parliamentarians and the Levellers of the English Civil War. Locke, its most systematic expositor, offered it in justification of the revolution of 1688. It was part of the accepted ideology of the American and French revolutionaries, and was expressed in the Declaration of Independence and the constitutional Bill of Rights in America, and in the Declaration of the Rights of Man in France. It was in the name of *The Rights of Man* that Tom Paine sought to rebut Burke's *Reflections on the Revolution in France*. Since that time, 'natural rights' have been subjected to a good deal of criticism; but many who, like J. S. Mill, discarded the ideology of 'Nature' have remained firmly attached to the rights claimed in its name, and have felt the need to find other, and firmer, ground on which to base them.

In the seventeenth century doctrine, rights were attributed to individuals as if they were intrinsic properties of men 'as men'. 'Thus we are born free as we are born rational,' said Locke.[11] Whatever rights are granted a man as citizen of this or that state, his natural rights go with him wherever he goes: they are said to be 'inalienable', 'imprescriptable', 'indefeasible'. No government or positive law can deprive him of them, nor can any higher claim prevail against them; if they are to be limited at all, it is only by the consent of their possessor. The contract theory of government was thus inextricably bound up with natural right theory.

What we have said in Chapter 3 of the weaknesses of natural law theory in general applies equally here, and needs no recapitulation. A theory of natural rights, however, has special problems of its own. If we attribute rights to individuals absolutely, we are incapable of resolving conflicts between them as they arise; in a famine, one man's right to life may well involve infringement, by the commandeering of food hoards, of another's right to property. If two principles, equally ultimate, absolute, and reasonable, conflict, there is *ex hypothesi* no further principle upon which a resolution or adjustment can be arranged. Social regulation is a continuous process of adjustment between conflicting claims; the theory of absolute natural rights would seem to make the process impossible.[12]

Natural rights, being rationally deducible from man's nature, were considered universally valid irrespective of differences in environment. Such a view is tenable only when the rights in question are vague enough to fit almost any set of concrete conditions.

The idea that 'man's nature' abstracted from environment, could yield a body of rights, has been attacked more fundamentally. Since there can be no right without a rule, to abstract man from society is to abstract him from the context of rules, and therefore to make a discussion of rights irrelevant. Since rights imply duties, they imply someone in a social relationship with their subject upon whom the duties can rest. Robinson Crusoe had no rights until he met Man Friday. However, not all seventeenth century theorists understood 'a state of nature' as being non-social, as did Hobbes and Spinoza. For Locke, the state of nature was already a social state, governed by the Law of Nature, from which natural rights derived.* Whenever men come into social relations, they acquire certain rights and duties arising from their very natures. Each recognizes intuitively the natural law dictating mutual forbearance for reciprocal advantage. This position is not open to the objection that it divorces rights from rules, or from society.

T. H. Green criticized it as non-social in another sense. Rights, he maintained, are made by social recognition; the claims we have on other men depend for their validity on the moral aims and standards generally accepted in the community. He did not deny altogether that there might be a right not generally recognized. He insisted, however, that every right must be justified in terms of some end which the rest of the community does in fact consider good, and which could not be achieved without recognition of the right.[13] Now it may well be that to have any hope of securing positive recognition of a right, it must be defensible in terms of moral standards acceptable to at least an influential part of the community. But this is quite different from saying that no right can be *valid* except on these terms. For the first proposition is a description of the probable social facts, i.e. it is a sociological statement; pronouncements about the validity of a right are legal or moral statements, prescribing or applying rules. If 'natural rights' are claimed on the grounds that they are 'reasonable', it is no answer to say they might be unpopular. Green treated 'X has a right to R' as if it always meant 'most people are (or could be) convinced that X has a right to R'. In this he was not, as might appear, simply stipulating a special usage for a word; nor was he predicting what sort of rights claimed by individuals are likely to receive positive recognition. His purpose was to commend the standards of the community, limiting criticism to comments on ways in which detailed practice is inconsistent with prevailing principles. It is an attitude that the piecemeal reformer might accept, but which must necessarily fail to satisfy the revolutionary. However appropriate it might have been to the 1870's, one can see that the men of 1789 or 1917 wanted something more radical and robust.

---

* Admittedly Locke says that all men enjoy some rights at least (like the right to life) even apart from society, simply as God's creatures. But he is able to postulate such rights because he also postulates a law of nature binding on all men, and imposing corresponding duties upon them.

D

Natural right theory has been criticized as non-social in a third sense. According, again, to Green, men possess rights by virtue not of their individual purpose, but as constituents of a common good; for Bosanquet, one's rights are the necessary conditions for the performance of one's moral function in the community, so that in a sense, they derive from one's duties. Laski takes the view that rights 'are correlative with functions. I have them that I may make my contribution to the social end.'[14] 'The claims I make must . . . be claims that are necessary to the proper performance of my function. My demands upon society . . . are demands which ought to receive recognition because a recognizable public interest is involved in their recognition.'[15] Each of these writers appears to be laying down, as a criterion or procedure for justifying claims, that they must contribute to a common good. They repudiated the classical theory of natural rights because, in divorcing the individual's interest from the community's good, it separated his claims from just that principle which would establish whether or not they were justified. Now it is not clear that all the rights that we should consider justified could be defended in terms of a common good, if by that we mean an advantage in which every member of the community will have some share. Neither is it clear that they must always be necessary conditions for the performance of a social function, however widely that phrase is interpreted. Even congenital idiots and condemned murderers might properly be said to possess some rights, though they make no contribution to any good that others enjoy, and, on the contrary, impose on the rest of the community the burden of feeding, housing, serving, and guarding them. There seems to be meaning of some sort, therefore, in speaking of the rights of men 'as men', as distinct from their rights as members of a community. Not indeed that this exhausts the possibilities; for many people would be ready to attribute rights to animals. We certainly feel that we have duties towards them, and this must strictly entail their having rights against us. A capacity to contribute to the welfare of others *may* be a necessary condition for *some* rights; but we do in fact ascribe 'rights' in cases where this condition is not satisfied.*

* It might, however, be argued that since the common good includes the well-being of the subject of the rights in question, any conditions benefiting him would to that extent promote the common good. But if these rights conflict with the claims of others, how do we decide between them? It is no answer to say 'Maximise the common good', for this is not something to be measured. In Chapter 12, we suggest that 'deciding in the light of the common good' is equivalent to judging impartially between claims in the light of the interests and needs of those affected. It is simply to apply the moral criteria discussed in Chapter 2.

(b) Natural rights and moral rights

The introduction of the word 'moral' into the discussion of 'natural rights' is suggestive. For the traditional criteria for a 'natural right' are that it should be rationally demonstrable and universal. This is reminiscent of the criteria of critical acceptance and impartial application which we suggested in Chapter 2 were the characteristics of moral rules. While denying that rights can be deduced logically from an examination of man's nature, we have nevertheless maintained that established rights and rules are open to reasoned criticism, and that implies canons from which rights—moral rights—may be derived. As to the universality of natural rights: though no right could be reasonably attributed to all men without qualification, we have argued that the characteristic of a moral rule is that it applies irrespective of purely personal considerations, and that differences and limitations in application must be relevant and rationally defensible. If, for example, we believe in democratic rights for white men, we must show good grounds for denying them to black; and the simple criterion of skin colour alone is not an obviously relevant ground of distinction. There may be other and better grounds—but the onus of proof rests on those who would limit the right, not on those who would give it universal scope. The close connection between the ideal of equality and natural right theory will become plainer in the next chapter.

The theory of natural rights was a special theory of moral rights, conditioned by the peculiar features of an age preoccupied with the mathematical sciences, and anxious to assert the value of individual enterprise, opinion, and belief against traditional political and ecclesiastical authority. Associated with some forms of protestant theology, it stressed the autonomy of the individual conscience; springing from a nascent capitalism, it defended individual property against authoritarian interference; and as the ideology of radical and revolutionary movements, it insisted on free speech and representative institutions.

Its influence on political thought and action has nevertheless survived the special conditions of its birth. Attempts to give formal expression to 'natural', 'fundamental', or 'human' rights did not cease with the French Revolution. Constitution makers ever since have regarded a Bill of Rights as an almost essential preamble or appendage to their work. The Preamble to the Charter of the United Nations reaffirms 'faith in fundamental human rights' (without, however, listing them), 'in the dignity and worth of the human person, (and) in the equal rights of men and women'. In 1948, after long discussion in the Human Rights Commission of the United Nations, assisted by an enquiry into theoretical problems conducted by Unesco, the General Assembly adopted a Universal Declaration of Human Rights.[16]

(c) General and particular ascriptions of rights

Before considering the purpose and status of such declarations, however, we must distinguish briefly between two ways of ascribing 'rights'.

'X has a right to £10 from Y' is a particular prescription, implying, but not stating, a general rule. If Y has undertaken by contract to pay X £10, and all conditions have been fulfilled, it follows as a conclusion or as a particular application, of the general rule 'Contracts must be kept', that X has a right to £10 from Y. To make the judgment is to settle the matter. 'Creditors have a right to be paid', however, is a general rule that requires application to the given case. The right attributed here is not absolute. Y may be able to defeat X's claim by showing, for example, that there has been fraudulent misrepresentation. Rules couched in the form 'All Xs have rights to R against Ys' are liable to limitation; claims arising under them are defeasible, and, in Prof. Hart's phrase, defeasible concepts are 'to be defined through exceptions and not by a set of necessary and sufficient conditions'.[17] 'Everyone has the right to choose his own employment' does not necessarily rule out military conscription, or even under emergency conditions the direction of labour. These are limiting or exceptional conditions that would defeat the right. It might be preferable, perhaps, to state the right with the principal exceptions included, but we simply cannot foresee all the conditions in which we should feel it proper to make exceptions. Moral and legal growth is very largely a process of discovery by experience; of refining rules of thumb by distinguishing the cases which, while apparently falling under a rule, are in relevant ways exceptional. We can never lay down, therefore, a single formula, however complex, to determine the conditions in which a right will hold, or conversely all the conditions that would defeat it. This is not a reason for rejecting all generalized statements of rights as useless, if only because it is a characteristic that they share with every general rule.

What is peculiar about declarations of natural or human rights is that the rules purport to apply to all men—not to creditors, debtors, landlords, tenants, doctors, etc., but universally. The very extent of the claim involves either or both of two conditions: *i.* that many circumstances must arise in which the rights would be defeated; *ii.* that being divorced from all particular circumstances, they will be so general as to square with very diverse applications under different conditions.

(d) 'Human rights'

What this means in practice may best be seen from a consideration of the Universal Declaration of 1948. The preamble offers it as a declaration of

> 'a common standard of achievement for all peoples and all nations, to the end that every individual and every organ of society, keeping this Declaration constantly in mind, shall strive by teaching and education to promote respect for these rights and freedoms and by progressive measures, national and international, to secure their universal and effective recognition and observance, both among peoples of Member States themselves and among the peoples of territories under their jurisdiction.'

The articles that follow vary from the very highest order of generality (e.g. Art. 1; 'All human beings are born free and equal in dignity and rights. They are endowed with reason and conscience and should act towards one another in a spirit of brotherhood') to reasonably specific recommendations (e.g. Art. 25: ' . . . the right to security in the event of unemployment, sickness, disability, widowhood, old age or other lack of livelihood in circumstances beyond his control'). These are not in any sense statements of fact; if we wanted to disagree with them, we should not have to *prove* that men did or did not possess these rights, in the sense that they possess arms and legs. Earlier formulations like the American Declaration of Independence, by using terms like 'self-evident truths' invited this sort of interpretation and gave rise to needless confusion. For these are obviously prescriptive statements which commanded wide support among member nations (or their governments), and which they were prepared to subscribe to, not as formulae by which their policies were to be determined, but as general aims, and 'common standards of achievement'.

The very generality of these statements of principle is, of course, the reason why they command assent from governments and individuals who, in their particular judgments and decisions, differ very radically.[18] For the way in which a rule is to apply in given circumstances is not deducible from its general formulation. Moral principles of this order lay down the terms in which discussion is to be conducted and decisions defended; agreement on the terms is no guarantee of agreement on particulars. The right to social security stated in Article 25 is not an injunction upon states to set up National Insurance schemes, or National Assistance Boards, for it might well be argued that if ordinary commercial or friendly society arrangements existed, an individual who in sickness was without means of support had only himself to blame—

that he 'lacked livelihood in circumstances which had been within his control'. It should be noted, in any case, that the Universal Declaration is not positive law (though it has been incorporated into the international law governing Trust Territories); it is a statement of objectives felt to be *generally* desirable. It is quite properly open to economically backward peoples to argue, for example, that while recognizing the desirability of working towards the ideal of a universal, free system of elementary education, required by Article 26, the rate of progress must be governed by the relative claims of other ideals upon their resources.

Formal declarations of rights are mainly directed not to the regulation of relations between private citizens, but to the duties of governments and legislatures. Where private relations are involved, the duty is laid on the legal authorities concerned to make positive law conform to the standards prescribed. In the seventeenth and eighteenth century, for instance, limits were prescribed for interference by governmental organs with the decisions of private persons. The rights of life, liberty, and property claimed by Locke, or to 'the pursuit of happiness', claimed by the Declaration of Independence, were intended as protests against imprisonment at executive discretion, taxation without normal legislative authorization, interference with trade, the quartering of troops, etc. Indeed, the bulk of the Declaration is taken up with enunciating the particular grievances of the American colonists, which in their view justified revolution, and which together constitute, by negation, the meaning of the general rights in this context. Since the eighteenth century, we have come to regard the state less as a hostile, if necessary, intruder in private affairs, and more as an instrument for promoting welfare. Accordingly, the duties imposed by more recent declarations require positive action, not merely non-interference. Whereas 'natural rights' required only that governments as well as private persons should respect a proper sphere of personal autonomy, 'human rights' also require positive performance for their realization. That duty may not necessarily fall upon governments; if churches provided free and universal education, making provision also for the children of 'rationalist' parents, the requirements of Article 26 of the Universal Declaration would presumably be met. The presumption, however, is that if the right is not otherwise implemented, the duty rests on the government by default.

IV. 'NATURAL RIGHTS' AND LEGAL THEORY

The theory of natural rights has had as profound an effect on legal as on political theory and practice. In the eighteenth century, Blackstone virtually identified natural rights with the rights of Englishmen in common law, a conservative interpretation which sufficiently accounts for Bentham's implacable hostility to the doctrine. It continued, however, to influence judges in England and America in the nineteenth century; English judges tended to interpret statutes limiting freedom of contract narrowly, and American judges to treat them as unconstitutional.[19] For the theory of natural rights found its way into the first ten amendments to the American Constitution, to provide criteria by which the Supreme Court could test the legal validity of statues. The Fifth Amendment (later extended to cover state legislation by the Fourteenth) provides, *inter alia*, that 'No person . . . shall be deprived of life, liberty, or property, *without due process of law*'. Laissez-faire economic doctrine combined with natural right theory to produce, in the second half of the nineteenth century, an interpretation that *prima facie* excluded from legislative competence any interference with freedom of contract.[20] By 1907, acts of the following types had been held invalid on this ground: (*i*) Acts forbidding interference by employers with their employees' membership of labour unions; (*ii*) acts prohibiting the imposition of fines on employees; (*iii*) acts regulating the mode of weighing coal to determine miner's wages; (*iv*) truck acts; (*v*) acts regulating hours of labour, except in special conditions.[21] On the other hand, it is only in the last two or three years that the Supreme Court has taken the view that racial segregation in schools is contrary to the rights guaranteed by the constitution.

The Supreme Court, by assuming the power to review legislation for constitutionality, has been virtually converted into a third chamber of the legislature, without the power of initiation but with an absolute power of veto. The extreme generality of the rights included in the Bill of Rights leaves room for enormous variation in interpretation, so that the way in which they apply to any particular case depends entirely on the political and moral attitudes of the majority of judges at any one time. Consequently, in appointing judges, a President is bound to look carefully at their political opinions. The Court's resistance to the New Deal policies of the 1930's persuaded President Roosevelt to attempt to enlarge the bench to include a more favourable majority; though the attempt was frustrated, several judges conveniently died or retired, with the result that since 1937 the natural and constitutional rights of American citizens have been defined in somewhat different terms. When the law of the constitution empowers a court to review legislation in terms of a very general statement of rights, it is in fact endowing it with the sort of discretion usually reserved in democratic states for elected and responsible assemblies.

V. CONCLUSION

In the first part of this chapter, we examined the relation of the concept 'rights' to rules, and showed how there could be moral as well as legal and customary rights. These latter raise no philosophical problems beyond understanding what is meant by saying that a man has such a right.

Concepts like 'human', 'natural', or 'fundamental' rights, however, are more puzzling, because they are not so clearly related to rules. Statements of rights of this type are statements of moral principles of a very high order of generality. No particular course of action ever follows as a necessary consequence of such a principle. Nevertheless, they draw attention to important interests which are shared by most men, like the interest in living and in being let alone, in security of person and security of property. To recognize these interests as 'natural rights' is to lay down that they can rightly be impaired only for very special reasons— that the onus of proof rests heavily on whoever would set them aside.

Since the seventeenth century, lists of such rights have tended to lengthen. In part, this may be because their authors have become aware of the very wide margin for interpretation permitted by very general principles, like 'the right to liberty', and have tried to make them more precise by listing their applications more particularly (like the right freely to leave and return to one's country). But this is not the only reason for the greater elaboration of such statements. With the enormous expansion in wealth since the seventeenth century, expectations have been greatly extended. Men have become more aware of how one another live, not only as between class and class but as between continent and continent. They have been led to challenge the fairness of privileges formerly taken for granted. Moreover the sense that poverty, disease, and ignorance need not be the inevitable lot of most of the world's inhabitants, and that they might be remedied by deliberate action, has led to the recognition of claims to certain minimal economic and social conditions as 'human rights'. In the chapters that follow, we shall examine what is implied in social principles of this sort.

PART TWO

SOCIAL PRINCIPLES AND THEIR IMPLEMENTATION

CHAPTER 5

JUSTICE AND EQUALITY

I. EQUALITY AND NATURAL RIGHTS

The theory of natural rights, which we discussed in the last chapter, is related closely to the idea of quality. The state of Nature, declared Locke, is

> 'a state also of equality, wherein all the power and jurisdiction is reciprocal, no one having more than another, there being nothing more evident than that creatures of the same species and rank, promiscuously born to all the same advantages of Nature, and the use of the same faculties, should also be equal one amongst another, without subordination or subjection . . .';

and the law of Nature

> 'teaches all mankind who will but consult it, that being all equal and independent, no one ought to harm another in his life, health, liberty, or possessions . . .'[1]

The American Declaration of Independence proclaimed, as self-evident truths, 'that all men are created equal, that they are endowed by their Creator with certain unalienable Rights'; the Declaration of 1789 echoed: 'Men are born and live free and equal in their rights'; and that of 1948: 'All human beings are born free and equal in dignity and rights'.

We have seen that the universality claimed for natural rights strongly suggests the criterion of impartiality for a moral rule. If, for instance, democratic rights were to be accorded to white men, we decided one must show good cause to deny them to black men. Where there are no relevant differences it would be unfair—or we might say *unjust*—to treat people differently.

In this chapter we shall begin by relating the concepts 'morality' and 'justice' to 'equality' as a social and political ideal. We shall then consider their relevance to problems of law and administration.

II. ANALYSIS OF 'EQUALITY'

The word 'equality' is used in one of its senses when we make comparisons. Now we can compare things only because they have some quality or attribute in common. We do not compare an elephant with a cabbage; we compare the relative size, weight, or colour of elephants and cabbages. It would, therefore, be as meaningless to say 'All elephants are equal' (in this sense of 'equal') as it would be to say 'Some elephants are more than others'. Neither statement is complete without a reference to some quality common to all elephants. What then of 'All men are equal'? If this were meant in this descriptive-comparative sense, it is difficult to think of a human quality—physical, intellectual, or moral— of which it could be true.

In social and political theory, however, 'equality' is more often prescriptive than descriptive. In this sense, 'All men are equal' would imply not that they possess some attribute or attributes in the same degree, but that they ought to be treated alike. But it is hardly likely that anyone would want to see all men treated alike in every respect. We should not wish rheumatic patients to be treated like diabetics. A poll tax is generally considered less just than an income tax, and a progressive tax fairer than a flat rate. There are clearly some differences that are proper grounds for differences in treatment. Equals (i.e. in the descriptive-comparative sense) ought to be treated alike in the respect in which they are equal; but there may be other respects in which they differ (or, are 'unequal') which justify differences in treatment. Men who make identical tax returns ought to be taxed alike, but if they suffer from different ailments they should be treated with different medicines. Injustice, said Aristotle, arises as much from treating unequals equally as from treating equals unequally. But if we agree to that, could it be right to treat *all* men equally in *any* respect, unless there were *some* attribute that they all possessed in the same degree?

It might well be asked whether there is really any respect in which a serious and responsible demand could be made for treating all men as if they were all equal in the sense of falling into one category. The obvious answer is that there are some demands like that of equality before the law which suggest just this. It might, therefore, be maintained that there must be some positive quality which all men have in common to *justify* them all being put in a universal category such as that of being a legal person. This would commit us to a search for some esoteric 'fundamental' quality in respect of which all are alike. Yet if this quality is so elusive, how can political theorists say with such confidence that all men possess it equally and ought accordingly to be treated as equals?

The difficulties arise, in our view, from putting the question in the wrong way. Consider Hobhouse's treatment of the subject:

'As a matter of the interpretation of experience, there is something peculiar to human beings and common to human beings without distinction of class, race or sex, which lies far deeper than all differences between them. Call it what we may, soul, reason, the abysmal capacity for suffering, or just human nature, it is something generic, of which there may be many specific, as well as quantitative differences, but which underlies and embraces them all. If this common nature is what the doctrine of equal rights postulates, it has no reason to fear the test of our ordinary experience of life, or of our study of history and anthropology.'[2]

Hobhouse seems to be making a distinction between all the particular differences between men, which he would treat as accidentals, and some essential or fundamental quality of 'men as men'—something called 'human nature', 'human dignity', 'personality', 'soul', etc.—by virtue of which they must be treated as fundamentally equal. But if we strip away all the qualities in respect of which men might differ, what is left? If from human nature we abstract talents, dispositions, character, intelligence, and all other possible grounds of distinction, we are left with an undifferentiated potentiality. To say that X is a person, or a human being, is to say that though we may not know enough about him to say whether he is wise or foolish, musical or unmusical, extrovert or introvert, we do know that he is the sort of object of which such things might be said. 'Human nature' implies a varying potentiality for a certain limited range of qualities ('limited' because it rules out having, say, the trunk and dimensions of an elephant); it is not another quality that all men possess equally, on account of which they should in some positive way be treated alike. 'The abysmal capacity for suffering' looks, on the face of it, a more promising candidate for universality. But while all human beings are liable to suffer, if some suffer more from a given cause than others, there would seem to be a case for unequal treatment, to protect the more sensitive. Conversely, the human species is not unique in this respect, yet we do not proclaim a fundamental equality between men and dogs.

It might be argued[3] that all men have certain basic needs, for food, clothing, shelters, etc., which must be satisfied if suffering is to be avoided; 'basic', in that, whatever the variety of their needs, these are common to them all: and further, if these are not satisfied, none can be satisfied. But while all men need *some* food, they do not all need the same sort, or even the same amount; and while in cold climates they need elaborate clothing and shelter, in warmer climates they can survive with none at all. Differences in circumstances create differences in needs, and it is no help to say that all men are equal in possessing basic needs, if they are needs for different things.[4]

(a) Equality of consideration

These difficulties arise from treating 'All men are equal' as if it were a positive prescription, i.e. as if it meant 'Treat all men alike (if not in all, at least in certain fundamental respects)'. For if it is unjust to treat unequals equally, there would have to be some sort of universal human equality, in the descriptive sense. Yet this is not to be found. The dilemma can be avoided, however, by re-formulating the prescription. What we really demand, when we say that all men are equal, is that *none shall be held to have a claim to better treatment than another, in advance of good grounds being produced.*

The only universal right, it has been said, is the right to equal consideration.[5] This is not a right in the ordinary sense. Its existence cannot be established by referring to law, for it is presupposed by the idea of law, as a rule of *general* application, and by the procedure whereby a judge must consider relevant evidence and apply a rule in order to reach a decision. We cannot show that such a right *ought* to exist in law by pointing to the advantages of recognizing it; for until we admit the principle of equal consideration we cannot know whose advantage would be relevant.

'Equal consideration' is really the 'impartiality', which we examined in Chapter 2, in a somewhat different guise. And this, we said, was one of the criteria implied in the idea of morality. Similarly, equality of consideration is implicit in the idea of justice. When we ask a judge, or anyone else making a decision between competing claims. 'Why do you treat A differently from B? 'we expect him to justify discrimination by showing in what relevant respects they differ. If there is no relevant difference, we consider that he has been unreasonable. If he answered: 'I decided in that way because I felt like it', or 'because I like A better than B', his answer would be unsatisfactory because it is either an explanation of his conduct rather than a justification, or a justification on irrelevant grounds. We are seeking a reason that will satisfy the criterion that differences in treatment must be based on relevant differences of condition: what we have been offered is an explanation or justification in terms of the judge's own feelings or preferences.

When we have to decide between claims, impose burdens or allot benefits, the only rational ground for treating men differently is that they differ in some way that is relevant to the distinction we propose to make. We cannot know whether they do until we have considered their claims impartially. To do otherwise would be to treat a man purely as a means for someone else's satisfaction (one's own, perhaps, or a friend's). If we refuse to consider his claims on their own merits, we presume an inequality without troubling to establish it. This is very like what Kant meant when he said: 'treat humanity, whether in your own person or in that of any other, in every case as an end, never solely as a means'. He did not mean that when every particular difference between men has been evaluated, there remains something of value in itself, a fundamental 'humanity'.

Understood in this way, the principle of equality does not prescribe positively that all human beings be treated alike; it is a presumption against treating them differently, in any respect, until grounds for distinction have been shown. It does not assume, therefore, a quality which all men have to the same degree, which is the ground of the presumption, for to say that there is a presumption means that no grounds need be shown. The onus of justification rests on whoever would make distinctions.

To act justly, then, is to treat all men alike except where there are relevant differences between them. This is not a formula from which anyone can deduce in particular cases, how he ought to act, or make decisions. For what constitutes a *relevant* difference, and what sort of distinction ought to be made in respect of it? So far we have achieved no more than a definition of 'justice' in terms of equality, and definitions cannot prescribe action, since they merely elucidate the meanings of words. At the most we have arrived at a rule of procedure for taking decisions: Presume equality until there is reason to presume otherwise. But this is a formal, not a substantive rule.

(b) 'Relevance'

Clearly, much depends on what we hold to be relevant. So far we have provided no guidance on this point. In asking 'Who shall vote?' a South African Nationalist considers race differences relevant; his critics deny this.

When there is a clear and accepted rule, the problem of relevance presents no difficulty. An Inspector of Taxes has no doubt that the size of a man's income, the number of his dependents, and his life insurance premium are relevant to his liability for income tax, because a clear rule of law makes them so. Similarly, most people would agree that a man with a starving family has a stronger claim on their charity than one who has not; for there is an accepted moral rule that we should do what we can to prevent people starving. When we speak of doing justice in cases of this sort, we mean taking into account only such factors as the rules sanction. But on that basis we should have to admit that a South African judge applying racial discriminatory laws was doing justice, so long as he decided according to the law and nothing else.

Justice, however, is not only a matter of applying general rules to particular cases. For the rule itself may be unjust. The Aristotelian principle lays it down that equals should be treated equally and unequals unequally. There are two distinct prescriptions here. The first is the requirement that a law should be a *law*; exceptions should not be made unless relevant grounds are produced. But the second is the requirement that there should be categories—e.g. categories created by law—and the problem is to determine what are *relevant* grounds for determining such categories. There is a distinction between unjust administration of the law and an unjust law. The judge may act justly in denying a man the vote because he has a black skin, if that is the law; but we can still question whether the criterion established by the law is itself defensible. This may not be so easily settled. Once again it is up to whoever would make distinctions to justify the criteria in terms of more general rules, and ultimately of a balance of advantage to all concerned. In the chapters that follow we examine the way we employ such criteria in distributing wealth, and in awarding punishment, how we apply them and how we must go about justifying them.

(c) *Justice as an 'equality of proportion'*

Suppose we can agree in a given case what differences are relevant; room for disagreement still remains, for we may not agree on *how much* they matter. Aristotle held that justice consists in an equality of proportion between persons and things assigned to them, i.e. that differences in treatment should be proportionate to the degrees to which individuals differ in relevant respects. Granted a loose, or metaphorical sense of 'proportionate', this is a useful way of putting it. In a stricter sense, however, it is misleading. For example, it would seem to suggest a flat rate tax on incomes—yet we usually regard a progressive tax as fairer. It may be urged that there are other factors relevant to tax assessment besides gross income, and that a progressive rate preserves an equality of proportion between the tax levied and some other, more fundamental factor. There are, of course, many other relevant factors (e.g. family responsibilities, incentives to effort and initiative, variations in living expenses between different groups, etc.), but these cannot all be reduced to one fundamental factor present in different degrees, to which tax should be proportionate. In constructing a tax schedule, we have to weigh one factor against another, and though we may be able to preserve strict proportion in respect of any given difference (e.g. allowing the same tax relief for each child), there is no way of showing what relative weights ought to be given to the various factors involved, except where there is already a rule laying them down. Similarly (as we show in Chapter 8), while judges try to preserve some sort of proportion in the punishments they award to different offenders, and while there are maximum sentences varying with the seriousness of the offence, the many factors relevant in assessing penalties cannot be expressed in a formula from which just sentences can be calculated with arithmetical precision. For in the end, doing justice calls for decision-making, not calculation: we have to *decide* what is relevant, and what consequences ought to follow—and though we decide according to rules, we are still doing something different from arithmetic.

Nevertheless, social theorists have hankered after an objective moral truth, analogous to science, ascertainable by rational techniques, and yielding prescriptions that anyone with intelligence and good-will would be bound to accept. Bentham's 'moral arithmetic' is an obvious example: if a decision could be shown to yield the greatest possible number of pleasure (or happiness) units for all the individuals affected by it—each to count for one, and for no more than one (the principle of impartiality) —it would be justified beyond reasonable dispute. Now if pleasure could be clearly identified, and if a generally acceptable technique could be devised for measuring it, and if everyone in fact agreed that all decisions ought to maximize it, Bentham's formula might achieve its object. We should then have an agreed technique for settling moral questions, just as the use of a foot-rule is the agreed technique for settling the height of a post. But whatever we mean by 'pleasure', we have no agreed technique for measuring it. Even more to the point, it is not universally accepted as the one criterion for justifying decisions, and there is no way of showing that it ought to be. Consequently, a Benthamite 'moral arithmetic' would not convince anyone who did not accept pleasure as the sole criterion.[6]

It is only in special cases, like taxation, that an arithmetic proportion between 'persons and things assigned to them' makes any sense. Even then, it may not be conclusive, for we prefer a progressive tax to a flat rate. But that is not to say that once the relevance of a criterion has been accepted, *any* difference of treatment would be justified. The degree of difference can still be the subject of arguments—and some arguments are good, some bad. A Chancellor of the Exchequer who proposes a shift in tax burdens has to give his reasons. Suppose he decides to lower income tax rates, while also drastically lowering dependents' allowances. He would not be altering the factors relevant to the distribution of the burden, but the relative amounts they were to count. He might defend the change by showing that incentives to effort were being frustrated by high rates of tax, and that this was so serious that the special claims of family men were of lesser account. Under some conditions, this might be reasonable. On the other hand, if other allowances were to remain unchanged, we might ask why he picked on this one in particular. What is a good reason is a matter of judgment, not of conclusive demonstration; but where reasons of any sort can be given, decision is not a matter of whim or arbitrary preference. Justice demands that we show what is loosely termed 'a sense of proportion'—an admittedly relevant difference in condition will justify only a reasonable degree of discrimination. There is no formula for determining what differences are relevant for any given purpose, or for measuring the degree of distinction they would justify; we can only formulate principles of procedure, namely, that particular distinctions must be sanctioned by rules, and that criteria enshrined in rules must be ultimately justified in terms of the generally beneficent consequences of adopting and maintaining them.

III. EGALITARIANISM

We have been concerned so far to elucidate 'justice' so that the principle reiterated in the historic declarations of rights that all men stand equal, can be reconciled with the plain fact that we feel it right to treat men differently. Equals should be treated equally, unequals unequally: but the respect in which they are considered unequal must be relevant to the differences in treatment that we propose. And so, until an inequality of attribute or condition has been shown to be relevant, it is improper to make it a basis of distinction. Impartiality involves not merely recognizing similarities, but know which differences ought to be ignored.

The demand for equality has never been intended in practice as a general plea that all men be treated alike. Egalitarians have always been concerned to deny the legitimacy of certain sorts of discrimination resting on some given differences, i.e. they have challenged established criteria as unreasonable, and irrelevant to the purposes for which they were employed. Claims to equality are thus, in a sense, always negative, denying the propriety of certain existing inequalities. When the Levellers urged that all Englishmen were entitled to the vote by reason of a birthright equality, it was clear alike to themselves and to most, if not all, of their opponents that they meant to challenge a property-owning franchise (not, for example, to extend it to women, or to question the distribution of wealth). Ireton retorted that since universal suffrage would endanger other property rights, property was a relevant criterion for allocating the right to vote.[7] Similarly, French revolutionary *Egalité* was aimed not at levelling property, nor, for many, at universal suffrage; it was a specific protest against the privileges of noble birth and clerical status, e.g. tax exemption. The idea of the career open to the talents was a rejection of the principle that the highest, or the most lucrative, posts in the state service should be reserved for aristocrats. On the other hand, the Declaration of the Rights of Man explicitly recognizes that superior talent and qualities of character are proper grounds for distinctions of wealth, honour, and power. And most of the revolutionaries accepted differences of wealth based on inheritance, and the consequent differences in educational opportunities. It is just these differences that are challenged in our own day by the demand for 'equal opportunities'. In the past eighty years or so, we have been busily dismantling an educational and social system by which opportunities of advancement depended on family means, and replacing it with one that makes skill in passing examinations one of the principal criteria. But some look askance even at this latest ground of inequality.

Out of context, 'equality' is an empty framework for a social ideal; It has content only when particularized.[8] That is why it is a mistake to think of history as a movement towards ever greater equality, in which one distinction after another is being borne down; as though the word stood for some essential idea which assumed a different shape in each generation, but which remained in some fundamental way the same, or of which every later manifestation somehow embraced and transcended all the earlier ones. For as fast as we eliminate distinctions, we create new ones—the difference being that the ones we discard we consider unjustifiable, while the ones we create seem reasonable. If we can be said to make progress in this matter, it is by criticizing existing distinctions, by creating new ones that conditions seem to justify, as well as eliminating the ones they do not; and this is rather different from aiming at a theoretical and universal ideal equality, within which all the differences in treatment we should wish to preserve are somehow reconciled.

The form in which an egalitarian ideal is expressed may draw attention to the specific differences between persons which are, but which ought not to be, the basis for important distinctions in treatment or rights (e.g. 'equality of race, or sex'); or it may point to the type of treatment, or the class of rights, in respect of which improper distinctions are being made (e.g. 'equality of opportunity', 'social equality', 'equality before the law'). There are obviously many possible forms of egalitarianism; we shall consider only those mentioned, which are particularly important in the modern world.

(a) *Equality of race or colour, and equality of sex*
These forms of egalitarianism have important common features. They

all deny that the class whose cause they champion (e.g. negroes, Jews, or women) is 'inferior'. Now 'inferiority' may be understood (1) wholly prescriptively, or (2) descriptively, with prescriptive implications.

(1) Where 'inferiority' is wholly prescriptive, it implies a simple refusal to extend the principle of equal consideration to the class in question. The Nazi who asserts that Jews are an inferior race may be saying simply that they are not to count, that they should not be considered, that injury to a Jew matters only if it affects a non-Jew. A limitation in the scope of the basic moral principle cannot in a strict sense be refuted, any more than we could refute (or demonstrate) that the principle ought to extend to animals or insects. Aristotle felt it compatible with his definition of justice that some men who were by nature slaves should be considered only as instruments for the satisfaction of others. Impartiality, as a criterion of morality, implies only that all those who are the proper objects of moral consideration be considered equally; but since it is the most general or the ultimate criterion, we cannot go behind it to show who are the proper objects of moral consideration. Consequently, the egalitarian cannot provide reasons for rejecting the Nazi limitation. But equally the Nazi can give no reason for adopting it. It is at this level that declarations like 'All men are equal in dignity and rights' are important—not as arguments but as exhortations. When discussion reveals disagreements at the very root of morality, rational moral argument must give way to the persuasive methods of preacher and prophet. At this level, to adopt a moral position is to make an ultimate choice—i.e. one in its nature beyond the limits of rational justification, where appeals must necessarily lie to the sympathetic emotions. The importance of Christianity in the history of morals lies in the persuasive force of the doctrine that all men, being alike the children of one Father, are *prima facie* of equal account. This cannot be a rational demonstration—common divine paternity no more entails the principle of equal consideration than common human paternity entails an equal patrimony. By appealing to the sentiment of brotherhood, to sympathy for sufferings, Christianity has been able to change moral attitudes at a level at which rational argument ceases; it is precisely on this account that its influence has been so tremendous.

(2) It is significant, however, that the Nazis were not content to leave matters thus. To lay down, as an ultimate principle, that Jews are not to count, would be logically unassailable; but equally it would be impossible to give any reason why anyone else should adopt it. In practice, the Nazis attempted to *demonstrate* the inferiority of the Jew by a mass of dubious biological and ethnological evidence, designed to

provide *grounds* for the inferiority.* But this is to abandon the first position. For to offer grounds is implicitly to admit that were good grounds lacking, there would be no case for discrimination, and this is to *extend* the principle of equal consideration to Jews and non-Jews alike. And thus, at this level of argument, the assertion of 'inferiority' becomes descriptive, as well as prescriptive. It is now maintained that in respect of some particular and relevant attributes, Jews (or it might be negroes, or women, according to the basis of distinction proposed) are inferior to others, and that this justifies discrimination against them. The argument is now vulnerable on the possible grounds: (*a*) that the evidence will not support the claim that all Jews (negroes, or women) are in the given respects inferior to non-Jews (white men, men); (*b*) that the respects in which they do differ are irrelevant to some, if not all, of the forms of discrimination made to rest on them; (*c*) where differences *are* relevant, the degrees of discrimination are out of all proportion to the degrees of difference.

The case for 'equality of the sexes' can be arranged fairly neatly under these three heads. (*a*) While there are admitted physical and psychological differences between men and women, there is no evidence that women are generally inferior to men in intelligence, business capacity, soundness of judgment, etc.; discrimination resting on such assumed inferiorities is therefore ill-grounded. (*b*) The admitted differences will not support discrimination between the sexes in respect, e.g. of voting rights, entry to the professions, educational opportunities, levels of remuneration, etc. Whatever distinctions are made in any of these respects should depend on criteria applying alike to men and women. Thus 'equal pay for equal work' means that men and women should be paid equally if and only if they work equally well. If women always worked less well than men in all jobs, then equal pay for equal work would invariably mean less pay for women. But then the criterion of differentiation would be that of performance, not sex. On the other hand, feminists do not complain because the law forbids the employment of women as coal miners, for the admitted difference in physique between the sexes makes this a reasonable distinction. (*c*) There are admitted biological and psychological differences between men and women that can properly support a difference in function within the family. A mother is expected to occupy herself with house and children

---

* Whether, in such cases where strong emotions are aroused, the grounds advanced are properly to be called 'reasons' or 'rationalizations' is another matter. This would depend largely on whether the Nazi would accept counter-arguments and act differently if his arguments were refuted. (See Ch. 9, Section II.)

authority

a father with earning the family living. Nevertheless, this does not justify elevating the husband into a lord and master, nor the complete sacrifice of the woman's personality to the demands of the family. The emancipation of women has expressed itself not only in law and economics, but also in changes in conventional marital relations. Many husbands now recognize that the domestic burden carried by mothers of families in previous generations was out of all proportion to the difference in function implied by the difference in sex. Their readiness to share the chores and the baby-minding is a sign of a practical extension of the principle of equal consideration.

Where, as in family life, sex differences are held to be relevant, the egalitarian is usually ready to accept differences in rights. The married woman is entitled to maintenance if her husband leaves her; he has no corresponding right. Family allowances are the property of mothers, not of fathers. English law safeguards the property rights of married women, protecting wives from the undue influence of their husbands, but not conversely. These distinctions are not called 'inequalities' because they are held to be justified; for the word 'inequality' in this sort of context usually has a pejorative force and we call a distinction an 'inequality' only when we have already decided to condemn it. This distinction between the pejorative 'inequality' and the neutral 'difference in treatment' is helpful in discussing egalitarianism in all its forms.

(b) 'Equality of opportunity'

Egalitarians are often charged by their opponents—usually unjustly—with wanting to treat everyone in all respects alike, irrespective of *any* differences. Accordingly, to make their position clear, they often use the phrase 'equality of opportunity'. It would be unjust, they admit, to treatment alike; justice requires only that they be given equal opportunities. But equal opportunities to do what?

One answer might be: 'Equal opportunities to achieve success in the career of one's choice'. This is the French revolutionaries' ideal of 'la carrière ouverte aux talents'. For them it meant careers open to all irrespective of rank by birth. Modern egalitarians scorn so limited an interpretation. What use, they say, is an equality that takes no account of differences in opportunities arising from differences in wealth? To achieve equality of opportunity we must compensate for such advantages by free education, university scholarships, etc. Success or failure must be made to depend only on the capacity and character of the persons concerned, not on the accidents of wealth.

So conceived, however, 'equality of opportunity' would be consistent with a single educational stream which everyone entered on the same footing, following it as far as his capacity allowed. This is not the theory (whatever the practice) of our present system. We aim, instead, at a number of streams, to provide educational opportunities appropriate to different types of ability, as well as different degrees. The system is not like a slope that people climb until strength gives out, but more like a transport system in which people are conveyed to different, and appropriate, destinations. And we do more than treat everyone as if they started on an equal footing: we attempt to compensate for some personal disadvantages, as well as giving preferential treatment to special talents. We have schools for disabled, blind, and deaf children, and we spend far more per head on them than we do on the average child. If this is not accounted 'inequality of opportunity', it is because the discrimination is felt to be justified.

The egalitarian may object that we are treating 'equality of opportunity' too narrowly—that it involves not one basic provision within which each does the best he can for himself, but a variety of patterns, within which each finds what is most suitable to him; 'equality of opportunity' is achieved only when there is an *appropriate* opportunity for each; what is to be equalized is not the opportunity to enter professions or to be successful in business but the opportunity to lead a good life, or to fulfil one's personality.

Now 'the good life for A' may well be very different from 'the good life for B'; and there is no element, signified by the term 'a good life', which, while taking different shapes, is still common to both. For the term signifies only that there is a way of life for A, and another for B, both approved (though for different reasons) by some third person, who accordingly calls them both 'good'. The element in common is the approval of the speaker, not some property of the ways prescribed, which must be made equally available to both A and B. But then, if I commend one way for A and another for B, I should recommend that *different* opportunities be made available to them. A, perhaps, should be sent to a technical school, with the opportunity, if he will, of becoming a mechanic; B to a grammar school and university, to become, if he will, a scientist. We carry out an assessment of children's capacities at the age of eleven, and send them accordingly to different schools. We accord them *the same* opportunities only in the sense that all are entitled to be treated alike until relevant grounds are established for treating them differently. Thus they all take the same examination—but its purpose is precisely to establish the different opportunities to be provided thereafter. This is a special application, in the fields of education and recruitment to the professions, of the procedure we have called 'equal consideration'. If we do not say that opportunities thereafter are unequal, it is because we see the point of the discrimination. Differences in opportunities are compatible with 'equality' if we see the point of them—they are 'inequalities' when we do not.

The man who presses for 'equality of opportunity' is urging that certain factors, like wealth, which have hitherto determined the extent of an individual's opportunities, should be neutralized. But he may very well be urging at the same time discrimination according to other criteria. Because in the mouth of the egalitarian 'equality' is a term of approval, he is bound to distinguish between differences in treatment that are reasonable, and therefore compatible with 'equality', and those that are not, and are thus 'inequalities'. His procedure is to criticize established criteria, and to elaborate new and more reasonable ones; and there is nothing wrong with it. But the statement of his objects in terms of 'equality', when his aim is to substitute reasonable for objectionable distinctions, is frequently misleading, not least to himself. His position is not greatly clarified by saying that he seeks not 'equality of treatment' but 'equality of opportunity': neither phrase means very much unless we know the criteria under attack. A negro from Alabama demanding 'equality of opportunity' may be attacking the educational colour bar, leaving wealth untouched; a South African white trade unionist using the same phrase may well mean the reverse.

(c) 'Social equality'

Socialist egalitarians commonly declare themselves for 'social equality', a term open to diverse interpretations. 'Equality of opportunity' is certainly one element in the ideal, the 'inequality' under attack being usually wealth, and particularly inherited wealth. Beyond this, they are attacking wide inequalities of income and property. The socialist rarely advocates equal incomes for all; on the contrary, he is in favour of using 'need' more extensively than at present as a criterion for distribution. His complaint is rather that some of the criteria currently employed are unjustified, or that differences grounded on reasonable and relevant criteria are often out of reasonable proportion.[9]

But it is not only in education and income distribution that the socialist finds groundless inequalities. He is critical too of class attitudes that make the respect due to a man depend on criteria like speech, dress, and eating habits, a man's old school, and the sort of work that he does. These problems arise more acutely, perhaps, in Western Europe, where an aristocratic tradition still lingers on, than in America or Australasia, where it has never existed, and where the highest respect is reserved for the materially successful.

The socialist who objects to such attitudes of inferiority and superiority can gain little consolation from the fact that the old class system in Western Europe is breaking down; for it is being replaced by a new one in which social status depends no longer on birth or breeding but on occupation and education. The scientist and the doctor may lack an ancient lineage; but they command considerable social prestige. This is not because of the money that they earn; for a car dealer could acquire wealth and lack such prestige. It is because of their education and occupation. In the Soviet Union a new class-system has emerged which is determined largely by criteria such as occupation and membership of the Communist Party. The clear-headed egalitarian can only argue, when confronted with such glaring social facts, that although society will always have a class structure in the sense that there will tend to be intermarriage, social intercourse, and similarity of dress, manner and outlook between people with similar occupations and education, this differentiation should not be accompanied by attitudes of inferiority or superiority. A dustman has a different job from a schoolmaster and is likely to have a different circle of friends; but he ought not to be considered to be an inferior sort of man. The egalitarian deprecates a social structure in which 'You are talking like a fishmonger's wife' or 'You have the manners of a dustman' are expressions of abuse. He strives to cut the lingering connection between people being different and people being better or worse. The ideal of the classless society,* at least among non-Marxist socialists, seems directed as much to eliminating social attitudes of this sort as to an economic re-ordering for its own sake. Ideally, the respect owed to a man should be determined by his moral qualities, not by social graces.† Accordingly the socialist egalitarian is suspicious of public schools and other institutions tending to foster the visible differences which are the badges of social grading.[10]

The term 'social equality' has been adopted by socialists largely to distinguish their objective from the earlier egalitarian ideals of the French Revolution. The men of 1789 sought 'equality before the law', which for them meant eliminating aristocratic legal privileges and feudal obligations. The Jacobins, and the nineteenth century Republicans on whom their mantle descended, sought 'political equality'

* The Communist can only claim that the USSR approximates to a 'classless society' because of the special definition of 'class' suggested by Marx. In his view a social class is determined by the relationship to the means of production. When all private ownership of the means of production has been abolished, all members of a society fall into one class—by definition. And where there is only one class, there is no class.

† There are, of course, some socialists for whom 'a worker' as such is the salt of the earth. But this is snobbery, not egalitarianism.

or universal suffrage. To socialists these ends by themselves seem in-adequate; they are at best ways of achieving 'real' equality—social equality. Without that, 'political equality' is an illusion. A wealthy élite would continue to exercise effective political power; judges and legislators would still be drawn from its ranks, and predisposed to favour it. Legal costs would put justice beyond the poor man's reach. Without social equality, 'equality before the law' would remain an empty form.

(d) 'Equality before the law'

'Equality before the law' is probably the most generally respected of all egalitarian ideals. For this reason, if for no other, it deserves a fairly full analysis. An ideal that everyone takes for granted will probably leave plenty of room for misunderstandings which lead to charges of hypocrisy and bad faith. In the analysis that follows, we distinguish several different senses of 'equality before the law'. In every case, however, what is meant is either a restatement of the purely formal principle of equal consideration, or a denial of the reasonableness and relevance of the criteria used to discriminate between the legal rights of different classes of persons in certain fields.

Two senses of 'equality before the law', must first be distinguished. It might apply (*i*) to the rules themselves, (*ii*) to the actual practices of legal administrators. For though the law might be formally just, the judges might be corrupt.

(i) 'Equality' in respect of the rules of a legal system

According to some writers, 'equality before the law' implies equality of rights and duties in law. Now if they meant that all men and women ought to enjoy the *same* rights and duties, it would be clearly untenable. Law creates classes with special rights and duties. Landlords have different right from tenants, policemen from sanitary inspectors, Members of Parliament from judges. As law is a system of rules for a society in which there is considerable specialization and division of function, such differences in rights are inevitable. In such a differentiated society strict equality of rights is not simply a Utopian ideal; it is in-compatible with the existence of such a society.

'*Equality of legal personality.*' Sir Ernest Barker has tried to express the idea in another way. What is significant, in his view, is that 'each legal personality is equal to every other in terms of legal capacity'. All legal persons do not enjoy the same rights, but all enjoy the same capacity for rights. Now, 'legal personality' is a legal term, with no necessary connection with 'person' in a non-technical sense. To say of

A (and A might be just as well a corporation as a natural person) that he is a legal person is to say that he has rights and duties of *some* sort, though what they are remains unspecified. Kelsen puts it thus:

'The legal person is the legal substance to which duties and rights belong as legal qualities. The idea that "the person has" duties and rights involves the relation of substance and quality ... In reality, however, the legal person is not a separate entity besides "its" duties and rights, but only their personified unity.'[12]

When therefore we say of A and B that they are legal persons, *we have not said enough to distinguish* what rights and duties they have, and consequently the respects in which they are unequal. If this is all we are to understand by 'equality of legal capacity', or 'equality before the law', it cannot be a criterion for evaluating legal systems, or an ideal to be realized, simply because it is necessarily entailed in calling anything 'a legal system'. At best it is the legal equivalent of the principle of impartiality, or equal consideration. It is tantamount to saying that there can be no legal basis for a decision until the legal status of the parties to a dispute has been investigated. But this is a formal property of any legal system, not a substantive one by which good systems can be distinguished from bad.

'Equality of capacity for rights' would be more than formal if it were taken to mean that a person might assume any rights he chose. But such an arrangement would be obviously unworkable. It would be a strange society in which anyone could assume at will the rights of judge or policeman, or in which a man might choose to be for legal purposes a married woman. Rights and duties can be assumed, of course, by contract, but even this capacity cannot be completely general. There are good reasons for limiting the contractual capacity of minors, and for prohibiting child marriages.

There is, however, one sense in which 'equality of capacity for rights' might be meaningful as an ideal, namely, in the sense that no human being, or natural person, should be altogether without rights. That is to say, every natural person should be a legal person. This would not necessarily be true of every legal system. The old penalty of outlawry, by putting a man outside the law, deprived him of all rights, and therefore of legal personality. A slave in the strict sense has no rights, his legal standing being that of an object of property rights vested in his master. 'Equality of legal personality' in this sense is not the equality of one legal person with another, but of all natural persons by the fact of their being legal persons. Even so, the equality is hardly more than formal. For to say that every man ought to have *some* rights is to say very little, and is not inconsistent with the actualities of slavery, even though the slave might have a *locus standi* in a court of law.

'*Equality of fundamental rights and duties.*' 'Equality before the law', according to Hobhouse, implies that all human beings should possess certain 'fundamental' rights and duties; special relations create differences, and special rights and duties may be voluntarily assumed; nevertheless, 'it is in the spirit of modern law to hold certain fundamentals of rights and duty equally applicable to all human beings'.[13] He instances 'equal protection of life and limb for every one under the law, and equal penalties on every one violating them'. But even this is open to objections. The condemned murderer, the traitor, and the soldier showing cowardice in the face of the enemy may have no right to protection of life. Penalties for violations of the law, for what may be technically the same offence, may vary enormously—first offenders usually get off more lightly than old lags. There are many criteria, besides the class of the offence, which help to determine the penalty.[14] What Hobhouse had in mind, however was that in modern law we do not distinguish the crime of homicide 'according as slayer or slain is high caste or low caste, noble, free or slave, man or woman, of the same or of different kindred, citizen or alien'.[15] These are differences that we no longer consider relevant in determining whether a killing is murder, and it is in respect of these that men stand equal before the law in matters of homicide. But we do make distinctions between sane and insane, and between judicial killings and private killings; if these differences are not 'inequalities', it is because we accept them as justified. Once again, the egalitarian ideal must be understood not in terms of some universal and fundamental respect in which all men stand equal, but in terms of the inequalities denied.

'*Equals in law should be treated equally by the law.*' While recognizing that the law creates categories involving differences in rights and duties, Hobhouse insists on one sort of equality, in the sense of universality:

> 'Whatever else it may be, law is a rule couched in universal terms and applied impartially, that is, with accurate equality, to all cases that fall within its definitions ... The law may prescribe that all murderers should be hanged, or that only murder with premeditation is a capital offence ... But in every case the rule is universal for the cases to which it applies, and this means that all persons whose cases conform to the rule are treated equally.'[16]

Now if this is taken to refer to the content of a legal system, rather than to the way in which judges actually reach decisions in operating it, it is a statement of what is necessarily implied by using the word 'rule'. Consequently, it is bound to be true of any legal system. A law simply could not prescribe that cases falling within the same category be treated differently: a rule that said that burglars should be treated according to the judge's discretion, for example, would be empowering the judge to create new sub-categories by which distinctions would be regulated. And this is consistent with the equal treatment of equals, for it would now be up to the judge to decide who were and who were not equals.

The principle that equals should be treated equally by the law is meaningful as a prescription, and not simply as a sort of definition of 'a rule', only if we adopt non-legal criteria for determining what is a relevant difference. 'Equality in law' is not an equality of attribute like equality in height, though by virtue of such specific equalities men may be equals in law. Legislation, however, is a selective process: it picks out attributes significant for the purposes the law is meant to serve and turns them into legal criteria for discriminating between persons. Other attributes, irrelevant to these purposes, will remain legally unrecognized. But though persons with different attributes may thus be equal in law, a change in the law recognizing these particular attributes would make them thereafter unequals. Whether given individuals should be equal or unequal in law and in what respects, must depend on what objects we believe law ought to serve. Men are equals in law when their differences remain, rightly or wrongly, unrecognized.

However, legal rules are not absolutely inflexible, laying down a fixed range of attributes as relevant for legal purposes. In applying law, judges are frequently creative, not mere calculating machines. In distinguishing precedents, in deciding to construe a statute narrowly, they may well be deciding to recognize as relevant, differences hitherto ignored. Apparent equals in law may turn out to be unequal after all, and therefore liable to different treatment.[17] The possibility of adapting the law by judicial interpretation is commonly regarded as a source of strength, not of weakness, for it makes the law more responsive to changes in conditions and in conventional moral attitudes. Yet if we admit that it is sometimes right for the judge to create new law when the old seems unjust, what point is there in saying that judges ought to treat equally those who in law stand equal? Whether they are equal now depends on the judge's own discretion, and on his ingenuity in distinguishing the case before him from unsatisfactory precedents.

If 'equality before the law' is regarded as a property of the rules themselves, rather than of the way they are administered, it cannot mean that in some respect all men ought to be treated alike. Either we find reasonable exceptions, or the principle reveals itself as a definition of a rule, or a necessary corollary of such a definition. In the latter case, it could not serve as an ideal, precisely because the conditions implied would be necessarily true of anything that we chose to call a 'legal system'. It becomes significant as a practical ideal only when we give up the search for a universal basis of equality, and interpret it negatively, as a denial of the propriety of making distinctions of a particular sort.

(ii) 'Equality' as applied to the actual administration of the law

Rules, we have said, apply impartially to all persons who fall within a given category; for that is simply what we mean by 'rules'. The impartiality of the men who apply the rules cannot be so easily assumed. The colour of a man's skin may have no legal relevance to a charge of rape; but it would be rash to assume that it would make no difference to an Alabama jury's assessment of the evidence. To be sure that irrelevant factors do not influence judicial decisions, we must look beyond the form and content of rules to the machinery for administering them. We must ensure, for example, that judges are free from political pressures, by insulating them from the executive and legislature; free from corruption, by training them in professional standards, professionally maintained; free as any human being may be from irrational bias, by appointing to the bench men of wide experience, humane sympathies, and trained intellect. Our jury system works on the assumption that twelve average men, with no advance knowledge of a case, and no axe to grind, are likely to be impartial assessors of the evidence presented. It works reasonably well if no bitter local prejudice has been aroused; and a case can be transferred to another area, if an impartial jury would be hard to find. Legal justice is not simply a matter of applying known rules to facts objectively given; it presents, too, the problem of devising institutions and procedures that will work impartially; that will elicit evidence and weigh it judicially, without presuming what has not been proved for the sake of arriving at a pre-determined conclusion; that will see the facts in the light of the law alone, without allowing judgment to be swayed by extraneous motives, like fear or bribery. These are technical problems of administration, to be solved empirically, rather than by the analysis of theoretical ideals.

Inequality in the administration of the law may arise not only from the partiality of judges and juries, but from defects of a different sort. If poor men are kept from the courts by the cost of a legal action; if a rich man can force a settlement on less favourable terms than a poor opponent would get in court, by threatening to carry the case to appeal; if the former's case is put by more skilful—and more expensive—

counsel than the poor man can afford; then the formal equality in law of rich and poor is contradicted by a substantial inequality of access to justice. The Legal Aid and Advice Act has gone a long way to eliminating such inequalities, but it has created a few new ones too. A successful defendant not in receipt of aid cannot recover costs beyond what an aided plaintiff may be able to raise on his own resources. Provided that he can make out a reasonable *prima facie* case, the poor man can now approach the courts confident that he has little to lose; the wealthier defendant is liable to lose whether he wins or not. Removing inequalities of one sort may create others on the way.

(e) *'Equality before the law' as a constitutional principle*
'Equality before the law', according to A. V. Dicey, is a fundamental principle of the British Constitution. It consists, he says, in 'equal subjection of all classes to the ordinary law of the land administered by the ordinary law courts'; it 'excludes the idea of any exemption of officials or others from the duty of obedience to the law which governs other citizens or from the jurisdiction of the ordinary tribunals'.[18] Now 'equal subjection to law' may mean that all classes, including officials, have the same rights and duties—which is clearly false and would be patently absurd; or it may mean that the particular rights and duties of individuals, no matter how they vary, derive alike from the law, and are to be determined in accordance with the law. But since *legal* rights and duties are in question, this is an unilluminating tautology. From the standpoint of law, there can be no rights and duties, and no exemptions, save those that the law itself creates. This is necessarily true of any legal system, and so cannot be a peculiar and commendable feature of any one in particular.

Dicey's insistence on 'the ordinary law of the land' was intended, however, to distinguish the English from the French system (which in fact he misunderstood). France, he argued, possessed a special system of administrative law, different from its 'ordinary law', from which the rights and duties of officials derived, and which gave them some kind of privilege and protection not enjoyed by other citizens. But French administrative law is certainly part of the French legal system and satisfies its criteria of validity. The difference between the French system and the English is that while in France disputes between officials and subjects are dealt with by a special division of the judicial system, in England they are dealt with (or they were in Dicey's day) by the branch dealing with disputes between subject and subject. There is no point in treating administrative law as 'extraordinary', while regarding civil and criminal law as 'ordinary'.

The real point of Dicey's case is that, in English law, officials are not immune, simply as officials, from responsibility for injuries they inflict. They are not, for example, in the same position as foreign diplomats (who, incidentally, would seem to be an exception to Dicey's 'equal subjection of all classes'). And what for Dicey was even more important, the tribunals before which they must answer are composed of independent judges, rather than fellow administrators who might be prejudiced in their favour. The real question is not then concerned with some sort of equality of rights and duties by which officials and others stand equal in law, but with the best way to ensure that administrators carry out their duties with integrity, and that private claims against them are impartially considered. Whether these purposes are best secured by bringing all cases to the same courts (which was roughly the British system in Dicey's day), or by setting up a separate branch of the judiciary to specialize in administrative law (as in France), or by *ad hoc* tribunals dealing with special administrative fields (the technique widely used in Britain today), is a matter for experiment and comparison of the working merits of each system wherever it has been tried.

IV. JUSTICE AND THE RULE OF LAW: PROBLEMS OF JUSTICE PUBLICLY ADMINISTERED

Earlier, we analysed what is involved in making, or discussing, 'a just decision'. Our conclusions might be summarized thus:

(a) It presupposes rules.
(b) Differences in treatment must be justified by reference to relevant differences of attribute or condition, i.e. differences recognized by the rules. Other distinctions would be legitimate only if by making them the rules were amended universally, i.e. there can be no particular exceptions, only an elaboration of criteria, creating new distinctions to be applied generally.
(c) Differences in treatment must be, in a loose sense, proportionate. That is, given the grounds of distinction, we may still challenge the degree of discrimination.

These criteria are rules not of substance but procedure. They do not prescribe specifically one act rather than another; but if we try to act justly, our deliberations must be conducted within this formal framework. For that reason, they apply equally to private decisions, on the basis of moral rules (e.g. a man deciding how he ought to divide his property when he dies), and to public, or institutionalized, decisions, reached within the framework of legal or other formally established rule systems.

Critical canons applying to techniques of public justice

Public justice, understood in this sense, raises special problems. To live in society is to be subject to rules not of our own choosing; we submit disputes that we cannot settle by agreement to the arbitration of rule-determined authorities, and are committed, or compelled, to abide by their decisions. We want some assurance that justice is being done, that public and enforceable decisions satisfy the formal criteria listed above; that judges or administrators do not decide cases in the light of personal considerations, like fear for their jobs, or hope of reward. But more than that, we want to be assured that, given the intention of impartiality, the criteria of substance employed are broadly those that we should recommend ourselves. Admittedly this condition could not be satisfied for everyone, since moral attitudes conflict. We can aim at best at ensuring that the criteria adopted will be *widely* and roughly acceptable.

Since the rules of a society are not only principles for determining disputes, but also guides to the probable results of our actions, it is important that we should be able to see fairly clearly how the rules would apply to our own cases. If the rules were secret, or so vague that all, or most, decisions were unpredictable, we could not plan our lives with confidence or security. On the other hand, for some purposes at least, we should not wish the rules to be so precise and inflexible that they cannot be adjusted to take account of unusual, but relevant, factors. It must be possible to distinguish the exceptional case from the standard type for which the rule is designed.

In brief, unless administration satisfies the criteria of integrity, acceptability, predictability, and flexibility, legal justice is unlikely to be truly just.

'*The rule of law*' and administrative discretion

Aristotle's famous distinction, between 'the government of laws' and 'the government of men', has become part of the great liberal tradition.[19] There is an obvious sense, of course, in which all government is by men; and a sense too in which all government is by law, for even the widest public discretion (like the 'sovereignty of Parliament') derives ultimately from law. The real choice is between leaving cases to be decided by the unfettered discretion of arbitrators (what is sometimes called 'cadi-justice'), and prescribing rules in advance to determine them. General rules may be inflexible; as no legislator can foresee all the

E

situations to which a rule will apply, it may be occasionally inequitable. On the other hand, discretionary decisions may be prejudiced by selfish interests and irrelevant preferences, by a too narrow departmental view of public policy, an unwillingness to complicate an aesthetically satisfying administrative pattern, or by sheer administrative self-assertion. Administrators may be influenced by powerful interests, or they may wish to placate political supporters. Whether this sort of thing happens or not, it is undesirable that public justice should be suspected of it.

For Aristotle, 'government by law' is government by 'passionless reason'. The phrase is misleading: the reasonableness of a law will depend on the wisdom and integrity of the legislators, who may discriminate as unfairly between classes as administrators between individuals. Nevertheless, a decision according to law must be justified by criteria which are matters of public knowledge; a discretionary decision is one in which the criteria are not public, at least in the same sense. There is thus more scope for bias and favouritism in the latter case, and less opportunity to criticize the criteria on which the decision rests.

'The rule of law' and rules of policy

There is a range of possible techniques between the rule-determined decision and 'cadi-justice'. In modern government, administrative decisions are rarely matters of simple preference.[20] Though the law may allow wide discretion, administrators act within it according to rules of policy, which correlate their decisions. Unlike law, however, rules of policy are not necessarily publicly known, and may consequently be changed without public discussion and explanation. Furthermore, the administrative technique differs from the judicial in that it is only in the rare case that creates public disquiet, like the Crichel Down case, that particular decisions have to be publicly defended.

These differences are important in two ways. Firstly, whatever his actual motives, the judge operating in full view, must give reasons for his decision that do not twist the known rules beyond recognition; and this provides some assurance of impartiality, beyond what a professional tradition provides. The administrator's impartiality must depend almost entirely on professional standards and safeguards within the departmental organization. Secondly, the privacy of the administrative process has the virtues and vices of flexibility. Within the vaguer rules of policy, the administrator can take account of the special features of the particular case. Since he is rarely called upon to justify himself publicly, he can stretch, or change, the rule to meet new situations. Though judges may enjoy some discretion, and are reluctant to ignore morally relevant features of a case, they are constrained by their consciousness that they are creating precedents for other judges, that 'hard cases make bad law'. They have a duty not only to do justice, but also to make their decisions conform reasonably closely to the law as generally understood (at least by their brother lawyers). For the law is not simply a guide for the judges; it is also a basis for prediction. The correlative of legal flexibility is uncertainty and insecurity.

The judicial procedure, then, provides safeguards against the simpler forms of corruption, and the subtler administrative vices. In matters closely affecting individual choice of action, it tends to be more strictly predictable than administrative action, because judges are reluctant to recognize the relevance of exceptional features without authority. And in private and criminal law, it is of supreme importance that the individual should know in advance what legal consequences his acts will have. Modern administration deals, however, with some matters, like town planning, where the special features of particular cases may well be more important than any they have in common; general rules can provide only the broadest guidance.[21] Administrative action in these cases affect private interests in unforeseeable ways; but if the policies are to be at all rationally implemented, predictability must yield to flexibility.

In these matters, the problem is to devise procedures that will elicit all the relevant facts, give interested parties the opportunity to state their claims, and ensure that the responsible official is without personal interest in the outcome. Broadly speaking, these are the criteria known in English law as 'the rules of natural justice'.[22] Justice might *conceivably* be done even though these rules were not observed; an official might have ways of assessing a person's claims without actually consulting him, and he might be sufficiently detached to discount a personal interest. But institutions cannot be designed on the assumption that officials will possess quite exceptional levels of imaginative insight and moral integrity. In any case, it is important, as lawyers never tire of pointing out, not merely that justice be done, but that it be manifestly seen to be done. It is doubtful whether the 'rules of natural justice', as understood in England, go far enough. Personal interest is not the only factor that may prejudice judgment; the rules of natural justice are no safeguard against the hidden political pressures on administrators, from which judges in the liberal democracies are generally insulated.

Quasi-judicial techniques
Within the last half-century or so, techniques have been developed to

combine the flexibility of administration with some of the characteristic safeguards of the judicial process. The 'quasi-judicial' techniques[23] of the public inquiry and the independent administrative tribunal provide for public hearings of evidence and legal argument; final decisions, however, are taken in the light of policy, rather than according to stricter rules of law. Reasons are sometimes given, but by no means always.* There is still the danger of political pressure, and the chance that, despite the public hearing, private claims may be set aside in favour of a narrow departmental view of the public interest. There is some safeguard where an appeal can be made to a tribunal independent of departmental influence, but this is by no means generally the case. Whether in the end decision should rest with the department, subject only to the political checks implied in ministerial responsibility to the legislature, or with an independent appellate tribunal, depends on a variety of particular conditions arising from the sort of issue to be decided. The full complexities of this problem cannot be investigated here; we are concerned only to point out that the choice between judge, administrator, and public inquiry, is one of technique, and must be related to the particular needs and difficulties of the given problem. The traditional British preference for the judicial process is soundly based in the fields where it has traditionally operated; but it does not follow that it is appropriate wherever modern government touches particular interests. Nevertheless, the extension of administrative discretion, operating according to the flexible rules of policy in the privacy of government offices, puts new emphasis on the need for officials with the integrity and impartiality that we are accustomed to expect of judges.[24]

Acceptability to the public of judicial and administrative decisions
It is desirable, we have said, that the criteria employed in public decision-making be broadly acceptable. On the face of it, one would expect that where judges administer laws made by a representative legislature, the criteria employed would be acceptable to most citizens. But where, as in the USA, judges can declare laws unconstitutional, legal decisions may lag behind the main trend of majority opinion. Just because the courts are insulated from political pressures, there are times when they are clearly out of sympathy with the dominant social ideals, and become strongholds of conservatism. English judges were much criticized in the 1930's for construing statutes limiting the Common Law rights of property and contract so narrowly as to defeat their plain intention.[25]

---

* But more frequently so, since the decision to implement the main recommendations of the Franks Report.

Administrators in the democracies are directly or indirectly answerable to the legislature for their decisions. It is the business of Parliament or Congress to inquire into administrative policies, and to demand that dubious decisions be explained and justified. They cannot do more, in the nature of the case, than inquire into broad policies, in a general and occasional way, ventilating particular grievances as they arise. Nevertheless, the political link between the executive and the legislature, while making administrative decisions susceptible to political pressure, is a way of keeping administrators sensitive to public opinion.

V. CONCLUSION

We have touched on a wide range of problems in this chapter. Common to all, however, is the notion of impartiality—the principle that discrimination must be grounded on relevant differences. Otherwise, men stand equal. A brief examination of egalitarianism led to the conclusion that 'Equality' as an ideal is intelligible only in a given context; that it is negative, in the sense of denying the legitimacy of certain kinds of discrimination grounded on differences held to be irrelevant. A positive egalitarianism, demanding similar treatment for all, irrespective of *any* difference, would clearly lead to absurdities. To sweep away all distinctions would be to commit injustices as inexcusable as any under attack. Moral progress is made as much by making new and justifiable distinctions as by eliminating established but irrelevant 'inequalities'. This is no less true of law than of other aspects of social organization. 'Equality before the law' is not a single ideal; its intention changes with the criteria under attack. But if we demand that legislators remove the disabilities of Roman Catholics, negroes, or women, we take it for granted nevertheless that judges should elaborate legal distinctions, create new categories with appropriate rights and duties, wherever there are reasonable and relevant differences not obviously provided for in the rules.

Authoritative institutions for settling disputes raise problems of another sort. It is not enough to prescribe formal criteria, to tell judges and administrators: 'Be impartial—close your ears to irrelevancies—do not let your judgment be influenced by friendship or enmity, fear, greed, or ambition.' Some assurance is needed that they will in fact approach their duties in this spirit. We suggested four critical canons, integrity, predictability, flexibility, and acceptability, by which public justice must itself be judged, and we examined briefly, in the light of these canons, some of the decision techniques and procedures currently employed.

Formal analysis yields no positive prescriptions. To act justly, we must seek guidance from rules of substance; and these, in turn, must be appraised in the light of more general rules, standards, or values, by which their consequences must be judged. Justice involves using rule criteria in making particular decisions, but the criteria themselves need justification. In the chapters that immediately follow, we shall be concerned with the application of the abstract principle enunciated in the earlier part of this chapter to the problems of distributive and retributive justice.

CHAPTER 6

JUSTICE AND THE DISTRIBUTION OF INCOME

I. JUSTICE AND THE ECONOMICS OF INCOME DISTRIBUTION

The general principles enunciated in the last chapter have practical applications in discussions of the ethics of income distribution. A society like a nation is, from one point of view, an organization for the co-operative production and distribution of goods and services, which is a process governed by rules. In the nineteenth century it was effected largely by particular wage (and other) contracts, supported by general rules like 'Contracts ought to be kept', or 'Individuals ought to be free to make the best bargains they can'; in the twentieth century collective joint negotiating machinery fixes wage rates which are themselves general distributive principles. We have in addition an elaborate state organization for income redistribution by taxation and social services.

We can ask of all these arrangements: are they fair? To justify them it would have to be shown that inequalities in income were related to criteria which were reasonable and relevant. For justice consists in treating equals equally, and in adopting as criteria by which men are to be considered equal or unequal, only such qualities or circumstances as can be reasonably justified. But what does 'reasonable' amount to in such a context? An examination of the criteria canvassed in this particular context will, it is hoped, serve a double purpose. It will provide first a working example of the way in which the procedural rules involved in the notion of 'justice' discussed in somewhat abstract terms in Ch. 5, can, and do govern the discussion of practical issues in moral terms. Secondly, it will help us to understand important controversial issues of modern social and economic organization. Whenever an arbitration tribunal considers a wage dispute, or a Chancellor a budget, or there is question of a change in pension rates, taxes, or social services, discussion is bound to turn on what is fair, as well as on what is economically possible or expedient. Clarification of the moral issues involved is, in our view, of great importance at the present time.

We must deal immediately, however, with a possible objection. Is it not a mistake to discuss these questions in moral terms at all? Are not incomes determined by impersonal and non-moral forces of supply and demand? What have morals to do with marginal productivity, which according to the economist determines wages?

Now some incomes are obviously not determined in this way. Any state pension or social service payment is the result of a deliberate policy of redistribution, and concerns the economic theorist only to the extent that it has economic consequences that can be broadly predicted. The economist is competent to advise on probable results; it is not within his province to make the moral choice involved in such a decision of policy.

Even with wages and salaries, the supply and demand situation is a limiting, but not a completely determining factor. If wages were fixed at levels quite unrelated to the market situation, there would no doubt be complications; in an otherwise free and competitive economy there might well be labour shortages in some fields and unemployment in others—but we need not assume an otherwise competitive economy. In our own economy, the market situation is certainly a necessary cause of the wage structure; for we do not conscript labour. The wages in a given industry must therefore be high enough to supply it with recruits in the fact of competition from others, and they cannot be so high that an industry, which must cover costs or face bankruptcy, cannot carry on. But the market situation is not a *sufficient* cause, i.e. it will not of itself alone explain the wage structure. Subsidies, import restrictions, and guaranteed prices, are only a few of the ways in which governments intervene, making wage rates what they would not otherwise be.

But since wages and salaries can be varied by deliberate decisions, even if only within certain limits, it makes sense to ask whether the present scales are fair; and that assumes criteria of fair distribution.

Moreover, collective bargaining and industrial arbitration, the procedures for settling most wage rates nowadays, are frequently carried on in terms of 'a decent living wage' or 'an adequate reward for skill and responsibility'. Concepts like these are normative, used to prescribe what workers *ought* to receive, not simply to indicate what they *want*, or hope to get in the present market situation. Though each party to an industrial dispute may be simply trying to squeeze as much as it can, it is very common for them to put up a case, i.e. to show *reasons* why their demands ought to be met. In this respect, collective bargaining resembles diplomacy, rather than the haggling of the bazaar; for the strength of one's bargaining position may depend, in part at least, on being able to convince an arbitrator, or perhaps a minister, that one has a good case. Unions and employers alike are anxious, too, to justify themselves publicly, in terms which imply that more questions can be asked than the straightforward economic one: 'What will the market bear?' or the prudential one: 'How much can we get out of this?'

It is not, of course, our intention to speculate on the extent to which moral considerations shape events. Neither of course do we support the thesis that all incomes are distributed in the light of moral criteria, or that regard for such criteria *necessarily* plays a part in determining the level of any income. Incomes from betting or dope-peddling are obvious examples to the contrary. Our contention is more limited; namely, that *some* incomes are fixed by practical men after deliberation. They do not just happen like the flow of the tide. Into such deliberations enter not only predictions provided by economists of what is likely to happen, but also considerations of what is fair.[1] And even where such considerations have not been taken into account in reaching a decision, it can still be criticized in the light of criteria of fairness.

It is not unrealistic, then, to examine the criteria generally employed in discussions of income distribution. We may classify them under three main headings:

(*a*) desert;
(*b*) need;
(*c*) property ownership.

We shall defer discussion of the last until Chapter 7, where it will form part of a more general discussion of property rights.

II. CRITERIA OF DESERT

'Desert' is a normative word; its use presupposes a rule having two components: (*i*) a condition to be satisfied; (*ii*) a mode of treatment consequent upon it. In questions of income distribution the condition is usually the performance of service (and in this respect it differs from 'entitlement' which is more general, since one might be 'entitled' to benefits under rules which prescribed need, or insurance contributions, or sale of goods, as the qualifying condition). We cannot estimate desert, therefore, in a vacuum; we must be able to refer to some standard or rule from which 'X deserves R' follows as a conclusion.

In dealing with individuals, our standard would normally be given by the rate commonly earned in the industry by people doing the same sort of work. We might reckon a particular worker deserved more than the current rate, because his output exceeded the average, or was of better quality, or because he worked longer hours; but it would be impossible to make any estimate at all of his deserts without at least starting from the standard rule—the rate for the job.

But how shall we decide what is the *fair* rate for the job? This is a question that confronts every arbitrator in a wage dispute. Since this is also a question of 'desert', though at a higher level of generality, it must be answered in terms of higher order rules or standards, governing the relative remuneration of various types of employment. Theoretically, we might arrange forms of employment in a hierarchy according to some acceptable criteria (such as the degree of skill, responsibility, etc.), but it would still be impossible to evaluate the fair remuneration of any one, unless the remuneration of some at least of the others were treated as given. In practice, of course, we never attempt such a wholesale reorganization of wage rates throughout the economy; variations are *ad hoc*, concerning at most all the occupations within one industry. It is inconceivable that we could ever draw up a new list from scratch, uninfluenced by traditional relativities and differentials.

In dealing then with the question of 'the fair rate' we should have first to accept some basis of comparison that seemed relevant. Industrial arbitrators, for example, use criteria like skill, responsibility, the length of training required, and some that we might call compensatory, which take account of the unpleasantness of a job, e.g. dirt or danger. But why should these criteria in particular be considered proper grounds for discrimination?

(a) Skill, responsibility, length of training
It is fairly generally held that greater skill and responsibility are good reasons why some men should earn more than others. These criteria are so deeply rooted in our social thinking that they are sometimes put forward as self-evident or absolute principles.[2] But we do recognize limits. Few people would consider skill at forgery or responsibility for managing a drug racket good reasons for favourable treatment, though both might be highly profitable as a matter of fact. Evidently the employment must be useful and desirable. Now principles that can be limited are not absolute; it is permissible, then, to ask why they should be appealed to at all.

We may be told that skilled or responsible services are 'worth more' to the community than others. This may mean no more than that people will in fact pay more for them, and this is not in itself a justification. In any case, what people will pay for an article or a service is not due solely to the properties of the thing itself. It depends on how much of it they already have, and how much is available, and whether there are effective substitutes. A domestic servant is worth a great deal more today than fifty years ago (even allowing for the fall in the value of money), not because the service is different but because there are fewer servants to be found.

'Worth' may be intended, however, in some non-economic sense.[3] It might be said, perhaps, that a scientist's work is more important than a miner's. As things stand now, if we had to choose between having fewer scientists or fewer miners, we should probably prefer to have scientists. But if the number of miners began to decline rapidly, the choice would become increasingly difficult. As the output of coal fell the services of the miner would seem more valuable, perhaps, than those of the scientist. But that is not the same as saying simply that people would want them more and therefore pay more for them. It is to say that the community would *need* them more. And to say what a community needs is to prescribe what people ought not to be without, not simply to decide what people want. What a man's services are worth to the community depends, then, on how much it needs them.*

The main argument for using skill and responsibility as criteria for income distribution would be that people would not take the trouble to acquire skills or undertake responsibility without economic incentives. On this view, income differentials would have to be justified as ways of regulating labour supply, with the ultimate purpose of satisfying consumer need. Of course, income may not be the only factor attracting people to particular jobs; they may be intrinsically satisfying, or offer long holidays. The case for financial inducements would then be correspondingly weaker.

Again, special effort or sacrifice to acquire training may not be in itself a ground for favourable treatment. A spare-time student who gains the same qualifications as one working full-time in easier and pleasanter conditions, may earn our admiration; he does not necessarily earn a higher salary. In general, however, because training calls for special application, and because trainees usually live less well than less skilled workers, it may well be necessary to hold out better prospects for trained workers, if the supply of recruits is to be maintained. But again, if the training has its own compensations, like the pleasure of undergraduate life, it may not require very large inducements to get people to accept it.

(b) Compensatory criteria

Some occupations, like dock labour, give extra pay for dirty or dangerous work. This is by no means universal, of course. The infantryman at the front gets no more than the orderly at the base. Nevertheless, there is a case to be made for the principle that nasty jobs should have

* Moreover, there are some sorts of 'worth' for which rewards in terms of income seem inappropriate. Great courage in battle is recognized by medals, not by increased pay.[4]

their compensations. It was widely held, during the depression of the 1930's, that miners, whose work is both dirty and dangerous, were scandalously underpaid on that account.

The use of compensatory criteria of this sort might be partly justified, like skill and responsibility, in terms of inducement. If unpleasant work is no better paid than other sorts, recruits might be hard to get. But this sort of work is often unskilled, and special inducements may be necessary only if labour of all sorts is scarce. There is, however, a different point involved. While unpleasant jobs have to be done, it seems hard that X should have to do them rather than Y. If circumstances or recruiting officers decide that one rather than the other must risk his life or his health, there may be a case in equity for giving some compensatory advantages. If two men are otherwise equal, special treatment, good or bad, for one seems to demand compensation to redress the balance. Admittedly, some men lack the job-getting qualities, and are forced to take the jobs that no one else wants. But lack of skill or personal charm may not be good enough reasons why a man should suffer the hazards of silicosis or a broken neck. It may be, then, that if such jobs must be done, they ought to carry compensatory benefits.[5] These need not be in the form of higher income, except that this form of benefit is the one which, as the most general, is the most widely acceptable.

(c) Traditional relativities in income distribution

At any given time, there is a socially accepted hierarchy of occupations with a traditional scale of income and prestige. It may not necessarily be justified in the terms suggested above, particularly if conditions are changing rapidly; but there will always be a good deal of resistance to any modifications of it. It tends to be regarded as intrinsically and prescriptively right.

There is a case, indeed, for avoiding drastic alterations in the traditional scale. Expectations, habits, and commitments depend on it.[6] People feel badly treated if they find their relative position on the scale worsening; they feel deprived of their reasonable expectations and their legitimate place in society. If they have undertaken training at a low income, expecting a higher one later, they may feel cheated if they are disappointed. Admittedly, they have no contractual claim on anyone, neither is the existing income scale an eternal scale of justice. None the less, a man normally chooses a career once and for all, with expectations for which he may have good grounds at the time of choosing. People who have established a way of life, made decisions and commitments in the reasonable expectation of being treated according to one rule, have a claim of a sort not to be disappointed. While then a traditional pattern of distribution cannot be sacrosanct or immutable, we ought not to approach the problem of altering it as if we were starting from scratch; this would lead us to ignore present claims which are relevant.

III. CRITERIA OF NEED

What we have called the 'desert' criteria of distribution are all related to the performance of service. Some nineteenth century socialists, like the Saint-Simonians, attached so much importance to these that they adopted the maxim: 'From each according to his capacity, to each according to his works.' This was mainly in protest against large incomes founded on property titles, the case for which we consider in the next chapter. It is clear, however, that 'to each according to his works' would be insufficient as the *sole* criterion of distribution, for it makes no provision for the aged and the disabled, who can make little or no contribution. The moral obligation to provide for those who cannot provide for themselves has been widely recognized, in forms ranging from the Mosaic law on gleaning (Deut. xxiv, 19-21) and the charitable work of the mediaeval monasteries, to the Poor Law and the National Assistance Board. Provision of this sort is not simply a question of establishing a common minimum, on the basis of arithmetical equality, which is to be satisfied before desert criteria began to operate. For charity and poor relief usually discriminate between the sick and the healthy, the young and the old, making different provision according to criteria of *need*.

Just as some socialists have stressed the criteria of desert, others, like Babeuf and Louis Blanc, adopted the slogan: 'From each according to his capacity, to each according to his needs.' Marx and Lenin paid homage to this ideal, though they rejected it as immediately unattainable, postponing its realization to the communist millennium that would follow the dictatorship of the proletariat.[7] Distribution according to need has a kind of moral persuasiveness which distribution by desert seems to lack. There is something attractive in the vision of a society in which men work for the love of the task itself and of their fellow men, in which financial incentives would be unnecessary, and in which incomes would be proportionate to needs, none enjoying luxuries until the necessities of all had been satisfied.*

* In such a system it might still be significant to say that one man deserved more than another, but what he deserved would not be extra income. Greater service might merit honour or respect, without their being linked to cash benefits. There is no logically necessary link between 'desert' and 'income'.

The Utopian maxim has the qualification, however, 'from each according to his capacity'. The reformers were as much concerned with the universal obligation to contribute to the community's well-being as with the universal

The claims of need are especially persuasive in part because of certain features about the way the concept is used. There is a close connection between 'needs' and income, which does not exist between income and 'desert'. When we state a man's needs, we prescribe, explicitly or implicitly, what must be done to satisfy them. To say that a man needs food is to indicate fairly precisely what must be done about it. Needs of this sort are thus logically related to income, since to state the need is to recognize a *prima facie* claim that only income could satisfy. There may be other needs, of course, which are not related to income in this way, like the need for freedom; but these could not be satisfied as a matter of fact unless the needs for food, clothes and shelter had already been satisfied. For dead men cannot be free.

Need criteria might be thought, then, to have two characteristics which desert criteria do not share.* In the first place, they seem *determinate* in a way that desert is not. What a man deserves depends on a rule, and there is no logically necessary connection between the performance of services, which is the condition of desert, and income. A system could be envisaged, for example, where men's deserts were recognized by awarding only honours or medals, or by appointment to public offices. It would not be nonsense to say 'A is more skilful than B, and B than C; A deserves to be an earl, B a viscount, C a knight'. The honours list does in fact make some awards on this principle. But it would be nonsense to say 'A needs more food than B; make A an earl'. The only award relevant to A's need would be food.

In the second place, there might seem to be an empirical test of needs. Whether a man needs food, clothing, and shelter would seem

---

claim to the satisfaction of needs. Distate for the parasite would survive, it seems, even where people worked for the joy of it alone; other things being equal, a man is expected to make some effort to support himself. But what degree of effort qualifies? Do we estimate 'capacity' by a man's own account that he is 'doing his best', by his past performance, or by a production target fixed by the works manager? If 'from each according to his capacity' is taken to be a condition to be satisfied before need criteria are allowed to operate, desert becomes a qualifying condition for any income at all.

* We are here referring to *individual* needs, which are appealed to *directly* as criteria of distribution. These should not be confused with the community needs referred to earlier in this chapter (p. 139) which were appealed to as justifying desert criteria. The difference between these two classes of needs is obvious enough. Educational policies, for instance, can be justified either as satisfying the needs of the individual child or as being related to a need of the community—e.g. for scientists or typists. Indeed the conflict between the claims of the individual and those of the community, which is a recurrent theme both in political theory and in Utopian satires, could be stated in terms of the conflict between these classes of needs.

to be a matter of fact, whereas his deserts depend on norms. Here again needs might seem to be more firmly grounded than claims based on desert.

A system of distribution must employ determinate criteria if it is to work as a public institution. Its rules must indicate fairly precisely what everyone ought to have, or justice will not be manifestly seen to be done. If it were true that need criteria always indicated precisely what a man ought to be given to satisfy his need, and if his needs could always be settled as objective matters of fact, a claim based on need might appear more cogent than one which turned on the answer to the difficult question, 'What rewards are appropriate to any given degree of skill?'

We shall try to show that this is a mistaken point of view. Needs are not simple matters of fact, but presume norms as much as do deserts. And though some needs, like the need for food, are reasonably determinate, others, like the need for relaxation or constructive occupation, are not. To use needs of the second sort as criteria of distribution would raise theoretical and practical difficulties that would be insuperable.

(a) Analysis of 'need'

We must first examine what in general we mean when we attribute to anyone a 'need'.[8] It is, first, to indicate the lack of something which it would be injurious or detrimental to the subject not to supply; alternatively, a lack which frustrates some end envisaged on his account. 'X needs food' implies that not having it is detrimental to him. To say that a carpenter needs tools is to say that he cannot fulfil a carpenter's functions without them. But to talk of 'injury' or 'detriment' (and, as we shall show later, of 'function'), is to imply a norm or standard by which states or achievements are assessed. Thus to talk of a 'need' implies the lack of something which prevents a person reaching or maintaining some state defined by the norm. It is this which distinguishes 'need' from 'want'. To say that a man *wants* food is simply to describe his state of mind; to say that he *needs* food is to say that he will not measure up to an understood standard unless he gets it.

Insofar, then, as needs are appealed to as criteria for distribution, there is no further justification possible for using them for this purpose. For in a moral discussion what else *counts* as a justification, apart from reference to the harm, injury, benefit or advantage promoted by rules or by their absence?* What must be done in such cases is to establish the existence of a need and to show that it is more urgent or more widespread than other needs. Conflicts about such matters can easily arise as we have already shown in the case of the possible clashes between an

* See Ch. 2, p. 55.

individual's needs and those of the community. But this is a case of a conflict between different people or groups of people whose needs are admitted. Another source of disagreement is the different conceptions of injury which are built in to different types of need. These could be classified in all sorts of ways, but as a matter of convenience at least three sorts of needs are worth distinguishing—biological, basic, and functional. This form of distinction is convenient not simply because in a context of justification it indicates why it is that some needs are regarded as being more urgent than others, but also because, as we shall show later, some sorts of need are more practicable than others to use as criteria for distribution.

(b) Biological needs
Biological needs are perhaps the most palpable in that they are related to a norm which is commonly, though not universally assumed—that of survival. For most people regard death as a disaster, as the supreme injury. Without food or oxygen we cannot survive. Biological needs would therefore be fundamental; for unless we survive we cannot satisfy any other needs or wants. 'Survival', however, is not the simple concept that it may at first appear. If we *meant* by survival *simply* breathing, eating, drinking, eliminating, sleeping, and doing the other things which are part of what is meant by 'being alive' then satisfying the biological needs would be part of the definition of survival. But usually being alive implies doing all sorts of other things that we want to do or think we ought to do. And if anyone queried the justification implied in an appeal to such biological needs he would surely have in mind a claim like that of Socrates that it is not mere life that is to be valued most highly, but the good life. And the good life means living *in a certain manner*.

(c) Basic needs
The notion of living in a certain manner as distinct from just keeping alive is closely linked with the concept of 'basic needs'. An example would be the need for love. Now men can live without love; the evidence shows however that if they have not had a certain amount of love in infancy they will be permanently stunted as members of society. They will be unreliable, incapable of forming lasting attachments, distractable, incapable of being absorbed in anything for long, and so on. In so far, therefore, as men have a 'basic need' for love they will be incapable of living in a certain manner unless this need has been satisfied. They will not enjoy the amenities of any sort of social life.

Usually, however, 'basic needs' are related to a more determinate conception of living in a certain manner. They suggest what seems the bare minimum for a 'decent' sort of life; and this varies from time to time and place to place. What seems the bare minimum for a decent sort of life in Britain today is a good deal more than what many Englishmen enjoyed a century and a half ago, and more, too, than many Asiatics enjoy today. This is important because it demonstrates the way in which the needs which we term 'basic' are related to norms set by different cultures. Differences of general prosperity, class-structure, and social habits are reflected in differences of view between societies about what needs are 'basic'. In California creditors in a bankruptcy case can no longer place an attachment on the family television set, which is now recognized as a necessity.

'Basic needs' are thus a function of the general living standards of the community in question, which yield norms like 'subsistence level', or 'a decent standard of living'. In any community there is a certain income (the median) enjoyed by the most numerous income group, which sets the minimum standards of expectation of that community. It comes as something of a shock, therefore, when we encounter in our community people well below that standard. We call them 'the needy', because they lack what the overwhelming majority enjoy—they fall below the norm. Whatever is necessary to bring them up to it then becomes a first claim on the community's resources.* The point, however, is that to find people suffering this need would not be shocking were it not that the norm is constituted by what is already widely enjoyed. In England we are shocked to find people who cannot afford a bed; it would not be shocking in China, where the norm, and therefore what constitutes a 'basic need' is pitched far lower. This is not to say that an Englishman in China would be satisfied by Chinese conditions, or that his view of what needs are basic for Chinese would be different from what he considers basic for Englishmen. But the standards he applies in China have been formed by English, not Chinese conditions. Again, when we say that 'basic needs' are governed by a social norm, we do not mean that they imply necessarily a uniform level of need. The norm admits of varied applications in special conditions, like sickness, which creates special needs. But here again the needs are 'basic' because

---

* This is not strictly accurate. The most numerous income group do not spend their incomes in exactly the same way. There will be a range of items of expenditure common to nearly all of them, and a further range which varies, for instance, with tastes and occupations. All buy a certain amount of food: some, but not all, buy bicycles, beer, or football boots. 'Basic needs' are for those things that everybody buys; anything that many people in the most numerous group contrive to do without cannot be basic. Consequently, public assistance, which is usually meant to cover only basic needs, can be expected to provide incomes smaller than the media.

the social norm is a state of health. Where poor sight is common and spectacles rare, there would be no basic need for spectacles.

Basic needs are thus fairly precisely determinate because they are related to norms set by conditions already very widely enjoyed. They are the needs for precisely those things that most other people have got. Beyond this minimum, however, needs becomes increasingly vague. A psychologist might say, for instance, that everyone has a need for relaxation, or for opportunities for acquisition. But is the need for relaxation sufficiently satisfied by a visit to the cinema, or does it demand a Mediterranean cruise? Is stamp collecting as good a way of satisfying the need for acquisition as collecting precious stones? Are there some people for whom the one will do, and others who need the other? Our point is not that such needs do not exist, but they are too indeterminate to provide criteria for income distribution.

(d) 'Functional needs'

There are certain needs which must be satisfied if a man is to do his particular job. Some of these at least are reasonably precise. A carpenter needs a plane and a saw, or he cannot *be* a carpenter. Accordingly functional needs enter into discussions of income distribution, and in particular of remuneration and taxation. People who travel for their living usually receive tax-free travel and subsistence allowances, directly related to their functional needs. If allowance is not directly made for such needs, we should expect earnings to be proportionately higher to cover them.

On the face of it, such needs seem to be matters of fact, independent of norms; but this is not the case. We are not likely to disagree about the functional needs of a plumber (though we might about his need for a car to get from one job to the next). Not all cases are as simple as this. *The Times*[9] supported an increase in judges' salaries on the grounds that the dignity of the bench must be upheld by a certain way of living, extending as much to their home lives as to their manner of travelling to and from the courts. On this view, a judge's function includes upholding the dignity of the bench, which he could not do if he travelled to the courts by 'bus and, presumably, helped with the washing-up. De Jouvenel[10] takes the view that a university professor is incapable of fulfilling his function unless his income permits him to entertain his colleagues and students in a comfortable and civilized manner. But not everyone would accept these accounts of the functional needs of judges and professors. Egalitarians might regard them as rationalized prejudices in favour of the traditional economic and social hierarchy.[11]

These are not disagreements about facts but about norms. When we speak of a social function, we are prescribing standards of achievement for anyone filling the role. Now while there is broad agreement about the standard for plumbers, there is not the same agreement about professors and judges. One might take a narrower view than de Jouvenel of a professor's function, and maintain that he has done his job if he has given his lectures, administered his department, marked his students' essays, and engaged in research. Civilizing his juniors (for de Jouvenel part of his function as professor) would on this view be supererogatory and the expenses incurred in doing it would not then count as meeting functional needs. Differences of this sort commonly arise between H.M. Inspectors of Taxes and taxpayers claiming relief for expenses 'wholly, exclusively, and necessarily incurred in the performance of their duties'.

The notion of 'a functional need' can be used, therefore, as a distributive criterion only where there is broad agreement on the interpretation of the function in question, and on the needs to be satisfied in order that the functional norm can be fulfilled. Beyond that, it is too vague to be of use.

It would be practically impossible, then, to use need criteria alone as a basis for distributing a community's entire income, as some socialists would like. They can apply only within the narrow field of basic needs and to a limited range of functional needs, where the function is so strictly defined as to yield broad agreement on what must be provided if it is to perform at all. For the level of basic needs is settled by what most people in the community already enjoy; and functional needs, in the narrow sense, must also be broadly satisfied already, if the functions in question are being fulfilled; it follows that there must normally be a surplus over and above a community's basic and functional needs put together.* Any needs beyond these are likely to be too vague to indicate the precise level of income necessary to satisfy them, and so could not function as distributive criteria. Moreover, at these levels of need, tastes become increasingly important elements for real satisfaction, and a system of distribution in which a person's tastes became an effective criterion of what income he was going to receive would be obviously unworkable, unless all goods were like air, in unlimited supply.

It would be possible, of course, to have a system by which, once basic needs had been met, the surplus was divided equally, so that everyone would have the same amount of money for meeting other

* This might not be the case if a community's income had been suddenly reduced, for example, by war, so that its standard of basic need could barely be met. It would then be possible to distribute its whole income by rationing according to need criteria formed in better times.

needs according to taste. But this would not be to use such needs as criteria of distribution. For that, there would have to be a way of giving more to the man who *needed* more, of distinguishing the man who needed to collect gems from the one who could be satisfied with stamps. Such criteria are obviously impossible to apply.

Equal distribution of the surplus would not be distribution according to need but a refusal to treat any criterion as relevant beyond basic and functional needs. At that point to treat people equally would imply that for all relevant purposes they were equal. Something like this was done in rationing petrol in wartime. The so-called supplementary ration varied according to certain criteria of need (mainly functional, but in the case of disabled persons basic). Any surplus was then distributed to give equal mileage to all car owners, above their needs.* This would be a possible method of distributing income in general. It is doubtful, however, whether the same total income would be available for distribution, once desert criteria had been abandoned, and economic incentives eliminated.

IV. INCOME DISTRIBUTION IN THE WELFARE STATE

The distribution of income is a field where many criteria operate, some of need, some of desert. (Property criteria will be considered in Chapter 7.) We must now briefly consider the relevance of these criteria to the actual techniques of distribution in the welfare state, as exemplified in Britain. Property apart, there are three main distributive (or re-distributive) techniques: the payment of wages and salaries, taxation, and social services. Each involves allocating income according to rules, which embody criteria of the types already discussed.

There is nothing exceptional about a system with multiple criteria, nor do we find undue difficulty in making decisions where multiple criteria apply. In drawing up his personal budget, for example, a man has to weigh what he owes to his family against the appeals of charity, or his need for books to help him with his job. There are no easy rule-of-thumb methods for arriving at right answers to such questions. A man's arrangements will reflect a scale of priorities which seems reasonable to him. But another might feel that, had he been in his position, he would have decided differently. But he would not necessarily condemn the first man as immoral or unjust on that account. Decisions of this sort are reasonable or unreasonable, rather than right or wrong.

* It is a curious paradox, in the light of our analysis, that the special ration related to need should have been called 'supplementary', and the share of the surplus 'basic'; the more so, because when petrol was in short supply, the 'basic ration' was withdrawn to ensure that supplementary rations were met.

Public decisions with multiple criteria are complicated, however, by the necessity for public justification. An individual making a personal decision may rest content with it if he has first given due consideration to all relevant claims; the arbitrator in a wage dispute has the additional worry of satisfying the parties to the dispute, and perhaps the public at large, that his decision is reasonable.

(a) The determination of earnings

The economists explain wage rates by reference to economic laws, but this account, as we have shown, does not exhaust the possibilities of discussion. We can still ask whether any given distribution is just, and within limits we can interfere with free market forces by deliberate wage fixing. Most wages are settled, however, by collective negotiations in which both parties are no doubt out to get the best terms they can. But they often feel called upon to show grounds why their claims *ought* to be met. For if they cannot agree, the parties may refer their dispute to arbitration or to the Industrial Court, or the Minister of Labour may appoint a Court of Inquiry, whose report will almost certainly influence the final settlement. At this stage, at least, the process involves appeals to distributive criteria of the types already discussed. Claims by higher paid workers usually appeal to the desert criteria of skill, responsibility, and length of training, or to some traditional scale of relativities supposed to be based on them. An increase in wages for work of comparable skill in one industry is generally regarded as a proper ground for an increase in another. Equals must be treated equally.*

Lower paid workers naturally put more stress on need criteria, especially during an inflation. The idea that all workers ought to get at least a 'decent living wage' is broadly accepted by workers, employers, and arbitrators.[12] What constitutes 'a decent living wage' is not, of course, a matter of plain fact, but a socially determined norm related to a conception of minimum needs. However, if a society recognizes a duty to see that everyone reaches a given minimum standard, it is reasonable that something related to that standard should be a criterion for minimum wages. For though it is possible to supplement wages by public assistance, as in the Speenhamland system, there are good social,

---

* Job comparability is not, of course, a simple matter. Jobs are held to be comparable if they call for similar degrees of skill, etc. But how can we really compare, say, policemen and firemen in these respects? What tends to happen in practice is that those jobs are held to be comparable which have traditionally been similarly paid. The notion thus tends to perpetuate the differentials and relativities established by tradition.

psychological, and economic reasons for not 'pauperizing' the lowest income groups.

We have seen that the case for meeting basic needs is hard to resist. When prices are rising, a wage claim on these grounds will always be a strong one. When Sir Stafford Cripps persuaded the unions to accept a partial wage freeze, he specifically excepted claims from the lowest paid workers. The result was that differentials for skill were substantially reduced. When the policy broke down, skilled workers tried hard to recover the ground they had lost, while the unskilled continued to claim increases every time the cost of living index made another jump. The result was a series of leap-frogging claims, the unskilled gaining an increase on the strength of need, the skilled using this as a case for a further rise to restore the differential. The unintended consequence was to intensify still further the pressure on costs and prices, a further round of inflation, and a further claim from the unskilled to meet it.

Arbitrators were very much aware of these difficulties, which arose in part from the use in wage determination of multiple and conflicting criteria. The Court of Inquiry into the engineering dispute of 1954 declared themselves unable to 'assess or quantify the dangers to the national economy which might arise from action which provoked a general and substantial increase in productive costs', and called for an authoritative and impartial body to consider 'the conflicting economic arguments' surrounding particular claims, 'to form a view upon their implications for the national economy', and to 'give advice and guidance as to broad policy and possible action'.[13] Later inquiries echoed the same plea. Writing from first hand experience of these difficulties, Barbara Wootton complains that arbitrators are 'engaged in the impossible task of attempting to do justice in an ethical vacuum'; that 'we cannot indefinitely dispense with some kind of general policy, indicating on social grounds ... the weight to be given to skill and responsibility in different circumstances'.[14]

It is misleading, however, to say that arbitrators are operating in an 'ethical vacuum'. They are faced not with a shortage but a plethora of criteria. What is lacking is any sort of authoritative rule or policy indicating the order of importance to be attached to them, which would be broadly acceptable to all parties. Such a policy could not, however, be laid down by any impartial and independent body of experts. This is clear from the mixed reception given to the first report of the Cohen Council,* set up to meet the sort of need expressed by the 1954 Court of Inquiry. For the order of priority the public interest requires is

* *Report of Council on Prices, Production, and Incomes,* 1958 (Non-parliamentary).

not a matter which, once established and explained, would command general assent as if it were an empirical fact. For one thing, economic prediction is a risky business, and the consequences of any given policy are almost always in dispute among the experts. But what is more important from our point of view, 'the public interest' is not an empirical but a normative concept. An egalitarian might welcome inflation as a way of reducing rentier incomes, even at the cost of some decline in international trade. Or again, the view of the Cohen Council that the public interest was compatible with (or even demanded) a moderate degree of unemployment was fiercely challenged by many socialists. In part the disagreement was about economic theory; but in part too it was based on different *evaluations* of the consequences of different courses of action.

In one sense, of course, arbitrators have always been free to arrange the criteria in whatever order they saw fit; for unlike judges and civil servants, they are not bound by rules of law or public policy, but enjoy a formally unfettered discretion. But this is the weakness rather than the strength of their position, for their awards carry weight only so long as the parties to disputes, and the public generally, can be persuaded to accept them. And this depends on their ability to show that they are reasonable in relation to accepted criteria. An independent decision to treat claims based on desert criteria as not, for the time being, in the public interest, would deprive them of the confidence of all those trade unionists, for whom differentials based on skill are part of a natural moral order.

A wage policy, of the sort that the 1954 Court had in mind, would have to be put forward authoritatively as government policy, by agreement with the principal unions and employers' associations, to have any chance of success. For the moral criteria that such a policy would assume are not proper subjects for expert pronouncements. That is why they are the stuff of political controversy, and why governments cannot evade responsibility for policies that appeal to them.

(b) Taxation

Desert and need criteria are relevant for taxaion, as well as for wage determination. Until the nineteenth century, taxation was simply a matter of raising money to cover government expenses, and ease of collection counted for a good deal more in the choice of a tax than concern for fair distribution of the tax burden. Indirect taxes, which bear most heavily on lower incomes, provided the bulk of government revenue. But there were plenty of protests, and the salt tax was among the best-hated defects of the *Ancien Regime*. The invention of the in-

come tax provided a way of distributing the tax burden on the principle
that those should pay most who could spare most, over and above their
minimum needs.

Our present system employs both need and desert criteria. Everyone
is entitled to a personal allowance, which may be supplemented by
marriage and children's allowances, all of which would be justified as
recognizing basic needs. Expenses incurred in doing one's job are free
of tax, as meeting functional needs. Desert criteria appear in the principle that unearned income is taxed more heavily than earned. Indirect
taxation, though conforming less closely to these principles, is so adjusted that it bears less heavily on the lowest incomes, and does not
impair the satisfaction of basic needs. Thus purchase tax is so graded
that essentials are taxed less heavily than luxuries. Until recent years,
basic foods, so far from being taxed, were directly subsidized.

The law provides inland revenue and customs officials with a code
to guide them. Their discretion is far narrower, therefore, than the
industrial arbitrator's. Though there might be two views about whether
a given item is to count as an expense necessary for employment, this
does not involve exercising wide discretion. It is another aspect of the
ordinary problem of applying a rule, discussed in Chapters 3 and 5.
The criteria to be applied are laid down, and the official has power to
interpret but not to vary them.

The industrial arbitrator's problems are more nearly paralleled by
those which face the Chancellor of the Exchequer, whenever he proposes
to modify taxes. If he has a budget surplus to dispose of, for example,
he can choose whether to allocate it according to need or desert. He
may decide to give relief to the family man; or he may seek to increase
incentives by reducing the higher rates of income tax, thus widening net
differentials between higher and lower paid workers. Decisions of this
sort are always highly controversial, precisely because different people
stress different criteria, some giving priority to need, others to desert.

(c) Redistributive techniques—taxation and social services

Taxation is no longer just a way of raising revenue. Since the end of the
nineteenth century, it has become in conjunction with the social services
an increasingly important way of redistributing income according to
need. Indeed, though need criteria do crop up in wage determination,
earnings are generally thought of in terms of desert; we deal with needs
specifically by carrying out a subsequent redistribution as a matter of
deliberate policy. There are various ways of doing this. The most
straightforward is the cash payment, either to meet special categories of
need, like child allowances, or to supplement incomes that would other-

wise fall short of the basic standard, e.g. through National Assistance.

Other services, like education or medical care, are provided directly to meet particular types of need. The fact, however, that some people reject such services, preferring private schools and nursing homes, suggests a practical limit to the technique of direct provision, related to the limitations of need criteria discussed in Section III. Beyond basic needs, which can be fairly precisely determined, consumers' preferences become increasingly important. If most people are satisfied that a state medical service meets their needs, at least as well as any arrangements they could afford to make for themselves without it, it is probably reasonable to go on providing it out of taxation. But where needs are less specific—like the need for entertainment—and where *what* is needed is very much a question of taste, direct provision becomes inappropriate. A standard service would leave the needs of many people quite unsatisfied; but a more varied provision, something to suit all tastes, would raise the awkward problems of relative cost that we discussed at the end of Section III. At this level of need, there would be little point in attempting to provide direct services, or, indeed, to allocate income on that basis at all.

When a service like education or medical care is provided free for everyone out of taxation, anyone who could otherwise afford the service out of his earnings or other income may suffer a net loss of satisfaction, since what he pays for in taxes may be different from what he would choose for himself. Alternatively, he is compelled (as in the case of parents with children at private schools) to pay for services he does not want at all. This is not a criticism of the principle of redistribution according to need, for it is concerned only with the service that the taxpayer himself enjoys, and which he has himself paid for. It is a criticism only of the technique of direct provision as against cash payments.* Direct provision is most useful when the need it meets is precisely determinate; the further it goes beyond that limit, the more likely it is to provide what many people do not want. Though what a man wants is not necessarily the same as what he needs, there is a

---

* The same objections apply, however, when the payment is tied to the service, rather than to the circumstances of the recipient. There would be little advantage in a system where patients paid their doctors and were reimbursed by the state. A patient who preferred unorthodox methods, like naturopathy, would be no better off. The system would meet this difficulty if it related payment, not to the doctor's bill (i.e. to a particular way of meeting the need), but to the patient's condition, e.g. by a sickness benefit. But this would be a standard benefit, and would not necessarily cover the whole cost of satisfying the need in the way that any given patient prefers. It would be clearly impractical, however, to cover the full cost of *any* sort of treatment the patient chose.

prima facie case for treating his own view of what he needs with respect rather than giving him what somebody else thinks will be good for him. This is surely implied by the general moral principle of respect for persons.

V. CONCLUSION

It is fairly generally agreed that, property incomes apart, our system of distribution by desert, supplemented by redistribution according to need, is right in principle. Differences of opinion arise mainly about the proper weight to be given to these criteria. On the one hand, some people complain that we so emphasize need at the expense of desert that initiative and enterprise are seriously discouraged, or lost by emigration to less 'need-minded' countries. Economic egalitarians, on the other hand, believe that we are too much bound up in our traditional assumptions, and that the gap between the extremes of income could be narrowed still further, stressing need more and desert less; or, beyond the point where need is a useful criterion of distribution, aiming at something nearer an arithmetical equality. They believe that this could be done without disastrous consequences; that on the contrary a greater equality of incomes would eliminate snobbish distinctions, and create a stronger sense of fraternity and social harmony. This controversy is closely bound up with the problems of property, which we deal with in the next chapter.

CHAPTER 7

PROPERTY

The last chapter dealt with incomes deriving from the performance of personal service and from need. We deferred the controversial issues of incomes from property until we should have made a preliminary analysis of property in general. In this chapter, we shall indicate what these issues are, and suggest ways of dealing with them.

Property and income are obviously related. For one thing, what a man receives in income is also his property; for another, property may be a source of income, or, as we shall see, it may be nothing but a certain sort of title to income.

I. PROPERTY AS A COMPLEX OF RIGHTS

(a) The natural rights of property

The classic declarations of natural and human rights, to which we referred in Chapter 4, have all given prominence to the rights of property. In order to survive, we must have access to things like houses, clothes, and food, as well as to land and machines necessary to produce them. Rights that settle how such things are to be controlled, who is to have the use of them, and on what terms, are clearly of the first importance. And life would be intolerably insecure if we did not know from one moment to the next what things would be available to us to serve our necessities. It is not surprising then that the authors of the classic declarations have felt that some property rights might be called 'natural', 'inviolable', and 'sacred'.[1] But what rights in particular are to be considered 'natural' is not always clear; and in practice, the rights of property have varied a good deal with time and place. Some rights at least, which would have been regarded as inviolable at one time are now subject to very strict qualifications. Locke would have been highly indignant had he ever been presented with a Compulsory Purchase Order. The UNESCO Committee of Experts, reporting on *Human Rights*, limited the 'fundamental rights of property' to what 'is necessary for (a man's) personal use and the use of his family; no other form of property is in itself a fundamental right'.[2] This is a good deal more restrained than, say, the Declaration of the Rights of Man, and is a sign of a wider recognition today that property rights largely depend on particular circumstances, and on the particular social system.

(b) The diversity of property rights

The term 'property' covers a very wide range of rights; we clearly mean something very different in saying 'This house is my property' from what we mean when we say 'The copyright in this book is my property'. Professor Tawney has made this point very forcibly:

'. . . in most discussions of property the opposing theorists have usually been discussing different things. Property is the most ambiguous of categories. It covers a multitude of rights which have nothing in common except that they are exercised by persons and enforced by the State. Apart from these formal characteristics, they vary indefinitely in economic character, in social effect, and in moral justification. They may be conditional like the grant of patent rights, or absolute like the ownership of ground rents, terminable like copyright, or permanent like a freehold, as comprehensive as sovereignty or as restricted as an easement, as intimate and personal as the ownership of clothes and books, or as remote and intangible as shares in a gold mine or rubber plantation.

'It is idle, therefore, to present a case for or against private property without specifying the particular forms of property to which reference is made, and the journalist who says that "private property is the foundation of civilization" agrees with Proudhon, who said that it was theft, in this respect at least that, without further definition, the words of both are meaningless. Arguments which support or demolish certain kinds of property may have no application to others; considerations which are conclusive in one stage of economic organization may be almost irrelevant in the next. The course of wisdom is neither to attack private property in general nor to defend it in general . . . for things are not similar in quality, merely because they are identical in name. It is to discriminate between the various concrete embodiments of what, in itself, is, after all, little more than an abstraction.'[3]

There is no single comprehensive list of rights, then, that could be offered as 'the rights of property'. Neither can one necessarily infer from 'ownership' the existence of any one 'essential' right. The right to alienate, by gift or sale, is very generally associated with 'property'; nevertheless, property which is entailed cannot be alienated. Similarly, property rights usually exclude the exercise of similar rights by anyone other than the owner, but this is not inevitably the case. If owners of 'old masters' were required by law to exhibit them publicly from time to time, others besides the owner would have a right to enjoy them; yet we should not consider that the ownership had been terminated on that account. However, in the ordinary or standard cases of 'property', we should expect the owner's rights of control and enjoyment to be exclusive, and we should expect, too, a right to alienate the object in question. If these rights were not in fact included, we should expect some specific qualification to make the point clear.

The rights involved in 'ownership' will obviously vary widely according to the nature of the thing owned; the possible uses of a pen are different from those of a gun. Property rights are never absolute—no society could work on the principle that a man might do what he liked with his own irrespective of the consequences to other people. The limitations vary not merely according to the nature of the object, but with place and time. The concept 'ownership' comprehends, therefore, a range of rights varying constantly with changing conditions and moral attitudes; but it implies, too, that within that range, there is for everyone else an obligation not to interfere.

(c) *Distinction between property rights of control, and property titles to income*

In asserting 'These clothes are my property' (or, more probably, 'are mine') I am making an exclusive claim to wear them, lend, sell or otherwise alienate them, destroy or modify them as I please. Property rights in respect of things are rights of control. But to say 'This pound note is mine' is more complex; an account of what might be done with a piece of paper would give but a poor idea of what it means to own twenty shillings. Cash is a title to a range of possible goods and services, and to possess it is to have potential rights of control over things, realizable at will. The control over goods and services to which one is entitled by reason of owning securities is still more remote. Unless I choose to exchange my title on the Stock Exchange for a cash title, its realization may be deferred for a long time, perhaps indefinitely. On the other hand, securities represent a claim to income in the future, to a regular cash title year by year so long as they remain unredeemed. There are some forms of property, like annuities, which consist wholly in titles to income and which entail rights of control only over the things that the income will purchase year by year (except in so far as they might be sold for cash on the open market).

It is convenient, therefore, to distinguish property as a system of rights of control over things, and property as a title to future income. The two aspects are often closely related (e.g. in the case of a one-man business) but are neither theoretically nor practically inseparable.

II. PROPERTY SYSTEMS AS WAYS OF ORGANIZING CONTROL OVER THINGS

(a) *Property systems distinguished, as forms of control*

A system of property, in the sense of a set of norms allocating control over the physical resources at its disposal, is essential to any community. In the state of nature, Hobbes assures us 'every man has a right to everything'. But where everyone has a right to everything, no one has a right to anything; significantly, Hobbes sees the state of nature as one of perpetual warfare. The transition from the natural state to civil society, according to Rousseau, 'changes usurpation into a true right and enjoyment into proprietorship', which is a roundabout way of saying that since property is a legal category, without a system of law, it is necessarily meaningless. Both writers imply that any society must allocate rights of control over the land and goods at its disposal, as a prerequisite of a social order. We must know who has the right to live in any particular house, or who is entitled to accept a tenant for it. To this extent the writers, both past and present, who have stressed the maintenance of property as among the most important functions of State and law, were justified. It does not follow, however, that the State ought to support the particular rights, or indeed the general pattern of rights, that these writers have been concerned to defend. For not only is there diversity in the particular rights associated with ownership; the notion of 'ownership' itself covers a multitude of different forms of organization.

The simplest type of organization is that of individual proprietorship, where exclusive rights of control vest in natural persons. On this pattern, the owner of an object is entitled, to the exclusion of other private persons, to decide what shall be done with it, except as he is limited by law, or by voluntary agreement (e.g. by the terms of a lease granted to someone else).*

The legal notion of a 'corporate person' involves a more complicated type of organization. Property rights, analogous to those possessed by individuals, are said to vest in corporations. Since corporations are themselves normative systems, the rights of control legally attributed to them as a whole (concentrated as it were, in the legal person as uniquely and exclusively as if it were a natural person) will in practice be exercised by men designated by the rules of the corporation, and may accordingly be divided and subject to conditions. Questions of responsibility then

---

* This does not exclude the possibility that the law may authorize other persons, as State agents, to exercise particular rights of control (e.g. by making a demolition order).

arise, for the agents may be required to justify their stewardship to the rest of the members, on pain of loss of office. There is no end to the possible specific variations of which the genus 'corporation' is capable. Joint-stock companies, co-operative societies, whether of consumers or producers, collegiate bodies, local councils are only a few of the possible varieties. Each constitutes a way of organizing control over physical resources, and the uses to which they are put are likely to vary with the pattern of organization. The rights of control may be limited, not merely by the general provisions of law governing the type of object in question (e.g. sanitary requirements applicable to houses in general), but also by the instrument of incorporation specifying the purposes for which the resources in question may be used.

Public property may be regarded as a special type of corporate property, where the corporate person is the State. As before, the law will define the persons authorized to exercise control, and will probably provide machinery for making the agents accountable.

It is clear that neither private nor public corporations (which, for this purpose, may include all State property organizations) necessarily confer on their members, taken severally, rights of use or other enjoyment of the property of the whole. Shareholders, whether of Woolworths or the local co-operative society, must pay for their goods, and there are no free rides for all on British Railways.

In some primitive communities, as well as in some experimental communist communities, property is held in common. As with more familiar corporate property organization, rights are enjoyed according to an established normative order, the main difference being that specific user rights are allocated to all members.*

While it is true, therefore, that a social order requires a system of property, the possible forms are endless. Which will yield the best results depends partly on the type of thing which is the object of control, partly on factors like the productive and administrative techniques employed. Individual proprietorship, for instance, may not work in a

* This is very different from the 'property in common' of the state of nature of seventeenth and eighteenth century writers, who pictured rather a world without property regulation, where anyone might pick the berries that grew wild, or kill the deer in the boundless forests of North America. The absence of a system of control is not the same as a system in which every member has agreed user rights. Locke was virtually making this distinction when he distinguished common in nature from common by compact (*Second Treatise*, Secs. 27–34). Fishing in the ocean, 'that great and still remaining common of mankind' was subject in Locke's day to no legal regulation. Since then, whale fishing on the high seas has been restricted by agreements forming part of international law, allocating fishing rights among the nations. What was once common in nature has thus become common by compact.

highly industrialized community; on the other hand, large scale corporate property organization depends on intricate and efficient administration, which can hardly be expected without good communications.

Discussions of the merits of private property too often fail to recognize such distinctions; it is tempting to assume that what applies to individual, applies equally to private corporate proprietorship, and to utilize arguments appropriate to personal goods to defend individual control of capital goods. Food, clothes, houses, pictures, and books are clearly in a different category from railway tracks, coal mines, and factories, and it would be strange if argument relevant to forms of control for the one were applicable to the other. It is often claimed, for example, that private property is a vehicle for the expression of personality; and when it is a question of clothes, furniture or books, the case is a strong one. Apart from retail trade, however, the one-man business has become too rare for the case to seem cogent when applied to capital. Similarly, the claims that the opportunity to acquire property satisfies a deep-rooted acquisitive instinct, or provides an incentive to effort, or provides a firm basis for the family, may all be cogent when applied to personal goods, but are relatively weaker when applied to capital goods. For capital goods are the instruments employed by other men in earning their living, and in satisfying the wants of the community at large; control over them is not merely a means of satisfaction; it is also an exercise of power, and to treat them on the same terms as personal goods is to ignore important differences which may weigh heavily on the other side.[4]

(b) The organization of control of capital goods

The classic case for private property in capital resources is in part a purely economic one. Classical economic theory assumed that the sole aim of the individual entrepreneur would be to maximize profits from the use of his property. In doing so, he would use it for the greatest satisfaction of consumer demand. His interest in profit was thus both an explanation for his behaviour and a reason for leaving capital under his control, since it ensured beneficial results for the community at large. This case was buttressed by Locke's argument that goods acquired value by virtue of the labour that went into producing them. Since a man's labour was his own, the goods he produced were also his own. Further, a man had a natural right to use the resources that Nature (or God) made available to sustain life. Accordingly, property rights of control in land (or capital) arose from man's need for the instruments of production, while property titles in the output derived from the labour expended. This argument was clearly appropriate for an economy of peasant proprietors: but it needed considerable modification and extension to justify mercantile capitalism.

The whole case, however, now has an archiac ring. The typical modern enterpreneur is neither a peasant proprietor nor an individual owner-employer, but a corporate person, like a joint-stock company. The divorce of ownership and management consequent upon the change has become a commonplace. The owners of capital are now holders of income titles, and of voting rights that many of them never exercise; the controllers are salaried managers* formally responsible to the shareholders, but often interested in other things besides the maximization of profit. Concern for efficiency for its own sake, the desire to build up an ever-expanding industrial empire, even a benevolent vision of workers and managers associated happily in a joint enterprise, with welfare schemes and sports grounds as its tangible expression—interests like these may conflict with those of the shareholder, concerned only with greater profits. This tension of interests is fairly typical, and those of the shareholders are not necessarily the strongest. The pursuit of efficiency for its own sake, it is true, need not cut across the maximization of profits; for the manager is accustomed to estimate efficiency by this very yardstick. Nevertheless when it comes to dividing profits between reinvestment and dividends the tension may become acute.

The interests of those who control industrial capital in a modern private enterprise economy are by no means so simple, therefore, as those of the entrepreneur of theory. Furthermore, monopolistic practices, like pricing agreements and output restriction, have invalidated, in some fields at least, the case for pivate ownership that the competitive theory was supposed to support. And if the main objective in capital control is not necessarily the pursuit of profit, other objectives, like the extension of industrial empire for its own sake, are not necessarily benevolent.

The socialist turns accordingly to other forms of property organization, in the belief that managerial interests can be turned into socially useful channels by making controllers responsible not to shareholders, whether active or passive, but to the political representatives of the nation in Parliament, to the workers in the industry (in producers' co-operatives and collective farms) or to the consumer (in consumers' co-operatives). Experience however, suggests that members of consumers' co-operatives are hardly more active in their own interests than

---

* The term 'manager' is used here of anyone competent to decide how capital resources are to be employed. Throughout this chapter, it may be taken to include boards of directors, whether of private or public enterprises, the executive committees of co-operative societies, and industrial policy-makers generally.

F

shareholders in a joint-stock company. But equally if managers were responsible to the workers, the objectives of control would not necessarily be any more beneficial to the community at large than under present arrangements. For the workers in an industry are, in relation to the consumers, as much a sectional interest as the shareholder, and are no less capable of manipulating market conditions for sectional advantage.[5]

The organization of British nationalized industries is an attempt to free industrial managers from their obligation to maximize shareholders' profits to the possible detriment of consumers' interests, while insulating them from too immediate political pressures that might introduce motives no more desirable. In the normal working of these industries, the managers are relied upon to maintain efficiency from considerations of professional pride and public service; in matters of major policy, they are subject to directives from Ministries ultimately accountable to Parliament. Though not primarily profit-making concerns they are required by the statutes incorporating them to break even, 'taking one year with another'. Failure to do so would therefore constitute a *prima facie* case against their efficiency. However, the possibility of falling back on public funds to meet losses might conceivably lead to less concern for costs of production than might be felt in private organizations. So far, the industries nationalized have been those which have been peculiarly liable to monopolistic organization, like the production and distribution of electricity and gas. There are also those which, like the coal industry, are of major public importance, and have suffered particularly from labour troubles and capital shortage, or similar special difficulties. Where such difficulties do not exist, and where market conditions stimulate competition, it cannot be taken for granted that organization by public corporation would necessarily serve the community better than more traditional forms. In any case, the possible forms of industrial organization have certainly not been exhausted, and the peculiar problems of particular industries might well yield peculiar solutions. Experiments in legislative and administrative control of monopolies, in this and other countries, offer possible alternatives to nationalization, even where the case against private control might seem strongest.

It is not part of our present purpose, however, to examine what conditions would justify nationalization, still less to suggest the organization most appropriate to any given industry; that would require a specialized treatment far beyond the scope of this book. We are concerned to argue only that from this standpoint at least, the organization appropriate to an industry is likely to depend on its special conditions. The question must be considered empirically, and dogmatic creeds are unlikely to produce universally valid answers.

(c) Industrial organization and human relations

It would be unfair to suggest, however, that the Socialist attack on private (or capitalist) industrial organization stands or falls with the hypothesis that it fails to achieve maximum satisfaction of consumers' wants. The Socialist tradition inherits from the French Revolution the ideal of 'Fraternity' and from Christianity 'the brotherhood of man'. While Socialists are inclined to take for granted that the elimination of capitalism would greatly increase production, many feel that, this apart, by making the pursuit of self-interest the motive force of the social order, capitalism poisons human relations and sets man against man.[6] Through all the varying prescriptions for reform there runs the Owenite ideal of a 'new harmony' in which men will work not each for himself but one for another.[7] Fourier's *phalanstères*, Proudhon's *mutuellisme* and all the other Utopian schemes for economic re-organization are alike in seeking to eliminate competition and rivalry and to substitute the spirit of mutual aid. One of the main driving forces of Marxism is the conviction that only in the working class is fraternity possible; for in the working class alone is there an identity of interest.

Yet the very nature of the problem they are trying to solve defeats them. For wherever there is a sharing out, one man's gain is another's loss: it is only with certain forms of wealth, like national parks or communal facilities generally, that one man's enjoyment need not preclude another's (and even a national park is pleasanter when there are few visitors). Where goods are of the sort that can be shared in, there need be no rivalry; but those that must be shared *out* invite competition. Some forms of economic organization stress the competitive spirit more than others; nevertheless, in any system in which income is related to satisfying other people's wants, the producer has something to gain by making the terms of satisfaction as stiff as possible. There is no reason to suppose, for instance, that in a syndicalist society the workers organized to control a given industry would not behave, in relation to the rest of the community, like any other sectional interest anywhere else. The Parliament of Industry, much canvassed by the Guild Socialists of the early 1920's might well have become an open battleground for competing interests, rather than an assembly dedicated to the high ideal of community service.

We are not maintaining that all economic activity is necessarily prompted by egotistic motives. We admit, too, that some forms of organization will stress them less than others, e.g. monasteries or, perhaps, producers' co-operatives.[8] The spirit of service and brotherly love could hardly be realized by the manipulation of economic organization alone, but some forms might favour it more than others; and if through playing down competition it proved necessary to accept lower standards of material welfare (which has not, of course, been proved), we might reckon the gain well worth the loss. The easy assumption, however, that fraternity and abundance necessarily go hand in hand merely obscures the moral choice that might have to be made. The difficulty encountered by social experiments designed to change human nature is that too often they depend for their success on the change having already been made.

(d) Liberty and industrial control

The right to decide how—and whether—capital resources shall be utilized is a source of power over workers who depend on them for their livelihood. It is not surprising, therefore, that socialists as well as anti-socialists have defended their particular creeds in the name of Liberty.

The anti-socialists are largely concerned with what would happen if the State became the sole employer in a community. A worker who gave offence, they argue, would lose all hope of another job, or would be compelled to accept whatever terms the State cared to offer. Now, while this might be true of a highly centralized economy, it is by no means an inevitable consequence of *any* sort of socialist system. A sound radio artist who loses the favour of the BBC might have to seek another type of employment, but an engineer who loses a job under one area gas board might possibly find one under another. 'The State' as employer is an abstraction: practice, industries must be organized fairly autonomously, and there is no more reason to expect a 'black list' of public than of private employers. This particular danger attaches to any monopolistic organizations, but it is not inherent in public owner-ship as such. There are, in any case, many forms of public ownership (e.g. municipal enterprise) which are not monopolistic, and there are, as we have shown, many forms of socialist organization other than the public corporation.

The socialist argument goes deeper, and is analogous to the case for political democracy. Profits, it is argued, mean less to the employer than wages to the worker; yet the decisions of the one might affect the other catastrophically, without his point of view having been considered. The worker must take orders made without his knowledge and without con-sulting him, for a purpose which may be to his detriment. As parlia-mentary democracy ensures that the needs of the governed are con-sulted, so industrial organization should provide for the needs of the workers. Others go further, and appeal to the principle of government by consent; a man is not free who must obey orders to which he has not consented, at least through representatives.

This case is surely somewhat exaggerated; for powerful Trade Unions can usually insist that workers' interests be considered. It is now very widely conceded that workers' representatives should be associated in some form with management. The joint production committee is fairly common, while a few firms have even carried 'co-partnership' to the lengths of including workers' representatives on the board of directors. Nevertheless, while managers remain formally responsible to shareholders, there will probably be strong resistance to workers' participation in management. And equally in the nationalized industries, workers' control was rejected, even by a Socialist government. Since that government's main intention was to protect the interests of consumers, it preferred to appoint independent managerial boards, rather than entrust control to the workers themselves, whose interests were potentially as restrictionist as those of private employers. Trade Unionists who join the boards, therefore, do so as private persons, not as representatives of the workers in the industry.*

III. PROPERTY TITLES TO INCOME

The disagreement between economic liberals and socialists over property is not limited to property as a complex of rights of control; it extends also to its other aspect, as a complex of income titles.

The relation between these two aspects can be exhibited if we consider how rights of control may be translated into income. Control, we have said, usually includes the right to alienate. Thus control over one thing can be bartered for control over another, or exchanged for cash, which is a potential control over any of a number of things. Or one can exchange control temporarily, or in part, by hiring or leasing in return for an income title. Such a title can itself be sold for cash, becoming a sort of property in itself, and like rights of control, a marketable commodity. Or again, cash may be exchanged for an income title, by lending at interest or investment, or by buying an annuity.

* That the form of workers' participation in management is no simple problem is borne out by the experiment of the Dock Labour Board. There, official trade union representation on the employing authority inhibited the union's function of expressing workers' grievances, with a resulting weakening in union discipline. Clearly, in an industry with a tradition of labour unrest, harmony cannot be quickly restored by simply substituting union representatives for the former employers. To the dock worker, the new unionist looks uncommonly like old boss writ large.

As before, any one justification will not necessarily be appropriate for all forms of property title to income. Patent rights, or an author's copyright, are much closer to rewards for skill than are interest and rent. The former, however, are rarely controversial; but the latter, which arise from purchase or lending, are often attacked by egalitarians because they are said to yield income without service.

(a) Justifying property titles to income

Justifying property titles to income is clearly different from justifying property rights of control. There might still be room for lending at interest, even if all private control of capital goods were abolished. Even Communist governments have borrowed private savings at interest.

The early Church condemned lending at interest as a form of avarice. If one's neighbour were in need, it was wrong to demand interest before supplying his wants. The growth of commerce, however, introduced complications; the borrower was no longer 'in need', but sought capital for use in profit-making. Gradually, the ecclesiastical prohibition was qualified. Where the borrower wanted money to make more money, it seemed reasonable that the lender should share in his gains.[9]

Looked at as a private transaction, commercial lending is of benefit to both parties, and need cause no heart searchings on either side. From the economist's point of view, too, interest has its function in directing the flow of investment into the most profitable and, on classical assumptions, the most socially advantageous channels; for interest is a cost, and only entrepreneurs who expect to make profits by satisfying consumers' demands will be prepared to incur it. From the lender's standpoint, interest provides the inducement to sacrifice present for future enjoyment, or, at least, to incur the risks and disadvantages of exchanging ready cash for assets that cannot always be immediately realized without loss. In the classical free economy, investment is possibly only if people can be persuaded to set aside part of present income in savings for the use of industry. Interest provides the necessary inducement.

There are, however, other ways of providing for capital investment. A prosperous firm may finance expansion out of accumulated profits or a government by taxation, or by creating new money. Again, we are not necessarily committed to interest rates as the only mechanism for determining priorities; government investment has never been deterred by rates of interest, and in the years following the last war new capital issues were regulated by government licence, rather than by the market mechanism. It is doubtful, however, whether these methods could be extended as a permanent feature of the economy, to cover the whole volume of present investment, without first introducing revolutionary changes in the pattern of capital ownership.[10] To dispense with the need for private lending would require a central regulation of investment and private incomes far stricter than any yet experienced outside the Communist countries. If, therefore, the present pattern of economic organization is worth preserving, interest can be justified by its function.

(b) Property titles to income and economic equality

Socialist criticism of interest and similar titles to income is not usually directed to the principle itself, however, but to the economic inequality with which it is associated. It does not seem patently unjust that a man should benefit from lending his savings; the injustice, if one exists, lies in the ability to save from large incomes without real sacrifice, and so to increase them still further without rendering any personal service to the community. It is not, in short, that property titles have no place at all, but that their present distribution is too limited, and that they make for undesirable income inequalities. Allied to this feeling of injustice is the belief that income inequalities make for social differences, dividing society into classes with little mutual sympathy and no sense of solidarity. Still worse, property titles, unlike those of desert or need, are transmissible by inheritance, so that families become congealed, as it were, in their class habits and attitudes. And even if a case might be made out for the founder of a large fortune, his heirs succeed to his advantages through no merits of their own. Inheritance apart, since the owner of a fortune is able to give his children advantages in education, and to use his influence to start them off well in life, the initial inequality is perpetuated by inequality of opportunity, while positions of leadership and influence become the prerogative of a limited number of families forming a wealthy élite.

The force of these arguments is practically acknowledged by our system of taxation. Estate duty is largely aimed at breaking up concentrations of capital on the death of their owners,[11] while progressive taxation considerably reduces the saveable surplus of distributed incomes. In distinguishing between 'earned' and 'unearned' incomes, our tax law seems to recognize that the claim of the latter is weaker, and that wide inequalities based on property titles may have undesirable consequences.

Some people feel that this levelling process has gone too far. They claim that the hope of acquiring property is an important incentive to production and that it is greatly impaired by steeply progressive taxation. Others argue that a nation without great property owners lies helpless at its government's feet. If wealth is power, it is better decentralized in private hands, than concentrated under a government's control. Individual liberties, and especially the rights of small property owners, cannot be preserved unless there are a few wealthy and independent men with the will and the means to defend them. The great property owner is the champion of the small one too, for he defends the principle of property—for instance, the Crichel Down inquiry resulted in better assurances for all landowners, small as well as great, that administrators would pay proper attention to their claims. But that inquiry would never have been held, and the abuses it revealed might never have been remedied, had not one of the property owners who had suffered these abuses been rich and influential enough to conduct a single-handed agitation against a government department.

This last argument may be two-edged, however, for it seems to admit that owning property gives some men a greater political influence than others; yet there is no reason to suppose that such influence would normally be used for any but self-interested ends. Power without responsibility must always be suspect, even when its exercise is of advantage to others besides its owner. Just because it is irresponsible, it may be used on another occasion to damage the very people it aids on this one.

Of far wider scope is the argument that without a wealthy and leisured élite a nation's culture degenerates. The greatest achievements of art and learning, it is argued, were produced under the patronage of a cultured and leisured nobility. A levelling of incomes, by eliminating the patron, either commercializes the artist and the scholar, or puts him at the service of public authorities. Such authorities, in the nature of the case, can be generous to the orthodox but dare not venture public funds in support of the heretic and the iconoclast. As M. de Jouvenel points out, it was the private income of Engels that enabled Marx to work on 'Das Kapital'.[12] For those who take this view it would not be enough merely to have wealthy men in the community; for a cultured class could not be produced in one generation. The attitudes and values of social importance must be nurtured as family traditions.* The aristo-

---

* The case was stated classically by Edmund Burke: 'A true natural aristocracy is not a separate interest in the state, or separable from it. It is an essential integrant part of any large body rightly constituted. It is formed out of a class of legitimate presumptions, which, taken as generalities, must be admitted for actual truths. To be bred in a place of estimation; to see nothing low and sordid from one's infancy; to be taught to respect one's self; to be habituated to the censorial inspection of the public eye; to look early to public opinion; to stand upon such elevated ground as to be enabled to take a large view of the widespread and infinitely diversified combinations of men and affairs in a large society; to have leisure to read, to reflect, to converse; to be enabled to draw the

cratic ideal which characterizes these noble families which have given voluntary public leadership and service over several centuries, is inextricably linked with the inheritance of fortunes. These form the economic base of the tradition. For those who take this view, economic and social equality is not a good but an evil. Every society, however democratic, has its élite, its leaders of opinion and taste, its governors and managers; without a propertied class, the élite will consist of men whose very success in an egalitarian world would testify to qualities of aggressive self-assertion which, untempered by liberal and humane traditions, might be ruinous to liberty and civilization.

This argument treats income neither as a reward for service, nor as a means of satisfying need, nor even as a means of meeting functional needs; it is rather a way of providing the opportunity for service. If it were true that fortunes based on inheritable property were indispensable for an élite of this sort, and if such an élite were really so valuable, the property system would be justified by its beneficent consequences. The argument would not be invalidated merely because some great property owners were boors, lacking both talent and desire for public service. Nor would this prove that income deriving from property was unjustly distributed. For if, to provide the cultured, liberal and talented leadership that society needs, it were necessary to support a given property system, then anyone possessing wealth according to the rules of that system would have a valid title to it. Whereas for the egalitarian differences of parentage are irrelevant grounds for inequalities of income, for his opponent they are relevant, because inheritance of property justifies itself, not in every case, but by its overall results. The

---

court and attention of the wise and learned wherever they are to be found; to be habituated in armies to command and to obey; to be taught to despise danger in the pursuit of honour and duty; to be formed to the greatest degree of vigilance, foresight, and circumspection, in a state of things in which no fault is committed with impunity, and the slightest mistakes draw on the most ruinous consequences—to be led to a guarded and regulated conduct, from a sense that you are considered as an instructor of your fellow-citizen in their highest concerns, and that you act as a reconciler between God and man—to be employed as an administrator of law and justice, and to be thereby amongst the first benefactors to mankind—to be amongst rich traders, who from their success are presumed to have sharp and vigorous understandings, and to possess the virtues of diligence, order, constancy, and regularity, and to have cultivated an habitual regard to commutative justice—these are the circumstances of men, that form what I should call a *natural* aristocracy, without which there is no nation.' (*An Appeal from the New to the Old Whigs*—Works (Bohn Edn. 1901, Vol. III, pp. 85–6). Mr T. S. Eliot puts a case not dissimilar in essentials, though modified for a more democratic age, in Chap. 2 of *Notes towards the Definition of Culture*. (1948.)

categories of the property system would then take their place in their own right alongside skill, function, need, etc., as criteria to be applied in determining what a person's income ought to be. Allow that, and the socialist argument, that inherited property enables some men to enjoy income without contributing anything to the common fund, would be quite beside the point; for it demands that one criterion shall be justified in terms of another, instead of by its own beneficial results.

The differences that divide the egalitarians from their opponents are partly differences of belief, and partly of attitude. Both parties accept, that wide economic inequalities produce a stratified society; but while the former believes that this *necessarily* implies class conflict, the latter attributes the conflict to misconceived envy, which a better understanding of the social order and a more generous outlook would eliminate. The one view criticizes the differences in individual material advantages; the other stresses the gains to society as a whole which are said to result from them. Most egalitarians, however, would repudiate the need for a leisured élite, arguing that if it has any advantages, they are limited to the wealthy class alone, while the rest of the population goes unconsidered. They tend to believe that an egalitarian society would raise the standards of taste and the values of the people generally, and, therefore, deny that it would involve cultural degeneration; for equality of opportunity would release so much new talent that it would more than compensate for expected loss. These are largely questions of fact and to choose between one social prophecy and another is not easy. According to the one, the egalitarian society is a collection of undifferentiated mediocrities, wrought to a common pattern of taste, culture and opinion; according to the other, it is an ideal order in which the special needs of individuals and groups are accorded infinitely more attention than they are at present.[13]

IV. CONCLUSION

With the addition of 'property', we can now draw together the account of the main criteria of income distribution which we began in Chapter 6. Ownership has this in common with desert, that in neither case is there any logically necessary connection with income.* The connection is established by rules which might conceivably be other than they are. The rules might be justified, however, if they create inducements for people to act in certain desirable ways. As desert titles offer incentives to

---

* There is no intrinsic reason, that is, why one should claim an income whenever one lends money or goods to anyone else. As we remarked earlier, lending a interest was a sin in the mediaeval Church.

hard work, to acquire skills and accept responsibility, so property titles encourage people to put their possessions at the disposal of other people who need them or can use them productively. If there are general advantages in adopting such criteria, they may provide good grounds for differences in income distribution. But if, as some socialists maintain, the whole system of income distribution and control over capital goods could be reorganized to achieve the same, or even better results without them, and without disadvantages to offset against them like a general decline in enterprise or in intellectual vigour, ownership criteria might not be justified, and distinctions based on them could be condemned as cases of 'privilege' or 'inequalities'. Absolute justice is no more at stake in financial rewards for lending than in financial rewards for skill.

Desert and ownership criteria both differ from need, which, we have shown, has a direct relation to income. Distribution according to need is not a way of influencing behaviour. Need criteria presuppose standards, which above the level of bare biological needs, vary from culture to culture. Basic needs rest directly on a conception of a mode of life that it would be thought injurious to fall short of. This mode of life is taken for granted; but the standards implied vary widely. Functional needs are in a sense secondary, since the standards to which they are related are not necessarily good in themselves, but serve some further valuable ends. Yet they are still different from desert and ownership titles because their justification is not that they encourage desirable performance, but rather that unless they are satisfied such performance would be impossible. For that reason it would be logically absurd to try to meet the claims of functional needs, as of basic needs, in any other way than by income distribution. This is not the case with either desert or property claims.

This analysis would have to be modified, however, if it were agreed that a society needs a wealthy élite based on inheritable property titles to income. In that case, ownership criteria would resemble functional needs, as providing necessary conditions for the performance of socially important functions. But in this case the functions would be those of a social class.

There remains to consider the case for prescriptive titles. Prescription is in origin a legal principle which recognizes a property title when the benefit in question has been enjoyed without dispute for a very long time. Now, on the face of it, mere de facto enjoyment of a benefit would not be a good moral reason why one should go on enjoying it. There is something to be said, however, in favour of respecting settled arrangements. We argued, in connection with traditional wage and salary scales, that men found settled habits and expectations on the basis of an established distributive system, and that sudden and radical revision of it might cause hardship, resentment, and social disharmony. The same might be said of property rights. We suggested at the beginning of this chapter that security in the enjoyment of property, of some types at least, has seemed so important as to find a place in all the classic declarations of fundamental rights. Moreover, in an economic system which still depends in large measure on individual decisions to defer present enjoyment for future advantage, a sense of insecurity about the future may have disastrous effects in discouraging long term investment Revolutionary adjustments in the distribution of property and income, such as accompanied the German inflation of the early 1920's, are more likely than almost anything else to disrupt a nation's solidarity, set class against class, and endanger all its settled institutions and traditional standards.

CHAPTER 8

PUNISHMENT

To do justice is to treat men unequally only according to the degree of their relevant inequalities. This has been a recurrent theme, particularly in the last three chapters, which have dealt with problems of distributive justice. Men differ in so many ways that no two are ever alike in all respects; yet to do justice we must disregard all differences except those that accord with the appropriate criteria in each field. And these criteria must be justified by showing that beneficent consequences can be expected to follow their operation as general rules. In Chapters 6 and 7 we considered those governing income distribution, and inquired how they might be justified, and how they applied to particular cases. Punishment, or retributive justice, presents a similar set of problems, but it is further complicated by the fact that to punish a man is deliberately to do something unpleasant to him, not as a dentist does, as a regrettable accompaniment to the long-term betterment of his condition, but as a matter of deliberate principle. We did not feel called upon to ask, in Chapter 6, 'What can justify distributing any income at all?' because we need make no apology for giving people things they want. But since people would generally prefer not to be punished, we are bound to ask 'What can justify ever punishing anyone at all?', before going on to consider the criteria for punishing in particular cases.

I. THE JUSTIFICATION OF PUNISHMENT

(a) 'Punishment' defined

'What can justify punishment?' is a moral, not a linguistic question, not therefore to be answered by analysing concepts. Nevertheless, some of the confusions which have made the question seem unnecessarily difficult in the past may be avoided by clarifying the way in which the word 'punishment' is most generally used. For instance, many people have insisted on the close connection between punishment and guilt for a crime already committed. It would therefore be wrong, they say, to justify it as a deterrent to crime in the future. But they have often failed to recognize that his reference back to a crime is part of the *meaning* of 'punishment'. (We deal with this point more fully later on.)

Professor Flew[1] has suggested five criteria for the use of the word 'punishment' in its primary sense, i.e. five conditions satisfied by an ordinary or standard case to which the word would be applied:

i. it must involve an 'evil, an unpleasantness, to the victim';
ii. it must be for an offence (actual or supposed);
iii. it must be of an offender (actual or supposed);
iv. It must be the work of personal agencies (i.e. not merely the natural consequences of an action);
v. it must be imposed by authority (real or supposed), conferred by the system of rules against which the offence has been committed.

To these criteria another might be added: that the unpleasantness should be an essential part of what is intended and not merely incidental to some other aim. While it is not a misuse of the word to talk, for example, about 'punishing the innocent', or of a boxer 'punishing his opponent', these usages, though related to the primary one, disregard one or more of the criteria ordinarily satisfied, and must be treated accordingly as extended or secondary usages. In considering the justification of punishment, we are confining the word to its primary sense, except where otherwise stated.

(b) The two main approaches to justification—utilitarian and retributive

The problem has been approached from two standpoints. One, the utilitarian, is typified by Bentham:

'All punishment is mischief: all punishment in itself is evil. Upon the principle of utility, if it ought at all to be admitted, it ought only to be admitted in as far as it promises to exclude some greater evil.'[2]

'The immediate principal end of punishment is to control action. This action is either that of the offender, or of others: that of the offender it controls by its influence, either on his will . . . in the way of *reformation*; or on his physical power . . . by *disablement*: that of others it can influence no otherwise than by its influence over their wills . . . in the way of *example*.'[3]

The other, the retributive approach, is exemplified in its most thoroughgoing form by Kant:

'Judicial punishment . . . can never be inflicted simply and solely as a means to forward a good, other than itself, whether . . . of the criminal, or of civil society; but it must at all times be inflicted on him, for no other reason than *because he has acted criminally*. A man can never be treated simply as a means for realizing the views of another man . . . He must first of all be found to be *punishable*, before there is even a thought of deriving from the punishment any advantage for himself or his fellow-citizens. The penal law is a categorical imperative; and woe to that man who crawls through the serpentine turnings of the happiness-doctrine, to find out some consideration, which, by its promise of advantage, should free the criminal from his penalty, or even from any degree thereof. That is the maxim of the Pharisees, "it is expedient that one man should die for the people, and that the whole nation perish not"; but if justice perishes, then it is no more worth while that man should live upon the earth.'[4]

There appears to be a serious difference of view here, the one looking for justification to the beneficent consequences of punishment, the other exclusively to the wrongful act. It remains to be seen whether the gulf can be bridged.

(c) Distinction between justification of punishment in general and in particular

It is important, first, to distinguish between a rule, or an institution constituted by rules, and some particular application of it. We can ask what can justify punishment in general, i.e. why we should have rules that provide that offenders against them should be made to suffer. But this is quite different from asking how to justify a particular application of such rules, in punishing a given individual. Though retributivist and utilitarian have tried to answer both questions, each in his own terms, the strength of the former's case rests on his answer to the second, of the latter's on his answer to the first. And their difficulties arise from trying to make one answer do for both questions.

(d) Justifying punishment in general

The retributivist refuses to look to the consequences of punishment for its justification. It is therefore virtually impossible for him to answer the question 'What justification could there be for rules requiring that those who break them should be made to suffer?' except perhaps in theological terms. For appeals to authority apart, we can justify rules and institutions only by showing that they yield advantages. Consequently retributivist answers to the problem can be shown, on analysis, to be either mere affirmations of the desirability of punishment, or utilitarian reasons in disguise. To the first class belong assertions of the type 'it is fitting (or justice requires) that the guilty should suffer'. For to say 'it is fitting' is only to say that it ought to be the case, and it is just this that is in question. To say, with Kant, that punishment is a good in itself, is to deny the necessity for justification; for to justify is to provide reasons in terms of something else accepted as valuable. But it is by no means evident that punishment needs no justification, the proof being that many people have felt the need to justify it. Again it might be argued that the concept 'a legal system' necessarily implies punishment; but even so, one might still ask why we should have systems of just that sort.

Some concession, however, might be made to Kant's point of view of a type which would be consistent with denying that punishment is a good in itself. For, although it might be argued, as by utilitarians, that the pain of punishment is something that requires justification, some grounds must also be produced for stipulating that such pain, if justifiably inflicted, should be confined to those who have committed offences. For it might be the case that the infliction of pain on the relatives of offenders or on their employers was a more effective deter-rent than inflicting it on the offenders themselves. In 'it is fitting that the guilty should suffer' stress should be put on 'the guilty' rather than on 'suffer'. It would then be a re-iteration of the principle of justice which, we have insisted,* must always go along with the consideration of interests affected by rules. For laws, by their very nature, are directed against people who actually do or are likely to do certain sorts of things. And these sorts of things are things like murder or theft which people can reasonably be said to *choose* to do; they are not things like measles that just happen to them. To inflict pain on people who have not, by their choice, put themselves into the category in question (e.g. of thieves or murderers) would be to discriminate against them on irrelevant grounds. It would be to disregard their claims and to treat them merely as tools for discouraging others. In so far, then, as the retributi-vists insist on the principles of justice, they have an element of a case in that they stress the injustice of treating people as guilty when they are in fact innocent. But what cannot be granted to them is their thesis that the infliction of pain on anyone at all is ever desirable without any further justification being given.

Some retributivists argue that while punishment is a *prima facie* evil, and thus in need of justification, it is less objectionable than that the wicked should prosper. This is to subsume the rule 'Crimes ought to be punished' under a more general rule: either 'The wicked ought to be less well off than the virtuous' or 'The wicked ought not to profit from their crimes'. But 'wickedness' involves assessment of character; we do not punish men for their wickedness, but for particular breaches of law. There may be some ignoble but prudent characters who have never

* See Ch. 2, Sections IV and V, and Ch. 5, passim.

broken a law, and never been punished, and noble ones who have—
our system of punishment is not necessarily the worse for that. We may
have to answer for our characters on the Day of Judgment, but not at
Quarter Sessions. The State is not an agent of cosmic justice; it punishes
only such acts as are contrary to legal rules, conformity to which, even
from unworthy motives like fear, is considered of public importance.
And if we offer the narrower ground, that the wicked ought not to
profit from their *crimes*, we are bound to justify the distinction between
crimes and offences against morals in general. What is the special virtue
of legal rules, that a breach of them alone warrants punishment? It
seems that the wicked are to be prevented from prospering only if their
wickedness manifests itself in selected ways; but how is the selection
made, unless in terms of its consequences? In any case, if we permit the
subsumption of 'Crime ought to be punished' under the more general
'The wicked out not to prosper', it would still be proper to seek justification for the latter. It would not help to say 'Justice requires punishment'; for this is but to reiterate that there is no need for further
justification. It might be argued that in such a universe, where the
wicked prospered, there would be no inducement to virtue. But this
move would merely defer the utilitarian stage of justification; it would
not render it superfluous.

A similar veiled utilitarianism underlies Hegel's treatment of punishment, as an annulment of the wrong.[5] It is not easy to see how a wrong
can be annulled: what is done cannot, in a literal sense, be undone. It is
possible to make restitution for some wrongs, but this is beside the point,
for punishment is the infliction of suffering not the exaction of compensation or restitution. A man may be sent to prison for injuring
another, and *also* be liable for damages. Punishment is not intended to
restore the fortunes of the victim. But if it were, the justification would
be in terms of the better condition of the victim, or of society in general
which would result from the punishment, and, like all utilitarianism,
this is forward looking. So also is another Hegelian argument, that the
idea of right, which law embodies, would be denied, unless it were re-
affirmed through the machinery of punishment. But why should it be
re-affirmed in precisely this form? Would not formal condemnation of
the wrong principle which the crime exemplified, be sufficient? In
evidence to the Royal Commission on Capital Punishment, Lord
Justice Denning declared: 'The ultimate justification of any punishment
is not that it is a deterrent, but that it is the emphatic denunciation by the
community of a crime.'[6] But 'punishment' does not mean 'denunciation',
nor does the necessity for denunciation, which may coincide with that
for punishment, imply a right or duty to inflict suffering on those

denounced. Even if it did, the justification would be utilitarian, since the need for denunciation rests presumably on the need to uphold law for the general advantage.

Others have treated punishment as if it were a sort of automatic reflex, a response of the social order to the crime, following in the nature of things like a hang-over.[7] But this is to confuse rules with scientific laws. It is in the nature of things that certain physical acts have certain unavoidable physical consequences; but the penal consequences of a breach of legal rules follow only because human beings have made that sort of a rule. We do not need to justify the laws of nature, because there is no way of making them other than they are; social rules must be justified because they are different in precisely this way. To treat punishment as a natural, unwilled response to a breach of law is to class it with natural phenomena, about which questions of justification do not arise; it is not to justify it. It is of course true that once we have agreed on the need for penal laws, any particular act of punishment might be justified (though not necessarily sufficiently justified) by reference to a rule that has been broken. This may explain how it comes about that people think that punishment is a sort of social reflex. But it is a point of view that presupposes a system of punishment that has already been accepted.[8]

Lastly, among so-called retributive justifications, we must consider one advanced by Bosanquet:

> 'Compulsion through punishment and the fear of it, though primarily acting on the lower self, does tend, when the conditions of true punishment exist (i.e. the reaction of systems of rights violated by one who shares in it), to a recognition of the end by the person punished, and may so far be regarded as his own will, implied in the maintenance of a system to which he is a party, returning upon himself in the form of pain. And this is the theory of punishment as retributive . . . The punishment is, so to speak, his right, of which he must not be defrauded.'[9]

Now it must be admitted that few criminals seek to destroy the entire social order, and the average burglar would no doubt feel indignant if his own house were burgled. He might even agree, in principle, that law-breakers should be punished. Yet his efforts to elude the police are evidence enough that he does not will his own punishment, in any ordinary sense of the phrase. He may be unreasonable and immoral in making a special exception in his own favour—but that does not justify constructing a theory of punishment on a hypothetical will (which Bosanquet calls his 'real will') that would be his were he reasonable and moral; for then he might not be a burglar. To treat punishment as if it were self-imposed is to offer a spurious account, in terms of consent, of something that, in the nature of the case, most criminals will always do their best to avoid.

To say, with Bosanquet that punishment is the 'right' of the criminal is to disregard one of the usual criteria governing the use of the word 'right', namely, that it is something which will be enforced only if the subject so chooses, the corollary being that it operates to his advantage. Only by pretending that punishment is self-imposed can we think of the criminal as exercising a choice, and only by treating it as reformative can we regard it as to his advantage. Indeed, Bosanquet does introduce a reformative justification in saying that punishment tends 'to a recognition of the end by the person punished'. But that is a utilitarian, not a retributive justification.[10] The acceptable part of Bosanquet's view is connected with a point which we have made earlier. Men put themselves into the category of offenders by choice; it is not something that just happens to them. It is odd to say that people choose to be punished; but it is their choice which has put them into a special category. In this respect they are relevantly different from other people who have not so chosen.

Retributive justifications of punishment in general are unsatisfactory, we have suggested, for the very reason that they refuse to look to the consequences of rules of this sort, denying thereby a necessary part of the procedure for justifying rules. And there is no reason why we should limit ourselves to the consequences for the criminal. It would be an odd sort of theory that was ready to accept punishment in principle, because of the good it did to criminals, but refused to consider possible benefits or damage to the rest of the community. We need not be put off by Kant's injunction that the criminal must be treated as an end, providing that in weighing advantages and disadvantages to everyone we do not lose sight of his welfare altogether; we are not bound to treat it as our sole legitimate concern. There is nothing in the utilitarian approach, as Bentham understood it, that denies this principle. The criminal must, like anyone else, 'count for one'; but he must not count for 'more than one'.

Bentham's case is that punishment is a technique of social control which is justified so long as it prevents more mischief than it produces. At the point where the damage to the criminal outweighs the expected advantage to the rest of society, it loses that justification. As a technique, it operates advantageously in three ways (though these need not exhaust the possibilities): by reforming the criminal, by preventing him (e.g. by death or imprisonment) from repeating the offence, and by deterring others from like offences.

i. *Reformation.* Not all theories dealing with the reform of criminals are theories of punishment, in our sense. We must distinguish theories dealing with reformative measures to *accompany* the punishment from those which hold that the suffering intrinsic to the idea of punishment is itself reformative. Detention in a mental hospital may not be in itself an essential part of the process of curing mental disorders, though it may provide a convenient opportunity for psycho-therapy. Similarly, prison reformers concerned with the moral re-education of criminals are offering theories of punishment in a strict sense only if they expect the suffering involved in loss of liberty, prison discipline, etc. itself to lead to reformation. This is important, for though reformative treatment might cure criminal inclinations by relaxing the rigours of punishment, it might still defeat the ends of punishment, if it reduced the deterrent effects for others.

'Reformation' is in any case ambiguous. A prison sentence may persuade a man that 'crime does not pay'; but in that case he is as much deterred by example as anyone who learns the lesson at second hand. He would be a 'reformed character' only if he showed remorse for his past misdeeds, and resolved not to repeat them, not through fear of further punishment, but simply because they were wrong. It is questionable whether punishment produces this sort of moral reformation in very many cases. Some offenders may be shaken by imprisonment into reflecting on their behaviour and resolve to do better; it is at least as likely, however, that the blow to self-respect, and criminal associations, may lead to moral deterioration. We attempt to reform first offenders by passing them over to the probation officer, rather than to the prison warder. There is, however, the further point that, no matter how humane the intentions of the officials providing reformative treatment, it will almost certainly be accompanied by some compulsion and carry some elements of stigma and rebuke, which would tend to act as deterrents.

This is not to say that punishment is never justifiable as reformative; but it is questionable, on utilitarian grounds, whether the reformative benefits alone of the institution would justify it.

ii. *Prevention.* Similarly, though we should not regard it as the *main* purpose of punishment to prevent crime by removing or otherwise disabling the potential criminal, this aim is recognized, in long terms of 'preventive detention' for hardened criminals, and in sentences of transportation and deportation. The death penalty is thought by some to be similarly justified. It is clear, however, that the case for punishment as prevention is convincing only for criminals with several convictions; for in other cases we are not entitled to assume that the offender would repeat his crime.

iii. *Deterrence.* The strongest utilitarian case for punishment is that it serves to deter potential offenders by inflicting suffering on actual ones. On this view, punishment is not the main things; the technique works by threat. Every act of punishment is to that extent an admission of failure, and we punish only that the technique may retain some effectiveness in the future. The problem of justifying punishment arises only because the technique is not completely effective; if it were, there would be nothing to justify.

Retributivists do not of course deny that punishment can act in these ways, nor that it has these advantages. They maintain only that they are incidental, and that a system of punishment devised solely on these principles would lead to monstrous injustices, which we shall consider in the next section. However that may be, it is evident that while the utilitarian can provide *some* sort of justification, the retributivist is either offering utilitarian arguments in disguise, or virtually denying that punishment in general needs any justification at all. Of course there is no arguing with him if he *consistently* takes his stand on the intuition that there ought to be punishment. If a retributivist just insists that it is morally repugnant that a man should do an injury to another man without suffering injury himself there is little more to be said. For by standing on such an 'intuition' he is claiming that there are no further reasons for his principle. The utilitarian can only point out to the retributivist that a great many people think that punishment requires some justification; that he can provide good reasons for punishing people; and that, though it is intolerable that there should be murder, rape, and dope-peddling, punishment is just one way of reducing the incidence of such admitted evils. He sees nothing intrinsically fitting about this particular way, which itself involves increasing the misery in the world. The strength of the retributivist position lies, however, in his approach to the justification of the particular act of punishment, which we must now consider.

(e) Justifying particular punishments

i. *Retributivist criticisms of utilitarianism.* Critics of the utilitarian approach contend that it would justify punishing not only the guilty but the innocent too. For if punishment is justified solely by its effects, would it not be permissible to manufacture evidence against an innocent man, in order to provide an example to others? If there were an outbreak of crimes particularly difficult to detect, and if people generally could be persuaded that an innocent man had in fact committed such a crime, would not the utilitarian conditions for punishment be adequately satisfied? Alternatively, if the advantages of deterrence could be achieved by merely *seeming* to punish a criminal, would it not be wrong to do more than pretend to punish him, since the advantages could then be had without the disadvantages?[11] Again, to the extent that the utilitarian relies on reformative or preventive benefits, would he not seem justified in punishing before a crime had been committed? If a man were thought to be contemplating, or even capable of, an offence, might he not be sent to prison and a crime thereby prevented, with the prospect of a reformed character thrown in for good measure?

If utilitarianism could really be shown to involve punishing the innocent, or a false parade of punishment, or punishment in anticipation of an offence, these criticisms would no doubt be conclusive. They are, however, based on a misconception of what the utilitarian theory is about. We said at the beginning of this chapter that 'punishment' implied, in its primary sense, not the inflicting of *any* sort of suffering, but inflicting suffering under certain specified conditions, one of which was that it must be for a breach of a rule. Now if we insist on this criterion for the use of the word, 'punishment of the innocent' becomes a logical impossibility. For it follows from the definition of 'punishment' that suffering inflicted on the innocent cannot be '*punishment*'. It is not a question of what is morally justified, but of what is logically possible.*

When we talk of 'punishing the innocent', we may mean: (i) 'pretending to punish', in the sense of manufacturing evidence or otherwise imputing guilt, while knowing a man to be innocent. This would be to treat him *as if* he were guilty, and involve the lying assertion that he was. It is morally objectionable, not only as a lie, but because it involves treating an innocent person differently from others without justification, or for an irrelevant reason, the reason offered being falsely grounded.[12] (ii) We may mean, by 'punish', 'cause to suffer'; we might use it, for example, of a case in which suffering is inflicted where there is no offence in question, and so where no guilt, actual or pretended, is implied. Further, suffering might not be the main intention, but only incidental to some other aim. In that case, it could not be said that as a matter of *logical necessity*, it is wrong to punish the innocent. To imprison members of a subversive political party, treating them *in that respect* like criminals, though no offence had been proved or even charged, would not necessarily be immoral, especially if the intention were not primarily that they should suffer, but to prevent them causing mischief. Persons believed by the Secretary of State 'to be of hostile origin or association' were detained, under war-time Defence Regulation 18b, though technically guiltless of an offence. Critics of the Regulation

---

* An analogous relation between 'guilt' and 'pardon' accounts for the oddness of 'granting a free pardon' to a convicted man later found to be innocent.

might have attacked this as 'punishment of the innocent'—but they would have been borrowing implications of the primary sense of 'punishment' to attack a type of action to which these did not apply. For it is only *necessarily* improper to 'punish the innocent' if we pretend they are guilty, and if suffering is essential to the intention, i.e. if we accept all the primary usage criteria. If we use the word in some looser sense, there might be a case for acting in this way in special circumstances.

We are arguing that in exceptional conditions it may be legitimate to inflict suffering as a technique of social control or policy, without relation to offences under rules, just as we detain lunatics or enemy aliens. Such suffering is not, however, in the primary sense of the word, 'punishment', and is not *therefore* objectionable as 'punishment of the innocent' (though it may be on other grounds). It is only when it is deliberately inflicted on the pretext of guilt that it is open to the retributivist objections. The short answer to the critics of utilitarian theories of punishment, is that they are theories of 'punishment', not of *any* sort of technique involving suffering.

It might be objected that we are seeking to answer a moral objection with a definition. For why should we stop short at inflicting suffering on *offenders*? Supposing we could protect society yet further by having a rule that authorized inflicting suffering on, say, the relatives of offenders, if the actual offenders had vanished or escaped abroad? Though it might be strictly inaccurate to describe such a system as 'punishment' it might well serve the same purpose as punishment. Such a system would be highly objectionable, at any rate in any ordinary circumstances; but could it not be justified by the utilitarian procedure of appealing to the net advantage of having such a system?

On a crude understanding of utilitarianism, it could; but it would leave out of account the considerations of impartiality and respect for persons which we have argued are as necessary to the idea of morality as regard for consequences. It is not inconsistent with regarding a man as a source of claims, with ends of his own deserving of respect, to have a system of punishment which lays it down that people who choose to break rules suffer penalties. In a sense, to have *rules* forbidding certain types of conduct commits us to doing *something* to discourage people from breaking them. As a responsible person, the potential offender can decide whether to put himself in the class of persons liable to punishment. But this is not the case if the victims of the suffering to be inflicted are not themselves offenders. They would be made to suffer only as instruments for inflicting suffering on the real offender. Their own claims would have received no consideration at all; nor would they have *put themselves* in the class of people liable to punishment. They would be passive levers employed by society to bring pressure to bear upon potential offenders, without themselves being offenders. This would be morally intolerable.*

ii. *The retributive theory*

We are now able to examine the strength and the weakness of the retributive position itself.

'If there is any opinion to which the man of uncultivated morals is attached' (wrote F. H. Bradley) 'it is the belief in the necessary connection of punishment and guilt. Punishment is punishment, only where it is deserved. We pay the penalty, because we owe it, and for no other reason; and if punishment is inflicted for any other reason whatever than because it is merited by wrong, it is a gross immorality, a crying injustice, an abominable crime, and not what it pretends to be.'[13]

What is misleading in this way of putting the case, is that it overlooks the extent to which this is a definition of 'punishment'. The 'necessary connection of punishment and guilt' is a logical connection. It would be more accurate to write 'Punishment is "punishment", only when it is deserved'—for the inverted commas indicate that the sentence is about the way a word is to be used, not about the qualities of the act. A. M. Quinton has put this point succinctly: 'It is not, as some retributivists think, that we *may* not punish the innocent and *ought* only to punish the guilty, but that we *cannot* punish the innocent and *must* only punish the guilty . . . The infliction of suffering on a person is only properly described as punishment if that person is guilty. The retributivist thesis, therefore, is not a moral doctrine, but an account of the meaning of the word "punishment".'[14] This is strictly true, but it presupposes the moral principle, which we have already allowed, that inflicting suffering on *offenders* is the only systematic way of inflicting suffering to maintain law which is morally defensible in most circumstances.

So long, then, as the retributive thesis is limited to saying that no act of punishment is justified that is not the consequence of a breach of

* It might be, however, that in very exceptional conditions one might take the claims of such people into account, but decide, nevertheless, that it was so important that the law should be upheld that they must be put aside. It is impossible to say, without reference to any particular context, that such a choice would be wrong. But it would have to be a *choice:*—maintaining the law would have to be quite deliberately chosen as more important than the claims of the innocents not to be made to suffer without having committed an offence. On occasion, a schoolmaster may feel justified in punishing a whole class of boys, if he cannot find the actual offenders and feels that it is vital for discipline that the guilty shall not escape unpunished.

law, it is unobjectionable—but its truth depends on the meaning of the words used. This is not however the only interpretation that could be put on retributive theory. For it might be held that the theory points to a close connection between punishment and *moral* guilt.[15] The connection however cannot be very close. For moral guilt is not a *sufficient* condition of punishment, there being many offences like lying, which are moral offences, but which are not dealt with as punishable offences, like making false declarations of income to the Inspector of Taxes. It is difficult to maintain even that moral guilt is a *necessary* condition for punishment. For since it is the duty of the judge to apply law as it is, not to question its morality, from his point of view at least it would be right to punish a purely legal offence. It would also be open to the utilitarian to argue that, though one might be morally guiltless in disobeying a mischievous law, punishment would be unjustifiable, not because of the absence of moral guilt, but because no mischievous law could justify the further mischief of punishment. It is not a question of what conditions a particular act of punishment must satisfy, but of the conditions that a *rule* must satisfy if punishment is to be properly attached to a breach of it.

It remains, however, to consider how the utilitarian approach should deal with the question of justifying the particular act of punishment. To ask, in respect of every particular case, that it be justified as preventing more mischief than it causes would be to miss the point of punishment as an institution. Once we agree that rules are desirable, and that they ought to take a particular form, there is always a *prima facie* case for applying them whenever appropriate occasions arise. For there would be no point in having rules if, on every separate occasion, we were required to balance the probable consequences of keeping them or ignoring them. Such a process would defeat the very purpose of the rule, which is to introduce regularity and predictability into human intercourse.[16] It would be especially self-defeating in respect of punishment. Punishment would not be an effective deterrent unless it could be relied upon to follow every breach of law, except in circumstances sufficiently well-understood for the exceptions not to constitute a source of uncertainty, diminishing the effectiveness of the threat. This is not to say that guilt should be a sufficient condition, nor even that no discretion should be permitted to judges in deciding whether a particular case called for punishment or not. It means only that guilt once established, there is a case for punishment which has to be defeated. Proof of an offence is sufficient to overcome the initial utilitarian presumption against causing suffering, and the onus of proof then rests on whoever would set the punishment aside.

II. DETERMINING THE APPROPRIATE DEGREE OF PUNISHMENT

The characteristic of a retributive theory of punishment, we have said, is that it looks backward to the crime, not forward to the consequences of the punishment. And this approach is linked by some, though not all, retributivists to a belief that liability to punishment ought to be related to moral guilt, i.e. that men ought to be punished for their wickedness, or at least, that only wicked men deserve punishment. The utilitarian, on the other hand, regards punishment purely as a way of maintaining rules, and judges it according to the degree that the suffering it prevents outweighs the suffering it inflicts. These two attitudes are carried over into discussions of the degree of severity of the punishments which ought to be inflicted for different offences.

One of the criticisms levelled against utilitarianism is that by relating the justification of punishment to its expected consequences, rather than to the crime itself, it would seem to justify penalties divorced from the relative seriousness of crimes. Thus, if the only way to deter people from trivial offences were to impose major penalties, it would appear justifiable, on a utilitarian view, to punish parking offences more severely than, say, robbery with violence. Bentham held that where detection is difficult, and the risk of punishment accordingly diminished, greater severity ought to compensate for the uncertainty. On this view, a serious but easily detected crime might warrant lesser penalties than a minor but secret one. This conclusion being to the retributivist intolerable, he contends that to escape it we must seek the measure of punishment in the crime itself, relating it to the degree of wickedness involved in committing it.

Once again it is important to distinguish criteria for the justification of rules from those for justifying their application in particular cases. To ask 'How much punishment is appropriate to a given offence?' is ambiguous; for the question may refer either to the punishment allotted by a rule to a particular *class* of acts, or to *one particular* act within that class. Penal laws generally emphasize the distinction; they rarely prescribe one precise punishment for every offence of a given type, but rather stipulate a maximum (and occasionally a minimum) penalty, leaving determination of particular penalties to the judge's discretion. Two questions emerge: one, the legislator's, asks 'What principles are relevant to the determination of maximum (or standard) punishments for offences of different classes?'; the second, the judge's, asks 'By what criteria, in addition to the maximum (and perhaps the minimum) penalty prescribed by the law, ought I decide the punishment appropriate to a given criminal action?'

(a) *Principles relevant to the determination of penalties for different classes of offences*

'The only case' said Kant, 'in which the offender cannot complain that he is being treated unjustly is if his crime recoils upon himself and he suffers what he has inflicted on another, if not in a literal sense, at any rate according to the spirit of the law.' 'It is only *the right of requital* (jus talionis) which can fix definitely the quality and quantity of the punishment.'[17] This is the most extreme retributive position, but its essential weakness is discernible in any more moderate attempt to relate the punishment directly to the nature of the crime.

The retaliatory principle of 'an eye for an eye' will work literally only in a few special cases, and in some of these it would be rejected as intolerably cruel. But if we are to take it in some other sense, 'in the spirit of the law', it involves a sort of arithmetical equation of suffering as impracticable as Bentham's hedonsitic calculus. Suffering of one sort cannot be *equated* with another, though it may be possible to prefer one to another (or to be indifferent as between one and another). I can certainly say that I would rather see A suffer in one way than B in another; or that there is really nothing to choose between the two. But this is quite different from saying that A ought to be made to suffer in exactly the same degree as B, whom he has injured; for this involves not a preference enunciated by some third person, but a quasi-quantitative comparison of the sufferings of two different people, treated as objective facts. And there is no way of making this comparison, even though the external features of their suffering may be identical. It is even more evidently impossible when the suffering of one is occasioned by, say, blackmail, and of the other by imprisonment.* Short of literal retaliation, there is no way in which the crime can be made the measure of the punishment, unless reference can be made to some predetermined scale. But the question then becomes that of drawing up the scale. This difficulty remains in the retributive theory as presented by Mr J. D. Mabbott. While admitting that there can be no direct relation between the offence and the penalty, he maintains that by comparing one crime with another we can make an estimate of the punishments *relatively* appropriate: 'We can grade crimes in a rough scale and penalties in a rough scale, and keep our heaviest penalties for what are socially the most serious wrongs regardless of whether these penalties . . . are exactly what deterrence would require.'[18] What, however, are we to

---

* Hegel virtually admits the impossibility of a rational answer to these questions (*Philosophy of Right*, § 101), but insists that there must be a right answer (§ 214), to which we must try, empirically, to approximate. But by what test shall we judge whether our shots at justice are approaching, or receding from the target?

understand by 'socially the most serious wrongs'? Part at least of what we should mean by that phrase is that we ought to do our utmost to prevent them. The most serious wrongs are the ones we are least ready to tolerate. Consequently, these are not only the ones we blame most severely; they are also the ones we feel justified in penalizing most heavily, in order to deter people from committing them. It is difficult to see, then, how deterrence could be left out in constructing or justifying such a scale. Again, there is surely no doubt that in allocating penalties for offences against, say, currency or import regulations, what is most relevant is not the severity with which we *blame* the offence in any moral sense, but the profit that the offender might expect to make on such a transaction. Crime must not *pay*, however mildly we might blame it. It is not easy, with offences of this sort, to know what degree of blame is appropriate, because they are offences against morality only because there is a *prima facie* moral duty to obey the law. It is difficult to feel very deeply about breaches of rules which might be quite different in six months' time; but that is not a reason for punishing them leniently, if that would destroy the effectiveness of the rules.

The retributivist's difficulty is that he wants the crime itself to indicate the amount of punishment, which it cannot do unless we first assume a scale of crimes and penalties. But on what principles is the scale to be constructed, and how are new offences to be fitted into it? These difficulties admit of no solution unless we agree to examine the consequences to be expected from penalties of different degrees of severity; i.e. unless we adopt a utilitarian approach. It remains to be seen whether this can be done without our having to concede the retributivist case that this might involve severe penalties for trivial offences.

For the utilitarian, arguing in deterrent terms, it is the threat rather that the punishment itself which is primary. Could we rely on the threat being completely effective, there could be no objection to the death penalty for every offence, since ex hypothesi there would be no occasion ever to inflict it. Unhappily, since no detection system is perfect, punishment can never be utterly certain, and we must reckon on some offenders taking the risk, and therefore upon the need to inflict *some* punishments, if the threat is to remain effective for others. We must suppose, therefore, for each type of crime, a scale of possible penalties, to each of which would correspond a number of probable occasions on which it would be necessary to carry out the threat, the number presumably decreasing (though at a diminishing rate) as the penalty increases. Ultimately, however, we should almost certainly reach a hard core of offenders who, by reason perhaps of a misguided certainty that they would never be caught, would remain undeterred whatever the penalty. We should then choose, for each class of offence, a penalty which will prevent too much damage to the community, without inflicting an intolerable amount of suffering on offenders. A little more, and we might prefer more crimes to inflicting it; a little less, and we should reduce the number of crimes by increasing it. (This is Bentham's principle of 'frugality'.)[19]

This statement of the case might appear to suffer from precisely the same weakness as the retaliatory theories, namely, that it involves a quantitative comparison of harm done to the community on the one hand, and the criminal on the other. But this is not so. We say something like this: To increase the penalty for parking offences to life imprisonment would reduce congestion on the roads by making people more careful where they parked. Nevertheless, the inconvenience of a larger number of offences would not justify so sweeping a disregard for the liberty even of a very few offenders. With blackmail or murder, the mischief of the offence is so great that the possibility of averting further instances defeats to a far greater extent the claims of the offender. One parking offence more or less is of no great moment; one murder more or less is.* We should consequently feel justified in inflicting heavier penalties.

This type of assessment does not involve the quantitative computations of retributivist theory. Whereas in that case we were asked to estimate the damage done by the crime, and then to inflict that amount on the criminal, here we are required only to choose between one combination of circumstances and another—between, say, a certain degree of congestion on the roads plus a certain amount of suffering to a given number of offenders, and a lesser congestion plus more suffering, though to fewer offenders. This type of choice may not always be easy to make—but many moral choices *are* difficult. The point is that there is nothing theoretically impossible, or even unusual, about asking people to make it. We are accustomed to expressing *preferences* between things incapable of quantitative comparisons; what is impossible is to assess how much one man has suffered by being blackmailed, and to inflict a similar amount of suffering on the blackmailer in terms of a prison sentence.

It is apparent that the criticism levelled at utilitarianism, that it would justify severe penalties for relatively trivial offences, is groundless. For

* If the difference between the death penalty and imprisonment for life could be shewn to involve even a small difference in the number of murders likely to be committed, the case for the former would be accordingly stronger. But the Royal Commission on Capital Punishment (1949–53), having weighed the statistical evidence, concluded that it was important 'not to base a penal policy in relation to murder on exaggerated estimates of the uniquely deterrent force of the death penalty'. Cmd. 8932, § 790 (3).

part of what we mean when we call an offence 'relatively trivial' is that we do not care so much about people committing that one as we do about others; and that, in turn, implies that we should be unwilling to inflict so much suffering to prevent it. Similarly, 'relatively serious' crimes are those that are relatively intolerable; and to describe them in this way is to say that we feel justified in going to much greater lengths to prevent them. If this is so, the proposition 'Trivial crimes do not deserve severe penalties' is analytic, being necessarily the consequence of the way we use 'trivial' in this context. Like the other retributive criticisms of utilitarianism discussed, it rests on a definition.*

(b) Criteria governing the allocation of penalties to particular offenders

We distinguished earlier between the legislator's question, which seeks criteria for determining maximum (and perhaps minimum) penalties for different classes of crime, and the judge's question, which seeks criteria for determining the penalty appropriate to a particular offender. Two men guilty of what is technically the same offence are not necessarily awarded the same punishment. On the principle that justice requires that equals be treated equally, this would seem *prima facie* unjust, unless we can suggest criteria, other than legal guilt, by which they might properly be considered unequal. Now judges do employ such criteria; it makes a difference whether a man has previous convictions, whether he has acted under strong provocation, or temptation, or duress. These considerations would be relevant not only to the determination of punishment, but also of blame, and the coincidence of criteria certainly lends colour to the retributive view that the degree of moral guilt, or blameworthiness, is relevant to the determination of punishment. If we are to continue to maintain the mainly utilitarian position that we have adopted hitherto, we must meet two possible objections arising from these considerations:

(i) Is it consistent with utilitarianism that we look to the particular conditions of the crime, and of the criminal, for the measure of punishment? From the point of view of deterrence, does it make any difference that X acted under temptation, or provocation? Should we not look forward to the exemplary advantage of the maximum penalty, rather than backward to the extenuating circumstances of the crime? And if we

---

* There are people who would rather suffer any crimes than inflict certain penalties, e.g. torture or death, which they regard as absolutely wrong. This need not mean that such penalties can *never* be right, but only that there are no *imaginable* circumstances in which their consequences could justify them. But some absolutists altogether deny that consequences are relevant; they are then makin gan ultimate judgment which cannot be discussed, and for which justification can be neither offered nor sought.

do not do this, is it not because we accept the relevance of criteria of moral guilt to the determination of penalties?

We argued earlier that once rules are accepted, there is no need to justify every particular application of them in terms of its beneficent consequences. What is necessary, then, in this case, is to justify in utilitarian terms the criteria of extenuation, not each application of them.

Now there are some conditions, like unavoidable ignorance or mistake of fact, lunacy, infancy, or irresistible duress, which completely exonerate an offender, both in morals and in law. We neither blame nor punish a person for breaking a rule unless the act is intentional and the offender a responsible person, who knows what he is doing and knows that it is wrong. For it is only in such a case that a man could be said to *put himself* in the category liable to blame or punishment. In the cases we are considering a person might be said, *prima facie*, to have broken the law and therefore to have placed himself in the normal category of law-breaker. But this case is defeated by any of the considerations mentioned which would make a relevant difference between this and the normal law-breaker. And justice demands a distinction in treatment. Consequently, no act committed under the conditions mentioned would be either punishable or blameworthy.

The recognition of such criteria, however, could also be defended in strictly utilitarian terms. If the principle object of punishment is to act as a deterrent, it can be effective only in respect of *deliberate* acts. Accordingly, if it is waived on any of the grounds mentioned, its effectiveness is not impaired. The same man contemplating murder gets no encouragement if a homicidal maniac escapes punishment, since the defence of insanity would not be open to *him*. It would be a pointless mischief, then, to make men suffer for any but deliberate offences.

Again, there are conditions like strong temptation or provocation which mitigate the degree of blame and would also justify a milder penalty. Unlike the conditions just discussed these extenuate rather than exonerate. They are, however, sufficiently like those conditions for us to feel, on rather vague grounds of fairness, that a distinction ought properly to be drawn between offences committed under them and the normal case. A utilitarian, however, would be reluctant to make such concessions unless he were assured that there would be no weakening of the threat. An offence committed under such conditions would be exceptional, and leniency could be expected only under similar conditions. And though these might not be such as to warrant saying that a person acting under them was not responsible, in such a state of mind he would be unlikely to take much account of the threat of punishment.

If that were so, it would be pointless to inflict the full measure of suffering provided for the offence.* Suppose, however, that it could be shown that crimes of passion could as a matter of fact be successfully discouraged by very severe penalties, such that the extra suffering inflicted on actual offenders was more than justified by the extra protection given to society, there would be a conflict between the vague notion of fairness which makes us talk of passion as an extenuating circumstance and the purely utilitarian considerations of prevention and deterrence.

(*ii*) The second possible objection is that since the criteria tending to mitigate blame and punishment coincide in so many particulars, should we not be justified in saying that men deserve punishment only to the extent that they are morally guilty (or wicked, or blameworthy)?

This would be so if there were a complete correspondence of criteria—but this is not the case. The question of motive is crucial. We generally regard a man as less blameworthy if, in breaking a rule, he does so 'from the highest motives', instead of selfishly or maliciously. A traitor prompted by conscientious political convictions might be blamed for wrongheadedness, but we might still respect his integrity, and blame him less than a merely mercenary one. Now this type of consideration is sometimes important in mitigating punishment (e.g. in the case of 'mercy-killing'), but by no means always. Sincere fifth-columnists cannot expect to be treated less severely than merely disgruntled or ambitious ones. A man's motives are frequently so obscure and so difficult to establish objectively, that leniency on this account might well invite the insincere to counterfeit sincerity, with no way of unmasking the cheat.† A man's

---

* Cf. Bosanquet, op. cit. pp. 214–5. 'The true reason for allowing circumstances which change the character of the act to influence the sentence is that, in changing its character, they may take it out of the class of offences to which it *prima facie* belongs, and from which men need to be deterred by a recognized amount of severity. If a man is starving and steals a turnip, his offence, being so exceptionally conditioned, does not threaten the general right of property, and does not need to be associated with any high degree of terror in order to protect that right. A man who steals under no extraordinary pressure of need does what might become a common practice if not associated with as much terror as is found by experience to deter men from theft.'

† Consider, in this connection, the difficulty of distinguishing the genuine survivor of a suicide pact, who has been unable to carry out his side of the bargain, from the 'cheat' who relies on a counterfeit pact to evade the maximum penalty for murder. (See the Report on Capital Punishment, §§ 163–176.) The same applies to 'mercy-killings': 'How, for example, were the jury to decide whether a daughter has killed her invalid father from compassion, from a desire for material gain, from a natural wish to bring to an end a trying period of her life, or from a combination of motives?' (Ibid. § 179). Nevertheless, where we feel reasonably sure that the motive was merciful, we expect leniency. Bosanquet's account is probably sufficient justification: a mercy-killing is not really in

high motives may sometimes be a reason for not punishing him at all;
but in other cases they may be a reason for punishing him as severely as
the law allows. For the conscientious offender may be the stubbornest
of all: his scruples may be far less easily overborne by threats of punishment than more selfish motives. Only the man of weak conviction is
likely to be put off by threats of punishment. The effectiveness of
government, if not its very survival, could well depend on its success in
coercing conscientious but recalcitrant minorities. In that case, conscientious motives could scarcely be admitted in extenuation of the
offence. On the other hand, the severity of the penalty necessary to
secure a high degree of conformity might be a mischief outweighing
the advantage gained. It might then be reasonable to give up punishing
conscientious offenders altogether, if they can be discerned from the
fakes. We no longer punish conscientious objectors to military service,
having learnt by experience that they are rarely amenable to threats, that
they are unsatisfactory soldiers if coerced, and that, given a rigorous
test of conscientiousness, there will not be enough of them to frustrate
the community's purpose. In this instance, the motive has been formally
embodied into the rule, such that anyone who breaks it conscientiously,
and in accordance with recognized procedures, does not in fact break it
at all.

Though there is a considerable overlapping of the criteria for awarding
blame and punishment, the case of motive seems to indicate that they
are not necessarily identical. The wide area of coincidence seems nevertheless to demand explanation. Morality, like law, is a system of rules
for guiding behaviour, and blame is to the one what punishment is to
the other. Many rules supported by blame (including self-blame, or
remorse) appear also as legal rules upheld by punishments; for the ends
of moral guidance are largely similar to those of legal control. But
qualities of character, and therefore the motives for actions, count for
more in moral than in legal judgments; for morality operates not merely
by prescribing or prohibiting certain classes of action, but also by
training character (and therefore conduct in general) by praise and
blame of 'the whole man'. We blame men for being bad-tempered; we
punish only for assault. Praise and blame, reward and punishment, are
nevertheless closely analogous, and since their functions are broadly
alike, it is not surprising that the criteria for allocating them should
largely correspond. But because we usually blame the criminal we
punish, it does not follow that we therefore do, or ought to, punish

---

the same class as a brutal murder for profit, and we may feel justified in tolerating
a few examples rather than inflict the maximum penalty on this type of offender.

G

according to the criteria of moral guilt. Analogous techniques are likely to employ analogous criteria: but since punishment is administered through formal machinery of investigation, proof, sentence, and execution, according to established rules, the criteria governing its operation are likely to differ in some important respects from those implicit in the informal and personal procedures by which we blame.

The very closeness of the analogy, however, leads us to slip easily in thought from one system to the other. Judges often speak and act as if the criteria of moral guilt were directly relevant to the determination of penalties in particular cases.[20] Conversely, the ordinary man may exclaim in indignation against an offence against morals, 'He deserves to be punished', though no law has been broken. We learn to obey rules in childhood by a mixture of praise and blame, reward and punishment, and we easily assume that the same criteria are appropriate to both types of sanction. But the legal process is a technique for controlling large numbers of people; it necessarily requires different criteria from parental and pedagogical discipline.

Nevertheless, law depends for its effectiveness on public confidence and support. In the nineteenth century, many people came to feel that penalties for trivial offences were often excessive. This led to a perversion of justice in the contrary direction, since juries would refuse to convict on clear evidence of guilt. In the twentieth century, the McNaghten Rules, which define 'insanity' as a legal defence against a murder charge, have been widely criticized, and judges have been known to encourage juries to bring in verdicts of insanity in cases clearly outside the Rules, but to which the death sentence seemed inappropriate on moral grounds.[21] A penal system which has to be applied by judges and juries, and which invites public criticism of its decisions, cannot remain effective if it departs too radically from conventional standards apportioning blame.

III. CONCLUSION

It has not been the purpose of this chapter to advocate or defend any particular set of penal arrangements, nor to suggest that those currently operating in this country are necessarily rationally justifiable. Instead, we have tried to indicate how to go about defending or attacking punishments, in general or in particular. We have asked, not whether this or that arrangement is justified, but what would be the appropriate procedure for justifying it; not, primarily, what criteria are, or ought to be, employed in fixing penalties, but how to go about choosing, or criticizing such criteria. Our main contention has been that punishment is a technique for preventing breaches of rules; like any technique, it must be judged by its results. On the other hand, like any system of rules, once adopted, it implies a *prima facie* case for implementation in particular instances, so that in any normal case it is sufficient to point to a breach of a rule of the appropriate type to justify a penalty. That is not to say that guilt is always a sufficient condition for punishment. There are other reasonably relevant criteria. These, however, must be compatible with the overriding conception of punishment as a technique for upholding rules. Not indeed that *any* penalty could be justified that upheld the rules—for the efficiency of a technique must be judged not only by its achievements but also by its costs. Whatever criteria we employ must satisfy the condition that, while upholding rules, they do not entail so great a measure of suffering that the rules are no longer worth upholding. We have seen that in allocating punishment to a class of offences, we are, in a sense, deciding how much crime of that type we are ready to tolerate, in preference to the alternative of a stricter penalty.

We have provided no short way to a decision on, say, capital punishment as a penalty for murder; we have only indicated the lines on which discussion must go. But if, as some maintain, to abolish it would not impair the effective deterrence or prevention of that crime, there would seem, on our analysis, no further argument by which to defend it.[22]

Finally; punishment is not the sole technique for ensuring that laws are kept. More people obey laws because they respect them than do so because they fear the consequences of breaking them. It is better to create conditions in which there are fewer potential offenders than to keep down the numbers of actual ones by punishing them. As a technique employing deliberate suffering, it must be counted, in moral terms, as costly, to be considered rather as a last resort than as the obvious and natural way of maintaining the social order intact.

CHAPTER 9

FREEDOM AND RESPONSIBILITY

We observed, in discussing the extenuating conditions of punishment, that both blame and punishment presuppose the deliberate intention of a free and responsible agent. Consequently, a case for either could be rebutted by showing that a man was not responsible for his actions. If, for instance, he had been compelled to act with a pistol at his back, or if he were insane and subject to uncontrollable impulses, we should say he could not help doing what he did—that he was not a free agent—and therefore not culpable.

Some people, however, claim that there is a sense in which none of us is free. Everyone, they would say, is formed by his past and by his environment. What he is and what he does can be accounted for by complex causes that go back to childhood and even beyond. Free will is thus an illusion; the choices made by normal men are as much determined as those of lunatics. We are all prisoners of the past.

This view has been widely held to be destructive of morality. For if we are not free to choose between right and wrong, what point could there be in saying we *ought* to choose the right, and *blaming* anyone for choosing the wrong? Similarly, it has often been thought to undermine the moral basis of punishment. For since we have allowed that no one ought to be punished who is not responsible for his actions, would it not seem to follow that if no one is responsible, punishment must be given up altogether, and replaced by remedial treatment? If, as William Godwin said, 'the assassin cannot help the murder he commits any more than the dagger', what point is there in concepts like guilt, responsibility, and punishment?

I. ANALYSIS OF THE TERM 'FREE'

The word 'free' is one which is often used, especially by politicians, but it is not always clear what is meant. Rousseau, for instance, said that man was born free but everywhere he was in chains. Did he mean the same thing by 'free' as Churchill when he advised us to 'set the people free'? All such uses of 'free'—these are only two examples—have something

we are not absolutely free - one is always bound by rules or laws, but as long as we keep within these rules, we are free - → contained freedom.

in common in that they recommend to us whatever state of affairs the term is used to describe. In other words, the word 'free' has a strong commendatory force; it is *prescriptive*. It expresses approval on the part of those who use it and creates an attitude of approval in the minds of the listeners. This also is the case with words like 'democracy'; but this common commending function is quite compatible with the term 'democracy' being used to *describe* quite different systems of government. For instance, people speak of eastern democracy and western democracy. Practically all that such terms have in common is the approval of the speakers for the system to which they are referring; *descriptively* they refer to quite different systems.[1]

The word 'free', then, has a commending function. But has it not some common descriptive meaning? Is there no common feature in the states of affairs *referred* to when we use the term 'free'? The trouble about the term 'free' is that it means too little because it means too much. In this respect it is like the terms 'equal' or 'same'. When we say that all men are equal or that all men are the same, we have not conveyed much information until we state the *respects in which* people are being compared. It is the same with the term 'free'. In general when we say that a person is free, we mean that, if a person *wants* to do something, he will not be impeded by some kind of constraint or limitation. But until we have stipulated what it is that he might want to do and what kind of constraint or limitation is absent, we have not conveyed much information. We have said too little because we have said too much. This is so often the case, especially with political arguments. When one person says that we are more free than we used to be and his opponent denies it, the discussion very often drags on interminably because different sorts of things are being referred to.

Indeed we could go so far as to say that it is only the context in which it is used that gives any sense to the word 'free'; for unlike words like 'square' or 'bovine' it indicates no positive characteristics. It is a word that is used to rule out some suggestion implicit in the context in which it is used. The suggestion would be of an impediment or constraint imposed on what a person might want to do. If we say, in general and out of the blue, that Jones is free, we are conveying no positive information whatever about him. And, if there were no question of a constraint and Jones could do whatever he might want to do, there would be no use for the term 'free'. Such a description only makes sense if we know that Jones has been in prison recently, or has been involved in divorce proceedings, or has been in quarantine for small-pox. In other words, the word 'free', like the word 'responsible', is used to rebut certain typical suggestions about actions.[2] Just as we use the word 'responsible' to rebut the suggestion that a man could not help doing what he did because of ignorance, compulsion, or other such extenuating circumstances, so also we use the word 'free' to rebut the suggestion that a man is the victim of certain typical sorts of limitations or constraints.

Now political philosophy, in the main, is concerned with social cons-straints which hinder us from doing what we want. In our first chapter we discussed different types of social constraint; we shall have more to say about them in the context of political liberty in our next chapter. There is a well established tradition in British political philosophy which holds that it would be advisable to use the word 'free' only in such contexts where the absence of some sort of social constraint is indicated. Hobbes, for instance, claimed that theologians had muddled up questions of freedom by talking about free-will. Properly speaking, he said, only a person is free, and this means that some kind of hindrance on his actions is absent. So, perhaps, it will be as well to clarify some of the issues at stake.

Questions of free will usually arise when being free is contrasted with being determined; for it is thought that if there is determinism in human affairs, then we cannot be really free. Spinoza and Hobbes, who were fascinated by the science of mechanics, suggested that human beings, like stones or watches, were part of a mechanical system of nature, and that all their actions were determined, as those of a clock are determined by its spring. Details of this picture of man were later filled in by Marx, who stressed the economic determinants of social action, and by Freud, who stressed the unconscious determinants of individual behaviour laid down in early childhood. Such theories—or more often popular misinterpretations of them—gave rise to a widespread conviction that human decision is impotent in determining what human beings do. Men were pictured as puppets at the mercy of forces which they could neither understand nor control. But is this postulated antithesis between being free and being determined really legitimate? What do we mean when we say that our behaviour is determined? And if our behaviour *is* determined, does this mean that it cannot also be free?

II. FREEDOM AND DETERMINISM

Problems connected with freedom and determinism are best clarified by examining what we wish to convey when we say that an action is 'determined'. For there are two different things, which are often con-fused, which 'determined' can mean. Firstly, there is what we might call 'causal explicability' and, secondly, 'unavoidability'. Many people have failed to distinguish these two very different strands in the meaning of the term 'determined', and they have often thought that 'determined' involves *both* of these things. When we say that our behaviour is determined, therefore, it is often assumed both that our behaviour has causes and that it is unavoidable. Let us, therefore, consider these two strands in the meaning of 'determinism' in turn, and we can then later show that simply because our behaviour has causes it does not necessarily follow that it is unavoidable.

(a) Causal explicability

Determinism to a scientist conveys the general proposition that every event has a cause. Whether this general proposition is true is a very difficult question to decide,[3] but it is certainly assumed to be true by most scientists. To say that an event has a cause is to say that there are universal laws together with statements about initial conditions prevailing at particular times, and that from these two together we can predict an event which we call an 'effect'. For example, given that under the conditions x,y,z, iron expands when it is heated, and given that the conditions x,y,z, prevail and that this is a case of iron being heated, we can make the prediction that iron will expand. Here we have a typical causal relation. The so-called 'cause' is then the event referred to in the statement of initial conditions. And these conditions are regarded as being *sufficient* to explain the effect, if it is a full-blooded causal *explanation*.

Have we such relations in human affairs? The initial difficulty about saying that we have is that it is difficult to maintain that there are any psychological or sociological laws which would enable us to make such definite predictions. There also difficulties connected with our knowledge of particular situations which constitute the initial conditions; for when we are dealing with stones and bodies falling, their past history is scarcely part of the present situation. But when we are dealing with human beings, their past history is very much part of the present situation, and it is very difficult to know whether a given case is really of the type to which the particular law we have in mind applies. Nevertheless, there are some generalizations in psychology and the social sciences which are reasonably well established.[4] They do not enable us to make detailed predictions; they merely enable us to state the sort of thing that will *tend* to happen under certain typical conditions. In this respect psychology is in no worse plight than other sciences like meteorology. The difficulties arise from the complexity of the subject-matter, and, it might be argued, can be remedied in time.

If, however, we look more closely at these so-called laws in psychology we find, in the main, that they do not give sufficient explanations of human *actions*, of what human beings do deliberately, knowing what they are doing and for which they can give reasons. Freud's brilliant discoveries, for instance, were not of the causes of *actions* like signing contracts or shooting pheasants; rather they were of things that *happen* to a man like dreams, hysteria, and slips of the tongue.[5] These might be called 'passions' more appropriately than 'actions', and in this respect they are similar to what we call 'fits of passion' or 'gusts of emotion'. Men do not dream or forget a name 'on purpose' any more than they are deliberately subject to impulses or gusts of emotion. One class of laws in psychology, then, gives causal explanations which seem sufficient to account for what *happens* to a man, but not for what he does.

There is another class of laws, however, which concern not what happens to men, but what they do—their actions, performances and achievements. But such laws state necessary rather than sufficient conditions. We have in mind here the contributions made by physiological psychologists and those who have studied cognitive skills like learning, remembering, and perceiving. Part of what we mean by such terms is that human beings attain a norm or standard. Remembering is not just a psychological process; for to remember is to be *correct* about what happened in the past. Knowing is not just a mental state; it is to be sure that we are *correct* and to have *good grounds* for our conviction. To perceive something is to be *right* in our claims about what is before our eyes; to learn something is to *improve* at something or to get something *right*. All such concepts have norms written into them. In a similar way, as we have previously argued,* a human action is typically something done in order to bring about a result or in accordance with a standard. Such actions can be said to be done more or less intelligently and more or less correctly only because of the norms defining what are ends and what are efficient and correct means to them. It follows that a psychologist who claims that such performances depend on antecedent physiological conditions or mental processes, can at the most be stating necessary conditions. For processes, of themselves, are not appropriately described as correct or incorrect, intelligent or stupid. They only become so in the context of standards laid down by men. As Protagoras taught, nature knows no norms. It may well be true that a man cannot remember without part of his brain being stimulated, or that learning is a function, in part, of antecedent 'tension'. But the very meaning of 'remembering' and 'learning' precludes a sufficient explanation in these sorts of naturalistic terms.

Furthermore the problem of the freedom of the will arose mainly in connection with a type of action that is palpably different from a mere

* See Chapter I.

movement or process—an action that is preceded by deliberation and choice. For, roughly speaking, a 'willed action' was usually taken to mean* one in which we think before we act, when we make up our minds in terms of considerations which are relevant to the matter in hand before we act. There are difficulties about developing causal laws for actions of this type which are additional to those already stated about actions in general. Such difficulties are similar to those which the social scientist, as well as the psychologist, has in predicting what human beings will do. This is connected with the fact that into the human being's deliberations about what he is going to do will be introduced considerations about what he is likely to do, which the social scientist may have published. A scientist may discover a causal law connecting the properties of clover with a certain effect upon the digestive organs of sheep. But, when he publishes his findings, the sheep cannot take account of them and modify their behaviour accordingly. But with men it is different. Many causal connections discovered by psychologists may only hold good provided that the people whose actions are predicted in accordance with the law remain ignorant of what it asserts. And it is practically impossible to ensure that this is the case. So, if people know the causes on which a prediction of a certain type of behaviour is based, and if they deliberate before acting they may do something different from what is predicted, just because they recognize these causes. A prediction may thus be valid only on the assumption that the people concerned remain unconscious of the causes on which it is based. Otherwise it may be no more than a warning.

But why cannot causal explanations *also* be given of such informed deliberations which precede actions? We are here confronted with the difficulty of accounting for *logical* thought in causal terms, of giving a causal explanation for rational actions done after deliberation which involves logically relevant considerations. This is an extreme case of the difficulty already cited of giving sufficient explanations in causal terms for actions and performances which involve norms and standards. Yet, as has already been pointed out, such premeditated actions are particularly important in the free-will controversy, as the exercise of 'will' has usually been associated with rational deliberation before acting.[6] When a man is solving a geometrical problem and his thoughts are proceeding in accordance with certain logical canons, it is logically absurd to suggest

---

* Whether the concept of 'a willed action' is a useful or clear one is another matter. Reference is here made to traditional controversies about freedom of the will such as that between Hobbes and Bishop Bramhall. (See R. S. Peters, *Hobbes*, 1956, pp. 178–89.)

that any causal explanation in terms of movements in his brain, his temperament, his bodily state, and so on, is sufficient *by itself* to explain the movement of his thought. For logical canons are normative and cannot be sufficiently explained in terms of states and processes which are not. Of course there are any number of necessary conditions which must be taken account of. A man cannot think *without* a brain, for instance. But any *sufficient* explanation would have to take account of the *reasons* for his actions. We would have to know the rules of chess, for instance, which gave some *point* to a chess-player's move. Indeed we would only ask for the cause of a chess-player's behaviour if he did something which could not be explained in terms of the rules of chess and the objective at which he was aiming. If, for instance, he refrained from taking his opponent's queen, when this was the obvious and the best move, we might ask 'What made him do that?' and we would be asking for a causal explanation, like 'he was tired'. But this would now be an explanation of what *happened* to him, not of what he did deliberately. We would not ask for such an explanation if there was an obvious reason for his move.*

This example can be generalized and the point made that behaviour is usually explicable not because we know its causes, but because people act in accordance with certain known rules and conventions and adopt appropriate means to objectives which are accepted as legitimate goals. We know why a parson is mounting the pulpit not because we know much about the causes of his behaviour but because we know the conventions governing church services. We would only ask what were the causes of his behaviour if he fainted when he peered out over the congregation or if something similar *happened* to him. Most of our explanations of human behaviour are couched in terms of a purposive rule-following model, not in causal terms. Moral behaviour, above all other sorts, falls into this purposive, rule-following category. For, as Aristotle put it in his *Ethics*, it is not a man's passions which are the object of moral appraisal nor his capacity to be subject to such passions; rather we praise or blame a man for what he does about his passions, for the extent to which he controls or fails to control them in various situations. Deliberation and choice may not precede every action, but habits are set up as a result of such deliberation and choice. It is for the

* Of course the category of 'action' is much wider than that of premeditated action, though it may be co-extensive with that of 'rationality'. For this covers the sort of things for which a man could have a reason—i.e. which fall under what we call the purposive rule-following model. Premeditated action is a particular case of action where action is *preceded* by rehearsals and deliberation; but often reasons can be given by people for what they do even though they do not deliberate *before* they act.

exercise of such habits that men are praised and blamed—for the ends which they seek and for the means which they adopt to bring about their ends. Punishment, too, as we have pointed out, presupposes that men can foresee the consequences of their actions and they they can learn to avoid those to which penalties are attached. Praise and blame, reward and punishment, act as rudders to steer human actions precisely because men deliberate and choose and can be influenced by considerations of consequences. There is a radical difference between actions of this sort and cases where things happen to a man—where he acts 'on impulse', has a dream, a vision, or lapse of memory, or where he is afflicted by a feeling of nausea or hysterical paralysis. Questions of the 'freedom of the will' do not arise where things happen to a man; only where a man acts and can be praised or blamed, punished or rewarded for what he does. Yet it is precisely in these cases of human actions, as distinct from passions, that causal explanations seem inappropriate as sufficient explanations.

Two sorts of objection might be mounted against this attempt to limit the role of causal explanations of human behaviour. In the first place it might be said that by substituting concepts like rule-following and the pursuit of objectives we were in fact introducing other sorts of causes. Now the word 'cause' can be used in this very wide sense. But the terminological question is largely irrelevant; for two sorts of explanations which are logically quite different would then be included under the enlarged concept of 'cause'. To follow rules, to take steps which are seen to be necessary to reach some sort of objective, to see the point of something, these may be 'causes'; but they are causes in quite a different sense of 'cause' from things like stomach contractions, brain lesions, acute pains, and so on. The types of explanation must be distinguished whether we use the term 'cause' to cover both or not. And certainly seeing the point of something is quite different—even if it is called a 'cause'—from the causes prevalent in the physical world. In the early days of the determinist controversy philosophers like Spinoza and Kant used the term 'self-determined' to distinguish rational actions from those which could be explained in terms of mechanical causes like movements of the brain and body. Indeed Kant's suggestion that man lives in two worlds, and is subject to two different sorts of causation, is a metaphysical way of bringing out the logical distinction between these two sorts of explanation.

The second objection is the suggestion that all reasons might be rationalizations—a smoke screen for what we are going to do anyway. We are, as it were, pushed by causes in the mechanical, physical sense, whatever we do; but sometimes we throw up an elaborate smokescreen of excuses which make no difference to what we in fact do. If, however, we say that *all* reasons are rationalizations, we make no difference between the behaviour of an obsessive or a compulsive and that of a rational man. If a compulsive believes that his hands are covered in blood and spends his time continually washing them, no relevant considerations will make any difference to his behaviour. All the known tests fail to show blood; yet he still goes on washing his hands. But a civil servant making a complex decision about policy does not proceed like this. He will change his mind and alter policy in the light of relevant considerations. Indeed it is only because people *sometimes* alter their behaviour because of relevant considerations that it makes any *sense* to talk of rationalizations as well as of reasons. A term like 'rationalization', which casts aspersions on the reasons given for action, is a verbal parasite. It flourishes because there *are* cases of genuine reasons with which rationalizations can be contrasted. Thus even if all behaviour has causes, in the sense of *necessary* conditions, there are objections to saying that all behaviour—especially rational behaviour—can be *sufficiently* explained by causes of the sort suggested by physical scientists, and by mechanistic philosophers like Hobbes.

Whether this means that there is *also* a case for freedom depends on whether 'free' can be equated, in any of its various senses, with 'not sufficiently explained in causal terms'. Kant and Spinoza, who spoke of self-determinism in the case of rational action, claimed that this is the proper sense in which men could be said to be free. A man is free or self-determined, they said, in so far as his behaviour is explained in terms of his rational decisions rather than in terms of purely mechanical causes. Such causes were viewed as movements which somehow pushed or impelled a man to act. In other words there was an implied contrast between rational actions and those which occurred as the result of some sort of internal push which acted as a quasi-constraint on a man. And this notion, that a man was somehow the victim of internal forces, fitted in very well with the other meaning of 'determined' which suggested that there was some sort of *unavoidability* about a man's actions.

(b) Unavoidability[7]

If a man is told that his actions have causes, he will probably agree. But if he is told that they are causally determined, he will demur. He will not complain about the verbal redundancy of the assertion but will picture himself somehow as a prisoner or a victim. This illustrates our contention that the concept of 'determinism' conveys more than the suggestion that behaviour has causes, or that it can be *sufficiently* explained in terms of its causal antecedents. To most people to say that actions are determined conveys the suggestion that they are unavoidable, that the individual in question cannot *help* doing what he does. Furthermore, it is often assumed that wherever causes can be found for a man's actions, then also his actions are unavoidable. And it has been argued, as a corollary, that once the causes of an action are known, blame and punishment are absurd.

This assumption that any action for which causes can be produced is therefore unavoidable is surely a mistake occasioned by the peculiar circumstances of the rise of science.[8] It so happened that scientific advance, which consisted in the discovery of far-reaching causal laws, coincided with the widespread theological doctrine of predestination and with the metaphysical picture of the universe as a vast piece of clockwork in which human beings, like cog-wheels, were pushed on in a set pattern of movement. God, as it were, constructed the clock and set it going. If the clock could be seen as a whole, men could see what the future had in store for them and what movements determined that their fate should be this and no other. Causal discoveries revealed the springs and levers which pushed men towards their appointed destiny. The tacit assumption therefore developed that wherever causes could be found for actions, they were also unavoidable. Causes, being pictured always as internal pushes and pulls, were thought somehow to compel a man. And this picture suggests compulsion whether such causes are properly to be regarded as necessary or as sufficient conditions for human action. Men were therefore regarded as being not free because they were the victims of a peculiar internal sort of compulsion exercised by the causes of their behaviour. They were thus not able to avoid doing what they did.

III. RESPONSIBILITY

To say that a man cannot avoid or help doing what he does amounts to saying that he is not *responsible* for his actions. In dealing therefore with unavoidability in relation to freedom and determinism we have in fact been dealing with the concept of responsibility. This can be shown in more detail by reference to Bradley's classic exposition of what we mean when we ascribe responsibility to a person.[9] Bradley laid down four main conditions:

(a) Self-sameness. There must be continuity of personal identity.
(b) The deed must issue from the will of the agent. By this he means that the agent must not be forced to do it. Compulsion he defines as 'the production, in the body or mind of an animate being, of a

result which is not related as a consequence to its will'.*

(c) The doer must be supposed to be intelligent. He must know the particular circumstances of the case. If a person takes somebody else's hat from a cloakroom, thinking that the hat in question is his own and having no prior knowledge that there was a hat in the cloakroom exactly like his own, it would be unreasonable to say that he was responsible for stealing somebody else's hat. (These two criteria (b) and (c) are as old as Aristotle and comply with the main criteria which he suggested for saying that an action is *voluntary*.)

(d) The doer must be a moral agent. He must be familiar with the general rules of what is required from his society. It is interesting to notice that these last two criteria are very similar to those of the McNaghten Rules, where in the case of people pleading guilty but insane, it must be shown that they suffer from a defect of reason of such a kind that they do not know what they are doing or do not know that what they are doing is wrong.

Bradley's analysis is interesting in that he lists three typical defences which might be used to support the plea that a man could not help or avoid doing something. These are the defences of compulsion, non-culpable ignorance of fact, and defect of reason. As Professor Hart has shown,[10] the concept of responsibility is not a positive one for which a list of positive conditions can be produced. Rather, like the concept of freedom, it is a term we use about a person's actions when we have satisfied ourselves that certain typical circumstances are absent. We conclude that a man is responsible for his actions when there is no case for saying that he acted under compulsion, in ignorance, under duress, and so on. All such exonerating circumstances support the plea that he could not help doing what he did, that his action was *unavoidable*.

Why then has the production of causes for actions tended to encourage the belief that men are not responsible? For the mere production of a cause is not of itself an exonerating circumstance. We often know what was a cause of a man committing murder; but it does not follow from this that he could not help it. The answer, I think, is that people like Freud and Marx who have exerted so much influence on modern thought by their causal speculations, spoke of causes as if they were mechanical pushes and pulls—economic forces or forces in the

---

* Of course, we often are forced to do things where we have *some* measure of responsibility for what we do. For instance, if we wittingly put ourselves in the position where what we do may depend upon another person's will, e.g. under hypnosis, we can then be held *partly* responsible for what we do under hypnosis.

depths of the unconscious which impelled a man to behave in a certain way. Men appeared, on Marx's theory, caught up helplessly in an unwinding historical pattern, or, on Freud's theory, as prisoners of their past. Their causal speculations incorporated the old metaphysical picture of man as a cog-wheel in a vast clock.

The result was that their causal speculations suggested an extension of the exonerating circumstance of acting under compulsion. The irresistible impulse, about which there was so much discussion following the report of the Royal Commission on Capital Punishment, is a reasonable extension of this type of circumstance; it might be regarded as extenuating rather than as exonerating. We shall say more about such extensions shortly. But the talk in Marx and Freud of economic forces beneath the social appearances, of wishes and impulses in the depths of the unconscious, suggested an *indefinite* extension of the concept of acting under compulsion. For if causes were conceived as mechanical pushes might not men always be acting under some sort of compulsion, as their actions always had causes, even if such causes are viewed only as *necessary* conditions of action?

As a matter of fact men *sometimes* do seem to be acting under this sort of compulsion. This is what makes the prisoner-of-the-past picture of determinism so plausible. For example, a man under post-hypnotic suggestion will do, when he wakes, what the hypnotist told him to do in his trance. He cannot be dissuaded or side-tracked by rational arguments. He will act as if there is something in him which *compels* him to act in this way. And it was because the language which Freud and Marx used to record their causal speculations—their talk of forces, drives, impulses, and so on—creaked with compulsion, that an indefinite extension of the concept of acting under compulsion was intimated. But we are inclined to say that a man is not responsible for his actions, after being hypnotized, not because we know their causes, but because he behaves so oddly when we try to get him to do something else. It is this which suggests compulsion or subjection to some irrational irresistible force. For irresistible impulses are those which, on the whole, people seem unable to resist. Very often, too, we speak of compulsives when we know nothing of the causes of their obsessive preoccupations. We describe their actions as compulsive because we apply a crude battery of tests to them, not because we have done a piece of detective work on their causes. For instance, if a man is really a kleptomaniac we have classified him as such because we have found that reward and punishment, praise and blame, rational argument, and so on, make no difference to his stealing. Causes in general must be distinguished from the special types of causes that have unavoidable effects. For there are *some* causes that do conform to this pattern. For instance, it is claimed by Bowlby of the Tavistock Clinic that certain kinds of deprivation of maternal care in early childhood, not only cause traits like unfriendliness distractability, and so on, but also constitute causes leading to unavoidable effects.[11] Deliberation and resolution, praise and blame, reward and punishment, change of environment—all these devices are of no use. Neither is the sufferer's knowledge of what he is likely to do in given circumstances, nor is his determination to do something different. His reasoning is irrelevant to what he does. In such cases there is some point in saying that a man cannot help doing what he does, that his behaviour is unavoidable. The causes, too, seem sufficient to explain his behaviour; for it falls into the category of something happening to him rather than of his doing something deliberately. But many have mistakenly generalized such sensational examples and have thought that whenever causes can be found for a person's behaviour, he cannot help doing what he does. But this does not follow at all. The facts even of this sort of case are highly disputable and psychologists have produced few other such examples of causes with unavoidable effects. The mere production of causes is of itself irrelevant to the question whether a man could reasonably be said to have been able to avoid doing what he did. It is only if we know *in general* that a certain type of cause trends to lead to unavoidable effects that the production of a cause is relevant to the question of responsibility. And then, of course, this *type of cause* must be produced; not just *any* cause. For most causes do not in fact compel. Perhaps the notion of compelling or impelling is itself only appropriate in cases where things *happen* to a man, where causal explanations are also sufficient.

There is thus, in general, no necessary connection between the two sense of 'determined'. Events whose causes are known are not necessarily also unavoidable. Indeed, very often, knowing a cause of something is a necessary condition of being able to avoid it. If we know that late nights cause irritability at breakfast, we know what to do to avoid irritability at breakfast. The assumed coincidence between discovering causes and unavoidability is due largely to the mechanical picture of causes. 'Free' or 'responsible' are only used appropriately as contrasts to 'determined' if by 'determined' we mean 'having causes of the compelling sort'. And such causes may well also be those which are sufficient because they are of things that happen to a man rather than of what he does deliberately.

IV. CONCLUSION

We are now able to relate our discussion of freedom and responsibility to our earlier discussion of blame and punishment. We observed, at the start of this chapter, that the suggestion that all our acts were determined might seem to strike at the roots of morality and punishment, since both presuppose a free agent. We can now see that this is misconceived, for though causes might be given for a person's actions, that fact alone does not entail that they are sufficient explanations, that his actions are unavoidable, or that he was not free. From the moral standpoint, then, a person can be properly blamed for doing wrong, unless there were present one or more of the exonerating circumstances which defeat the presumption of responsibility. These conditions apart, to know some causes of his action is not the same as to know that he could not help doing it. To understand all is not necessarily to pardon all. It may well be the case, however, that if a causal explanation is sufficient, blame is inappropriate. For this would be a case of something happening to a man rather than of a deliberate action.

Questions of responsibility and extenuating causes arise most often, and most controversially, in the context of punishment. With the growth of medical psychology, there has been steady pressure from penal reformers to enlarge the range of exonerating circumstances recognized by law—to acknowledge, that is, further conditions in which an offender could plead that he was not responsible. We suggested, in our discussion of punishment, criteria for determining which pleas of this sort might be admissible. If it could reasonably be held that a person in a given condition would be unmoved by the threat of a penalty (especially if it were certain), that he would be incapable of reflecting on the consequences of his action, or that such reflection could not be expected to make any difference to what he does, then there would be no point in inflicting punishment. For then it would necessarily fail to deter anyone in a similar condition in the future. Such a condition would then be properly admissible as an exonerating circumstance and we would regard such a man as a patient, in the literal sense, rather than as an agent. Of course, in marginal cases, like so-called 'irresistible impulses', it may be very difficult to say whether these criteria are satisfied or not. For any impulse that was not resisted might be said by someone to have been 'irresistible'. We therefore tend to regard such circumstances as extenuating rather than as exonerating. But we might insist, as a minimal requirement, that the person should have *tried* to resist such an impulse and failed. For it is only in the extreme and undoubted cases of irresponsibility (like lunacy) that trying is impossible.

Similar conditions apply in the case of blame. It would be pointless to blame anyone if blame could make no difference to his conduct. Morality is a system of rules by which each man prescribes, not only for himself, but for everyone else too. And so, when we blame we do not simply note that another man's conduct has failed to conform to the standards we set for ourselves; we also express disapproval of the wrong-doer, implying necessarily that he ought not to do the same again. Such an implication would be absurd, however, under any conditions where exhortation, remonstrance, or a rational appeal to the rules could make no conceivable difference.

What distinguishes blame and punishment alike from remedial treat-ment, of the sort we might give to offenders who cannot help themselves, is that they presuppose a capacity on the offender's part to act on rational decisions rather than to be merely a patient, subject to emotions and other forms of stimulation. Some writers, including Hegel and his disciples, have been so impressed by this distinction that they have treated punishment as a sort of tribute to the criminal's moral auto-nomy, as a kind of fundamental right.[12] Others have repudiated the reformative approach to punishment because they feel that it treats the person who has the capacity to make his own rational decisions as if he were a lunatic or a child. To punish or to blame, they would say, is com-patible with respecting a man's dignity as a moral agent; to undertake to reform his character is not. Though such views might not be accep-table on other grounds, they do rightly stress the close relation between punishment and responsibility, which distinguishes it from remedial treatment, like that administered by the 'straightener' of Butler's *Erewhon*. They implicitly admit the distinction we have stressed between what a man does, which conforms to a rule-following purposive model, and things which happen to him which can be sufficiently explained in causal terms.

We have tried to show that this important distinction between punish-ment and remedial treatment still holds good. Though psychological discoveries might possibly extend the range of extenuating conditions, they do not affect the distinction in principle. For to show the causes of human behaviour is not to show, save in exceptional cases, that men are not free agents. It is only because causes have been regarded as sufficient explanations of human actions as well as of human 'passions' and have been pictured—mistakenly—as quasi-compelling forces, driving a man to his destiny, that this has ever been in doubt. Men can be said not to be free if they are constrained by arbitrary tyrants, by laws, by tradi-tions, or by economic victimization; but not merely because their actions have causes. These *social* limitations on freedom are the subject of the next chapter.

CHAPTER 10

FREEDOM AS A POLITICAL IDEAL

I. FREEDOM, POWER, AND AUTHORITY

(a) Introductory

Chapter 9 dealt with 'moral freedom', or 'free will'; but, as T. H. Green pointed out, 'every usage of the term to express anything but a social and political relation of one man to others involves a metaphor'.[1] A man who is the 'slave of his passions' is a 'slave' only by analogy. In this chapter we shall deal with the primary sense of 'freedom' as a relation between one man and others, and more particularly with the problems of freedom as a political ideal, as an object which political and social institutions ought to be designed to preserve or achieve.

Two points in the analysis of the term 'free', which opened Chapter 9, need repeating here, for they cast light on our present problems. First: 'X is free' says very little about X, unless we can tell from the context what sort of restraint he is free from, and what sort of course he is thereby free to follow. There are as many sorts of freedom as there are ways of completing 'free to . . .' and 'free from . . .'. Consequently, when we meet the assertion that, for example, political freedom is not 'true' or 'real' freedom, but that some other sort is, we must understand the writer to mean, not that a mistake has been made about the meaning of the word, or in describing the facts of a situation, but that it is more important to be free from some other sort of restraint than from political restraints. But to say that one thing is 'more important' than another is to recommend or prescribe, not to describe. Secondly: in most contexts 'free' has strong commendatory force; exceptionally, as with reference to an escaped criminal, we might say 'Alas, he is free!', but we should be surprised to hear 'Alas, I am free!', because we should hardly use the term unless we were glad about it. (Existentialist doctrines seem paradoxical and striking because they treat 'I am free' as a ground for anguish.)

This feature of 'freedom' accounts in part for the difficulty some political theorists have had in reconciling themselves to the need for government. If freedom is a good thing, what can justify a few men exercising power over others, to prevent them doing what they want to do? Tom Paine thought that government was a necessary evil; if we agreed with him, we should have to decide just how much limitation of our freedom that necessity would justify. An important task of political theory is, in fact, to decide between the claims of liberty and authority, and to fix their proper frontiers.

The problem has been approached in various ways. The most naïve, perhaps, is that which seeks to distinguish between 'liberty' and 'licence': 'liberty' is good, but to be free to do undesirable things is to enjoy not 'liberty' but 'licence', and that is bad. Unfortunately, this does not help us to decide between claims, but only substitutes, an unfavourable word for a favourable one according to the speaker's preference. The words do not describe different things, but they prescribe or evoke different attitudes to them.

People who approve the spread of state regulation in recent years often try to reconcile it with 'liberty' by re-defining that word in terms of opportunity. 'Absence of restraint', it is said, is too limited a definition; freedom has a positive as well as a negative aspect.[2] If education is expensive and the parents are poor, it makes a mockery of freedom to say that one is free to educate one's children, merely because there is no law or custom against it. Choice may be *formally* unlimited; there can be no freedom unless it is also *effectively* unlimited. To remove any hindrance to people doing what they want to do thus counts as an extension of freedom. To provide a cripple with an artificial leg, an ignorant man with education, an unemployed man with a job, all count as positive extensions of freedom. Legal compulsions are then a small price to pay for positive freedoms of this sort; for we yield a little only to receive back more. And the absolute goodness of freedom remains intact.

The trouble with this interpretation of freedom as a political ideal is that it excludes nothing. Any condition can be described as the absence of its opposite. If health is 'freedom from disease', and education 'freedom from ignorance', there is no conceivable object of social organization and action that cannot be called 'freedom'. But the price of making 'freedom' all-embracing as a social end is to drain it of all descriptive meaning, and to leave only the prescriptive overtones, to make it synonymous with the vaguest terms of approval like 'good' and 'desirable'. Now to say that the proper object of law is to do the most good is not to say much; and if we understand 'freedom' in this broad sense, to say the end of law is to make people as free as possible is to say very little more. If we want freedom to remain significant as a moral demand, we must be prepared to see it rub shoulders with less exalted ideals, like personal security (which President Roosevelt called 'freedom from fear'), full employment ('freedom from want'), and so on, without wanting it to swallow the lot. There is much to be said, then, for the classical tradition of English political theory, which interprets 'freedom' negatively, as the absence of restraints imposed by the power of other men.[3] But in that case the problem of mapping the frontier between liberty and authority remains.

A way of sidestepping the difficulty has been to define 'liberty' so as to make it coincide with submission to some authority of which the author approves. For Rousseau it consists in obedience to the General Will; for Hegel, in obedience to the law of the land. The problem is thus made to disappear; but at the cost of a curiously paradoxical denial of conflict between the wills of the individual constrained and of the constraining power.* Law may be a necessary condition for liberty, since one man's freedom depends on the law's restraints on others. But if the law must restrain some to protect the liberty of others, liberty cannot *mean* submission to law.

(b) Law as a constraint upon constraints†

The 'positive' interpretation of 'liberty', that we criticized above, has this virtue, that it recognizes that there is more than one way in which freedom can be limited. In a complex system of social relations, freedom enjoyed by one man may operate as a constraint on another. A trade union or an employer may constrain us by threatening our livelihood; or we may live at the mercy of gangs like Chicago in the thirties, or be subject to the terror of a Ku Klux Klan, or in fear of a press that can blackmail us by threatening our reputation. These are arbitrary constraints, springing from power unlimited by rules, and we look to rules of law to defend us from them. Law can equally release people from the constraints of custom or conventional morality, as when Turkish law was amended to forbid confining women in harems, or, as in England, when the Married Women's Property Acts helped to weaken the customary authority of the Victorian husband. It is the paradox of freedom that we must set a constraint to catch a constraint.

The history of the idea of freedom is characterized by a shifting emphasis, as first one and then another constraint is relied upon to weaken the grips of others. Thus Hobbes relied on the force of sovereign coercive

---

* For a fuller treatment of General Will theories, see Chapters 11, 12, and 14.
† For the purpose of our argument 'constraint' and 'restraint' can be used indifferently. If you stop a man doing what he wants, you *restrain* him from doing it, and equally you *constrain* him to desist.

power to constrain the arbitrary power of individuals and associations, harnessing all lesser arbitrariness by one supreme arbitrariness that spoke through the law. But he was interested too in weakening customary constraints. For in saying that men are free in all those matters upon which the law is silent,* he was really rejecting customary constraints on freedom to change social status, or religious limitations upon free enquiry, unless they were also law. Hobbes the legal absolutist was also a radical individualist, for whom all social relations were essentially contractual.

With Locke the emphasis is different. Sovereign coercive power is itself suspect, and it is law that must restrain it, like all other arbitrariness. So for Locke liberty and law are not incompatible: 'The end of law is, not to abolish or restrain, but to preserve and enlarge freedom. For in all the states of created beings capable of laws, where there is no law there is no freedom. For liberty is to be free from restraint and violence from others; which cannot be where there is no law: and is not, as we are told, a liberty for every man to do what he lists.' 'That ill deserves the name of confinement that hedges us in only from bogs and precipices.'[4] Now this is valuaole and important; but it is open to two criticisms. In the first place, it stipulates a definition of freedom, resembling somewhat the distinction mentioned earlier between 'liberty' and 'licence', that makes it impossible for law (or at any rate, for 'law in its true notion') to be a genuine restraint at all. There is to be all gain and no loss of freedom from the law. But to separate the restraints of law from 'restraint . . . from others' is too simple: for laws are made and applied by men, and freedom may be as much curtailed by law as by any other technique. And it is too much to ask that law should prevent *all* constraint of one man by another; the power of the employer over his employee, of the voter over his MP, of the captain over his crew, and, some would say, of the trade union over the would oe blackleg, or the party whip over the rebel, are all, within some limits, reasonable and defensible restraints on liberty that the law should allow. It might be said that ideally it is the purpose of law to restrain in one direction only to enlarge liberty more in another. But liberty is not a commodity to be weighed and measured. I am free to do x, y, and z, but not p, q, and r—but there is no substance called 'freedom' of which I can therefore possess more or less, according to the particular combination of things permissible and things forbidden. All that can be

---

* 'As for other liberties, they depend on the silence of the law. In cases where the sovereign has prescribed no rule, there the subject hath the liberty to do, or forbear, according to his own discretion.' *Leviathan*, Blackwell edn. by M. Oakeshott, p. 143.

said is that I am free in some ways and not in others; that some are more important than others; and that the condition of being free in some ways is that I should not be free in others. But there is no way of casting a resultant sum of freedom.

The second objection to Locke's formulation of the 'end of law' is that it confines it too narrowly to the restraint of arbitrary power. A food rationing scheme is aimed, not at restraining power but at securing a distribution of scarce commodities according to need. Public health regulations are not aimed at controlling power but at preventing disease. Such activities can be described as removing restraints only if we slip into the sort of usage that we have already condemned when discussing 'positive freedom'. Locke's account obscures the fact that there might be other reasons for imposing a legal restraint besides the control of arbitrary power. This is what we meant when we said earlier that if 'freedom' is to remain significant, we must be prepared to see it rub shoulders with other ideals.

(c) *Liberty and executive power: The problem of freedom in seventeenth and eighteenth century terms*

Law, then, ought at least to protect every citizen from the arbitrary constraints of others. To achieve this, there must be within the state (as Hobbes rightly insisted), a concentration of power committed to enforcing the law, and great enough to overwhelm any potential law-breaker. In any normal circumstances, this power is bound to be at the disposal of a relatively small group of 'state managers', the executive, whatever the constitution of the state in other respects. From this stems the dilemma: How can those who wield the power necessary to enforce law be themselves confined within the law?

The modern state emerged from the baronial and religious wars of the fifteenth and sixteenth centuries. It was characterized by just this central concentration, under the control of kings, that Hobbes called 'sovereign power'. Could Leviathan be chained? In Hobbes' view, the question was absurd; for only a greater power could restrain it, and that would itself be sovereign. To attempt to limit, divide, or counter-balance state power would be to invite a return to the lawlessness from which the modern state had rescued us.

If we think only of power, Hobbes was right. In a revolutionary situation, the only effective restraint on armed force is a larger force. And it would be a strange and unstable constitution that established a second army under independent command to coerce the regular force under executive command should the latter act unconstitutionally. Yet once in control of state power, Hitler made short work of the merely legal restraints imposed by the Weimar Constitution. Revolutions, however, are the exception and not the rule, and in ordinary situations governments rely on authority rather than on power—on pronouncements, commands and decisions rather than on the machine gun. The recourse of power, we have suggested, is usually symptomatic of a breakdown of authority. It may well be the case, of course, that *the ability* to dispose of power is almost a necessary condition for the effective exercise of authority; and conversely, *de facto* authority within an order like the state may be a source of power. A government's authority over the army is obviously a source of power. We shall call power of this sort 'institutionalized power'.*

Now the problem of controlling the executive was not discussed by classical writers like Locke in a manner which did justice to the niceties of distinctions involved in the use of terms like 'power', 'authority', and 'sovereignty'. When stated in our terms it appears as the problem of confining the executive's use of power and *de facto* authority within the limits of its *de jure* authority. In a revolutionary situation, when institutions are breaking down, this may be possible only by a greater force than it can itself muster. But if what is in question is not the destruction of the constitution, but the gradual extension of executive power, by imprisoning opponents on trumped-up charges, illegal taxation, the suppression of criticism and so on, the problem may not be insoluble. Law may restrain executive action in two ways: governors trained in a liberal tradition are likely to be inhibited, by their own respect for legality, form unblushingly violating it; and, to the degree that their *de facto* authority and power derive from public recognition of their legal authority, they will be ill advised to trespass too obviously beyond the legal limits.

Locke saw the problem of liberty in something like these terms. Writing in defence of 1688 and 1689, and enunciating what was to become the standard Whig view of the Constitution, he saw the executive

* Just as 'authority' is predominantly a normative term which, in its *de facto* sense, approaches to being used descriptively, so 'power' is predominantly a descriptive term which sometimes has a normative use. We have already noted that there are many ways in which men may constrain others—by economic pressure, by blackmail, by force, and so on—and these are all forms of power.

'Power' in this sense has no normative reference; it is defined wholly in terms of the actual ability of one man to induce another to take a desired course. It must be distinguished from the sense in which we speak of 'the Council's power to make a Compulsory Purchase Order under the Town and Country Planning Act'. This is normative, resembling 'right' or 'entitlement'; we might equally well say that the Council has 'authority' to make such an order. These words imply the existence of a rule system in accordance with which action is taken.

as the principal enemy. Parliament, as a representative body making general rules, would have little interest in invading freedom (though he provided that the people might overthrow a Parliament should the unlikely happen.)* If the law-makers can be trusted, the vital thing is to make the executive subject to law, denying it authority to alter, suspend, or dispense with it at will. There may be emergencies when a prerogative discretionary power might be properly exercised by the executive for the public safety, but normally its discretion would be very narrowly defined. Add to this legislative control of supply, and the executive can be held in check at least to the point where it is prepared to risk blatantly illegal tax-raising by force of arms.

Montesquieu's famous doctrine of the separation of powers is an elaboration of these principles. Like Locke, he defines 'liberty' as 'the right to do anything that the laws permit'[5]: he has little fear of the legislature except when it is combined with the executive.† But he adds to Locke's separation of these two the further separation of the judiciary, in the long run perhaps the more important principle of the two. For if the limitation of executive power depends on maintaining the Rule of Law, it is of the first importance that there should be an appeal to an independent tribunal when power is abused. If the *de facto* authority of a government depends on its credentials, on its *de jure* authority, an independent tribunal competent to declare that no authority for an act exists will be a very real check on it. The Act of Settlement of 1701, which gives English judges a security of tenure that the early Stuart judges had not enjoyed, is rightly regarded as one of the fundamental features of the Constitution safeguarding the Rule of Law.

The doctrine of the separation of powers was primarily aimed, then, at restraining the institutionalized power of the state within legal limits. It was built into the Constitution of the United States, in the provision for separate election of President and Congress. Short of impeachment for 'high crimes and misdemeanours', each is independent of the other for tenure of office, and each is to that extent independent of pressure from the other in the discharge of constitutionally authorized

---

* See Ch. 14, p. 327.

† Montesquieu had his doubts, however, about a unicameral representative legislature: 'There are always in a State men distinguished by birth, wealth or honours. If they are submerged in the people, and have only one voice each like the rest, the general liberty will be for them slavery, and they will have no interest in defending it, for most decisions will be taken against them. The part which they have in legislation must therefore be proportional to the other advantages they enjoy in the State: and this will be achieved if they form a body with the right to veto the people's enterprises, just as the people have the right to veto theirs.' *Spirit of the Laws*, Bk. XI, Ch. VI.

functions. Though Supreme Court judges are appointed by the President with the assent of the Senate, they hold office thereafter 'during good behaviour'. The essential point of this arrangement is that the governmental process requires the concurrent action of three sets of officials, each of which derives its authority directly from the Constitution, without the mediating authority of another.

Montesquieu had seen the same sort of separation in the English constitution of the early eighteenth century. But even in his own lifetime the pattern was beginning to change. The independence of the legislature was in some measure undermined by royal patronage; but, on the other hand, it became conventional for the King's ministers to sit in Parliament, and to resign if they lost its confidence. Executive control over the legislature was not impaired with the elimination of patronage, for patronage was replaced by the evolving party system. The divorce of legislature and executive, which had largely been effected by the constitutional struggles of the seventeenth century, proved in practice intolerably inconvenient, and would have become even more so as the functions of government expanded. Legislative assemblies need leadership; they cannot really make policy, for realistic policy making can only emerge from the experience and responsibility of administration. But if they cannot be induced to accept executive policies, nor possess the authority to remove the executive, the result will be deadlock. In the United States, the gulf has had to be bridged by a variety of extra-legal expedients, like the use of Presidential patronage as a way of exerting pressure on Congressmen. In Britain, the solution has been found in Cabinet government, depending on a strong two-party system. Here, the simple divorce that Montesquieu envisaged has been replaced by a complex and delicate balancing of authority and party power: on the one hand, the legislature has the authority to deprive the executive of its credentials by a hostile vote; on the other, members are bound to their party by ties of political loyalty and personal interest, and the assembly as a whole can be dissolved (though not reconstituted) at the discretion of the executive. And constantly in the background of the modern political process, there is the reserve authority of the electorate.

(d) Liberty and legal restraints

So long as the content of law is not in question, the problem of safeguarding liberty is the institutional one of devising checks on power concentrations that might otherwise run wild. In the seventeenth century, however, the law was relatively static; little positive action was demanded of government, and there was no occasion for a legislature in almost constant session busily making laws. Parliament represented satisfied propertied classes, and though it might take a strict view, perhaps, of what constituted sedition, it could be relied upon in general to interfere little enough with people going about their daily business. By the nineteenth century, however, there were signs of change. The extending suffrage conferred a measure of power on classes who had something to gain from legal interference in daily affairs, and by the close of the century it was accepted that the state had a legitimate and positive part to play in promoting welfare. Law, now a vehicle of social reform, could no longer be taken for granted.

Some, indeed, were confident that a democratic legislature could not, by its nature, constitute a threat to liberty. Rousseau had argued that where the people is itself the sovereign legislature, 'the sovereign power need give no guarantee to its subjects, because it is impossible for the body to wish to hurt all its members', nor 'any in particular';[6] and though Rousseau would not have said the same for a representative assembly, his Jacobin disciples ignored the distinction. Thus Soviet constitutional apologists have argued that with the disappearance of class conflict and the emergence of a true general will, which finds expression in the Party and the state, the need for internal checks on government disappears.[7]

Others, like de Tocqueville and John Stuart Mill, viewed emerging democracy with less complacency. 'Such phrases as "self-government", and "power of the people over themselves",' wrote Mill, 'do not express the true state of the case. The "people" who exercise the power are not always the same people with those over whom it is exercised; and the "self-government" spoken of is not the government of each by himself, but of each by all the rest. The will of the people, moreover, practically means the will of the most numerous or the most active *part* of the people; the majority, or those who succeed in making themselves accepted as the majority; the people, consequently, *may* desire to oppress a part of their number; and precautions are as much needed against this as against any other abuse of power . . . "the tyranny of the majority" is now generally included among the evils against which society requires to be on its guard.'[8]

Mill's remedy is in part institutional: plural voting and proportional representation to strengthen the vote of those minorities which are peculiarly vulnerable to majority tyranny.* But this is not enough. The

---

* The prospect of wide, or universal, suffrage had worried many liberal political theorists long before Mill, particularly as implying a threat to property. Madison had warned against the possibility of majority tyranny in the debate preceding the adoption of the Constitution of the USA—see *The Federalist* No. 10. Madison's problem is discussed more fully in Chapter 15.

spirit of democracy is plain not only in governmental institutions, but also in the mass pressure which upholds conventional standards. Though outrageous opinions may not lead us to gaol, they may still put us out of business. 'Society is itself the tyrant—society collectively over the separate individuals who compose it—its means of tyrannizing are not restricted to the acts which it may do by the hands of its political functionaries.' Against social pressures there can be no institutional safeguards; 'social tyranny . . . leaves fewer means of escape, penetrating much more deeply into the details of life, and enslaving the soul itself'.[9] The majority, whether acting politically or socially, must be persuaded to mind its own business. But what is its business? We are back to the philosophical problem of liberty. Can we define limits beyond which it is wrong for one man to try to restrain another?

II. THE PHILOSOPHICAL PROBLEM OF LIBERTY

Mill's argument rests on two principles that need analysis.

(a) 'All restraint, *qua* restraint, is an evil . . . leaving people to themselves is always better, *caeteris paribus*, than controlling them.'[10]

(b) 'The sole end for which mankind are warranted, individually or collectively, in interfering with the liberty of action of any of their number, is self-protection. That the only purpose for which power can be rightfully exercised over any member of a civilized community, against his will, is to prevent harm to others. His own good, either physical or moral, is not a sufficient warrant.'[11]

We must not interpret 'self-protection' too strictly, however. Mill admits that it might be right to compel people to perform actions the neglect of which would be harmful.[12] It is a fair extension of the principle to allow compulsion where it can yield a positive advantage to others. The point of the 'self-protection' principle is that it distinguishes two spheres of action; one, where the individual's conduct is likely to affect the interests of others, when interference is legitimate; the other, where conduct is wholly 'self-regarding' and affects others for neither good nor ill, when interference would be illegitimate.

(a) 'All restraint, qua restraint, is an evil'

Mill offers no justification of the first principle; he treats it as self-evident. It is therefore beside the point that freedom may yield benefits; and similar whatever benefits may arise from restraint, they are purchased at a cost. Now a self-evident principle requires, by definition, no evidence or argument to support it; if it is possible for anyone who has rightly understood it to doubt it, it cannot be self-evident. At least one competent critic has found it possible to doubt Mill's assertion. J. D. Mabbott writes:

'I am still doubtful how far liberty is to be valued for itself and how far I am really counting on the ... good effects of variety and experiment to which Mill so often appeals. For if liberty itself is what I value it must have this high merit equally in the bad action and the good, and I cannot feel sure that, in a case where I knew I was doing wrong, it was at least one good element in the situation that no one tried to stop me.'[13]

There is something curiously paradoxical about this which derives, in our view, from the language employed. Calling freedom to act 'One good element in the situation', Mabbott treats it as if it were an ingredient in a composite whole, as one might say: 'Though the cocktail was largely made up of vitriol and spirits of salt, the lemon juice was wholesome enough.' But freedom to act is not a constituent of a situation separable from the thing done, and therefore capable of possessing distinct value. What is implied by Mill's principle is not that there is some value in the worst action if it is done freely, but that the onus of justification must always rest on the would-be restrainer, and not upon the person restrained. It is not that freedom of action is necessarily valuable in itself, but that there is always an initial presumption in its favour that must be overcome. And this is an accurate account of the way we carry on discussion in these matters. A writ of *Habeas Corpus* invites a gaoler to show good cause why his prisoner should not be released; the onus does not rest on the prisoner to make out a case for liberty. Similarly, in moral terms, if we find one man interfering with another's actions, and if we know nothing to start with about either, we should expect an explanation from the interfering one, not an account from the victim of why he should not be interfered with.

The presumption in favour of liberty is thus closely analogous to the presumption in favour of equality, discussed in Chapter 5. And the reason for it is the same, namely, that it is implied in the definition of a *moral* justification. Morality, we have observed, entails treating others as ends, never solely as means, or instruments. We do not ask a carpenter to justify using his plane simply as a tool, nor a biologist to justify the detention of an amoeba on a slide. But we do object to treating men in this way; and if the only reason that can be given for constraint of one man by another is 'I want to', the one is treating the other as a tool. Between the amoeba and the man there is an area of uncertainty. Many people today would feel it reasonable to ask a man to justify chaining up a dog; on the other hand, Aristotle was happy to defend slavery on the ground that some men were fit only to be the tools of others. To ask for a justification for a man's exercising a constraint upon another creature, is to recognize a moral relationship between them. One of the most important changes in moral attitudes since Aristotle's day has been the progressive extension of the class of beings that we treat as moral persons, so that now we not only include all human beings but, with some inconsistencies, the higher animals too.

The maxim 'All restraint, *qua* restraint, is an evil' appears, on this analysis, as a way of saying that any restraint of a being who is a fitting subject of moral judgments, must be justified in moral terms. And this is logically entailed by the criteria defining the sphere of moral discourse Consequently, it is a purely formal, or procedural maxim. It indicates where the responsibility for justification lies: it does not help us to decide whether a justification is adequate.

(b) The 'self-protection' principle

This problem, then, remains. Mill's 'self-protection' principle is offered as a minimal answer, i.e. that any interference with purely self-regarding acts *cannot* be justified (which does not mean that all other interferences can). And this though the act in question may be morally wrong, like suicide or drug-taking; for the injury concerns no one but the doer.

This principle has been vigorously contested. Fitzjames Stephen, one of Mill's severest critics, roundly declares:

'There are acts of wickedness so gross and outrageous that, self-protection apart, they must be prevented as far as possible at any cost to the offender, and punished, if they occur, with exemplary severity.'[14]

The problem can be clarified by distinguishing, as we did in Chapters 2 and 8, between particular and general justifications. As a criterion for interference in particular cases, Mill's principle would be clearly at fault; where there is a rule, legal or moral, requiring or permitting interference with conduct of a given kind, it is not necessary to show that any particular instance of it is harmful to others, and we depart from the strict letter of the rule only in the exceptional case where it would tend to defeat its spirit.* The utilitarian consideration of 'protection' arises only when the rule itself is in question.

In considering whether a rule is justified, we have to ask whether the over-all consequences would be bad if the type of conduct it pro-

---

* Elsewhere Mill accepts this view of justification of the particular instance. But he does not make this distinction in the essay *On Liberty*.

hibited became general. The sexual relations of A and B might be regarded, in a sense, as entirely their own business, if neither had marital or family ties. Yet there might be good grounds for banning relations of that type if the consequences to society generally would be bad, were they to be widely practised. Promiscuity or homosexuality could in many cases be defended as affecting no one but the parties taking part; but were the pressures of law and opinion relaxed, there might well be serious consequences for family life and the social structure, which on the whole we wish to preserve.

We have argued that to justify conduct of a given sort, we must consider with impartiality the consequences that would follow for everyone affected were it accepted as a general rule. On this basis, the class of immoral actions that affect no one but the doer—the class that Mill seeks to protect from interference—cannot exist; for if, considered as general social practices, they still affected only the doers, they would not be immoral. The only objection that could be raised to such practices is that they frustrated the doer from doing other things that he very much wanted to do. They would then be imprudent. They could only be thought immoral if the activities so prevented promised benefits for people other than the doer.

We have been seeking an interpretation of Mill's principles that would side-step the objection of their critics; they emerge as re-statements of the criteria of 'morality' established in Chapter 2, namely, that 'morality' involves respect for persons, and the critical assessment of conduct in terms of the consequences for all concerned if it were adopted as a general social practice. Unimpeachable as these principles are as procedural or formal criteria for moral judgment, they cannot provide the substantive rules for interference and non-interference that Mill expected of them. The most they will do is to rule out certain reasons for interference as morally insufficient. Thus it is not enough to say: 'I forbid your way of worship because I do not like it', since mere preference is not a *moral* ground for action. Since many people want to interfere with others simply on account of an unreasoned prejudice, the connection between freedom and the criteria of moral justification may be well worth while pointing out. Similarly, it would not be a moral reason for interference with religious worship, to say 'Your way is forbidden by Holy Scripture'; for it remains to be proved that any manner of worship so unauthorized would be harmful if generally adopted. An appeal to the authority of scripture may constitute a religious, but not a moral reason for an action or judgment. The distinction between moral and religious reasons has been of the first importance in the development of religious toleration.

Nevertheless, Mill did not do what he set out to do, and the main question remains unanswered: What actions, that admittedly affect others and so are the proper subjects of moral judgments, ought nevertheless to remain uncontrolled either by governmental or social pressure? What we have said so far does suggest that any restraint must stand up to objections of the following types:

(*i*) in the case of a particular application of restraint, that the act in question infringes no rule;

(*ii*) in the case of a general application of restraint, by a rule,

(1) that the object of the rule is bad;

(2) that while the object of the rule is good, the means proposed cannot reasonably be expected to attain it;

(3) that though the object is good, and the proposed means would secure it, it is not of sufficient importance to warrant the degree of restraint proposed.

These are still formal principles rather than guides for conduct. And we cannot expect to get further than this so long as we continue to speak simply of 'freedom', without completing it with particular references to the things that we are to be free, or not free, to do. For in applying formal principles, we must supply all the substantive details, the conduct proposed, the attendant circumstances, and an evaluation of the object of the proposed restraint. So far as we have gone, it has been impossible to produce any general theoretical principles that lead necessarily to the conclusion that the classic freedoms of speech, thought, worship, assembly, etc., ought not to be infringed.

III. THE DEFENCE OF PARTICULAR FREEDOMS

The stubbornness with which men have sought to defend these freedoms suggests, however, that a case might be made for them that is more substantial than the purely formal one; that is, that over and above the general presumption against any restraint whatsoever, there are special reasons for resisting limitations on these particular freedoms. Those reasons must be pragmatic; they must show that whatever immediate or limited advantages may be gained from restraint in given cases, there are good utilitarian reasons for adopting these freedoms as general rules. It would then require a very weighty argument to warrant setting them aside in any given case. And in fact Mill offers reasons of just this sort in defence of freedom of thought, discussion, and the allied freedoms of association, public meeting, etc.

The principal case we shall advance is that these freedoms are especially important because they provide safeguards against the abuse of power *in other ways;* that where they are denied, those in authority need not justify either their objects or their methods.

(a) Freedom of thought

It has been argued that to treat freedom of thought as an ideal is absurd, since we cannot, in the nature of things, be deprived of it. Speech, writing, even gesture, are public; what a man thinks, he alone can know, unless he chooses to tell.

For all that, men have been persecuted for dangerous or heretical thoughts. Elaborate inquisitorial techniques have been devised for inducing a man to let out what it would be safer for him to keep to himself. If punishment follows, it is clearly aimed not at the utterance but at the thought itself. The attempt to censor thought in this way is wrong, if only because the means is unsuited to the end. The threat of punishment may persuade a man to recant, as did Galileo, but it will not persuade him that he is mistaken.

Thought can be negatively controlled by depriving men of access to the ideas of others, by censorship of books and discussion. This point can be left until we deal with freedom of discussion in general. Coupled with this, however, we have seen in the present century the development of subtle techniques of mass persuasion that, in the hands of a Goebbels, can paralyse the critical faculties of a nation. Individuals have been subjected to 'brain-washing' processes that are capable of completely, if not permanently, altering moral attitudes and critical canons. Koestler and Orwell have sufficiently explored the sinister possibilities of both techniques. Recent experiments in sub-liminal advertising have been aimed at influencing a television audience by split-second flashes of which the viewer is unconscious. This technique might also be very attractive to governments.

How do such techniques differ from more ordinary methods of persuasion? It is not that they seek to influence thought by methods other than rational argument, for that is true of some quite legitimate religious and moral exhortation. The main difference is that whereas evangelism leaves it open to the subject to preserve a critical detachment if he makes up his mind to do so, these techniques deliberately seek to destroy detachment, or, as in the television case, to by-pass it. Now altering a man's mind in such ways is not always and necessarily wrong. There is nothing wrong in exceptional conditions with brain surgery and electric shock treatment, although unlike psycho-analysis they alter attitudes and personality by side-stepping reason. Our antipathy to nineteen eighty-four methods may be due in part to the evil ends with

H

which we associate them, or with the physical and mental cruelty involved in particular techniques. But to see the issue clearly, we must set these considerations on one side, and suppose a wholly painless technique (the television method will serve as an example), aimed at some laudable object like creating a universal resolve not to go to war. Now given such an object, we might conceivably overcome our ordinary repugnance for such methods—but if we still feel in doubt, that is evidence that the repugnance is based on something more than a detestation of less worthy objects or crueller methods.

And we are right to suspect any technique that alters attitudes, not with the object of restoring the critical faculty, like psychotherapy, but of numbing it. We have argued in earlier chapters that morality requires respect for persons, a willingness to treat everyone as an end, and not solely as a means, and therefore a readiness to attend to their needs and listen to their claims. Anyone who conditions a patient without consulting him must, even on the most charitable estimate, have decided what was good for him without having let him speak for himself. Psychotherapy aims to bring about a healthy state of mind, and there are agreed criteria, although of rather a negative sort, for estimating its success.* This is its saving feature. Where the patient is unfit to state his own case, we do not give the therapist a free hand to make whatever he likes of his mind, as he thinks best. For benevolent mass conditioning, however, there are no agreed canons; moreover, it may be necessary for the success of painless conditioning that the patient should be unaware of what is being done. At best, then the operator is bound to make his own choice of what is good for others, regardless of what they would think.

But more than this: mental conditioning techniques are liable to frightful abuses. They make it possible not merely to overcome resistance in the present, but, by paralysing the critical faculty, to disarm it for the future, transforming the patient into the passive tool of the operator. This danger is in itself a sufficient ground for a strong general presumption against them. By threatening the critical faculties, they threaten not only freedom of thought, but every other interest too.

(b) Freedom of discussion

From the standpoint of politics, freedom of discussion can be defended in similar terms, as necessary to the defence of other interests. But this is not the whole story. In the *Letter on Toleration*, Locke distinguished 'practical' and 'speculative' opinions, arguing that the duty of toleration is not the same in both cases. 'Both sorts,' he says, 'consist in the know-

* We have in mind criteria like diminution of unconscious conflict, ability to hold down a job and to maintain reasonable social and sexual relationships, etc.

ledge of truth, yet these (speculative) terminate simply in the understanding, those (practical) influence the will and manners.'[15] This is an important distinction between descriptive, factual, or scientific beliefs, and prescriptive or normative beliefs or attitudes.*

Mill does not follow Locke in distinguishing descriptive and prescriptive beliefs, and his case for freedom of discussion is correspondingly weakened; for, as we hope to show, the cases must be treated differently. He argues that to suppress a belief may deprive humanity of a valuable truth. Even were the belief false, to suppress it is to prevent believers in the truth finding out for themselves how to refute it. Without that, the accepted truth tends to become lifeless dogma, and degenerates, in time, into error, because it is never overhauled. We can feel confident of a truth only after watching opponents trying, and failing, to refute it.

Now this is a strong case for scientific freedom. Indeed, it could be said to be implied in the very methods of scientific inquiry; for science makes progress by having research workers advance hypotheses which are then subjected to tests, to determine truth. And even the theory that is ultimately proved false may be valuable in stimulating useful research, and perhaps a better theory. To censor scientific publications is to prevent scientists from doing their job. Similarly, Mill's case is good for freedom to teach, for rigid orthodoxy in teaching will not produce sceptical, yet inventive, research workers. It could be argued, of course, that a teacher with eccentric and improbable beliefs about his subject—a flat-earth geographer, for example—might properly be dismissed for inefficiency. But the argument is so liable to abuse that it needs to be used cautiously: what was more improbable for the sixteenth century than Copernicus's view that the earth went round the sun?

The main point, however, is that Mill never meets the real case for persecution of opinion. Though some men have certainly been persecuted for false beliefs, many more have suffered for dangerous ones. And the dangerous ones are those that prescribe conduct, not those that simply describe facts. It might be wrong, indeed, to suppress a book condemning the existing social order and urging revolution; but it would clearly raise issues altogether different from the suppression of an unreliable text-book on histology.

---

* Nevertheless, it may be confusing to say that prescriptions 'consist in the knowledge of truth', for prescriptions are 'right' or 'wrong', rather than 'true' or 'false'. It might also be necessary to recognize a third, intermediate class of belief, namely, one that purports to be factual, but which, because of moral attitudes already adopted, would imply (and might be intended to imply) a prescription. Thus: 'The Soviet bloc is working for world peace' looks like a simple statement of fact (true or false); but since most people favour world peace, it might well be a covert invitation to support the Soviet bloc.

Mill argues that to suppress an opinion is to assume infallibility for oneself, which would be monstrously absurd. Now this might be true of the suppression of a descriptive opinion, but it is mistaken when applied to prescriptions. A government that decides to suppress a book that would have a morally pernicious influence is deciding to use its power to combat evil. This is a moral choice, and questions of infallibility simply do not arise. If we have a duty to combat an evil when it is within our power to do so, it is pusillanimous morality that shrinks from acting upon conviction, on the principle: 'who knows? the other fellow may be right after all'. It would be wrong not to consider the merits of his case before reaching a decision; it would be just as wrong to postpone decision indefinitely, or to shrink from acting on it, on the grounds that had one not been oneself, or had he put some other case than the one he did, one might conceivably have taken a different view. To make a moral judgment is to commit oneself to a course; the claims of tolerance may persuade us that the right course is not to interfere: they cannot persuade us that, though the right course is to interfere, we ought not to interfere because the right course might be wrong.

The case for freedom of discussion cannot be absolute; we are quite ready to exclude defamation, or the publication of military plans. But it can be a very strong case all the same. Leaving aside any special arguments for freedom of discussion in any particular field, the strongest general argument, in our view, is that it guards against the abuse or mis-use of authority or power. We mean by 'mis-use' the employment of authority with benevolent intentions but in a misguided way. A ruler may wish to do his best for his subjects, but if he does not permit them to communicate their needs and experiences, he is as likely to do them harm as good. We mean by 'abuse' the use of authority for immoral purposes, like self-aggrandizement or enrichment, revenge, or spite. Freedom to criticize sets limits to *de facto* authority, and restrains the tendency of power to corrupt. The power to suppress criticism rests with authorities like governments, ecclesiastical governors, university councils, and the like, the very people whose activities, by their far-reaching consequences in so many fields, demand the closest scrutiny. But they are the less to be trusted with the power of suppression because it is so evidently in their interest to suppress anything that tends to weaken their *de facto* authority. By building up a strong disapproval of suppression of opinion, liberal societies inhibit their rulers from acting as though the preservation of power were a legitimate end in itself.

The case so stated will admit of exceptions, like the law of libel. The need to watch public authorities does not automatically entitle every man to pry into his neighbour's affairs and publish them to the world.

A defamatory statement is not excused merely by its being true; making it must serve some public interest. If we publish the details of X's shady past from spite, we cannot claim the protection of 'free speech'; but if X is a candidate for Parliament, it becomes a matter of public concern to know what sort of man he is.*

Though we concede that there are grounds for limiting freedom of discussion in certain directions, the enormous importance of the principle in general demands that the exceptions be defined as closely as possible, and that they be narrowly construed. Where the responsibility for suppressing rests with established authorities, we cannot afford to leave them with wide discretion in exercising it.

(c) Freedom of assembly and of association

The general case we have made out for freedom of discussion will apply with almost equal force to these freedoms too. (The special problems of freedom of association will be treated in Chapter 13.)

Public assembly presents more difficulties than discussion. Since public meetings may degenerate into riots, there is often a better case for suppressing them. The Prime Minister does not shake in his shoes whenever a newspaper makes a personal attack on him; but the same sentiments from an orator to a crowd in Trafalgar Square may lead to broken windows at No. 10. Freedom of assembly and association are necessary if criticism is to be heard and produce results, but for that very reason they need to be more strictly limited than simple freedom of discussion. The most elementary duty of a government (as Hobbes saw more clearly than some of his critics) is to preserve the public peace; when a public meeting threatens to turn from airing grievances to smashing windows, the time has come to disperse it. And when an association moves from advocacy and lobbying to criminal conspiracy to assassinate Ministers, any but the most cynical of governments must feel not merely personally interested, but obliged to suppress it for government's sake. Since what is permissible cannot be closely defined, a fairly wide discretion must rest either on the police or on a judge, in deciding when the limits of tolerance have been reached. Consequently, there is likely to be more disagreement about particular infringements of the freedoms of assembly and association than about similar infringements of freedom of discussion.

* 'Public interest' is ambiguous. We do not mean that any publication is justified if there are people 'interested', i.e. curious, to read it; we mean that it must be justified in terms of public advantage. The point may seem trivial, but the tasteless intrusion of the press into private grief has often been defended on the grounds that these matters are of 'public interest'. Perhaps such interest should go unsatisfied.

IV. LIBERTY AND SOCIAL RESTRAINTS

We observed earlier in this chapter that the 'non-conformist' may be as much restrained by public opinion, applying conventional standards, as by institutionalized power, and we quoted Mill's view that the tyranny of the majority is 'not restricted to the acts that it may do by the hands of its political functionaries'. His relations with Harriet Taylor, and his heretical religious opinions, made him particularly sensitive to the social pressures of Victorian morality. The essay *On Liberty* was as much concerned with social as with the legal restraints with which we have been mainly concerned so far. We must now turn to the power of opinion, operating as an informal but effective technique of social control.

To adopt a moral attitude entails condemning conduct inconsistent with it. The question is, what forms ought condemnation to take? Should we silently disapprove, or remonstrate, or should we actively penalize the offender by ostracizing, refusing to employ, or otherwise making life a misery for him? If we adopt the conventional code as our own moral standard; if we are convinced that it provides necessary rules for good social living, ought we not use what pressure we can to see that the rules are kept?

This is to look at morality on the analogy of law, as a technique of control with its own deterrents. But would it not be better, if a rule is important enough to seem to demand deterrents, to incorporate these in law? And in that case, would it be defensible to inflict for the one offence the double punishment of a prison sentence, followed by ostracism?

To take the second question first: it must be admitted that for many people the fear of public reproach or loss of friends may count for more than the fear of prison, and if the one penalty did not exist, it might mean stiffening the other, or the total deterrent effect would be reduced. As things are, the social penalty constitutes a part of the total that society imposes for offences against the law.

This need cause less concern than the operation of social sanctions in cases where the criminal law is silent. Legal punishment depends on proof established before an impartial tribunal, after expert inquiry into law and fact. One can be reasonably confident that when social penalties accompany legal ones, they at least do not fall on the innocent. (It is nevertheless too common for a person acquitted by a court to be treated socially as if he had been proved guilty, merely on the basis of his having been accused.) Social penalties outside the scope of the law are imposed with less discrimination: passion has a bigger part than reason in judgment, and where popular prejudice, religious or racial hatred, is engaged, justice will be rough. 'Lynch law' is only social pressure gone to extremes. In times of popular excitement a mere suspicion of, say, 'un-Americanism' can mean economic and social ruin for the unfortunate suspect, without benefit of trial or possibility of appeal.

As a coercive technique of control, social pressure is a blunter instrument than the criminal law, less discriminating and less reliable in its operation. It has, however, advantages of its own. Its very informality enables it to deal with offences like gross ingratitude and disloyalty to friends, too vague for legal definition, and hard to prove on evidence in a court of law, but which might nevertheless be dealt with satisfactorily by the rough and ready judgment of those who know the circumstances.* Further, morality is concerned as much with dispositions as with particular acts. We praise or blame men for their characters as well as for particular actions; we put them on trial only for their offences. By encouraging men to cultivate desirable dispositions, and by bringing pressure to bear on the owners of disagreeable ones, conventional morality exercises an influence for which the criminal law could never offer a substitute.

Generally speaking, however, Mill was rightly suspicious of the pressure of conventional opinion. It is not that it is never right; it is rather that it is so much more liable than legal techniques to be wrong. Conventional opinion can—and logically must—operate by exhortation and remonstrance. It does not need to rely on other sanctions, for it instils in most men a set of attitudes that restrain, as it were, from within. Society controls us through our own inhibitions, and we absorb and reproduce the standards of our moral environment as unconsciously as we breathe.

But suppose, in a given case, such social training has failed: suppose I know for a certainty that an employee of mine has been guilt of gross, though not criminal, immorality, have I not a duty to the community at large to sack him, as an expression of disapproval and an example to others? Particular cases, particularly considered, might support this view; but if they are advanced to justify action of this sort as a general rule, they must be suspect. The occasions on which we know the facts for a certainty, without the benefit of police investigation and cross-examination, may be fewer than we suppose; the desire to do the right thing is often mixed with the desire to be rid of an embarrassment, or to indulge a favourite prejudice. A society in which every citizen is the

---

* Social pressures of this sort are likely to be most effective in small and static societies; in large ones, where there is plenty of movement, one escapes ostracism by going to another town.

censor of his neighbour's morals is likely to be an inharmonious one at best, and cursed with blackmailers at worst. To make it a general rule that private persons should employ whatever power they have to uphold morality, is to rely upon a technique of control liable to grave abuses.

This is not to argue that we have no business with anyone's morality except our own; for this would be to reject an admittedly important technique of guiding conduct. We are not questioning the duty to remonstrate and exhort, to praise and blame, but the desirability of reinforcing such influences by the wayward use of private power.

PART THREE

PRINCIPLES OF ASSOCIATION
AND THE DEMOCRATIC STATE

CHAPTER 11

INDIVIDUALS IN ASSOCIATION

1. THE PUZZLING FEATURES OF 'SOCIAL WHOLES'

We said, in Chapter 1, that what we call a human society is a number of individuals bound together by a normative order, or body of rules. This account must now be amplified. In succeeding chapters we shall be concerned particularly with states, with their relations with associations of other sorts and with one another, and with the rights and duties we attribute to them as 'social wholes'. As a preliminary, we devote this chapter to a study of some of the puzzling features of the idea of a social whole.

We frequently speak of a society as if it were a sort of person. In law, corporate persons, like joint-stock companies and borough councils enjoy rights and duties, own property, are liable in tort and contract, much as if they were individuals. To attribute rights and duties in this way is clearly not the same thing as to attribute them severally to the individual members, as we saw in our discussion of property rights in Chapter 7. A limited company can be bankrupt without each of its shareholders being bankrupt. It is not only in law that the question of corporate personality arises. In everyday speech we say things like 'The TUC takes the view that...' or '...has decided to...'. Does this mean that all the trade union members of Britain take such a view, or a majority of them, or perhaps only the members of the General Council, or even only a majority of *them*? Or is it something different from all these?

Puzzling too is the way in which an association can outlive the individual associates. As Burke said of the state, 'it becomes a partnership not only between those who are living, but between those who are living, those who are dead, and those who are to be born'.[1] These perplexities yield fairly easily to the sort of normative analysis that we have employed in earlier chapters, in dealing for instance with authority and with the problem of rights. Acts attributed to associations are, in the end, the acts of those 'in authority'—acts of individuals duly authorized by rules; and the identity and 'life' of an association is to be found in its rules, and not in any spirit or super-personality above its particular members.

There are other problems, however, that require different handling. There is an obvious sense in which an agent or official of an association can commit it, as for example when he signs a contract on its behalf. 'Commitment' in this sense can be satisfactorily analysed in terms of authority given to some and obligations placed on other individuals by the association's rules, or by a greater rule system like law which includes it. In a different sense, however, the particular members may *feel* committed by such an act. Now we cannot account for feelings or attitudes, like loyalty or solidarity, simply by analysing rule systems. When men feel loyalty to their nation, or devotion to their church, what sort of attitude are they adopting, and what does it mean in terms of their behaviour? It is surely not the same as loyalty felt towards every member severally. This raises conceptual problems in psychology rather than in institutional analysis; for we are concerned here not with rule systems but with mental attitudes. The importance of this distinction will be apparent when we come to examine nations and nationalism, later in this chapter.

II. TWO APPROACHES TO ASSOCIATION

We shall distinguish first two ways of looking at an association. On the one hand, we may take the obvious line and say that an association is a number of individuals acting within the same rule system. This approach focuses attention on Brown, Smith, and Jones, each with his own interests and goals, which may be conditioned by the rule system, but which are nevertheless, from this point of view, the aims of these particular individuals. Alternatively, we may concentrate on the rules themselves. The picture is now different. In place of Brown and company, we see a normative system which constitutes 'roles', often within a hierarchical structure of authority.[2]

In the first account, whatever is done can ultimately be described in terms of the actions of one or more individuals. Whatever intentions, purposes, or will we attribute to the association will be located in the end in some or all of the members considered severally. They may appear now in the capacity of fathers, now as landlords, tenants, judges, and so on; but however we describe them, the history of the association will be the history of its members' actions, and nothing else.

In the second account, individuals disappear; for this is not a 'biographical' but a sociological or anthropological approach. The association now appears as a pattern of rules and procedures, abstracted from the individuals who may happen at any given moment to be operating within it. The system, we have said, constitutes roles—that is to say, there are within it foci of rights and duties to which labels attach, like father, landlord, judge, and we can talk of these without reference to any particular persons who may at any time fill them, just as we can discuss the role of Hamlet without considering whether the actor is Olivier, Gielgud, or Garrick. Thus, when we say 'The Prime Minister may recommend a dissolution' we may not be referring specifically to Mr Macmillan, or Sir Anthony Eden, but to *anyone* qualified to fill the role or office of Prime Minister. There is a sense in which the statement is timeless, divorced from particular events or men, just as a critique of Hamlet may have no reference to particular interpretations of the part. (In another sense, however, statements about the functions of roles would not be *true*, as descriptions of an effective system of rules, unless events and actions over a fairly long period tended to conform to them.) Roles may be grouped into institutions, forming co-operative procedure systems for the performance of certain understood tasks.[3] Thus a police force is constituted by a number of roles, like constables, inspectors, and so on, each with its own part in an integrated programme that would be set in motion whenever, for example, a crime was committed.*

Now both accounts of association, in terms of individuals and in terms of rules, are equally valid, and can describe the same facts, though from different points of view. But it is important to keep the distinction clear; we shall see later the sort of perplexities which arise from failing to do so.

III. THE ACTS AND PURPOSES OF ASSOCIATIONS

(a) 'Acts'

Evidently, to attribute an action to an association is not to attribute it to every member severally. Acts are ascribed to an association when they are done by agents authorized by its rules, according to prescribed procedures. An act of a state is simply the act of someone in authority, or a number of such acts by different authorities, related by constitutional procedures. 'The United States made a treaty' means that individuals qualified to act in the roles of Secretary of State, President, Senators, and so on, have performed acts appropriate to their offices

---

* The distinction between 'institution' and 'association' is not a clear one—which term we apply depends very much upon our standpoint. Thus a family may be regarded as an association, as a normative order though of a rather informal sort. But if we were describing, for instance, a tribal community, we might treat the family as one of its institutions, through which it organized property relations and the rearing of children. Similarly, the police force is an association of policemen, but it is also a state institution.

according to the prescribed procedure, together constituting 'an act of treaty-making by the United States'. Other acts attributable to the association may involve other officials; what makes them all 'acts of the United States' is their authority under the constitution. On the other hand, the individual cast in the role of President may also act in other roles—as father of his family, member of his golf club, etc. These acts will be defined in terms of other normative orders, and will not constitute 'acts of the United States'.

In essentials, this is the account that Hobbes gave of the unity of an association, and of the sense in which acts are attributable to it:

> 'A multitude of men, are made *one* person, when they are by one man, or one person, represented; so that it be done with the consent of every one of that multitude in particular. For it is the *unity* of the representer, not the *unity* of the represented, that maketh the person *one*. And it is the representer that beareth the person, and but one person: and *unity*, cannot otherwise be understood in multitude.'[4]

But he unduly limits the analysis in making the authority of the agent depend on the consent of every member; for authority springs from rules, and an association can exist effectively even though some of its members disapprove both of their 'representer' and of the rules authorizing him. Rules will be effective, of course, only if they are generally recognized; but that means only that they are the basis for expectation— that in a given situation men *look for* the sort of action that the rules demand from the person that the rules appoint, even though they might *prefer* things otherwise.

(b) 'Purpose'

Similarly, when we speak of the *purpose* of an association in a particular act or policy, we refer to goals envisaged by its authorized agents, which some at least of its members may not share. If we ask 'What was Britain's purpose in sending troops to Suez in 1956?' we can only mean 'What was the intention or conscious aim of the individuals for the time being acting as H.M. Government?' Of course, many people approve of it and many others did not—but how many there were on each side is irrelevant to the analysis of the original question.

But now, suppose we say 'The purpose of the Metropolitan Police Force is to prevent and detect crime in London'. We do not necessarily mean that this is the *intention* of whoever is for the time being Commissioner of Police—for we may want to take him to task for lacking such a purpose. The point is that 'purpose' means something different here from what it meant in the first case. There it meant the goal envisaged by individuals in choosing a course of action in a given situation; here it means the *function* of an institution in a range of possible situations.[5] We have moved from the biographical to the sociological account of association, from talking about individuals to talking about roles and institutions.

When we speak of the 'function' of an institution, we do not necessarily imply anything about anyone's aims or intentions. 'Function' may be understood in at least two ways, but neither involves purpose in the sense of conscious aim.[6] We might say, for instance, that a policeman's function, *qua* policeman, is to prevent crime, or that of an army to protect the country from invasion. To attribute a function in this sense is to indicate an end which the institution *ought* to bring about; it lays down a standard for assessing performance. A particular policeman may neglect his duties; he may be corrupt and criminal. His actual objectives, in short, may not square with his function. To define the function of a role is not, therefore, to say that any individual filling it necessarily wills the fulfilment of the function, or is even aware of what it is. This is even clearer in the second sense of 'function', which is analogous to the way in which a physiologist might speak of the heart's function in maintaining the supply of blood. 'Function' in this sense indicates an end actually brought about by an institution, though it may be quite unintended. Thus an anthropologist might describe the function of a ritual as maintaining tribal solidarity, though the intention of the performers is to placate evil spirits. Or it might be said of some armies that their function is to enhance the prestige of the aristocracy. This need not mean that anyone necessarily intends this result, but rather that this is one of the things that the army as an institution does in fact do, which helps to give the society its particular character. In certain instances functions in both these senses may coincide. A police force has the function of keeping order, in the sense that this is what it ought to do; if it is not corrupt, it will also have this function in the second sense, since it will in fact be helping to give the society its particular character as an orderly whole. But in neither sense is there any necessary imputation of an aim or intention to any one policeman, or to policemen in general. For policemen might fulfil their function even though their aim was only to demonstrate their own importance, providing their method of doing so prevented breaches of law. It is clear, too, that to impute a function to an institution does not imply the existence of anything that might be called a collective mind or spirit, immanent or transcendent, that has the function as a collective aim. Biologists arguing whether the function of a polar bear's white coat is to conserve heat or to camouflage it from its prey are not seeking to penetrate the mind of a transcendent creator, or even of an immanent evolutionary life force.

There is, admittedly, a third sense of 'function' which is subordinate to aim, namely, the sense in which we might say that the function of a knife is to cut. Here there is a deliberate intention on the part of the knife-maker to make a tool that will do a certain job. And some institutions may be deliberately designed in this way, as when an Act of Parliament establishes a Board with the function of administering a nationalized industry. But not only do many institutions (like the British Parliament itself) not originate in this way, but even those that do may subsequently develop quite different functions from those intended. The present functions of the United States Congress are a good deal more extensive than anything envisaged by the Founding Fathers.

This analysis clears up some of the confusion in the theory of the General Will, or at any rate in the Idealist version of that theory. According to Bosanquet's account, for example, an association has a purpose which is the expression of a collective or social mind. Institutions are 'principles' or 'ideas' which are different aspects of the social mind and purpose, mediating between the universal and the individual mind. The latter can be 'analysed' into 'features each of which should be an individual case of a universal principle'.[7] He means that every role in which an individual appears is a particular manifestation of some institutional principle, and thus some aspect of the collective purpose. Thus in assuming such institutional roles, an individual participates in the social mind and purpose, in a General Will, which Bosanquet calls his 'real will', distinct from his particular (or 'actual') will as a *mere* individual. And so, in fulfilling his institutional duties, he necessarily conforms to both the General Will and his 'real will' and is therefore free. If his actual will conflicts with it, he may *feel* constrained, but only because he is ignorant or careless of what he 'really' wills.

Now there is something very odd about saying that an individual has two wills. He can, of course, set himself mutually frustrating goals through ignorance of the true conditions of choice; or he may be unable to decide which of them he wants most; or he may even refuse to face up to the need to choose. Bosanquet's dual will is not, however, the outcome of mere ignorance of fact or psychological ambivalence. The 'real will' may not be a conscious, or even a sub-conscious intention: for he infers it not from a study of a man's mind, but from his social roles. It is as if anyone filling a role must *of necessity* will the General Will, and psychological facts have really nothing to do with it. Now if we interpret the General Will as a functional concept, this makes sense of a sort. Bosanquet would then be saying that a society is a system of functionally related roles and intitutions, and an individual cast in any given role could then be said to have an appropriate function in relation to the whole system. As we have seen, his actual objectives may not correspond to that function, i.e. his 'actual will' and his 'real will' may diverge. However, to state the function of a role is quite different from imputing an intention—a will—to its particular occupant. Strictly speaking, 'will' is out of place in the vocabulary of roles and institutions—it belongs to the 'biographical' vocabulary by which we account for the behaviour of individuals. Consequently, we are right to be uneasy at the paradoxical use of 'freedom' which makes a man 'free' whenever he is performing the duties of his roles, whatever his apparent wishes. The conscripted pacifist is not the more free for being compelled to perform the duties of his role of soldier. For anyone occupying a role does not necessarily desire to fulfil its functions; and if a man is compelled to do so, he is forced to act *against his will*, not in accordance with another will which is also his, inferred from the role he occupies. In the theory of the 'real will' the confusion of biographical with functional analysis has led to a moral outrage.

IV. THE SOLIDARITY OF ASSOCIATIONS

(a) The General Will as collective decision

For Rousseau, however, the General Will is more than a functional notion, though it is that too. On the one hand, it is the function of the ideal state, directed to the Common Good. Every man, in his role of citizen, shares in it, whether or not he or anyone else in the state seeks, as a matter of fact, to realize it. The General Will is indestructible, 'constant, unalterable and pure'; but it may nevertheless be mute, i.e. the individuals acting in their political roles as citizens may have no intention of fulfilling their functions. We noticed above that statements of function are, in a sense, timeless: 'The purpose of the state is to realize the Common Good' may therefore be true, though it may not be the intention of any of its members at any given moment.

On the other hand, Rousseau's General Will is also a series of decisions, in which every member of the state directly participates in a legislative assembly. But though all collective decisions reached by majority vote are expressions of the 'will of all', they are not all expressions of the General Will. The General Will is expressed only when those participating direct themselves to the question 'What is for the advantage of the whole association?' instead of to the question, 'What is for the advantage of myself, my friends, or my party?' The General Will is expressed, then, only in decisions taken in a special way, or by people acting in a special frame of mind.

This is one of the important differences between Rousseau and Hobbes. For Hobbes, an association is merely a framework of rules and procedures sanctioned by coercive power, within which individuals pursue self-interested goals. For Rousseau, it creates the possibility of morality; for it provides the individual with a possible interest outside himself, in the welfare of the association as a whole, and through it, in the welfare of each of its members. The General Will will not emerge unless the members realize this possibility, and vote disinterestedly.

We have argued that 'an act of an association' is ultimately the act of its authorized agents according to authorized procedures. Thus 'The committee has decided . . .' may mean simply that a majority of qualified members have outvoted a minority. This is equivalent to Rousseau's 'will of all'. But it could also be the case that no member, if the choice were his alone, would decide in precisely the way that the committee has decided. Each might find some opposition to his own policy, and a solution might be sought which, while satisfying no one completely, would meet most of the objections, and give everyone the sense that what he felt to be important had not been neglected. In the process, individual attitudes might change; each member might no longer want simply the adoption of his own policy—he might come to attach as much importance to finding a solution acceptable to everyone. The process of deliberation might produce a decision that could not have emerged otherwise. Once a decision has been reached in this way, every member may well feel committed even though the course is one with which he might formerly have disagreed, and 'committed' not merely because majority decisions bind minorities, but in the sense that he has an interest in it, feels bound to defend it from outside criticism, and feels bound to help carry it out. Anyone who has had experience of Quaker business meetings will recognize these procedures and attitudes and will distinguish them without difficulty from those of the *Assemblée Nationale*. A decision reached under these conditions might usefully be described as 'the sense of the meeting' or 'a general will'. But it would be quite another thing to say that other decisions reached through constitutional procedures expressed a general will, just because all parties were committed by their acceptance of the procedures. For the minority might remain dissatisfied, resolved to campaign for a reversal of the decisions at the earliest possible moment, though submitting for the time being.

A 'general will' in the sense we have allowed could emerge only in rather special conditions, e.g. where deliberations are face-to-face, where there is assurance of good faith, and where there are no fundamental moral disagreements. It might be found in some families and some committees, and even in larger gatherings, of village or tribe, where the members are intimately involved with one another over a wide range of interests. It may have been possible in the classical city-states (which Rousseau certainly had in mind in *The Social Contract*), or in the communities of the Middle Ages. It is significant, perhaps, that in those epochs it was a commonplace to describe associations by organic analogies, stressing participation in collective action, rather than in the contractual terms of the seventeenth and eighteenth centuries, with their emphasis on individual goals privately conceived though co-operatively pursued.

To seek a general will in our present sense in the mass associations of the twentieth century is surely to be misled by inappropriate analogies. It is sometimes said, for example, that the democratic state is governed by discussion; that deliberations in Cabinet and Parliament reflect deliberation in the country, in local meetings, in the press, in radio discussion, and so on, from which emerges a general will. But the sort of consensus that sometimes emerges from face-to-face discussion cannot be expected from nation-wide debate. In the course of controversy, some may be wholly persuaded, and others may modify their views; nevertheless, political opponents set out to win majority or influential backing, not primarily to reach agreement. Even a compromise is rarely more than the best that can be wrung from the other side—and there will always remain a disgruntled minority unreconciled and suspicious. These attitudes are obviously different from one that values other people's views and feelings instead of seeing them as annoying obstacles. For this seeks not merely to prevail but to do so with the widest possible agreement. Yet it is something like this that Rousseau asks of his sovereign assembly; it is surely unreasonable to ask it of anonymous millions. Clearly, participation in a decision-making process does in itself amount to subscribing to the final result, and in so far as the Hegelian terminology of 'General Will' and 'Real Will' suggests that it does, it is grossly misleading.

(b) The solidarity of the mass association, and the associative image

To say, however, that the acts of a mass association are simply those of its authorized agents, and its personality merely the unity of its rule structure, would not explain why members feel 'committed' by their leaders' decisions, as if they shared responsibility for them. It would account neither for the attitude 'My country right or wrong', nor, conversely, for the shame of a man who feels that his leaders have committed him to immoral policies. That is not because the analysis is wrong, but because it is concerned not with the psychological facts of solidarity and loyalty, but only with the formal unity of a common system of rules.

The solidarity of a mass association, whether trade union, church, or state, does not derive from the unity of a collective general will, by virtue of which every member mysteriously participates in, and subscribes to, every decision attribute to it. Nor is it merely a conscious submission to the procedural requirement that minorities must submit to majorities. It derives rather from the loyalty of the members to an ideal 'image' of the association, with which each identifies himself. The name of the association is for its members a focus for a set of ideal characteristics, as if it were indeed the name of a person. It is associated with a system of personifications and symbols, each representing a set of standards, capable of inspiring respect, and even reverence. And, of course, such ideal characteristics and standards are, to a certain extent, abstracts from the actual traditions and purposes of an association. An Englishman's 'England' might be compounded of symbols like the Queen, the lion, the imperturbability of the London policeman, Whittle and his jet-engines—even an ideal 'Englishman'. With all these he is emotionally involved, and the loyalties which are felt for them are not necessarily irrational.

Similarly, the images which people have of political parties have been shown in recent studies to be of great importance in explaining how people vote. In the short run at least, the party image counts for a good deal more than the party programme. This is not to say that men are loyal to the fictions of their own imaginations, which exist, ghost-like, only because simpletons believe in them. It may be based on a party's record, on a reputation built up over the years by adhering to consistent and distinctive principles. The image, however, is a myth in the sense that it tends to realize itself just because men believe in it.[8] To hold its supporters, a party must cultivate the image; its leaders cannot do violence to it too openly and too frequently without disillusioning their followers.

The personification of associations, by which we attribute to them unity, life, and will, may obscure the complex realities of decision and procedure; but it represents, at the same time, an important psychological fact, for it is a principal source of that emotional involvement with leaders, which we call 'loyalty'.

V. 'ASSOCIATIONS' AND 'COMMUNITIES'

(a) Associations with limited purposes

Emotional involvement with the associative image, is not, of course, of equal importance for all associations. We should not expect the share-holders of a joint-stock company to feel deeply committed, in an emotional rather than a financial sense, by their board of directors. Their interest is not likely to go much beyond the size of the dividend and the security of the capital. Only a very few members of the average co-operative society feel at all deeply involved in the conduct of its business. Thus many associations can be described fairly adequately in terms of procedures whereby individuals co-operate for limited and privately conceived ends. The contractual analogy, which was commonly used in seventeenth and eighteenth century accounts of association, is particularly appropriate in such cases. A business contract involves the assumption of obligations, on the understanding that others will fulfil theirs; it is intelligible only if we suppose that each party expects to get out of the arrangement benefits which more than compensate for what he puts in.

Associations of this type have a relatively narrow range of interests. For that very reason their members feel less deeply involved with them than with, say, their families or their nation. Their rules will generally be formally established; membership will be determined by clearly understood criteria (like payment of a subscription, or a formal under-taking) since only those who clearly accept its obligations will be entitled to the association's benefits. This sort of association was for Locke the standard pattern of all societies except the family—and even the family became contractual once the children reached the age of reason.

(b) The family

This account of associations becomes less and less adequate, however, as we move from joint-stock companies and sports-clubs towards the family and the nation. The differences between these two types have seemed so important that some writers reserve the term 'association' to the first, using 'community' for the second.[9] However, there are so many intermediate possibilities between the two extremes, like churches, Communist parties, and even trade unions, that sharp distinction in nomenclature may suggest a more clear-cut classification than the facts will allow.

Nevertheless, the differences between the two extreme types are brought out clearly when we consider the family. Kinship determines its membership, but beyond that the criteria are vague. Does a family extend, for example, to second cousins or relatives by marriage? Again, the rules which constitute its order are ill-defined, and vary considerably from one family to another; yet there is no criterion for determining with precision whether a given rule is part of a family order or not. The functions of the family are extremely varied; they extend from the care of children to the regulation of property and religion. The aims, too of a member of a family are irrelevant to his membership. One becomes a member of a cricket club because one is interested in cricket. But to be a member of a family one does not have to have any specific aim or interest.

The analysis of the family as an association has become increasingly difficult through the modern tendency to moralize relationships within marriage. There have, of course, always been considerable variations in the pattern of family life within different strata of society. But super-imposed on these traditional differences are those introduced by the introduction of moral considerations of justice, and equality between the sexes. The husband is no longer lord and master with his rights and obligations prescribed by predictable traditions. The wife is often a wage-earner as well; so she is seldom prepared to play a purely sub-servient role. The result is that, to a certain extent, married couples have to mould their own marriage in terms of what they consider 'fair', whatever the traditions of their parents may have been. This introduces a great variety of patterns of adjustment even within the same social class. There is great variation, too, in the manner in which the up-bringing of children is undertaken and their conduct regulated. Some believe in treating the child as far as is possible as a being in his own right whose independence should be encouraged and respected. Others still regard children always as adults in the making whose conduct needs to be carefully controlled and supervised. In some families the child-ren's claims and demands are seriously considered in matters of family policy; in other families the adults always know what is best. All such divergences, due to the intrusion of moral as well as purely cus-tomary or fashionable considerations, have tended to complicate the over-all picture of family life and to make any simple analysis im-possible.[10]

Nevertheless, members of a family, for some period of their life at any rate, are deeply involved with it. This is because membership en-tails many rights and duties, which begin at birth and end only in death. Much stress has been laid by anthropologists and psychologists[11] on the importance of methods of child-rearing in passing on the standards of a culture and shaping its basic personality type. Loyalties are first learnt in the family. The rights and duties which define one's position in the family are therefore very difficult to repudiate, and they lay down a pattern for more general social duties. Some psychologists believe that attitudes like that of a subordinate to his superior officer in the army are often a continuation of attitudes to the father.

(c) Nations and nationalism

It is therefore easy to see how one becomes deeply involved with the family, even though individual aims are irrelevant to membership, and the functions of the family and its membership criteria are vague. Determining what constitutes a nation is even more difficult. What is a nation for? Is it *for* anything? Or is it simply a complex of institutions like the state, church, or trade union, each of which taken separately might be assigned functions, but which together amount only to something very vague indeed, like 'a way of life'? What are the criteria for membership of a nation, and which normative relations fall within the national system, and which outside it? These difficulties largely disappear if we identify 'nation' and 'state'; but since we commonly talk about 'subject nations struggling for independence', i.e. to become states, there are apparently grounds for distinguishing the two concepts. It seems strange, however, that a type of association so ill-defined as the nation could be considered of such enormous importance in modern politics.[12]

'The nation' is a relatively modern conception, just as nationalism is a modern political ideal. In the Middle Ages, men did not think of themselves as Englishmen, Frenchmen, or Germans, but as vassals of their overlord, subjects of their king, and ultimately members of a universal order of Christendom. Gradually the monarchs of Western Europe strengthened themselves against the Emperor and the Pope on the one side and their barons on the other, each building up an increasingly centralized structure of political authority, and becoming a more important focus for loyalty than any competitor. At this stage, the idea of nationality was co-terminous with political allegiance. In 1789, the Abbé Sieyès wrote: 'What is a nation? A unity of combined individuals who are governed by *one* law and so are represented by the same lawgiving assembly.'

Until then, the conception of 'nationhood' was compatible with an individualist view of association, and the contractual analogy was not inappropriate for describing it. Membership of the nation-state so conceived might not be voluntary, but it might be thought of nevertheless in Locke's way, as essentially a collection of individuals pursuing private ends within a structure of rules, which provided the advantages of co-operation and eliminated mutual frustration in return for the acceptance of obligations.

Towards the end of the eighteenth century, however, a new view of nationhood was emerging, particularly in Germany, that seemed more appropriately expressed by organic than contractual analogies. The basis of this approach was cultural and linguistic rather than political.[13]

The individualism of Hobbes, Locke, Voltaire, and the Encyclopae-
dists, and their contractual analogies, came under heavy fire. Because
such individualist theories supposed a pre-social individual in a state of
nature and put him into society by a fictitious contract, they were said
to deal not with men but with unreal abstractions. The cultural cosmopolitanism associated with such theories emasculated literature and art,
because it uprooted the artist from the national tradition that made him
uniquely himself. The ideal 'humanity', which it put in place of national
tradition, deprived the artist of all character, and stripped the concept
'man' of its meaning and substance. Literary critics and philologists,
like Herder, who sought to revive—or create—a culture rooted in
German mediaeval tradition, language, and folk-lore, saw the artist
instead as a medium through which a national spirit spoke—a Volksgeist developing itself for the enrichment of mankind. In broader terms,
they saw a man not as an abstract 'individual', but as a manifestation of
the national spirit. This is what linked him with other members of his
nation who were different manifestations of the same spirit. And it also
distinguished them all from members of other nations. Analogously, an
oak tree might be said to be a principle or 'spirit' variously manifest in
its leaves, bark, and roots, which exists through them, and gives them
unity and identity. By virtue of this principle we can speak of 'oak
leaves, oak bark', etc. But equally, this principle is what distinguishes
them from sycamore leaves, roots, and bark. The national spirit is
manifest in language, customs, laws, and ideals. According to Hegel, it
cannot be fully expressed and conscious of itself as a corporate personality unless the nation becomes also a state, in which form it is capable of
will and self-assertion against others.[14] Other associations like the family
or the economic guild are also organic in structure, but they are more
like organs within the national body than organisms in their own right.

This view of the nation is the basis of European nationalism of the
nineteenth century, which resulted in the formation of the German and
the dismemberment of the Austrian and Turkish Empires. It provided,
too, an ideological framework for Nazi expansion: no matter who ruled
them or where they lived, all German-speaking people were members of
the German nation, and their proper place was within the German
state, the institutional manifestation of the Volksgeist.

The metaphysical basis of this account is dubious and its practical
consequences have been in many ways disastrous. Nevertheless, it
emphasizes the important distinction we have already noted between
associations like the family, the church, and the nation, and others, like
joint-stock companies and cricket clubs. Where the social contract
theory was weak was in assimilating all associations to the latter type.

It treated the goals and interests of individuals as if they could always be understood apart from the particular society, which was itself only a convenient vehicle for pursuing privately determined ends in co-operation. The strength of the organic analogy is that it appreciates the degree to which membership of a society can mould the aims and interests which each member sets himself. Indeed, much of what he does may be for no other reason than to conform to the rules of his society, or to live up to standards which are his simply because he is a member of this one rather than another. A Catholic's ideals are different from a Jew's precisely because they belong to different religious communities. The Church is not simply an organization used by individuals for satisfying privately conceived religious needs. For those born into it, at any rate, it stimulates and forms the needs themselves. The Catholic needs the Church in large measure because the Church has made him what he is. Similarly, the aims sought by Germans when they vote in elections may, in a sense, express individual interests as they see them; but these interests have been conceived within a context of national ideals and aspirations which distinguish them sharply from goals sought by American or English voters.

Common cultural and linguistic characteristics are evidently important in defining a nation. But a nation is not just a group with common characteristics, like the class of red-headed men or rice-eaters. It is not a logical class, but an entity whose existence is mainly in the minds of those who believe that they belong to it. The class of English-speaking people are not one but several nations. On the other hand, Walloons are not Frenchmen, but form, with the Flemings, a Belgian nation, despite their cultural affinities with the French. Though many people in Central Europe in the seventeenth century habitually spoke German, and shared other common patterns of behaviour, it is still true to say that no German nation existed until German nationalism created it. When Germans began to regard their common characteristics as particularly important, distinguishing them as a group from other men, they began to form an idea or 'image' of the German nation, with which they were emotionally involved. They became self-consciously German. 'German' then became more than just a label for classifying people with certain common features, like 'cannibal'; it became a focus for loyalties. The national image was closely connected with a sense of sharing in a common tradition, and an awareness of a common history with which members identified themselves. A nation's history is a sort of myth, holding up heroes for reverence and imitation, and thus setting standards and ideals. The sense of common history is also a bond of sympathy between those who share it. Germans feel that Frederick the Great 'belongs' to them, as Englishmen feel about Nelson or Frenchmen about Joan of Arc. Yet in another sense it might be said that Germans 'belong' to the tradition which Frederick symbolizes for them. This is not a matter of ancestry in the strict sense, for though a man's forbears may have been foreigners, he may still share in the tradition.

The national image may vary; aspects important for some may count less for others. For instance, in the Suez crisis of 1956 there were some Britons who felt humiliated because the 'lion' qualities of majesty, mastery and pugnacity—so well symbolized by Churchill during the Second World War—had been betrayed. There were others, however, who felt humiliated and ashamed because things were being done in Britain's name that were unworthy of the ideal image of Britain as the law-abiding protector of the weak. These differences are related to different aspects of a common tradition. The British believe that though they acted rather like brave adventurers in acquiring their empire, they also always brought the rule of law and protected the weak, once they had acquired it. A nation could hardly survive as an association without a fairly close correspondence between the images which members have formed of it. For it is created by and itself helps to create and perpetuate many strands of a common tradition.

The national 'image' is thus at once a focus for loyalties and a set of rough linguistic and cultural criteria which determine who belongs to the nation. The group thus formed has a corporate solidarity and mutual sympathies that it does not extend to outsiders. Such sympathies would not be enough, perhaps, in themselves to constitute an association in a strict sense; but once common interests are recognized, the nation rapidly develops exclusive institutions, like cultural associations and national political parties. Desiring to pursue its common interests and ideals in the most effective way, the nation aspires to self-government or statehood. This need not be the case, however; there are nationally-conscious Welshmen and Scots who are not politically nationalists, but who are anxious nevertheless to preserve their cultural traditions.

The growth of Indian nationalism was different. The subjects of the British Raj had neither linguistic, ethnic, nor religious unity, but only a common resentment of alien governors who treated them all as inferiors, but who also provided the political pattern within which national self-consciousness could grow. (In the event, Hindu and Muslim were too deeply divided to be united even by similar aspirations towards independence of the British, and two nations and two states emerged.) Though there were varied reasons why Indians were hostile to the Raj, there formed, within the many-sided opposition, a common national image, a new focus for sentiment and loyalty. And so the institutions which gave 'the Indian nation' meaning as a normative order were evolved in the struggle for independence. As in Western Europe, political organization preceded national consciousness. And this is again obviously true of Nigeria, which had no identity in any sense until British administrators created it, but whose peoples are now well on the way to forming a Nigerian nation, despite considerable cultural and linguistic diversity.

To sum up: when men say they belong to this or that nation, they are not always saying quite the same things. They identify themselves with a group image, and through it with other men for whom they feel sympathy and loyalty not extended to outsiders. But the criteria for identifying fellow nationals vary considerably. We have noted three sorts of national self-consciousness; it may spring from recognition of similar cultural interests, not necessarily related or directed to political organization (e.g. the Welsh); it may spring from common membership of a political association (the French version, as enunciated by Sieyès); or it may spring from the unity of purpose discovered in striving for independence of a common alien ruler (as in India, Malaya, or Indonesia). These do not exhaust the possibilities, nor are they mutually exclusive.*

Whatever the sense of 'nation', however, we should hesitate to refer to a group as a 'nation' unless a fairly large proportion of its members considered themselves such. The French-speaking people of Quebec are not a French-Canadian nation, neither are they French. French, German, and Italian-speaking Swiss are simply three sorts of Swiss: their national image transcends or embraces linguistic differences, and it would be odd to make distinctions of nationality where they make none themselves.

VI. STATES, NATIONS, AND 'SOCIETY'

'State' and 'nation' are related concepts—sometimes so closely related that in some contexts the words are interchangeable. In law, there is no distinction between membership of a state and of the corresponding nation. On the other hand, although in law Greek Cypriots are British nationals (more precisely, 'citizens of the United Kingdom and Colonies'), in a non-legal sense they are Greeks under British rule, for their national image is Greek not British. An Englishman, however, would rarely distinguish his own state and nation, unless he were engaged in political theorizing; 'country' certainly embraces both.

* Thus Arab nationalism is compounded of a group of closely-related languages, Islam, a consciousness of the glories of the mediaeval Arab empire and a hostility to alien rulers and commercial influences.

Hegelians, as we have seen, would say that ideally 'state' and 'nation' coincide; or rather, that a nation has not become fully self-conscious until it has achieved statehood, but that then the state includes the nation. In terms of individuals, 'state' and 'nation' would only be different ways of referring to the same collection; in terms of normative orders, the nation would be included within the state order. Liberal individualists, however, have usually insisted on a more limited definition of 'the state'. A people living in a given territory 'under one law', with a single governmental system extending to all of them, and to no one else, are then members of a state; but the state as an institution does not embrace *all* the roles in which they appear, but only political or legal roles.

Now admittedly we do distinguish legal roles, like voter, judge or policeman, from others, like father, shop steward, and accountant, which are not primarily legal though they may have legal standing, i.e. legal rights and duties may attach to them. Similarly, Parliament and the Civil Service are *primarily* legal institutions or associations, while the National Union of Railwaymen is not, though it has legal standing, and its rules provide legally recognized principles upon which a judge might settle a dispute, e.g. a question of wrongful expulsion. However, there is a sense in which there are no legally neutral acts or roles; everything is legally permitted or legally prohibited. So legal recognition cannot provide a strict criterion for distinguishing 'state' from 'non-state' acts or roles.

A more satisfactory distinction perhaps could be made between roles with governmental functions and others, defining the state in terms of governmental roles. There would be borderline cases, of course, like employees of nationalized industries, hospital boards, and corporation dustmen. But such classification is not dictated by the facts themselves, for social facts may be classified in any number of ways, according to choice and convenience. We shall find it convenient, for our present purposes, to treat the state as one institution, alongside others, like trade unions, churches and scientific associations, through which the national society operates. But this is by no means the only way of looking at it. Kelsen, for example, identifies state and law,[15] making other associations subordinate normative orders within the legal order—and from a lawyer's point of view, this is probably the most useful way of classifying the facts.

But if all that is at stake is convenience in classification, why should some liberal theorists[16] attach such importance to the distinction between state and society? Political theorists in the past have tended to hypostatize the state—i.e. they have treated it as if it were 'a thing', with the special characteristic that underlying all its acts was the threat of armed force. Consequently, some writers have feared that by defining 'the state' to include all the rules and roles of social behaviour, the way might be opened for the compulsory regulation of many activities that liberals prefer to leave to individual initiative, free choice, and voluntary organization. Furthermore, governmental decisions—state decisions—might then be regarded as the most authoritative statements of the public interest, against which no counter-claim could stand, a doctrine thought to be somehow involved in the theory of state-sovereignty. (We shall deal with this aspect of the matter in the next chapter.)

Now the state is not a 'thing', but a system of rules, procedures, and roles operated by individuals. Admittedly, when we speak of 'state regulation' we often think of rules backed by coercive sanctions. We have already argued, however, in Chapter 3, that in many legal matters coercive sanctions are besides the point. The difference between state and private schools turns only very remotely on coercion; the main differences lie in the ways they are financed, and teachers appointed. Whatever we mean by 'the state', we shall almost certainly mean an organization through which armed force is exercised; but that is not so say that it functions *only* in this way. In the days when the state was conceived mainly as a policing agency, for enforcing peaceful arbitration of disputes, preventing violence, and protecting property, it made sense to characterize it simply as a coercive institution (though this would never have exhausted its functions altogether). There was a point, too, in marking out a field in which coercive action was appropriate, and allocating that to the state, reserving other activities for 'society', i.e. for voluntary organization and individual initiative. From the core of policing institutions, however, has developed an elaborate and varied organization for social welfare, economic planning, fostering the arts and conducting scientific research. The nineteenth century liberal conception of the state, as an organization working through general rules backed by coercive power, needs considerable amendment. Its distinction between state and society would seem to exclude from 'state activity' some of the most important aspects of modern government.

The state has no 'essential' mode of operation. Its techniques range from the classic coercive procedure of the criminal law to the persuasive methods of the Road Safety and National Savings Campaigns, from industrial management to Arts Council subsidies and DSIR grants for research. One cannot say in advance whether a given task would more properly be left to individual initiative, or organized by governmental agencies. That depends on what can be done with the techniques available. If we define the state in terms of coercion, and then permit it to function only where it can coerce, we stipulate a definition and then make it a reason for a policy. This is not, of course, a criticism of all liberal political theory. The case for leaving certain fields to voluntary associations or private initiative can rest on better grounds than an arbitrary definition of what constitutes state action. A more positive treatment of this question will be found in the chapters that follow.

CHAPTER 12

SOVEREIGNTY AND THE MORAL BASIS
OF STATE SUPREMACY

I. THE STATE AND SOVEREIGNTY

(a) From the primacy of law to the supremacy of the state

In the last four or five hundred years, kinship and locality associations, in Europe and elsewhere, have steadily declined, and there has been a corresponding growth in the importance of mass associations, and particularly of the state. Family, village, guild, and parish, which at one time regulated nearly all the activities of most men and women, have become increasingly restricted in scope. The guild has disappeared altogether. The family was once a multi-functional organization within which men and women found their work, amusements, and religion under patriarchal government; but nowadays in many western countries at any rate its functions have dwindled to little more than the regulation of sexual relations and the procreation and care of children. Even the care of the aged and the sick, once an essential family function, is passing into other and more specialized hands. What is implied by the concept of 'the family' has narrowed accordingly to cover little more than an association of parents and children. It has little significance as a normative system if it is stretched to cover more remote relations. In more primitive societies, the roles of uncle and cousin may carry the duties of blood feud vengeance or the payment of compensation to the victims of their relatives' misdeeds; they now extend in England little beyond attendance at family ceremonies and giving presents at Christmas. The tight-knit communities of earlier times have been replaced by numerous specialized associations; the impersonal 'firm' has replaced the family business; trade unions, political parties, and special groups, like the RSPCA and the AA are the natural outcome of growing mass interests. Regulating and controlling them all, defining and delimiting their rights, is the modern state, which has itself wholly or partly absorbed many functions formerly performed by other associations—such as education, the care of the poor, sick, and aged, and economic production. A claim to an over-riding allegiance is made on its behalf, and there are those who regard it as the concrete manifestation of high ideals like liberty, equality, and justice.

The pre-eminence given to the state in the modern world contrasts sharply with the mediaeval outlook. In the feudal world the primary concept was not the state but law—a law not made by politicians but part of a universal and eternal order, to be discovered by a study of custom and precedent. Kings, councils, and judges found and formulated it but could not make it; for to create new law would be to impose a new obligation by an act of will, and only God could do that. Political authorities—i.e. those exercising legal authority backed by coercive power—were regarded as being as much under law as any other corporate institution; for law was not thought of as the creation of the political order, nor as linked to it any more intimately than to any other. Law was thought of as the eternal and objectively valid normative system within which all associations were contained, and from which all roles drew appropriate rights and duties. No feudal king could have said, with James I, 'Kings are not only God's lieutenants upon earth, but even by God himself they are called gods'; or with Bossuet, 'O rois, vous êtes des dieux'. Such pre-eminence as the feudal king possessed dervied from the privileges and prerogatives of his legal status in the social hierarchy. Until about the thirteenth century, when the notions of Roman law were rediscovered and began to penetrate western legal thinking, no distinction was drawn between private and public law, between the king's private rights as an individual with a certain status, and his public authority as representing the whole community. The idea of a political order—a state—different in kind from kindred, feudal, or economic groupings, hardly existed. The commonwealth had its law; the king was *primus inter pares* among his barons; his subjects were variously associated in their corporations, each of which was thought of as a partial expression of the law. Society was a hierarchy, organically conceived, within which everyone had economic, military, and religious functions deriving from customary status.

Aquinas in the thirteenth century thought in terms of a universal legal order, in which human law was the local manifestation of Divine law. Divine law as a body of universal truths might be known through reason or revelation and local customs were particular instances of it. By the end of the seventeenth century, this approach to political theory had been radically transformed. Locke saw the law of reason, natural law, as a standard by which human law was to be judged, and in terms of which it might well be condemned. Positive law—the law 'posited' or laid down by men—was no longer 'given'; Sir Edward Coke was probably the last English lawyer of importance to deny that the King in Parliament had the authority to amend the customary Common Law by legislation. Without the revolutionary idea that valid law might be created by an act of will, and not simply discovered by an act of understanding, the modern theory of the state could scarcely have emerged.[1] For once it is admitted that law can be made, and made specifically by the political authority, the political order no longer stands on an equal footing with other associations. If these derive their powers from law, the political authority as law-creator must be, in some sense, above the law, and superior to other associations. Thus the theory of sovereignty, as developed in the sixteenth and seventeenth centuries by Bodin and Hobbes, involved the logical divorce of law and custom, and the pre-eminence of the community's political organization. The law-making state became the source of legitimacy for all other forms of social organization; as the locus of sovereignty, it was unique.

(b) The theory of the determinate sovereign

'Sovereignty' is an ambiguous word, and the theories associated with it are complex and often puzzling. Our main concern in this chapter is to consider how the state can be related to other associations as a sovereign body to other subordinate ones. It will be convenient to consider first, however, the special theory, associated particularly with the names of Bodin, Hobbes, and Austin, that in every state there must be a determinate sovereign, i.e. that sovereignty must be located in some determinate person or body of persons, exercising 'supreme power over citizens and subjects, unrestrained by law'.

This (Bodin's) definition of 'sovereignty' shares the ambiguity of 'power' that we have already noted in Chapter 10.[2] By 'supreme power' we may understand either (a) supreme legal *authority, competence* or *entitlement* (i.e. a *de jure* use of 'power'), or (b) a supreme ability to induce men to take a desired course of action, by bringing some sort of pressure to bear upon them (a *de facto* use). To attribute sovereignty to anyone, in the first sense, would be to give an account of the provisions of a normative order, e.g. a constitution; to do so in the second sense would be to give an account of the actual determinants of political behaviour. On June 2, 1793, the French Convention, exercising sovereign legislative authority, ordered the arrest of the leaders of the Girondin party—but only after the President had led them with the other deputies from one exit to another seeking a way of escape from the armed mob that surrounded the Tuileries. Sovereign legal authority, it seems, is not proof against intimidation; the supreme power to determine other men's conduct may lie elsewhere.

I

i. Supreme legal authority. We have already touched on the notion of legal sovereignty in connection with the Austinian command theory of law, in Chapter 3. We observed that with federal constitutions in particular it is doubtful whether supreme legal authority can be located anywhere, unless in the constitution itself. Furthermore, in so far as the Austinian theory is directed to formulating a scheme for criteria of legal validity, what is required is not a sovereign legislator but a supreme norm, from which all other rules of law derive validity. To this extent sovereignty must always lie in the constitution, even where an institution is competent to amend it, since the amending competence itself derives from the constitution. Sovereignty as attributed to a constitutional norm we might term 'legal sovereignty'. To say, then, of the British Constitution, that Parliament is sovereign means that any rule Parliament enacts shall be deemed valid, even though it may conflict with previous statutes or rules of Common Law, or any other rule whatsoever. This norm is fundamental. Nevertheless, though a Parliament may be sovereign, a court may still argue (as did the South African Supreme Court in 1952)[3] that if the procedures laid down by the constitution have not been observed a rule purporting to be an Act of Parliament is not so, and the body passing it not a Parliament. The conditions of sovereignty derive from law, even when, in the sense of 'legislative sovereignty', it is attributed to an omnicompetent legislature.

Such a sovereign is not logically necessary to a legal order. For a constitution might divide legislative competence between co-ordinate organs as in a federal state, or place certain matters beyond the competence of any organ, e.g. by a Bill of Rights which *no* legislature may infringe; and in these limiting respects the constitution might be unamendable. (For if any organ *were* competent to amend the constitution in these respects, it might be held omnicompetent, because it could determine its own competence.)

It should be stressed, in any case, that to ascribe sovereignty to a legislature in this sense is not to attribute to it *de facto* 'power', but only a legal capacity; it is to say that a judge is required by law to give precedence to any rule it makes. It is a statement about the formal structure of a legal system, not about the ability of the actual legislators to determine the actions of other men.

Of course, law-making *is* one way of determining conduct. A sociologist or a historian would have to take account of a society's statutes in explaining its members' behaviour; for men may act as they do only because a particular rule is a statute. Legislators usually do determine other people's behaviour in the ways they intend. But there is no warrant for inferring that the *de facto* authority or power arising from supreme competence will also be supreme. It is not necessarily true, for instance, that the men operating the 'sovereign' organ are more generally obeyed than men operating a 'subordinate' organ. The amending organ in the USA—Congress together with three-fourths of the states—is omnicompetent (or very nearly so), yet the prohibition Amendment was a good deal less effective than most Acts of Congress, which is a subordinate organ when acting alone. Nor can we assume that supreme legislators are necessarily freer to do what they want; they may be subject to more non-legal pressures limiting their effective freedom of choice, than members of subordinate organs. Because they have wider competence more people will find it worth while putting pressure on them.

ii. Supreme power de facto. Consider now 'sovereignty' not in the sense of 'supreme legislative authority' but in a *de facto* sense. By this we mean an ability to determine the actions of other persons in intended ways by exerting some sort of pressure, without being oneself subject to similar determination from others. *De facto* power is of many sorts— it arises, for instance, from the ability to allow or deny others a chance to earn a living; or from the ability to make or mar a reputation; from the belief that salvation depends on a priest's good offices; or from the ability to inflict physical injury or impose physical constraints by the use of armed force. This last we shall term 'coercive power'.

We should hesitate to call any organization a 'state' that did not provide for the institutionalized use of coercive power—to that extent coercion is a necessary characteristic of a state. And obviously, a regime will not last long if its opponents control greater armed force than it does itself. But is it in any sense necessary, as Hobbes maintained, that in every state there must be a *determinate* person or body wielding coercive power great enough to overcome any possible opposition—i.e. a sovereign? Now it is not easy to see how to answer this question. Consider an army commander responsible to a minister, who is a member of a Cabinet responsible to an elected legislature. Where in this chain do we stop and say 'Here is the supreme coercive power?' It might be argued that the commander need obey the minister only if (or so long as) he accepts his authority, and that supreme coercive power therefore rests with him. But it is equally true that his subordinates obey *him* because they accept *his* authority. Without that he would be powerless. We can talk with confidence of 'supreme coercive power' only when the chain of authority is unbroken. (And then, since the coercive forces of the state are normally the only organized forces in its territory, it is trivial to say they are supreme.) In any state there will be determinate institutions competent to decide to use force; and normally the armed forces obey orders and do not act independently. The structure of *de jure* authority is normally authoritative *de facto*.

But the relations between the professional soldiers and the politicians vary considerably from state to state, and from time to time. The pre-eminence of civil authority is normally taken for granted in most of the great constitutional democracies, though not always in France. In some South American and Middle Eastern states, however, civil authority counts for less with the army than the authority of its own officers. In those countries, military revolts are not unusual. In such a state, the government must surely feel its freedom of choice somewhat circum-scribed within the limits of what the generals will stand. But in trying to understand the importance of military power in politics, it may be more interesting, in such cases, to look at the interplay of pressures *within* the armed forces, than to lump them together as the 'supreme coercive power'.

Even where generals can be relied upon to submit to duly constituted authority, the government does not have, on that account, a free hand. The analysis of political relations in terms of supreme power tends to be misleading, because it suggests that someone, or some determinate group, enjoys an unfettered choice. This is never the case. On the one hand, submission to authority is hardly ever absolute; men may submit with reservations. On the other hand, coercive power is not the only sort of power, and in the day-to-day running of a state, it may be less important than others. We shall look at these two points in turn.

In the first place, in a state men in the main submit to authority; they do not have to be subjected to coercion or other forms of power. And such submission to authority depends mainly on the recognition of its legitimacy. Power may well be one of the causes of obedience; but it is a regulatory device which is both distinct from authority, and is usually most effective when those who wield it are authorized to do so.*

> 'No man,' wrote Hume, 'would have any reason to *fear* the fury of a tyrant, if he had no authority over any but from fear; since, as a single man, his bodily force can reach but a small way, and all the further power he possesses must be founded either on our own opinion, or on the presumed opinion of others.'[4]

Men obey, either from 'opinion of interest' like the expectation of re-ward or punishment, or from 'opinion of right' (what we should term a belief in the legitimacy of the authority). But the first depends on the second, since 'the magistrate's authority must be antecedently estab-lished, at least be hoped for, in order to produce this expectation (of

* See Chapter I Section III and Chapter 10 Section I(c).

interest)'. Thus, support for revolutionary leaders grows as their chances improve; in the end there may even be a rush for the bandwagon; but the support they receive in the early stages must always be grounded on some principle of legitimacy or right. And conversely, as the established government loses authority, it loses power. The more people reject its legitimacy, or prefer other grounds of legitimacy than those it rests on, the less it can rely on the instruments of coercion. The constitutional legitimacy of the government of the Fourth Republic meant less, in 1958, to many Frenchmen, and certainly to many soldiers, than de Gaulle's claim to speak for 'the sovereign people', for the solid and permanent interests of France, like order, discipline, and national unity. Constitutionality carried less weight than the direct appeal to the ends which the constitution was designed, but had failed, to serve.

Behind power, then, lies authority, and behind authority some conception of legitimacy or right. But a principle of legitimacy need not be absolute and unconditional. In a constitutional order people are usually prepared to accept lawful authority, but they expect it to operate only within certain understood limits. And there is no reason why it should be exclusive; other organizations, as we shall see, constitute their own authorities, their bishops and their national councils and congresses, with claims to legitimacy in their own spheres.

According to Hobbes, there must be one, and only one, original legitimate authority in any society, to whom obedience is owed absolutely. This would be understandable as a prescription: Plan your constitution so that it provides a determinate omnicompetent authority, and then give it unqualified obedience. For an age of disorder, it would no doubt have its appeal. But Hobbes presented it as a necessary property of *any* state. In this he was clearly mistaken, not only because constitutional authority may well be divided between many lawful institutions, but also because governments can survive even though their subjects give them only qualified obedience, on condition that they do not trespass on the preserves of other authorities. Bodin and Hobbes sought to give the state supreme authority to settle the explosive religious differences of the sixteenth and seventeenth centuries. But they were wrong in thinking that religious peace required the submission of religious authorities to the sovereign. In fact, the state and a variety of churches came to accept that allegiance would be divided between them, each having its own proper sphere.

The sovereign power analysis is misleading in a second respect. Stressing legal forms or coercive power, it obscures the interplay of power of other sorts which determines political decisions. Whatever a government's legal competence, and whatever the coercive power at its disposal, it never has a free hand. It is exceptional for a legislature to be coerced, like the 1793 Convention, by a mob at the doors; but no post-war British government could freeze wages in the face of trade union opposition, even with the full support of the armed forces and a majority in Parliament. Governments are subject to diverse pressures, and strikes are only one of many types of non-coercive power that can be mobilized against them. In many of its activities, a government relies on active co-operation from banks, associations of industrialists, universities, and research establishments, as well as from thousands of voluntary workers of all sorts. Faced by a widespread refusal to co-operate, a government would be forced to make concessions. And in a democracy, a sectional organization representing a significant block of voters can exert strong pressure on elected representatives.

Some political theorists accept this criticism of Hobbesian or Austinian analyses, but attribute sovereignty instead to the people as a whole. This is a complicated idea, which we consider later in the context of democratic theory. The important point here, however, is that 'popular sovereignty' does not imply that there is a determinate person or group able to make its own independent decisions, free of any external pressure. Politics is the interplay of pressures, rather than the assertion of sovereign will.

This is true not only of democratic governments but also of dictatorships. Dictators can govern only so long as they satisfy the expectations of their party, their armed forces, their technocrats, or whatever other groups provide their support. Within the governing group, sectional or factional pressures are pitted one against another. The purges in Communist states are only the outward signs of a continual struggle for power. The dictator survives so long as he can hold the support of whatever faction is for the time being dominant, and his policies may well reflect the shifts of power within his party. It might be said, of course, that the party, the armed forces, and perhaps the industrial managers collectively constitute the sovereign power—but this would obscure rather than illuminate the question of how political decisions come to be what they are.

In brief, 'sovereignty' may be an important and useful concept for juristic analysis, and though there may not be a determinate sovereign in a juristic sense in every state, it is neither meaningless nor misleading to say there might be. It *is* misleading as a political concept, at least if sovereignty is understood to reside in a determinate person or institution, because it suggests the wrong questions. To ask where sovereign power lies would seem to imply that someone or some group can regularly get their own way if they insist on it, no matter what any-one else may want or do. This is unrealistic. What a government can do depends very largely on what people believe it ought to do, and what powerful sectional interests want it or permit it to do. Political action is always the result of a conflict of wills, never an expression of a single independent will.

(c) The state as a sovereign order

Political theorists who accept these criticisms of the Hobbesian theory of sovereignty may attribute sovereignty, nevertheless, to the state as a whole as an association, distinguishing it thereby from non-state associations. Whatever this may mean in detail, it gives the impression that the state is in some way especially important, so that it is reasonable to talk of 'the state and other associations', as though what distinguishes the state is of greater moment than anything which distinguishes non-state associations from one another. We shall now examine what might be involved in such a claim.

i. *The state as a 'total order'.* For Kelsen, the state differs from other associations as a whole differs from its parts:

> 'The relation between the total legal order constituting the State . . . and the juristic person of a corporation is the relation between two legal orders, a total and a partial legal order . . . To be more specific, it is a case of delegation.'[5]

Given Kelsen's terms this is necessarily true, for it means only that the *legal* validity of a non-state order consists in the *legal* recognition of its rules. Kelsen treats 'state' and 'law' as different ways of saying the same thing. The state is not the source of law, it *is* the law. 'The dualism of law and State is an animistic superstition.'[6] Consequently the legal vali-dity of an association is its authorization by the state. Thus from the legal standpoint the state is a total order, and the only total order, pre-cisely because state and law are identified. Speaking legally, to call law (state) a total order is to say that we do not have to seek extra-legal validation for it; to call other associations partial is to say that their validity derives from law. This is logically necessary, but only because it is *legal* validity which is in question.

But we need not speak legally. Exactly the same might be said of *any* association if we care to adopt the appropriate standpoint. From a church's own standpoint, its order is complete or 'total'—its rules have their own, not a derivative validity. It prescribes its own canons of vali-dity, and in so far as the state enters its sphere, the state could be said to be legitimized by the church. This will sound highly theoretical, if not improbable, to a twentieth century Englishman, but it would have seemed clear enough to a thirteenth century ecclesiastic. When the power of the Church was at its peak, and the Pope was engaged in a bitter struggle for supremacy with the Emperor, it was seriously argued that all secular authority drew its legitimacy from the Church. The Church claimed to be the sole earthly source of all legitimacy, itself deriving authority from the ultimate source, God. The theory of sovereignty was foreshadowed in the papal claim to *plenitudo potestatis*. Similarly, a revolutionary association today might prescribe the limits within which its members should obey the law, and impose its own duties running counter to law; it would then be extending its own authorization to part of the law, and withholding it from the rest.

Of course, to ascribe sovereignty in this sense to non-state associations seems highly artificial. In the first place, few specialized orders need explicitly recognize more than a tiny sector of the legal system and it seems more natural to adopt the standpoint of the more comprehensive rather than the less comprehensive whole. Secondly, most associations are composed of law-abiding men who have no wish to challenge state authority; consequently, their constitutions will be presumed not to conflict with law.* Alternatively, we might say that the members of the association recognize the legitimacy of the state as well as of their own order, though on different grounds.

Once again, it is important to distinguish a juristic from a political analysis. From a lawyer's point of view, non-state associations may well be viewed as subordinate parts of a greater legal whole, which is the state. If an association's rules conflict with law, they are invalid, but that has no necessary bearing on their validity for its members. In Eastern Europe, the Catholic Church has been engaged in a long struggle with the Communist states in which it has sought to define for Catholics the conditions for state legitimacy. Conversely, the state has sought to impose its terms for legal recognition of the Church. The individual has had to decide where his ultimate duty lies, or which authority is ultimately binding. Some governments have sought to resolve the conflict, not by suppressing the Church (too many of their subjects regard it as legitimate for that to succeed) but by trying to capture its authority by installing officials of their own choice, who would accept legal recognition on the state's own terms.

These difficulties rarely arise in this country because there is wide agreement on the spheres to which associations, including the state,

---

* If we look at this strictly from the standpoint of the association, we might say, theoretically, that the association's constitution implicitly adopts the legal system as part of itself.

should confine themselves. It is a long time since an association felt the need to call on its members to set their loyalty to the association above their loyalty to the state, or, what amounts to the same thing, to prefer a non-legal to a legal authority. This is as much because of self-restraint exercised by the state as by other authorities. If Parliament in 1926 had declared general strikes illegal, and relied on its legal authority backed by coercive power, it might have broken heads, but never the strike. The passing of the Trade Disputes Act in 1927 banned general strikes in the future, which suggests that Parliament had held back more from prudence than from principle. In 1926 such an Act would have pitted state against union authority, in what the unions would have regarded as an impudent raid on their own proper terrain. When the strike had collapsed, the unions were too discredited to put up a real fight against the Act.

In normal conditions Englishmen would put state authority before any other. This is not because the state makes other associations legitimate, but because all parties avoid conflict by respecting one another's jurisdiction. And if the frontiers of jurisdiction are uncertain, it will not help at all to say that all associations derive their legitimacy from the state. Legality is only one sort of legitimacy, and not necessarily the most compelling one in all situations.

One of the most important functions of government is to keep a balance between the various sectional authorities which might otherwise wreck the social order in a crude conflict of power, like the religious wars of the sixteenth century. The state has its own great authority, as well as great power, for this purpose, but not independently of the whole complex of authorities. Its own can be used and preserved only by lending its weight now to one, now to another, avoiding, if it can, forcing upon its subject a choice between conflicting loyalties. An umpire's authority prevails over the players' loyalty to their teams only so long as his decisions are intelligible according to the rules of the game. A government is more than an umpire; but its authority will prevail only if it takes account of the claims of other great associations, whose *de facto* authority in their respective fields may be no less than its own.

ii. *The state contrasted with 'voluntary associations'*. The state as a compulsory order is frequently held to be different in essence from other associations which are voluntary. Its compulsory character involves two things; first, that its members cannot deny its jurisdiction by resigning, and second, that it punishes rule-breaking. The criterion of 'voluntariness' is more complex, however, than it at first appears.

Consider first the question of membership. Any association must prescribe, formally or otherwise, criteria for membership, and it could be said that a voluntary differs from an involuntary association because its members must have freely entered into membership, e.g. by a formal act of joining. No one else would be considered by the association as bound by any obligation it may impose. Such an understanding of 'voluntary' would clearly exclude the state, for except in the relatively few cases of naturalization, we do not choose to become members of any particular state. To be born of parents qualified as members, or to be born within territory under the state's jurisdiction is usually enough. Moreover, one cannot resign from the state as from a club. It may be possible to leave the state by leaving its territory, especially if one can become a naturalized member of another state. But some states prevent free exit; so that the right to resign is still subject to the state's consent; and if it refuses to recognize naturalization, the subject remains in its view one of its members to the end. Again, the state's jurisdiction, unlike that of other associations, extends to anyone in its territory. 'Membership of the state' is therefore a more complex idea than membership of most other associations, which impose obligations only on their own members.*

However, the state is not altogether peculiar in these respects. The family, the tribe, and some churches claim jurisdiction over anyone whose parents are members or who has been ceremonially inducted into the association in infancy. Unlike the state, however, theirs is not a territorial jurisdiction. But like the state, membership does not depend on a deliberate decision to join, and they may provide no recognized way of leaving. A man may be a member of a family, in the sense that he has a family status with appropriate rights and duties, though he may have no interest in it and acknowledge none of his obligations. Similarly, in Jewish law, a man born a Jew remains a Jew, even though he actively repudiates membership. A formal distinction can be drawn, then, between voluntary and involuntary associations, according to whether a formal act of joining is a necessary condition of membership, and whether they recognize the right of members to renounce their jurisdiction by resigning. But in neither of these respects is the state the only involuntary association.

A further distinction might be made between associations which punish rule-breaking, and those whose only sanction is expulsion.

* It might be simpler, though contrary to generally accepted ways of looking at the matter, to treat everyone in a state's territory at any given time as an involuntary member, with rights and duties varying between citizen and alien members. Of course, citizens 'feel' members, while aliens do not, but how they feel does not affect their legal status nor the effectiveness of their obligations.

But again, the state is not the only association that provides punishments short of expulsion. Trade associations and trade unions fine their members; churches impose penances; in a family, children forfeit their pocket-money, and even an adult may be cut off with a shilling. In any association, however, which, unlike the state, allows a member to leave the jurisdiction by simply resigning, every sanction is, in a sense, subject to the member's acquiescence. For he may always prefer to leave or be expelled, rather than pay.

These are *de jure* distinctions, not *de facto;* for they depend only on formal criteria of membership. Voluntariness in this sense might still be consistent with an association's having *de facto* power to prevent a member resigning, or to compel him to join. In a sense, of course, expulsion from any association may involve a sort of loss, especially if there is no substitute catering for the member's interest. But expulsion from some associations, which are nevertheless voluntary in a formal sense, may involve very severe loss, not only by denying the member the opportunities and facilities that the association offers, but also by deliberate punitive action, designed to prevent resignations. Such action may also be used to induce outsiders to join. A powerful trade union or trade association may deliberately prevent non-members from earning a living in their own trade or business. There are places, too, where a man who leaves a dominant church, or repudiates its authority, may suffer a social and economic boycott from the faithful. In this respect the coercive power of the state and the compulsion exercised by other associations may differ only in degree. This point is of great importance for the problems of the relation between the state and other associations which we discuss in our next chapter.

iii. *The state's monopoly of coercive power.* 'The essence of the state,' wrote Herman Finer, 'is in its monopoly of coercive power, declared and enforced as the only legitimate monopoly; in its very existence, which is an immanent threat; or in its active use in the naked form of force when the members of the society ... threaten the main values and are about to disrupt the society by exercising force against each other. This, then, is the state; and its supreme power and monopoly of coercion (which it can devolve in many ways on its own terms) is *sovereignty*.'[7]

In intention, at least, the state allows the use of force only to its own coercive institutions, except in cases like self-defence. The reality does not always square with the intention, of course. One regime after another has tried to crush the Sicilian Mafia, with at best temporary and limited success. Nevertheless, if the state is to make good its claim to universal jurisdiction within its territory, it must be able to discipline recalcitrants, and it cannot tolerate an organized force that might resist or challenge it. Further, given that a basic function of any state is to keep order, it must maintain a force of its own sufficient to prevent the settling of disputes by violence.

But as we have already pointed out, to monopolize coercive power is not to have a monopoly of all power. This has two implications. Firstly, the state must often defer to other sorts of power, exercised by associations whose goodwill it must have. Secondly, precisely because the state has vast coercive power, as well as a great *de facto* authority, many other associations will be anxious to manage the state. In the liberal democracies political parties are organized for just this purpose. Their power derives immediately from the votes they win, but their capacity to win them depends very largely on their wealth; and so they are themselves open to the pressures exerted by associations and individuals who finance them. Churches and trade unions sponsor political parties, and other interests subscribe liberally to their funds. The vast sums spent in an American Presidential election are not all subscribed out of disinterested idealism.

Political parties apart, sectional interests bring steady pressure to bear on policy makers, either by lobbying the legislature or by deputations to a minister. Some pressures are less scrupulous, ranging from bribery to blackmail. In some of the newer states of the Commonwealth tribal and family loyalties can put the administrator under intolerable pressure to make exceptions in favour of his own people.

Competition for sectional benefits is not, we shall argue, necessarily a bad thing; but it is important that sectional pressures should not escape publicity. Further, the state should be so constituted that it cannot fall altogether under the control of a single interest group. Lenin described the state as a coercive organization for preventing the conflicts of economic classes from breaking out into open violence. At its worst, the state can be merely that; inevitably, it must be at least that. The real question is whether it can provide a way of adjusting the conflicts equitably, instead of simply lending its power to one interest group to suppress the rest.

II. THE MORAL BASIS OF STATE SUPREMACY

(a) *Aristotle—Rousseau—Hegel: The state as a total moral order*

The picture we have given above of the modern state buffeted by competing sectional interests, if not their open battleground, does not fit Rousseau's ideal of a state serenely governed by a citizen body self-lessly expressing a General Will to the Common Good. Rousseau belongs to a tradition in political theory, stretching from Aristotle to

Hegel, and beyond to the totalitarians of the twentieth century, which sets the state above other associations, because its ideal object is the good of all. The goals of other associations either conflict with this ultimate good, in which case they are illegitimate, or they are partial expressions or aspects of it, in which case the end of the state will include and transcend them. 'If all communities aim at some good,' wrote Aristotle of the *polis*, 'the state or political community, which is the highest of all, and which embraces all the rest, aims, and in a greater degree than any other, at the highest good.'[8]

Rousseau's belief in the supreme moral end of the state made him unequivocally hostile to other associations.

'As long as several men in assembly regard themselves as a single body, they have only a single will which is concerned with their common preservation and general well-being. In this case, all the springs of the state are vigorous and simple . . . there are no embroilments or conflicts of interests; the common good is everywhere clearly apparent, and only good sense is needed to perceive it . . .
'But when the social bond begins to be relaxed and the state to grow weak, when particular interests begin to make themselves felt and the smaller societies to exercise an interest over the larger, the common interest changes and finds opponents: opinion is no longer unanimous; the general will ceases to be the will of all; contradictory views and debates arise; and the best advice is not taken without question.
'Finally, when . . . the meanest interest brazenly lays hold of the sacred name of "public good", the general will becomes mute.'[9]
'When factions arise, and partial associations are formed at the expense of the great association, the will of each of these associations becomes general in relation to its members, while it remains particular in relation to the State: it may then be said that there are no longer as many votes as there are men, but only as many as there are associations . . . Lastly, when one of these associations is so great as to prevail over all the rest . . . there is no longer a general will, and the opinion which prevails is purely particular.'[10]

Rousseau was a democrat; in his ideal state the popular assembly would exercise supreme legislative authority, reaching decisions by majority procedure. He was uneasy, however, in case a majority should put its particular interests before the common good. His problem was to ensure that the will of all, which was the combined wills of the majority, would really give expression to the general will to the common good—that voters would ask themselves 'What will be the best for everyone?' rather than 'What will be the best for me, or for the group to which I belong?' He saw sectional associations as the greatest dangers; for a man who would hesitate to put a wholly *selfish* interest before his duty to the common good might nevertheless put his group loyalty before his loyalty to the state.

'It is therefore essential, if the general will is to be able to express itself, that there should be no partial society within the State, and that each citizen should think only his own thoughts . . . But if there are partial societies, it is best to have as many as possible and to prevent them from being unequal.'[11]

The influence of Rousseau is evident in the speech of the deputy Le Chapelier to the French Constituent Assembly, when on June 14, 1791, he introduced the law to prevent the formation of trade unions and employers' associations: 'it should not be permissible for citizens of particular occupations to assemble for what are claimed to be their common interests . . . there is now only the particular interest of each individual and the general interest. It is not permissible for anyone to suggest to citizens an intermediate interest, to separate them from the public body by a spirit of corporation.'[12] Three months later, the same deputy prevailed on the Assembly to pass a more general law restricting the political activities of non-state association. 'No society, club, or association of citizens,' it declared, 'can have, in any form, a political existence, nor exercise any influence on the acts of the established powers and legal authorities; they may on no pretext appear under a collective name to submit petitions, sponsor deputations, participate in public ceremonies, or for any other purpose.'[13]

For much the same reason, Plato had decided that the guardians of the Republic should have no family ties, in case these should interfere with their devotion to the state. Though Hobbes' approach to politics was very different, he was just as anxious to keep a close watch on lesser associations for the sake of state unity and sovereign power: a 'great number of corporations . . . are as it were many lesser commonwealths in the bowls of a greater, like worms in the entrails of a natural man'.[14]

Aristotle and Hegel saw the problem differently. For Aristotle, the end of the state includes all lesser ends, like those of the family or the village. These are too small to provide a man with everything he needs for a good life, but the state could not meet those needs without them. They have essential functions in the life of the greater organism. And this was also Hegel's view, though the Prussian state was very different from the *polis*. For Hegel, men approach membership of the state through membership of their corporations, or economic associations.

'Particular interests which are common to everyone fall within civil society and lie outside the absolutely universal interest of the state proper. The administration of these is in the hands of Corporations, commercial and professional as well as municipal, and their officials, directors, managers and the like. It is the business of these officials to manage the private property and interests of these particular spheres and, from that point of view, their authority rests on the confidence of their commonalties and professional equals. On the other hand, however, these circles of particular interests must be subordinated to the higher interests of the state, and hence the filling of positions of responsibility in Corporations, etc., will generally be effected by a mixture of popular election by those interested with appointment and ratification by higher authority.'[15]

For Hegel, every association has its function, but one that is subordinate to that of the state itself. The state must accordingly guide and control all other associations to serve its own greater purpose. This is broadly the attitude of modern totalitarianism. The Nazis smashed the independent trade unions, and replaced them with the German Labour Front, which was virtually a department of state. The Corporations of Fascist Italy were closely controlled by the state and the party. Again, trade unions and the scientific and artistic academies of the Soviet Union are closely tied to the state by the Communist Party. The Party permeates every organization, making sure that its policy is in line with the state's. Thus all associations are auxiliaries of the state, each with its specialized contribution to make towards the goal of 'the common good'.

All this presupposes that 'the common good' is an objective that can be precisely defined, that everyone has an overriding duty to pursue it, and that the state is peculiarly fitted to achieve it. But even so, it might still be said of any given state (e.g. by a Marxist in a capitalist state), that whatever its ideal possibilities, it was actually being used for sectional or class interests rather than the public interest or the common good.

(b) The concept of 'the common good'

But what does 'the common good' (or 'the public interest') mean? If a government's policies were directed to the interests of a class, a party, or any other minority, and disregarded other interests, one might say that it was sacrificing the public interest to a sectional interest. It ought to be directed, one might say, to realizing the interests of everyone. But can this be done?

Now there are certainly some governmental functions which benefit everyone, or nearly everyone. Defence, order, good roads, preventing epidemics—these might be called 'common goods'. But when people talk of promoting '*the* common good' they do not mean simply the sum of these particular common goods. For in the first place, '*the* common good' is generally thought to justify services like education, old age pensions, and perhaps free medicine, and these may involve serving the interests of some at the expense of others. Again, the government would have resented being told in 1957 that decontrolling rents was not for the common good. But the government clearly had to choose between the interests of the landlords and the interests of the tenants. Whether or not it chose rightly, it did little good to the tenants. If it chose 'for the common good', the phrase must mean something different from an interest which everyone shares. Political problems very often demand a choice between conflicting interests. And though there may be good reasons for a given choice, it can rarely be one in which all interests are harmonized in a transcendent interest, 'the common good'. Again, even where the objective is of general benefit, a truly 'common good', it does not follow that it should therefore override all other claims; yet this is precisely what Rousseau felt about *the* common good. For instance, the common good of defence might not be a good enough reason for uprooting a hundred families to make a rocket range. It might be better to compromise for the benefit of the few, and make do with a somewhat less efficient range elsewhere. The common good of defence would not then be conclusive; other claims would prevail against it. But perhaps this too could be reconciled within the concept 'the common good', if this is understood as a sort of compendious objective in which all other valid ends are harmonized and adjusted.

But this is not really a solution, for it is questionable whether the common good is properly speaking an objective at all. We might say that the state should set itself the objective of full employment, or a healthy nation, or a prosperous agriculture—these aims are intelligible because the terms have a fairly clear descriptive meaning. Opinions may differ about what percentage of unemployment is consistent with 'full employment', but the dispute is only about the exact scope of a term. With 'the common good' it is different. Two politicians may each say, with perfect sincerity, that he is seeking the public interest, or the common good, though one proposes to expropriate private capital and the other to defend it to the death. Does one of them have to be wrong, believing the common good to lie where in fact it does not? Is the disagreement about fact at all? It may be—for there is room for some disagreement on the economics of socialism. But the probability is that this is less important than a disagreement on moral principle. One holds private capital to be an immoral thing in itself, the other that it represents the legitimate fruits of thrift, industry, and other economic virtues. The difference, in short, is almost wholly prescriptive, and not about the facts of the situation.

What then have the two politicians in common, that enables them to appeal, with equal sincerity to 'the common good'? Only this: each is denying that his prescription is prompted by a purely sectional concern. He is saying, in effect, that having considered the claims of *all* sections in a spirit of impartiality, the balance of advantage lies in the course he recommends. They *may* differ about the nature of the consequences to be expected from their respective policies; but they need not do so. They may simply attach different values to them. They agree, however, that the effects on all members of the community must be considered before the balance of advantage can be struck, and each will probably accuse his opponent (not necessarily justly) of attending only to the interests of a section or class. When political parties are accused of being class parties, the imputation is that they care *only* for the welfare of one class, neglecting altogether the claims of others.

Understood in these terms, 'the common good' is not an objective in which all particular objectives are somehow reconciled and in which everyone shares. Nor would anyone necessarily be worse off, even on a long-term view of his interest, if he always satisfied himself rather than serving the common good. Neither is the common good merely the good of the majority; for we often think it right, for example, to tax the majority to relieve a needy minority; and we should condemn majority action if it took no account of suffering, inflicted on the few merely because they were a few. On our interpretation, 'to seek the common good' means to try to act justly, in the sense of 'justice' that we analysed in Chapter 5.

It follows, however, that the prescription 'seek the common good' is not of the same type as 'maintain full employment'. Whereas the latter is a counsel of substance, the former is one of procedure. We may have different ideas about the way to maintain employment, but we are clear what the world would be like with it and without it. 'Seek the common good' is different, not because it is vaguer or more general, but because it does not *describe* a determinate goal at all. It is an instruction to approach policy-making in a certain spirit, not to adopt a determinate policy. To say that the state should seek it is to say only that political decisions should attend to the interests of its members in a spirit of impartiality.

(c) The state's arbitral function

What becomes then of the claim that the end of the state, the common good, embraces and transcends the ends of other associations? Associations other than the state might be said to be limited interest organizations, that is, they exist primarily to promote the interests of their own members. This is ambiguous, however, and partially misleading. A trade union exists to promote the advantage of its own members, but the Discharged Prisoners' Aid Society promotes the advantage primarily of non-members. Its members' interest, *qua* members, is not in their own advantage but in that of others for whom they have a special concern. Nevertheless, it is true that the activities of associations other than the state are generally more limited; within the nation, at any rate, their objects extend only to some people, whether their own members or not, and are usually directed to satisfy specific claims or needs. The RSPCA limits itself to protecting animals, the NSPCC to protecting children, the NUR to protecting railway men. And their objectives sometimes conflict, as do those of a trade union and an employers' association.

States, however, are multi-purpose associations; it would be impossible to sum up in a phrase the whole extent of a state's functions. It is useless to say that its end is the common good, because this is empty of descriptive meaning. Again, the state is the only organization having effective jurisdiction over everyone resident within the national territory. While other associations have special regard to the needs of their own members, or of those for whom they have a special concern, we expect a government to show concern for everyone in its territory.

Thus far Rousseau is justified: within the national territory, all non-state associations are partial, in that they promote some special interest. If an association's members are satisfied that its objects are legitimate, and the association is a legitimate instrument with which to work for them, they will have special obligations towards it and a special loyalty to fellow-members. The stronger it is, the better the prospect of realizing its objectives. That is not to say that they would be justified in ignoring altogether the claims of non-members—there are moral limits to special concerns—but the interests and loyalties they share give them quite rightly a sense of solidarity and a special concern for one another's welfare. This is surely the force of Rousseau's contention that 'the will of each of these associations becomes general to its members, while it remains particular in relation to the state'. Because the state alone has universal jurisdiction in its territory, a moral obligation rests upon its government, as upon the agents of no other association, to consider equally everyone within it.*

---

* On the other hand, the state is not justified in ignoring altogether the impact of its activities on other nations; within the world of states, every state is a sectional interest. The problems suggested by this reflection are treated in the Appendix.

The government is therefore in the position of an umpire. Committed equally to all within its jurisdiction (except, perhaps, for aliens, whose claims might be thought weaker than those of its own members), it should deal impartially with competing sectional claims. Not that it is altogether peculiar in this. Every association must in some degree arbitrate between its own sectional interests. ASLEF, the footplate workers' union, can seek consistently to increase wage differentials for skill and responsibility, but the NUR, which includes both skilled and unskilled workers, must weigh the claims of one against the other. What distinguishes the state is the diversity of interests between which it must arbitrate, and its unique ability to make its decisions effective throughout its territory.

We are not suggesting that the *only* function of the state is to arbitrate between the competing claims of other associations. In matters like foreign affairs and defence, the initiative in action will normally be the government's. And in other matters, the state ought not take account only of claims presented by organized bodies; investigatory commissions must try, for example, to discover how unorganized sections of the community would be affected by the courses favoured by sectional associations, and the same is true of the policy makers generally. Indeed, in the economic sphere, in arbitrating between highly organized producers' interests, the government itself holds a watching brief for the virtually unorganized consumer.

Furthermore, there are some interests which competing groups have in common, but which are unattainable without state co-ordination and guarantees. In Hobbes' state of nature, men lived in fear one of another. This was because they lacked an authority to co-ordinate their interests and guarantee security. Everyone yearned for security but none could attain it so long as anyone acted independently. Similarly, in the competition of trade unions and employers' associations, stability of profits and wages may be unattainable without a co-ordinating economic policy, which only the state can impose. While each acts independently, the advantages it seeks may constantly recede in an inflationary trend to which it is itself unavoidably contributing, and which may, in the long run, defeat its objectives altogether. A stable price level could thus be said to be a common good, which only the state can achieve, because without state regulations no sectional association can be sure that its own enlightened restraint would be matched by that of others.

To function as arbiter or co-ordinator between competing interests is not, however, to have a further interest, the 'public interest', embracing and transcending all the rest. For a group called upon to make a sacrifice, the public interest often means somebody else's interest; on balance the latter may be more important in a given situation, but the former ought never to be ignored altogether. School construction may justify compulsory purchase of land, but the expected advantage will be that of the children and their parents, not of the owner; and mere numbers do not settle the matter conclusively, for we should not approve of expropriating the owner, or paying less than compensation at market rate, simply because every ratepayer (the owner expected) would be the better off thereby.

If we accept the arbitral view of state function, several things follow:

1. A sectional association is not likely to be persuaded to forgo its claims merely because 'the public interests demands it'. It must be shown why on this occasion the claims of others are to be preferred to its own, and it must feel assured that, had circumstances been otherwise, the decision would have been more favourable. It must be persuaded, in short, not of the moral supremacy of the state's purpose, but of its *impartiality*.

2. The state must not be allowed to fall into the hands of men concerned only for the interest of a limited group. It must be sensitive to all, without succumbing to any one or to any limited coalition of interests. Rousseau's fear of the dominant partial association was not unfounded. We shall consider in a later chapter how far the danger can be met by constitutional devices. It is evident, however, that great associations must either exercise self-restraint in the use of power, or must expect restraints to be imposed by the state in defence of its own independence and of other interests.

3. The problem is not only that of preserving the state from selfish domination. Because 'the public interest' is not a matter of fact but of moral valuation, there may well be two opinions about the rightness of any given decision. If state authority is monopolized indefinitely by a group with one set of values, the state will seem a poor umpire to men with different values. If they feel that their legitimate interests are consistently disregarded they will be *morally* dissatisfied. If they are powerful enough, they will try to change the constitution to secure more favourable umpires. Revolutions are made and resisted in a spirit of righteous indignation. The state will remain at peace only if the government's policy is morally intelligible at least to the more powerful interests that it affects. We shall argue later that one of the virtues of liberal democracy is that it tends to produce governments which share the moral attitudes of at least the strongest groups within the community.

In so far, therefore, as the supremacy of the state over other associations can be said to have a 'moral basis' and in so far as this is connected with promoting 'the common good', this amounts to little more than the procedural principle of impartial arbitration between sectional interests. And this is no more a substantive guide to policy than the same basic principle of morality which we showed at work in the guise of justice and equality in spheres of individual interests and claims. Nevertheless, reflection on the conditions in which political activity is generally carried on may well suggest certain substantive criteria which must be satisfied for a state to be able to act as an impartial arbiter and coordinator. How, for instance, could a state act impartially if its government could be threatened by private armies? We shall consider such matters further in the next chapter.

CHAPTER 13

THE STATE AND OTHER ASSOCIATIONS

I. THE CASE FOR ASSOCIATIVE FREEDOM

We have rather assumed, up till now, a general freedom to associate for sectional purposes. But we have shown, too, that some philosophers, like Rousseau, have been very suspicious of sectional associations, or, like Hobbes, have been positively hostile. Their attitudes were linked, however, with certain ideas about state sovereignty or moral supremacy which we have rejected. Nevertheless, the case for associative freedom needs to be examined. In this chapter we relate the general criterion implied in the notion of morality—respect for persons as sources of claims, and as morally autonomous beings—to the actual conditions of organized social action. Though it would be a mistake to say that freedom to associate for sectional purposes was, in a strict sense, entailed by such a general criterion, we believe that it can be supported by showing that people are more likely to be respected, and their claims receive due attention, if such a right is admitted in principle. Nevertheless, because sectional associations are authority structures, they may come into serious conflict with state authority. And because they often wield power, they may affect the liberty of others. In its capacity of umpire and co-ordinator, the state cannot leave them entirely to their own devices. On what principles can such conflicts be resolved?

We argued in Chapter 10 that there is always a *prima facie* case for freedom; because men must not be used merely as tools, the onus of proof always rests on whoever wants to limit it, not on those enjoying it. We must assume then, until we are proved wrong, that if men want to associate for sectional purposes they should be left unmolested. But it is easy to think of particular types of association, like robber bands, for which a contrary case could certainly be made out.

But there is also a special case for freedom of association over and above the formal *prima facie* case for not interfering, analogous in some respects to the special case for freedom of discussion.* The weight to be attached to this case will depend, of course, on such things as the

* See Ch. 10, Sec. III (b).

type of interest that any particular association is designed to serve, and its impact on other interests.

Men are social animals, or, as we said in Chapter 1, rule-following animals, because so few of their needs can be satisfied except by co-ordinated and co-operative actions. But their needs and interests vary enormously, and there is no ideal pattern of 'the good life' which would be right for everyone. If the structure of a society like a modern nation is to satisfy such diversity, it must be immensely flexible, providing for an enormous variety of activities. Rousseau was hostile to sectional associations because he took the state to be a possible and sufficient form of organization for all the legitimate interests that men might have. Even if such an assumption could be defended in the case of the highly simplified life of the *Social Contract's* ideal city-state, it could scarcely be defended in the case of the modern nation-state. An attempt to construct a monolithic organization would certainly collapse before the sheer complexity of the interests it must cater for. It could overcome its difficulties only by trimming all interests to the convenience of the administrator. 'The holistic planner,' wrote K. R. Popper, 'overlooks the fact that it is easy to centralize power but impossible to centralize all that knowledge which is distributed over many individual minds, and whose centralization would be necessary for the wise wielding of centralized power ... Unable to ascertain what is in the minds of so many individuals, he must try to simplify his problems by eliminating individual differences; he must try to control and stereotype interests and beliefs by education and propaganda. But this attempt to exercise power over minds must destroy the last possibility of finding out what people really think, for it is clearly incompatible with free thought, especially critical thought. Ultimately, it must destroy knowledge; and the greater the gain in power, the greater will be the loss of knowledge.'[1]

If we accept the principle that men are sources of claims to be respected, and not tools to be used by their rulers for so-called higher ends like national glory, such a solution is intolerable. A man should be treated with respect as having ends of his own, not used just as a means to the ends of others; and though he may not *always* know best what is good for him, it is surely incompatible with that principle, unless he is a lunatic or an infant, to try to do him good without consulting him on the matter. Clearly, this is possible in a great association like the state only very indirectly, and in a very small degree. Wherever needs in a particular sphere call for very varied provisions, organization must be highly decentralized, and it is doubtful whether any single authority structure could contain the vastly complex system of institutions that would be needed. There would seem, therefore, to be a strong case for leaving individuals to form their own associations for such purposes, and to leave them to organize their activities as they think fit.

As long ago as 1835, de Tocqueville foresaw the vital role the voluntary association would have in the democratic state, to save it from a stultifying orthodoxy, and the individual from complete subordination to impersonal administrative machinery.[2] What he saw in America convinced him that minority interests would be stifled under a dead weight of majority opinion, unless dissidents of every sort could organize to make their voices heard. Through voluntary associations individuals can make their claims audible; without them they are inarticulate, or drowned in a confused babble of voices. If the state itself is to satisfy their diverse needs, free associations provide the channels through which its members' experiences and claims can be expressed. The lonely individual confronting the state is dwarfed and overawed; its vast impersonality induces a sense of hopeless frustration. By association, he gains strength to bend state policy to cater more for his interests and preferences. Alternatively, by voluntary organization he can often do for himself what he might wait indefinitely for the state to do for him, and with a more vigorous sense of active participation in meeting his own needs.

Freedom to associate so as to serve sectional needs and interests is the more important when the activity in question depends for its value on spontaneity and conviction. A state monopoly of economic organization is less obnoxious than a state monopoly of religion, art, or science. Though people disagree about the efficiency of state enterprise in economic fields, there is nothing inherently impossible about it. If a planned economy required state wage-fixing in place of collective bargaining, there would be nothing inherently impossible about that either, though the planners might be well-advised to consult free trade unions before deciding.* But a state monopoly of religion would be absurd, because the value of religious organization depends on the free surrender of the *believer*. In prescribing a civil religion for the state, Rousseau saw that the only possible course with heretics was banishment. Experiment, invention, and originality in science and art depend so much on the free development and criticism of individual interests and ideas, that to subordinate them deliberately to a state policy is likely to devitalize them. Cultural institutions for the exchange of ideas, set up under state auspices, are always in danger of having a state orthodoxy imposed on them.

* The Polish October Revolution and the Hungarian revolt of 1956 both showed that the integration of trade unions with the state only muffles discontent; it does not eliminate it.

For de Tocqueville, voluntary associations were important not only as vehicles for the expression and satisfaction of sectional needs, but also as counter-weights to state authority. Rousseau had argued that in a well-ordered state, law would express the general will, and no other will might legitimately stand against it. The state's supreme authority rested on its moral supremacy, and would rightly exclude all other authorities. De Tocqueville, however, shared the belief of Locke, Montesquieu, and Burke, that liberty depended on a delicate equilibrium of authorities. Whatever the ideal, any actual state is potentially tyrannical. Even a democratic state may oppress its minorities. In earlier times, the authority of the king had been limited, both in fact and in law, by the authority of great aristocrats, who in extreme circumstances could rally opposition to tyrants. But this authority had suffered at the hands of absolute monarchs like Louis XIV, and had been finally destroyed in the triumph of revolutionary egalitarianism. In the democratic state that was just emerging, if state authority was not to overwhelm all opposition, the authority of the aristocrat must be replaced by that of the great associations, which could effectively challenge an oppressive government. Freedom of association, then, like freedom of discussion, is a bulwark against the invasion of other freedoms.

Freedom to associate is not enough, however. If associations are to fulfil the functions suggested, they must be recognized by the law. They must be able to own property, make contracts, and employ servants. Their funds must be protected from peculating officials, their collective reputation protected by the libel laws. The law must provide ways in which their accredited agents can appeal to the courts on their behalf; without the legal recognition of collective personality, redress would require independent action by all the associates, clearly an impossible situation for a great association. We are not concerned here with the varied and ingenious legal devices for extending legal personality to associations and the problems created by them. The principal point is that, granted the legitimacy of voluntary association for sectional purposes, such associations must be given an appropriate legal status if their aims are to be realized. In extending legal recognition the state in a sense adopts an association as part of its own system; but this is simply a matter of subsumption under rules, not a proof that the association is a subordinate part whose purpose must be integrated with the whole by the superior association. As J. N. Figgis wrote:

'The State may recognize and guarantee . . . the life of these societies —the family, the club, the union, the college, the church; but it no more creates life than it creates the individual, though it orders his birth to be registered.' 'The theory of sovereignty . . . is in reality no more than a venerable superstition . . . As a fact it is as a series of groups that our social life presents itself, all having some of the qualities of public law and most of them showing clear signs of a life of their own, inherent and not derived from the concession of the State.'[3]

II. LIMITATIONS ON THE FREEDOM OF ASSOCIATIONS

We have argued that it is practically impossible that a hierarchy of authority on the scale of the modern state could be flexible and sensitive enough to meet all the diverse needs of its citizens. It is unlikely, too, that associations would offer adequate channels for the expression of unorthodox opinions and minority needs, if they were closely controlled and supervised by the state, as Hegel recommended, and as happens in totalitarian states. In such conditions, individuals who do not conform to any of the standard patterns are likely to be sacrificed, without consideration, to the needs of the majority, or to the technical needs of mass administration.

Nevertheless there are certain types of restraint and regulation which a state would be justified in imposing, in its role of umpire, and to protect freedoms of other sorts. We have already noticed that associations may wield considerable power, over their own members and over outsiders. The greater the power, the stronger the case for regulation.

(a) State regulation in self-defence

We have argued that the state, as the only association exercising an all-embracing jurisdiction within a given territory, is in the position of an umpire, competent to decide between conflicting claims, whether of individuals or of associations. And to say that it ought to 'pursue the common good' implies that it should have an impartial regard for all claims. If it is to satisfy this condition, it must clearly resist any attempt by a sectional group to appropriate its authority or to coerce it for its own purposes. For this reason it must not only possess armed force; it must surely aim to monopolize it, since this is its ultimate defence against other pressures. And further, it must prevent attempts by other associations to spread disaffection amongst its forces. It might be justified, too, in protecting itself from pressures of other sorts; for physical force is not the only kind of power. For instance, whatever the case for recognizing the right to strike, the state can hardly admit its exercise for purely political purposes, i.e. where the object is not to wrest a wage increase from employers but to force a change in state policy, or, by a syndicalist general strike, to make a revolution by paralysing the economy. Again, a church must be free to criticize state policy in the light of its religious beliefs; but if it uses its authority to force a change of policy by fomenting civil disobedience or disorder, it is exercising a form of power which can properly be met by power. Though the state's own function as umpire requires that any association shall be free to press its point of view, it requires even more that the state shall preserve its own freedom to decide against a particular association in favour of stronger claims. Freedom of association can be justified by the need to gain a hearing; it does not justify putting so much pressure on the state that it denies an impartial hearing to anyone else.

(b) State regulation of associations to protect non-members

Secondly, because some associations exercise power, the state may properly limit their freedom as it effects the freedom of non-members. For instance, the anti-trust laws of the United States and the Restrictive Trade Practices Act in Britain are designed to protect independent traders and consumers from the power of monopolistic producers' associations. By combining, producers can increase their bargaining power, and so put unorganized consumers at a disadvantage, but only if no significant number of producers (or none producing a significant proportion of the total output) remain outside the organization, to benefit by undercutting.* Consequently, associations of this sort may aim, by restricting supplies or by a deliberate policy of temporary undercutting, to force independent producers either into the association or out of the industry. The trade union 'closed shop' works in much the same way, by members refusing to work with non-members.

There are two issues involved here. On the one hand, there is the need to protect the consumer; on the other, to protect the man who would prefer not to join the association if he had the choice. As regards the consumer, the state may have to weigh his claim to the cheapest product, against, for instance, a claim by producers that, in given conditions, a free market price would be too low for the industry to survive. There may be a case, in the short run at least, for allowing an industry to restrict output or fix prices to save it from general bankruptcy. Alternatively, in the case of the 'closed shop', if the state refrains from wage fixing, collective action by the workers may be the only way of securing 'a living wage'.

It is clear, however, that if an association can constrain outsiders to join by economic pressure, it can hardly be called voluntary, except in a

* This is not the only reason why producers associate and adopt common market policies. Some monopolistic practices are not necessarily objectionable.

purely formal sense. That does not necessarily condemn it; but it means that a government must look very carefully at an association's case for using such constraint so far as it is within its power to control it. It may, of course, be its policy to encourage union organization as a way of ensuring a just distribution of income; or it may encourage an industry to 'rationalize' itself through its trade association, just as it encourages solicitors to maintain professional standards by making membership of the Law Society a statutory condition for practising. It might be argued, in such a case, that freedom to stay outside the association would defeat the approved policy; or, in the case of the 'closed shop' that non-members might enjoy all the advantages of union organization, like improved wages and conditions of work, without accepting its obligations. A minority's freedom to abstain from membership is not an absolute right; it might reasonably be abridged if it prevented the rest from achieving legitimate and desirable ends. Nevertheless, there is something anomalous in upholding a formal legal right to abstain from membership, while condoning the use of economic pressure to frustrate it. If it is the state's view that in any given case such a right ought not to exist, it would do well, perhaps, to change the law, instead of leaving associations to press abstainers into membership by using extra-legal power.

(c) State regulations in the interests of members of an association

The case for free association is also a case for leaving associations to settle their own domestic affairs in their own way. But here again there are qualifications. In the first place, in recognizing an association as a legal person, capable of owning property, making contracts, and so on, the state *must* take notice of its rules. Indeed, as we have seen, the association *is* a legal person only by virtue of its rule system. This is therefore a part of the law, though a part which the association may itself be competent to amend according to its own procedure. The rules of the association establish rights and duties as between the whole and its members severally, which are also legal rights and duties (Lawyers have developed and adapted legal concepts like contract and trust to cover such relations). Because an association's officers are bound by such rules, the state cannot be indifferent to the way they apply them. The rights of members are thus *prima facie* the business of the courts. There are two broad issues in question here: on the one hand, the degree to which the administration of an association's affairs should be left to its discretion; on the other, the extent to which it should be left free to vary its objectives, in the face of objections from some of its members.

i. The degree to which the state should supervise the administration of an association's affairs will depend, in part, on the degree of hardship involved in resignation or expulsion. Injustice in a tennis club is no great matter, for members can leave it without great loss; it is probably better to leave tennis clubs broadly free to do as they wish, rather than subject them to the straitjacket of the law. Trade unions and trade associations, however, are another matter. A man's rights in his union may be as important to him as any legal rights he has, and they are the more in need of protection because he can rarely afford to resign. Lord Justice Denning stated the case for judicial review of union rules and administration in Bonsor v. Musicians' Union:

'On this appeal our task is to construe the rules of the Musicians' Union which constitute the contract between the member and the union; but in approaching this question of construction I desire to say that these rules are more a contract in theory than a contract in fact. In order for there to be a true contract, there must be the agreement of parties freely made with full knowledge and without any feeling of constraint. This was not so here. The Musicians' Union was a "closed shop". In order that a person should be allowed to work at his trade he had to sign a document agreeing to the rules. He had no option but to sign. The plaintiff himself said "I did not want to be a member of it . . ." When one remembers that the rules are applied to a man in that state of mind, it will be appreciated that they are not so much a contract, as we used to understand a contract, but they are much more a legislative code laid down by some members of the union to be imposed on all members of the union. They are more like by-laws than a contract. In these circumstances, the rules are to be construed not only against the makers of them, but, further, if it should be found that any of those rules are contrary to natural justice, or what comes to the same thing, contrary to what is fair and reasonable, the court would hold them to be invalid.'[4]*

ii. The second issue arose in the Free Church of Scotland case. There, a majority in the Church decided to amalgamate with another church whose doctrines were different from their own in certain important respects. The state became involved when the minority group claimed the Free Church funds. These were held in trust, they argued, not for *any* church, but only for one whose doctrines were specified in the trust. The House of Lords supported this view, on a strict interpretation of the law of trust. We are not here concerned with the legal merits

---

* Bonsor v Musicians' Union established the right of a member wrongfully expelled from a trade union, not only to reinstatement but also to damages for breach of contract and consequent loss of earnings.

of that decision. It gave rise, however, to a remarkable controversy which raised the whole question of the right of an association to define and develop its own aims, without legal interference. Critics of the House of Lords decision, like Figgis, maintained that an association possessed 'real' corporate personality apart from its state-created legal personality, and that it was absurd to confine the living association within the narrow limits of a legal definition of its aims.[5]

On the face of it, it *is* absurd, for it would prevent a significant majority of members from profiting from their joint experience, and modifying their original objectives accordingly. Again, the pursuit of a common objective might stimulate other related interests which the association might serve, even although they might not be stated in its constitution.

But there is a strong case too on the other side. A minority may be deeply committed to an association, by interest or sentiment. If it changes its objectives so radically that they can no longer share in its activities, they may suffer hardship or loss (like the loss of their church premises).*

In the Osborne case (1909), a trade union was forbidden to use funds for political purposes not specified in its declared aims. This raised similar problems, and a compromise solution was provided by the Act of 1913, which permitted unions to raise a political levy, from which objectors could 'contract out' without losing their normal rights as union members. If an industrial organization sets out to safeguard workers' interests, it might reasonably use political methods. But if unwilling members can be made to join by economic pressure, they should not also be made to subscribe to political purposes which they dislike.†

The broad choice for the state in such cases is between leaving associations free from interference that may be unsympathetic to their aims, and regulating and supervising them in its role of umpire, to protect the rights of members under the association's own rules. The more power an association has over its members, the stronger is the case for regulating it.

(d) State intervention in conflicts between associations
Because the state has the functions both of umpire and of preventing

---

* The Free Church controversy was finally settled by a special Act of Parliament, which divided the trust funds between the two parties. This was a reasonable settlement, but it might not be easy to do the same in all similar cases.

† It is often said that in some unions the legal safeguards are nullified by the pressure of opinion. But the law can hardly protect those who are too weakminded to exercise their rights for fear of being unpopular. The most it can do is to prevent the more blatant forms of intimidation.

disorder, it provides peaceful procedures for settling disputes which cannot be settled by agreement, and it forbids settling them by force. This has not always been the case. In Saxon times, the king's authority was insufficient to prevent the private settlement of quarrels by force, and the law went no further than to lay down limiting conditions for private wars. Duelling remained an accepted way of settling a quarrel until a much later date. The modern state, however, will not recognize an agreement to fight as a legitimate way of settling a difference.

Some disputes are still fought out, however, if not by force of arms, at any rate by methods not much less harmful to the community at large. Great business corporations, especially in the United States, have engaged in 'price wars', deliberately incurring losses by underselling competitors, in order to drive them out of business or buy them out at a bargain price. The most obvious examples of economic conflicts, however, are between rival trade unions and between unions and employers' associations. Though machinery for peaceful settlement often exists in such cases, it remains open to a union or to an employers' association to refuse arbitration, and to resort to the weapons of the strike and the lock-out.

It is important to distinguish here between the right of an individual, or a number of individuals acting separately, to refuse to work for an employer (a right which is not in question), and the collective right of an association to call a strike, in order to force concessions from employers. 'A strike' means a collective act, not just a sum of individual acts. Its whole point depends on its being organized for a collective end. And similarly, a 'lock-out' is not like a case of a firm's closing because it has run out of orders. Its end is an essential element in its definition: it is an act of war. Thus, to deny the right to strike would not necessarily mean supporting the conscription of labour, or attacking a man's right to change his job.

So long as the state held aloof from the market, leaving wages and prices to be determined wholly by private contracts, there was a clear case for permitting workers to remedy the weakness of their separate bargaining positions by collective action, including the strike.* But the theory of *laissez-faire* is now quite dead. Nowadays workers and employers are both highly organized. And the state takes an active interest in promoting the peaceful settlement of industrial disputes, which otherwise cause inconvenience and hardship to millions not directly involved. The right to fight it out, in these conditions, seems no less of

---

* Cardinal Manning wrote to Ben Tillett, in the 1890s: 'If for a just cause, a strike is right and inevitable, it is a healthful restraint on the despotism of capital. It is the only power in the hands of the working men.'

an anachronism than the duel or the vendetta. The considerations of public interest which have made the state the proper umpire in private quarrels would seem to apply as forcibly to industrial disputes. There would seem, then, to be a strong case for compulsory arbitration.

But the problem is more complicated than it looks at first. There is a long tradition of militant trade unionism, which cannot easily be overcome. The war-time restrictions on the right to strike were respected by responsible union officials; but their authority could not prevent unofficial strikes called by unofficial leaders of *ad hoc* militant organizations.* In wartime, everybody could see the damaging effects of strikes, and the authority of the state stood especially high. If at such a time state and union authority combined could not prevent strikes, is it likely that the state alone could do so, with perhaps, union authority ranged against it? We have pointed out in the last chapter that the state's authority is by no means exclusive, and that the authority of other associations in their own fields may be stronger than the state's. What the state can achieve as umpire depends in such cases on not forcing a major conflict of loyalties. This is the more true in the present case, because the conflicts of labour and capital are close to the heart of political controversy. The state's *de facto* authority depends very largely on confidence in its impartiality; but no government can avoid being thought to take sides in economic conflicts. And this is particularly true in the case of nationalized industries. So long as unions and employers can reserve the right to reject abritration if it seems unreasonable, they are usually ready to accept it. But while they continue to suspect bias, or differ from the government on broad economic policies, they are unlikely to submit readily to compulsory arbitration. If the state's *de facto* authority fails in a matter of this sort, it is unlikely to succeed by coercion.†

* Cf. O. Kahn-Freund: 'Should Strikes be Prohibited by Law?', *The Listener*, Vol. LIV (1955), p. 142. 'Under the law of the Weimar Republic, the liability of the unions for breach of collective agreements was coupled with a system of compulsory arbitration, and . . . in the event of a failure of negotiations, the award of an arbitration tribunal was . . . considered as a collective agreement. The union could then be faced with this dilemma: either yield to the pressure of its members and support a strike against the terms of the award and, by doing so, risk an action for breach of contract and jeopardize its funds, or, alternatively, urge its members to comply. This would preserve its funds but might lose it the loyalty of its members. They will cease to regard the union as a representative of their interests and begin to consider it as a sort of government agency. And this, I should say, was part of the story of how the German trade unions collapsed.

† Nevertheless, in the United States, and in some European and Commonwealth countries, the state has gone farther than in Britain in regulating industrial relations. In the United States, employers have a legal obligation to bargain

III. THE STATE AND OTHER ASSOCIATIONS AS COMPETING AND COMPLEMENTARY TECHNIQUES FOR PROVIDING SERVICES

The state, then, assists other associations by giving them legal recognition and imposes on them limitations and duties in its capacity as umpire. But this is only part of the story. The modern state provides many services, like medical care, poor relief, unemployment insurance, and education, which might still be provided by other associations, as they once were. It engages, too, in various forms of economic activity which were formerly left to non-state associations. Many people fear, with de Tocqueville, that the state is fast becoming for its members

> 'an immense and tutelary power, which takes upon itself alone to secure their gratifications, and to watch over their fate . . . For their happiness such a government willingly labours, but it chooses to be the sole agent and the only arbiter of that happiness: it provides for their security, foresees and supplies their necessities, facilitates their pleasures, manages their principal concerns, directs their industry, regulates the descent of property, and subdivides their inheritances—what remains, but to spare them all the care of thinking and all the trouble of living? . . . The will of man is not shattered, but softened, bent, and guided: men are seldom forced to act, but they are constantly restrained from acting: such a power does not destroy, but it prevents existence; it does not tyrannize, but it compresses, enervates, extinguishes, and stupefies a people, till each nation is reduced to be nothing better than a flock of timid and industrious animals, of which the government is the shepherd.'[6]

These words first appeared in 1840. De Tocqueville seized on political and economic egalitarianism as the dominating force in modern politics. He foresaw that when, in a nation of many millions, a majority came to resent the way in which wealth and opportunity were distributed, the state would be pressed to provide a variety of social services, involving a great extension of its authority. Egalitarians are not satisfied if the state merely guarantees minimum standards: they protest that any special advantage that can be bought, like a public school education, or medical treatment in a private ward or nursing home, is an offence against social justice. Consequently certain activities hitherto undertaken by non-state associations are not merely supplemented by state provision;

---

with unions in good faith, and various anti-union practices, like victimization, are prohibited by law. Furthermore, employers' federations and unions are legally liable for a breach of collective agreement.

K

they are now in danger of total absorption in the quest for uniform standards.

This picture may be distorted, but it certainly alarms many people. They fear that men become demoralized as they come to depend on the state for more and more of their needs. According to the critics, they no longer bother to provide for old age and sickness, for themselves or their families. They demand ever greater material advantages while seeing no need to exert themselves to get them. From protecting the helpless, the state has become the guardian of those perfectly capable of helping themselves, undermining as it does the solid bourgeois virtues of thrift, foresight, responsibility, and independence.

What the critics object to is that the state, in providing such services, has insisted on making them compulsory. Where formerly a responsible person joined with others to safeguard his own interest by deliberate choice, now he pays what is virtually a tax, and receives benefits which do not seem directly related to it, and which he has made no deliberate personal effort to obtain. Not that he is debarred from making supplementary arrangements (through life insurance, for example) if he chooses; but the inducement is diminished, and, according to the critics, will diminish further as the habit grows of looking to the state to meet every crisis that life brings. Of course, such criticisms presuppose a moral position. They rest like Mill's attack on paternalism, on the belief that individual initiative and personal responsibility are valuable in themselves. For Mill, nobility of character (or we might call it 'virtue') was at least as important as happiness—or rather, it was a necessary constituent of real happiness. But the noble character was one that was independent and responsible, active and experimental; and to be these things, a man must be trained to take responsibility for his own welfare, rather than to rely, like a child, on others.[7] It would be no answer to these criticisms, then, to point out how few old people go hungry nowadays, how much more healthy children are, how the fear of poverty through unemployment or sickness has ceased to poison the times of prosperity and health, as once it did for millions. For the critics would say that security is purchased at the cost of responsibility, virtue, and personal initiative. From this point of view, whatever the superior technical advantages of state provision, voluntary activities are better just because they are voluntary.

Considered, however, simply as a technique for providing certain types of service, the state has evident advantages over other forms of organization. Whenever there is a case for a uniform standard of service, as with the relief of poverty, or whenever a service can be administered more efficiently and economically on a large scale or on a territorial basis, such as social insurance and fire services, or, especially, if it is intended that the cost of the service should be spread unevenly, so as to effect a re-distribution of income, the state, having compulsory and universal jurisdiction within its territory, has an advantage over other associations. Again, the social stigma attaching to 'charity', humiliating the recipient and restraining many in genuine need from seeking it, does not seem to attach to state administered benefits, especially if, as with free education and school milk, it is received as of right, as part of a universal service without means test.

On the other hand, it is difficult to keep state services flexible, meeting different sectional and local needs differently, without conferring a wide discretion on local administrators. Such a discretion tends to produce corresponding variations in the standard of service rendered. Educational decentralization in this country has been criticized precisely because it results in differences, as between one local authority and another, in the numbers of grammar school places and university awards per head of the population. The very egalitarianism that tends to concentrate functions in the state tends also to press for centralized and uniform administration. It is difficult, too, for a state service to be experimental. A public authority sensitive to criticism cannot be expected to try out new and experimental techniques; experimental schools, like Dartington and the Outward Bound Schools, are rarely sponsored by public authorities.

In deciding the part it is to play in providing a service, therefore, a government must consider whether a voluntary association might possibly provide it more efficiently than it can itself, whether it might be more ready to experiment, or more adaptable in meeting varied requirements and changing conditions; or whether the service requires a uniform standard throughout the country. If a minimum (but not a uniform) standard of efficiency will suffice, the best arrangement may be a system of inspection supported by grants-in-aid. There may be grounds for adopting parallel provision, e.g. a system of state and non-state schools existing side by side, the one offering sound and sufficient education on orthodox lines, the other operating, in effect, as a sort of experimental laboratory. But if the state accepts such a partnership, it must see that its partner is not forced out of business. There may be a case for, say, tax remission, to enable experiments to continue. In some cases, the state's part might be to encourage and guide existing organizations, e.g. by subsidies to approved bodies, rather than to supersede them. Because the British are very sensitive on the subject of academic freedom our universities remain relatively independent, and state subsidies are administered through the mainly academic University Grants Committee.

Similarly, the arts are subsidized not directly by a government department, but through the Arts Council. But in other countries, like France, universities are often under the direct control of the Minister of Education, while in nearly every European country there is a state opera house and a state theatre, under direct state administration.

The choice of administrative technique is not altogether a matter of choosing the most efficient means for a given end. Where the state and other associations are together interested in providing a given service, it might appear in this light if considered in isolation. But if the critics of the modern welfare state are at all justified, there would seem to be a case for treating voluntary provision as having a positive value in itself, weighing against (though not necessarily decisively against) any state scheme tending to weaken it, as the National Insurance Scheme weakened the friendly societies. In such a case, it might be worth sacrificing something in efficiency in order to encourage voluntary associations on a basis of partnership, as the Ministry of Education encourages the Workers' Educational Association, rather than by-pass them and institute a rival scheme.

There are some functions, however, which no voluntary association could undertake on its own, because they call for co-ordinated efforts from many interests. Thus an attempt to attract tourists would call for joint action from the catering trades, from local authorities, transport undertakings, chambers of commerce, and so on. None of these could achieve anything alone; it is unlikely that any would even consider initiating such a policy unless it could be sure of co-operation from the others. It would tend to look to the state as a matter of course to take such an initiative, or at least to take over the job of mobilizing the joint effort. Co-operation in matters of mutual concern does of course occur without state intervention, but when the object demands large-scale organization, considerable outlay, and the co-operation of a very varied set of interests, authority and guidance are often indispensable. And where, as in the case of water supply, one body may be in a position to frustrate joint action by a large number of others, there may be a case for compelling it to join in, if the objective is an important one.

IV. THE STATE AND THE FAMILY

We have been considering mainly the state's relations with specialized mass associations, like trade unions and churches. We have maintained that, in principle, the state will do well to leave them to manage their own domestic affairs, intervening as umpire mainly in defence of other interest, or of individual members, if the association abuses its power.

Beyond that, it can usefully co-ordinate activities which might otherwise be mutually defeating, and initiate enterprises which would be
impossible without co-operation from many associations.

The problem of the family is superficially somewhat different. Unlike mass associations, its ties are informal, but it inspires powerful
loyalties all the same; its authority is effective although it is exercised
within a very indefinite rule structure. Families regular such intimate
and personal matters, and so many of their rules are vague understandings arrived at by experiment and mutual adjustment, that there
seems to be an especially strong case for leaving them alone. Any
general rule would seem beside the point in very many cases. The legal
rules, for instance, governing the property rights of husbands and wives
are quite irrelevant in families where all property has always been
pooled.

Nevertheless, the state has built around the family an elaborate legal
structure: it prescribes a minimum age for marriage and forbids marriage between close relatives; it prohibits bigamy; it makes dissolution
of the marriage association (and the forming of a new one) subject to
strict conditions and procedures, or in some states forbids it altogether.
It obliges one associate, the husband and father, to support the others,
at least while they are unable to support themselves; it regulates property relations between members, while at the same time treating the
family as a whole in some measure as a property owning unit; it may
even prescribe limiting conditions for the transmission of family property from one generation to the next, though it upholds in principle the
freedom of testamentary disposition.

One reason for this close interest is that the procreation and rearing
of children, which is a principal function of the family, is of interest to
others besides the parents. Precisely because children are automatically
members of a family and can have no choice in the matter, and because
they are subject to parental authority, their interests must be guaranteed
by the state, as it must guarantee the rights of a member of any association which exercises effective power. Moreover, other citizens have an
interest in the matter, for it is of general concern that children should be
equipped to become reasonably social and useful men and women.

In secular terms, it is difficult to see what concern the state would have
with marriage but for its procreative aspect. Some states have made
adultery and fornication criminal offences, but it is doubtful whether
such a law could be effective; on the whole these matters are probably
best left to conventional rather than legal control.* The concern for

* There may be a case on grounds of public health for legal control of prosti-
tution; but this is another matter.

children apart, there would be little point in drawing a legal distinction between informal sexual relations and formal and recognized marriage. Religious considerations are not here to the point; marriage may be distinguished by its sacramental character, while other sorts of sexual relations may be sin—but that is a distinction to be drawn by a church, not by any state that adopts a position of religious neutrality.

The state is concerned, of course, for the wife as well as for the children. Where the husband exercises a strong customary authority, as in early Victorian England or in Arabia, the state might be right to establish legal safeguards to protect the wife. But because the law in such matters is always a reflection of custom, that protection rarely exists in fact. In some legal systems, a wife's status is more like that of an object of property rights than of a party to a contract.

The legal rights of married women against their husbands were considerably extended in this country in the nineteenth century as part of a general emancipation of women, in custom as well as in law. But the need for legal protection diminished as the protection itself increased. Today, it is no longer so shocking or so difficult for a married woman to work for her living, as once it was. She is therefore less subject to the economic power of her husband. Easier divorce, too, has partially opened up a legal way of escape. There would seem to be less reason today, then, for legal protection for married women than there was a hundred years ago.

Nevertheless, a husband is still legally obliged, in principle, to support his wife, and she has special property rights against him. But what grounds could there be for this continuing interest of the state in a relationship which is rapidly becoming a partnership of equals, rather than a subjection of one to the power and authority of the other? One answer may be that the wife's independence lasts only until she becomes a mother. For then she usually loses the ability to fend for herself, except at her children's expense, and becomes again dependent on her husband and in need of protection.

Similarly, though divorce is easier than it once was, the state still imposes fairly strict conditions. Marriage in English law is a rare case of an association which cannot be dissolved by mutual consent of its members. Where there are children, the state can rightly intervene on their behalf (though the children of a wrecked marriage are sometimes better served by dissolving it). In the case of a childless marriage, however, there seems little point in insisting on the legal tie where neither party has the will to preserve it. It is true that marriage has functions other than procreation and the care of children—the control of sexual intercourse, regularizing a relation of deep personal affection, regulating property and inheritance, and the division of labour connected with the household. But most of these are either better taken care of by custom or are impossible to control legally, although laws may help to promote such aspects of marriage by setting authoritative standards. Stable marriages are no doubt desirable for the parties themselves and for society at large; but a broken marriage is not the less broken because the law does not recognize it as such. When the welfare of children is not involved, there is no much of a case for maintaining the legal existence of an association which serves no one's needs, and which must be either voluntary or else becomes a pernicious oppression.

The case for maintaining the façade of marriage when the association is marred by sexual maladjustment or personal incompatibility is weaker under modern conditions than it has ever been. For, on the one hand, many of the functions previously fulfilled by the family have been taken over by the state; and, on the other hand, marriage itself is now entered into in Western Europe predominantly by personal choice rather than by family arrangement. The diminution of its social functions together with the strong emphasis on personal choice, which is enhanced by the film and the popular novel, have combined to make it a much more private, personal and intimate association than ever before. These two trends both militate against stability. For on the one hand much store is set by 100 per cent compatibility; and on the other hand the functions of the family have so diminished that little is left to do save for couples to live in harmony and bring up the children.

A further cause of the instability of the family is the tendency for modern marriage to become *moralized*. Before women achieved some sort of equal status with men the norms for behaviour within marriage were prescribed by custom; personal adjustments had always to be made, but they were made within a framework of fixed traditions. Nowadays couples have increasingly to make their own rules as well as their own temperamental adjustments. Matters of principle can arise over the washing up as well as over the control of the family finance, and there are great varieties in the patterns of rules even within similar income groups. The result is that a modern marriage calls for a higher degree of personal responsibility on the part of those who undertake and maintain it than was the case when marriage was a more stable and uniform institution completely regulated by custom. It has become increasingly a sphere of personal choice and decision. There is correspondingly a case for leaving more to individual decision when the question of its dissolution arises.

In view of such considerations it seems logical either to make it easy to get married and also easy to get divorced, as is the case in the USA.

Or, if it is difficult to get divorced, it should also be much more difficult to get married. It would be difficult to envisage laws, under modern conditions, prohibiting marriage without parental consent at a later age than that prevailing at present. But certainly much could be done by public opinion to discourage early marriages without adequate thought and preparation. A corollary of such a change in public opinion might be a more tolerant attitude towards responsible pre-marital sex relations. But this raises wider issues which lie outside the more specific topic of the relation of the state to lesser associations[8] with which this chapter has been concerned.

V. CONCLUSION

We have approached the relations of the state with other associations from this standpoint: free association is necessary if the claims of all persons are to be attended to, because it is a practical impossibility for the state itself to attend to them all, and give each its due. When a state attempts to do so, directly or by harnessing associations to its own conception of 'a good life', it becomes a monstrous tyranny. Nevertheless, in its role as arbiter, it must regulate and interfere in the running of sectional associations, because it cannot leave extra-legal power dangerously free to invade the freedoms of others.

The case for interference presupposes, however, an impartial approach to sectional claims, and a regard for the persons whose interest the association exists to promote. But some governments regulate only to bend all associations to their own purposes, to deny expression to inconvenient claims, and to establish more firmly their own exclusive authority. This, we believe, is an abuse of state authority.

What guarantee could there be, however, that rulers will approach their task in the proper spirit? Though some men may go in for politics with the highest motives, some are concerned only for a sectional interest, and still others are devoted to the idea of power for its own sake. The finest antidote to state worship is to study dispassionately some of the men who govern states. Nevertheless, we recognize a general obligation to submit to those in authority, irrespective of their motives for seeking authority. And we expect them to show impartiality and concern for the welfare of those they govern, even though they so often disappoint us. What could justify such an obligation to submit? And what assurance can we look for that our governors will behave as they ought? Should we seek out men of high virtue and trust them utterly? Or should we seek institutional safeguards against the untrustworthy? These questions will concern us in the two chapters that follow.

CHAPTER 14

THE GROUNDS OF AUTHORITY
AND POLITICAL OBLIGATION

I. AUTHORITY AND ITS JUSTIFICATION

(a) De facto and de jure senses of 'authority'

We have distinguished in earlier chapters between a *de facto* and a *de jure* sense of 'authority', and further between each of these and 'power'.*
We took as an example of *de facto* authority that is not also *de jure*, the case of a man who takes charge in a cinema fire, and is obeyed without question by people who have never seen him before and know nothing about him. His authority, in this sense, consists in the fact that people are ready to accept his proposals, not because they have thought them over and agree that they are good ideas, but because he inspires confidence; they do what he says without question. This is clearly distinct from an exercise of power. In exercising power, a man secures compliance by force, threats or bribes; in this case men comply for no reason but that the leader is the sort of man he is.

We use 'authority' in the *de jure* sense when we speak of someone 'in authority', or of 'the authorities'. The factual question, whether people do in fact fall in with his proposals, obey his commands, etc., is not immediately to the point. He is 'in authority' because a rule, or a system of rules, authorizes him to give orders, and constitutes for others a duty to obey, at any rate so long as the commander remains within his authority or competence. So long as the rule is generally respected authority *de jure* will tend to be also *de facto*, i.e. people will fall in with the official's suggestions because they recognize in him a man appointed and entitled to give orders; though they might not respect the man, they might yet respect his office. In a strictly voluntary association (if such a thing exists), a man might exercise a *de facto* authority to the extent that members respect the rules that confer on him a *de jure* authority; but against the man who rejects the rule he may have no remedy. But if an association is able to enforce a sanction, authority *de jure* may also be a

---

* See Chapters 1, 10, and 11.

source of power, not in relation to those who accept but in relation to those who reject the authority. To the extent that *de jure* authority gives the official *de facto* authority over some at least of the members of an association, it tends to give him power over the rest. This is what we meant when we said, in Chapter 12, that coercive power is intricately bound up with authority; for governments would be powerless if they had no authority *de facto* over the armed forces—and its usual basis is the authority conferred by law.

(b) *Authority de jure and political obligation*

To speak of authority *de jure* presumes, then, a rule, or a system of rules, authorizing an agent to issue commands, or pronouncements, or to make proposals, etc., and placing on others an obligation to obey or accept them. When the authorizing rule is a law, and the association a state, we call this 'political obligation', though the term could well be extended to cover similar relations in other spheres. In the case of such an obligation, and while discussion is limited to the requirements of the rule system, we cannot ask whether a command is wise, prudent, or otherwise desirable before obeying it. The only permissible questions are ones like: 'Does the person giving the command, etc., really satisfy the conditions laid down by the rule, or is he an impostor or a usurper?' or 'Does his competence really extend thus far?'

Some writers have taken the view that these are the only questions that can properly be asked about authority—and presumably about the corresponding obligation to obey.

> 'Questions about the origin of authority,' wrote T. D. Weldon, 'in so far as they are sensible and answerable questions, are concerned with existing rights, laws, and political organization generally.' 'The position indeed is exactly parallel to that of the cricketer who asks "Why should I obey the umpire? What right has he to give me out?" One can answer only by expounding the rules of cricket, the position of the MCC and so on. Beyond that there is nothing to be done except to say "This is a game of cricket, isn't it?" '[1]

However satisfying an answer this might be in respect of cricket, it certainly seems to close the discussion prematurely when applied to the sort of authority exercised in states, and perhaps in churches and trade unions. Even in respect of cricket one might conceivably ask why the game should be played in precisely that way—or indeed whether the game is worth playing at all, if that is the only way to play it. Certainly, many political philosophers in the past wanted to ask questions on these lines, and would have been dissatisfied with Weldon's answer. They tried to get behind the particular set of rules to some other, more general criteria, to ask questions like 'What is the point in having rules that give some men authority over others, and particularly authority to coerce them?' and 'What *general* conditions (i.e. beyond any particular constitutional ones) must be satisfied for one man to possess authority *de jure* over another?' They distinguished legal and political obligation, making one depend on the other (as the natural lawyers made positive law depend for its validity on natural law). They sought fundamental grounds of authority and obligation that would validate a claim to obedience, and would also settle whether, and under what conditions, it might be legitimate to disobey, and perhaps to resist.

A short way of dealing with such aspirations has been suggested by writers like Margaret MacDonald and Professor J. C. Rees.[2] Political theorists like Locke, Rousseau, T. H. Green, etc., made the mistake, they say, of looking for grounds of political obligation which would be necessary and sufficient whatever the circumstances. These are not to be found. We can answer the question 'Why should I obey *this* government?' by looking at the constitution that authorizes it, or by considering the relative merits of obedience and disobedience *in the particular situation*; but if we divorce the question from all particular contexts, there is no way of answering it. For whether or not we ought to obey *must* depend on the circumstances. A fervent democrat might have a duty to accept a dictatorship if it were the best of the possibilities available in the circumstances.* Nothing is gained, say the critics, from highly general statements of the ends that governments ought to serve, like 'the greatest happiness of the greatest number' (Bentham) or 'the highest possible development of all the capacities of personality in all of (the society's) members' (Sir Ernest Barker); for they suggest no specific tests for determining whether in a given situation the end is being served, and whether, therefore, we should obey or not. The suggestion, however, is not that Locke, Rousseau, and the rest were writing empty nonsense. On the contrary, 'the value of the political theorists is not in the general information they give about the basis of political obligation but in their skill in emphasizing at a critical moment a criterion which is tending to be overlooked or denied'.[3]

Now it is certainly true that works like Locke's *Second Treatise* or Rousseau's *Social Contract* were not simply academic treatises, but essays in advocacy, adapted to the urgencies of a particular situation. Men rarely question the legitimacy of established authority when all is going well; the problem of political obligation is urgent when the state is sick, when someone is seriously contemplating disobedience or revolt

* Polish democrats probably felt like this about Mr Gomulka in 1956.

on principle. The advocates understandably saw the problem in terms of their own times. They often wrote as if the criterion 'overlooked or denied' were the one condition, without which no government could be legitimate, or as if, this being satisfied, nothing else mattered. For they clearly believed that they were enunciating principles of universal validity which were peculiarly fitting to their own times. There must have been something of universal importance in what they said; for they still have a power to move and persuade, which suggests insights transcending the particular context. Nevertheless, it can scarcely be maintained that the *specific* tests of legitimacy which they suggested have such validity. For there is no reason why there should be any one specific criterion or set of criteria for political obligation, to be satisfied in all cases, and which if satisfied is sufficient.

But it is doubtful whether the criteria suggested by the great political theorists should be understood only as specific criteria of this sort. Bentham's formula is certainly not in this class, and we shall argue that while the theory of consent has generally been associated with fairly specific prescriptions for political organization, there is another, more general side to it that may better account for its very great influence.

We argued in Chapter 2 that rules of a very high order of generality —at the level at which we speak of 'principles of procedure'—define the terms of discussion, rather than provide unique and unambiguous prescriptions for particular cases. They indicate the sort of criteria that will be admitted as relevant. For this very reason they can appear strikingly important in a very wide variety of situations. Precisely because they are formal rather than substantive and specific, they are least tied to particular circumstances. We shall try to show that the perennial discussion on the grounds of political obligation is more than a bandying of specific criteria, each significant for its own time and perhaps for others too, but each necessarily partial and inconclusive on its own. For there is a more fundamental disagreement. What is missing, for instance, from Margaret MacDonald's account of the discussion is any recognition that the criteria proposed are of different types, and belong to different frameworks of discussion. Appeals to Divine Right are different from appeals to tradition; and both are different in type from appeals to principles backed by reasons, rather than by higher authorization. Now many such principles might be found, such as the need for order, or the importance of consulting the interests of the subject. But they would all be different from criteria deriving from Scriptural authority or tradition. The perennial discussion of political obligation has been concerned, then, not merely with how a specific criterion is to be applied, nor merely with which specific criterion is the more important, but also with the *sort* of criteria which should be admissible. The fundamental disagreement has been about the framework within which the discussion is to be conducted.

We shall consider theories in which political obligation is discussed, first in a religious or metaphysical framework, next in a traditionalist framework, and last in a framework of moral concepts.

II. RELIGIOUS AND METAPHYSICAL GROUNDS OF AUTHORITY AND OBLIGATION

(a) 'Divine right'

We observed in Chapter 1 that it is only at a fairly advanced stage of civilization that distinctions are made between different modes of social control. At a more primitive level, all rules are alike religious, customary, and legal. Thus among many African peoples the chief or king is selected from one royal family, and may be required to demonstrate his divine appointment or 'charisma' by prowess in arms or other visible, customary sign. He is then formally acknowledged by his people, as the gods' gift to them, not merely to guard the social order, but also as a sort of talisman according to whose virtue the crops will be good and the seasons favourable.[4] His authority stems not simply from inheritance according to custom, or from popular acclamation; these are regarded as the consequences rather than the grounds of authority. The true source is divine, and his authority is therefore independent both of human choice and custom. (The relics of this association of monarchical and divine authority are still to be seen in the British rite of coronation.)

A more sophisticated version of this approach to authority is found in the sixteenth and seventeenth century doctrines of the Divine Right of Kings. The appeal to divine right implied that authority was not a matter of human will, nor was the obligation to obey of human choosing. We could know God's will in this matter on the authority alike of scripture and nature, and it was the only will *finally* binding upon men. For some, this ruled out any challenge whatsoever to a properly consecrated hereditary monarch. But the theory of the Divine Right of Kings was only a special application of a more general doctrine. 'You do not even begin to understand typical sixteenth century thought,' wrote J. W. Allen, 'till you have grasped the fact that to a vast majority of the thinkers of that period, all right was "divine" . . .' Obligation may be, primarily, to oneself, or to another, or to one's country or to all mankind; but it must ultimately be to God. It was inconceivable that there could be any obligation merely to man. For this reason, and for no other, it may be said that all right is divine. 'The King's right is, of course, divine; so are the rights of his subjects, if they have any.' On this understanding, it may follow that even the right to rebel is a divine right, arising from a breach of obligation 'unless, indeed, rebellion be conceived as a positive duty . . . . as it was by Knox'.[5] It was generally admitted that God had instituted government because men needed it. But in that case, might it not follow that Divine authorization depends on the king's governing in the interests of his subjects?

The appeal to Divine Right was thus inconclusive. The theory that authority is divinely instituted does not exclude the possibility that under some conditions God would similarly authorize resistance. The general theory is thus no more than a definition of the terms in which the case must be argued. If *all* obligation is religious, what is to be done when there is an apparent conflict of obligations, as, for instance, when the king commands what is contrary to God's law? If scripture were unequivocal, the way might be clear; but precisely because the prescriptions of scripture are taken to be of universal application, they are general and flexible, not particular and precise injunctions.* The command 'Render unto Caesar the things that are Caesar's, and unto God the things that are God's' necessarily leaves open the question, what things are Caesar's, what God's? To choose between the different interpretations of such maxims recommended by opposing parties we must seek elsewhere—in 'nature', perhaps—for further evidence of the Divine will.

Thus Sir Robert Filmer argued the case for absolute royal authority by analogy with patriarchalism—or rather, by claiming the direct descent of all kings in the senior line from Adam. In his opinion, kings inherited Adam's original authority as father of mankind. A father's authority is of nature, and therefore of God. But Locke retorted that paternal authority was of nature only while his children were in infancy; when they reached the age of reason, patriarchal authority must be freely conceded by the children themselves.

The problem of political obligation was posed in urgent form by the breakdown of settled attitudes and institutions, by schism and persecution. It is understandable that it should have been debated in terms of divine authority, in an age which made little or no distinction between religious, customary, legal, and moral duties, or which derived all the rest from the first. But this in itself settled nothing; divine right cast in a conventional ideological mould much of the same sort of arguments

---

* Dogmatic appeals, like Luther's, to 'the plain words of scripture' were merely refusals to consider objections. Rules may be 'plain' and still be equivocal in particular situations.

about the hazards of rebellion and the dangers of obedience as appeared later in the secular forms of contract, natural right, general will, and so on. Controversy was carried on by bandying scriptural texts; but the choice and interpretation of texts was governed by immediate and practical issues.

Accordingly, though Divine Right was used by some to assert the unconditional authority of princes, it in no sense entailed this conclusion. On the contrary, it was eminently suited to a theory of conditional obligation, since the prince's authority derived from the benign authority of God. The terms upon which a beneficent God would place men under an obligation to obey authority, the final cause of which was their own good, remained open to argument. And in a sense, this was not a weakness in the theory but a strength. For in a revolutionary situation, there is not much point in simply re-affirming the absolute claims of established authority. If men are disposed to doubt, they want reasons related to their situation, rather than dogmatic assertions that everything is as it ought to be. Any approach to political obligation that left no room for discussion in the light of the particular situation might confirm the faith of the faithful; it could not convince the doubter.

(b) The mystique of leadership
i. Charismatic theories of political authority.

The Divine Right of kings in particular, however, as urged, for instance, by Bossuet and by James I at his most extreme, was a claim to a special appointment, grace, or 'charisma', which marked kings out from other men. It has secular parallels in theories which see the leader as a man marked out by Fate or History for a special mission, ascribing to him unique insights or intuitions, or identifying him personally with the progressive forces moulding the future. In religious or secular forms, claims of this sort have been made for an astonishing variety of leaders, from Christ and Mohammed to Napoleon, Hitler and Stalin.

To attribute charismatic authority to a leader is not, on the face of it, to derive the obligation to obey him from a normative system of any sort. As Max Weber pointed out his authority rests on 'devotion to (his) specific and exceptional sanctity, heroism, or exemplary character' extending therefore to 'the normative patterns or order revealed or ordained by him'[6] but not itself deriving from any order. On the contrary, in the purest cases of charismatic authority the leader is in revolt against the customary or legal order, and the authorities deriving from it.

Yet charismatic authority is not simply authority *de facto*.* For the

* See Chapter I, Section III.

leader's disciples believe that *it behoves* them to obey—and more, that it behoves everyone else to do so too. The authority is held to imply a corresponding obligation, and that would be absurd if it meant only that the leader could get his followers to obey him as a matter of fact. But there is no normative system from which the obligation derives, and which could be said to justify it, unless 'charisma' has become institutionalized as in the case of the tradition of the Messiah. The appeal to the leader's Divine Right or historic mission is not a reason in a strict sense, for no proofs can be adduced that he possesses it, other than that he is the person he is. It is as if to say 'Look at him, then tell me, if you can, that you still doubt your duty!' In extreme cases, such as that of Hitler, this is put forward as an absolute and unconditional prescription. To fail to recognize the quality of such a man is not just to be a poor judge of character; it is a dire dereliction of duty.

ii. *'The Historic Mission.'* The appeal to 'the historic mission' adds nothing of substance to the case, though it may make it more persuasive. It treats history not simply as a succession of past events, but as an inevitable evolution towards an appointed goal, as the working out of an 'Idea', or of 'forces', which if fully grasped, whether by intuition or scientific methods, would enable us to know the future. The process is to be seen as a whole, with its own 'historic laws'. And it is the leader's insight into these laws that justifies his authority.

If the insight is intuitive, as with certain Fascists doctrines, nothing is added to the initial demand for faith. For if the leader possesses an intuition denied to lesser men, no reasons can be given for his authority that lesser men could understand. His assurances that the future will be thus and thus must be taken on trust.*

In the Communist version of the doctrine, however, the insight is said to be scientific. The historical drama is played out by conflicting classes of which one, the proletariat, is the revolutionary agent that will bring about the inevitable classless society. Leadership belongs as of right to the Communist Party as 'the most active and politically conscious', 'the vanguard of the working people in the struggle to strengthen and develop the socialist system'.[7] Its role is that of the most dynamic force in history, conscious of its mission and assured of ultimate victory. All this can be proved, it is said, by its science of history—dialectical materialism.

---

* This was also Plato's problem, in *The Republic*. Since the guardians' authority would be justified by their special insight into an esoteric philosophic truth, how could lesser men know the genuine authority from the spurious? Plato advocates indoctrinating the people with myths, which, in Rousseau's phrase, will be 'capable of constraining without violence and persuading without convincing'.

In this doctrine everything depends on the claim that by studying history scientifically, we can discover laws of development which will illuminate an inevitable future. Professor Popper has shown that this rests on a mistaken view of scientific method.[8] We can refer here to only a few of his criticisms. The procedure of science is to compare and generalize from particular situations. These generalizations are scientific laws. Historicist accounts go astray, according to Popper, just because they seek laws describing the development of history *as a whole*. For as a whole, history is unique; there could be only one particular, then, from which to generalize—which is absurd. We can isolate particular situations, and, by ignoring their peculiarities and concentrating on their similarities, we can discover sociological or economic laws. But these laws state only functional relationships between variables and must always state the limiting conditions within which alone they would be true. Unlike prophecies, therefore, which are unconditional forecasts of particular events, predictions based on such laws could always be upset if factors emerged which were not covered by the limiting conditions. Similarly, it is perfectly possible to see a trend in history, over a given period, and to make a prediction assuming the trend to continue. But trends themselves require explanation in terms of economic and sociological laws and whether they continue depends on other conditions remaining unchanged. We have shown in Chapter 9 how a psychological prediction could be upset by a person's becoming conscious of the causes on which it was based. Similarly, economists might predict famine in fifty years' time, given present trends in population and food production. But this would be a warning, not a prophecy It might be invalidated by some unexpected event, like an epidemic which resulted in widespread sterility, or deliberately defeated by encouraging birth control or food production.

If, then, there are no historical laws, but only sociological or economic ones, there can be no *scientific* insight into social forces moulding an inevitable future.* To the extent, therefore, that Communist or other claims to authority are based on the historic mission of a leader, class, or party, they receive no support from science. They are of the same religious or metaphysical order as claims to Divine Right.

---

* Of course, some of Marx's predictions were successful. It might be possible to explain those that were not (e.g. the progressive impoverishment of the proletariat) by showing (as Lenin did) that conditions assumed constant had in fact varied. But that is to admit that Marx did not study 'history as a whole', but adopted empirical sociological methods, without realizing perhaps exactly what he was doing. Marx's weakness lay not in the method he used, but in his own account of it.

(c) The claims of leadership

It would be a mistake, however, to underestimate the persuasive force of such theories as incentives to action. For morale feeds on the assurance of ultimate success, and success often comes to those who believe that they will succeed, simply *because* they believe it. And in a sense, every leader must believe in his star, his destiny, his mission, or simply in himself, if he is to generate in his followers the confidence that amounts to a *de facto* authority. M. de Jouvenel[9] has pointed out that to attribute divine or providential authority to leaders is a sort of recognition of the importance of leadership in any social enterprise. There is a sense in which some men are marked out by their personal qualities as leaders, and without them societies would not be formed, could not cohere, nor would any policy be initiated or pursued. We have seen* that individualists like Locke are prone to treat societies as aggregates of autonomous individuals bound by contracts which they arrange between themselves to suit their private ends. Such a view is unrealistic in part because it leaves the role of leader out of the picture. The leader creates associations by canvassing for support; he whips up enthusiasm by his own devotion to the cause; he initiates action; he keeps up the drive to carry it through. His authority as umpire saves the association from cracking up under internal tensions. He *is* a leader because he feels he is a man with a mission. If we too believe in the mission, this is the sort of man we follow; we vote for him for the good of the cause. Cause and leader merge, each lending authority to the other. Whether in any given instance we *ought* to behave like this is another matter. A man's capacity for leadership can only be grounds for an obligation to obey him if we are satisfied that we ought to go where he is going. His mission is, after all, self-imposed; we ourselves have to decide if it is worth supporting. But given a cause we believe in, or an association we value, the man with the marks of the leader upon him has a sort of claim on our allegiance accordingly.

Some political theorists, like Plato and Machiavelli, have been profoundly impressed by the role of leadership in political associations. They have been preoccupied, accordingly, with the question 'What sort of man is entitled to rule?', and have tried to lay down the personal qualifications necessary for a good leader. Anyone who possessed them would have a better title to authority than anyone else. Once such a ruler had been found, the best thing would be to give him his head. Others, like Locke and Bentham (who referred to rulers as 'plunderers'), have been far more suspicious of authority. Granted the need for leaders, they said, how can we organize political institutions so that bad or

* See Chapter 11.

incompetent rulers can be prevented from doing too much damage? Plato speculated brilliantly on the selection and training of perfect rulers; Machiavelli was mesmerized by the charisma of successful and glamorous leaders, like Cesare Borgia, Locke and Bentham were perhaps more realistic. They recognized that political institutions cannot be safely constructed on the supposition that actual rulers would be perfect. Leaders are not chosen by ideal tests of character and ability; they are designated, like hereditary monarchs, by traditional rules, or they are elected or otherwise chosen by followers as imperfect as themselves. It is important then to see that they do not abuse their authority, and to have institutional devices for getting rid of them if they do. The question of the personal qualities that rulers should have, may thus be less important for the problem of political obligation than the question of the type of rules which should authorize and limit their authority.*

III. TRADITIONALIST GROUNDS OF AUTHORITY AND OBLIGATION

For the traditionalist, an authority is legitimate if it is sanctioned by custom; no further questions need be asked. On the other hand, traditionalism is consistent with substantive limitations on authority, provided they too are traditionally prescribed. The English barons resisted King John to prevent his trespassing beyond the bounds of his customary authority, and the justification for deposing Richard II was that he had broken the fundamental laws of the kingdom.

A traditionalist is not therefore committed to an absolute acceptance of constituted authority, whatever it does. Given the customary rule, it is still possible to discuss how it is to apply. Burke could defend the Revolution of 1688 as necessary to preserve the traditional constitution of England from subversion by James II. To force a king to flee, to declare that he has abdicated, and then to invite a foreign prince to succeed him—this may not be according to the letter of customary obligation (and certainly not of legal obligation), but in unusual circumstances it may yet be consistent with the spirit of the tradition. Traditionalism understood thus broadly offers no unequivocal prescriptions for particular situations. It is certainly not a die-hard attitude, as Burke's Speech on Economical Reform eloquently testifies. It leaves considerable latitude for differences of opinion, and for discussion in the light of particular circumstances. On the other hand, it places limits on discussion, for it admits only those arguments that can be expressed in

* Cf. Spinoza: *Tractatus—Politicus*, Introduction, Section 6: 'In fact it makes no difference to the stability of a state what motive leads men to conduct its affairs properly, provided they *are* conducted properly.'

terms of customary and established standards. Thus Burke was willing to defend the traditional rights and liberties of Englishmen, and even of the American colonists, in revolt against English authority. What was inadmissible was a revolution like the French, avowedly in defence of 'the rights of man'. For that appealed to universal standards, divorced from any national tradition, conceived *a priori* and in the name of Reason, and without authority of prescription. Such an appeal could only be rash and impertinent nonsense.

The supremacy of tradition over reason in politics was asserted uncompromisingly by de Maistre:

> 'There is a sense in which reason is useless: we need knowledge of matter to preserve society; we have made advances in the science of number and in the so-called natural sciences; but when we leave the circle of our needs, our understanding becomes useless or uncertain. The human reason, ever in labour, puts forth systems which succeed one another without cessation: we see them born, shine forth, fade, and fall like leaves from the trees ... And amid this uncertainty in morals and politics, what can we know, what can we do? We *know* the morality we have received from our fathers as a collection of dogmas or useful prejudices adopted by the national reason. But for this we owe nothing to the particular reason of any individual. On the contrary, whenever such reason intervenes, it perverts morality.
> 'In politics we *know* we must respect authority, established we know not how nor by whom. When time brings abuse capable of altering the principles of government, we *know* we must suppress the abuse without touching the principles.'[10]

The function of reason, or philosophy, in politics is to strengthen the 'dogmes nationaux', in the role or ally or faithful servant; 'it is detestable when it appears as a rival or an enemy'.[11]

A traditionalist can give as a reason for a rule either that it is long-established or that it is authorized by some other rule that is. If he is a reformer, he reforms the detailed abuse in the spirit of a higher order rule or standard, embodied in the tradition. What as traditionalist he cannot do, is to appeal to standards universally valid, apart from the custom of any given culture.

Justifying traditionalist attitudes

A traditionalist might feel the need, however, to defend his attitude as a whole. To do this, he must go beyond appeals to custom and tradition; for justification of a whole system cannot be sought *within* the system. (We made an analogous point in Chapter 3, when we argued that one could not logically seek for a *legal* principle that would validate a whole legal system.) Burke and de Maistre justified traditionalism in part by appealing to religious principles. They saw in history a 'Divine tactic'— a providence that worked through generations for the well-being of mankind. Every nation was thus led to create for itself institutions appropriate to its genius, without fully realizing, perhaps, at any given stage, exactly what it was about. The traditional order was thus a religious order, i.e. one divinely sanctioned. That is why they condemned the rationalists of the Enlightenment and Revolution not merely for being mistaken, but as blasphemous and presumptuous.[12]

i. *Traditionalism as the highest prudence.* But traditionalism can also be defended on grounds of expediency or prudence. This case has been put most powerfully by Burke. In the first place, society is far too complex a system to be tinkered with. A people's constitution is the result 'of many minds in many ages. It is no simple, no superficial thing, nor to be estimated by superficial understandings. An ignorant man, who is not fool enough to meddle with his clock, is however sufficiently confident to think he can safely take to pieces, and put together at his pleasure, a moral machine of another guise, importance, and complexity . . . Men little think how immorally they act in rashly meddling with what they do not understand.'[13] A society is a delicate organism, developing and adapting itself to circumstances. To interfere with any major institution would start a chain of repercussions throughout the whole system, with results no man could foresee. It is more prudent, then, to accept the structure as we find it. It has been pieced together laboriously out of the conflict of competing interests. It is a balance worked out by practical men, a pragmatic compromise, not a vision dreamed up by theorists.

For that reason, there is everything to be said for not discussing it as if it could be interpreted in terms of abstract principles. Discussion must be kept within the bounds of tradition. Burke condemns the radical critics of the constitution for 'teaching the people to believe, that all ancient institutions are the result of ignorance; and that all prescriptive government is in its nature usurpation'. For the mass of men 'are not formed for finding their own way in the labyrinths of political theory, and are made to reject the clue, and to disdain the guide. Then will be felt . . . the ruin which follows the disjoining of religion from the state; the separation of morality from policy; and the giving conscience no concern and no coactive or coercive force in the most material of all the social ties, the principle of our obligation to government.'[14] Criticism which attacks the fundamentals of the tradition puts all in doubt. It would loose the bonds of society, and relase the worst passions in men, which only reverence, habit and 'useful prejudices' can keep in check. We must 'venerate, where we are not able presently to comprehend'.

But reform is not, on that account, impossible. It must seek, however, to conserve the spirit, and act piecemeal, not by radical change. It is important, too, never to insist too far on formal rights—even on prescriptive rights. For prudence counsels moderation in all things, even in the exercise of prescriptive authority. In attacking imperial policy on America, he refuses to discuss the legal aspects of the case: 'The question with me is, not whether you have a right to render your people miserable; but whether it is not your interest to make them happy. It is not, what a lawyer tells me I *may* do; but what humanity, reason, and justice tell me I ought to do.'[15] But even here he can appeal to tradition; for though Parliament may have a legal right to tax the colonies, the liberty that the colonists claimed to tax themselves was itself part of the English tradition which they had taken with them across the sea. Parliament would act with the highest prudence if it put aside its formal claims, and respected that tradition.

For Burke, prudence and prescription usually coincide, for prescription is the accumulated prudence of previous generations. That is why it is always safer not to appeal to abstract theories and principles, but to confine discussion within the limits of accepted standards. 'We are afraid to put men to live and trade each on his own private stock of reason; because we suspect that this stock in each man is small, and that the individuals would do better to avail themselves of the general bank and capital of nations and of ages.'[16]

Unhappily you cannot stop a volcano erupting just by sitting on it. When a society, like pre-revolutionary France or Russia, is already split by class antagonism and conflicting ideologies, and when many people feel there is no future for their ambitions, praising the sacred wisdom of the past will not silence their criticism. Locke had already answewred Burke, a century before:

'People are not so easily got out of their old forms as some are apt to suggest . . . it is not an easy thing to get them changed, even when all the world sees there is an opportunity for it . . . (But) when the people are made miserable, and find themselves exposed to the ill usage of arbitrary power, cry up their governors as much as you will for sons of Jupiter, let them be sacred and divine, descended or authorized from Heaven . . . the people . . . will be ready upon any occasion to ease themselves of a burden that sits heavy upon them.' 'Revolutions happen not upon every little mismanagement in public affairs.' But in the face of a long train of abuses 'it is not to be wondered that they should rouse themselves, and endeavour to put the rule into such hands which may secure to them the ends for which government was at first erected, and without which, ancient names and specious forms are so far from being better, that they are much worse than the state of Nature or pure anarchy'.[17]

But Burke was justified to this extent: a state whose consitution is permanently in question is permanently on the brink of revolution. Where the constitution is held in low esteem, power is unbridled by opinion, and government will tend to fall into the hands of the most vigorous and ruthless minority. Conversely, dictators who treat their constitutions as political manifestos, to be used or disregarded according to convenience, are likely to find that their opponents have as little respect for the rules as they have themselves. Setting an example of contempt for the rules from which their claim to authority derives, they must remain in a permanent posture of defence against sedition. The adjustments and compromises of routine politics proceed with the least friction when the parties to the business take its procedural framework for granted. Political authority would have little meaning if at every turn men asked themselves whether the authorities and the order that established them really ought to be obeyed. But true as this may be, it is irrelevant when men of normally unreflective temperament are moved by their situation to ponder the extent and grounds of their obligation to the existing order. At that stage, the routine of adjustment and compromise is already breaking down. It was Burke himself who declared, of Ireland: 'People crushed by law have no hopes but from power. If laws are their enemies, they will be enemies to laws; and those who have much to hope and nothing to lose will always be dangerous, more or less.'[18]

ii. *Historicist grounds for traditionalism.* Hegelian traditionalism is related to a more elaborate view of history than Burke's. For Hegel, the idea of morality evolves concretely in the customs and institutions of nation-states; the established order is justified as the latest stage in this historical process. The individual, as a particular manifestation of the social whole, has carried out the whole of his duty when he has done what society expects of one in his station. The only valid standards are those conventionally accepted, from which therefore criticism must necessarily begin, if indeed it can begin at all. 'We should consider,' wrote F. H. Bradley, 'whether the encouraging oneself in having opinions of one's own, in the sense of thinking differently from the world on moral subjects, be not, in any person other than a heaven-born prophet, sheer self-conceit.'[19]

A nation's institutions at a given time are thus the expression of an

ideology or spirit of the age. This pervades all its thought and organization, and is the highest, because the latest stage in a historically necessary evolution of morality and mankind towards perfection. But though
this point of view has for some been a justification for conservatism,
others have seen in it revolutionary possibilities too. For if every moral
order is only a stage on the road to perfection, it is yet imperfect, and
has within its inconsistencies and contradictions that will only be reconciled at a later stage in history. The 'heaven-born prophets', Christ,
Mohammed, Luther, or Marx, seem to confront the world with a new
revelation, re-making its morality and institutions. A radical Hegelian
might explain that such men crystallize the latent conflict in the existing
ideology, bring it to a crisis from which emerges a higher synthesis. So
far from issuing from outside the stream of historic evolution, they are
its essential instruments, giving expression to real and dynamic aspects
of the moral idea which the established order overlooks. Their un-
orthodoxy is as much a part of their society and their age as the orthodox
establishment.

Leaving aside the difficulties of Hegelian metaphysics, and the question of whether history can properly be treated as the evolution of an
Idea, it is clear that the argument remains inconclusive with respect to
political obligation. Even given that the established order is the highest
stage of the development of the moral idea so far, we might yet claim
freedom to criticize it in the interest of the stage to come. In a sense,
the critical criteria we employ would be a product of our environment
and tradition, but it makes nonsense of 'traditionalism' to say that we
are therefore all traditionalists.

iii. *The traditionalism of Professor Oakeshott—Politics as the 'Pursuit of
Intimations'.*[20] The point of the last sentence will emerge more clearly
from a consideration of Professor Oakeshott's approach to politics, the
effect of which is to deny that political action can ever be anything else
than traditionalist, whatever it might pretend to be. Politics, he says, is
'the activity of attending to the general arrangements of a set of people
whom chance or choice has brought together'. As an activity, it is more
like a skill, something we learn by practice, rather than a body of knowledge to be learnt or taught by theoretical maxims or systems. The sort
of politics we learn is the sort practised in our own society—for that
is the sort we practise almost from babyhood. We can comprehend
other people's politics only within the framework of our own. Political
reflection cannot exist, then, in advance of political activity, and a
political ideology must be understood 'not as an independently premeditated beginning for political activity, but as knowledge (in an abstract
and generalized form)'—elsewhere styled 'an abridgement'—'of a

traditional manner of attending to the arrangements of a society'. '*What* we do, and moreover what we want to do, is the creature of *how* we are accustomed to conduct our affairs.' The principles expressed in, say, Locke's *Second Treatise* were thus a brilliant abridgement of the British traditional way of practising politics. The error of the French revolutionaries was to accept them as a 'preface to political activity', as a statement of 'abstract principles to be put into practice', rather than as a 'postscript (whose) power to guide derived from its roots in actual political experience'. The meaning of the abridgement, in short, lay in the concrete details it summarized; its 'freedom', for instance, was a system of procedures of a certain kind, like Habeas Corpus, not a premeditated ideal independent of experience: 'it was what was already intimated in that experience'.

Politics is thus 'the pursuit of intimations'. It consists in 'guessing from a few moves of a game the strategy being followed and the moves to come'. For example: 'The only relevant reason to be advanced for the technical "enfranchisement" of women was that in all or most other important respects they had already been enfranchised. Arguments (either for or against) drawn from abstract natural right, from "justice", or from some general concept of feminine personality, must be regarded as either irrelevant, or as unfortunately disguised forms of the one valid argument; namely, that there was an incoherence in the arrangements of the society which pressed convincingly for remedy.'

The ideological style of politics, seeking to deduce the direction of political activity from abstract general principles, is thus based on a confusion of thought. We cannot proceed radically from first principles, for the principles are only meaningful *a posteriori*; we can only draw on existing experience, on our political tradition. It is a mistake to draw up ambitious programmes: we shall do better to guess at the trend of change, and move with it. 'Men sail a boundless and bottomless sea . . . the enterprise is to keep afloat on an even keel . . . the seamanship consists in using the resources of a traditional manner of behaviour in order to make a friend of every hostile occasion.' (Professor Oakeshott thus rejects the Hegelian conception of a rational Idea in history. There is change and adjustment to change—there is no built-in purpose, and, *sub specie aeternitatis*, no progress.)

His case seems to amount to this:

(a) There can be no political activity, even the most revolutionary, that does not derive from an existing style of politics, from a tradition.

(b) Specific prescriptions cannot be deduced from general and abstract principles. The latter have meaning only in the context of a tradition of behaviour. Viewed in the light of another tradition, they will mean something quite different, or nothing at all.

(c) Therefore, the best style of politics is that which consciously seeks to do no more than grasp trends in the given society and go along with them. This is the 'pursuit of intimations'. Politics can never be more than that, and if we seek to make it more, by adopting programmes based on abstract principles, we suffer from illusions that may be disastrous.

(a) Now it is *necessarily* true that all political activity occurs within a tradition. We are all creatures of our age and environment, however revolutionary our aims. If we are to engage in political activity at all, we must take for granted some at least of the rules and traditions which delimit it as a specific activity. The arrangements we take for granted 'always far exceed those which are recognized to stand in need of attention'. There can be no dispute about this. But according to Oakeshott, this rules out radical attempts to 'solve problems', for these suppose that we can start afresh, and ignore how much must be taken for granted. The most we can do is to 'remedy incoherences'. This is surely a mistake. For how could one recognize 'a problem' except as a difficulty or an 'incoherence' emerging within an otherwise accepted set of arrangements? A problem is precisely a situation where an established expectation is disappointed or an accepted tradition breaks down. 'Solving problems' and 'remedying incoherences by pursuing intimations' are really different ways of describing the same thing; they differ only in the sort of procedure they recommend. For 'solving problems' suggests the rational discussion of ends and means; 'remedying incoherences by pursuing intimations' suggests acting on hunches. The terms are differently loaded, but the difference is one of prescription, not description.

Again, Oakeshott's use of 'traditional' says too little because it says too much. For if *all* political action consists in working out the intimations of a tradition, what sort of activity would not be traditional? Oakeshott makes it an analytic truth that all politics is traditionalist; that is, it is necessarily implied by the meaning he gives to his terms. But then he cannot offer it as a reason for preferring one style of politics to another. He manages to do this, however, by using terms like 'traditional' and 'the pursuit of intimations' in two different senses in the course of the same argument. In the first instance, it covers any sort of political activity, whether in the style of Disraeli or of Robespierre; for both pursued objectives necessarily conceived within a given traditional

context. Yet it would surely be paradoxical to say that the only difference between a Robespierre and a Disraeli is that one believes himself
to be acting according to principles, while the other knows that he
acts on the hunches suggested by political experience. Oakeshott
thinks the difference to be more than that, for he thinks the Robespierre
style may be disastrous. One important difference is that anyone
consciously 'pursuing intimations' might be expected to move cautiously and to reform, if at all, piecemeal. Appeals to principle, on the
other hand, are more likely to lead to bold sweeping changes. The
difference is not just between two ways of describing political activity,
but between acting in different ways. It is at this point that Oakeshott
alters the meaning of 'acting within a tradition'; for having used it
generally of all political activity, he now confines it to the cautious
style, which he wishes to commend. But if we are all traditionalists of
necessity in one sense of the word, that cannot be a reason why we
ought to be so in quite another.

The weight of Oakeshott's case rests on our necessary inability to
escape from our own experience. We cannot ever learn from others
without assimilating their experience to our own. Thus he argues that
though we may study other people's ideals, we cannot act on them, because their ideals *are* simply abstracts of the sort of arrangements they
in fact have, and in the context of our tradition they would mean something else. Again, this is a necessary truth. For to understand another
person's experience *means*, among other things, seeing it in relation to
our own. And, of course, just because we look at other people's ideals
and institutions from the outside, we are the more liable to misunder-
stand them. But this does not necessarily invalidate a rationalist approach to politics, or appeals to principles and wider experience, as
Oakeshott seems to imply. When Montesquieu looked at the British
constitution, and particularly at its separation of powers, he only partly
understood what he saw. But he was very well aware that foreign institutions could not be imported. He believed, however, that one could
draw useful analogies, or discover principles of government, from the
study of foreign institutions, and that the British analogy could help
Frenchmen to recast their own, to secure an analogous liberty. When
the Revolutionaries came to apply the principle of the separation of
powers, they carefully reversed the British practice by insulating the
executive from judicial review. Their reasons were implicit in French
and not in English experience. But they were trying to guarantee individual rights against arbitrary executive power under rules of law, to
abolish *lettres de cachet*, and to limit executive power by a representative legislature. And these lessons they learnt from England and America.

What they meant by 'Liberty' was the rights that Englishmen and Americans enjoyed and Frenchmen did not. In the long run, this is what they achieved. Adapting English ideals to French conditions was a painful business, full of mistakes and false starts. And much of course they left untouched, though hardly unaffected. Whether they would have done better to have explored the intimations of the *ancien regime* is a matter of opinion. What they did was to envisage and create a political and social order radically different from it, and modelled in important respects on other systems which in general they preferred to their own. If they acted on abstract principles, they knew fairly clearly what they meant by them in concrete terms, though they did not all mean the same things. What most of them meant was certainly not to be had without very drastic changes in their existing arrangements. To describe political action in this style as the pursuit of traditional intimations is to make 'tradition' so wide as to be meaningless.

(*b*) Oakeshott's second ground for rejecting rationalism in politics is that general principles yield no specific prescriptions. They are 'abridgements' of an existing tradition, not a source from which new prescriptions can be deduced. But this again is a necessary truth, for it is another way of saying that rules do not determine their own application—a point we made in Chapter 3. But because it is necessary, it cannot be a guide to political activity.

For Oakeshott, 'pursuing intimations' (in the narrower of his two senses) consists in meeting new situations by looking for analogies in existing arrangements. This is different, it seems, from applying principles. But how is it different? In recognizing an analogy, we implicitly accept a principle. To say that the case for giving votes to women was that in most other important respects they had already been enfranchized, might be described either as recognizing an analogy between their admitted rights (to enter the professions, to hold property, and so on), and their claim to votes; or it might be described as implementing the principle of equality between the sexes. For equality between the sexes *means* just this sort of thing. When the radical appeals to sex equality to justify women's suffrage, he appeals to just that principle which makes the analogies of equality in the professions and equality in property rights appropriate. Conversely, one might argue that the principle of sex equality could not be properly extended to votes for women, because there were relevant differences to be considered, or that the analogies were inappropriate (i.e. that this was not what the tradition intimated).

But the effect of stressing 'intimations' at the expense of principles is to discourage argument of any sort. For analogies or intimations are things apparently perceived by intuition, and intuitions are beyond discussion and justification. We must rely, it seems, on the insight of those most skilful in politics, appeals to rational principles being ruled out. For by denying that 'ideologies' can mean anything beyond what is already established, Oakeshott denies the possibility of justifying decisions by appeals to rules or principles. And this is the only way of justifying one's choice of one analogy rather than another.

Similarly, though political activity proceeds by 'remedying incoherences', Oakeshott suggests no way of recognizing an 'incoherence' when we see one. But surely we should call a distinction, like an inequality between the sexes, 'an incoherence' (or an anomaly) only if we could see no way of justifying it. We see nothing incoherent about denying women the right to work in coal mines, because we could justify the discrimination by appealing to a principle. Oakeshott's suspicion of principles inhibits moral discussion because it rejects its procedure. But in refusing to appeal to principles he does not abolish them. He only leaves them inarticulate, and immune from criticism.

(c) What reasons can Oakeshott offer, then, for commending traditionalist politics? The answer probably lies in his estimate of success in political action: 'the enterprise is to keep afloat on an even keel'. As with Hobbes, order seems to matter above everything. The aim is to adjust the tradition to a changing environment, to ease stresses as they appear, all with as little disturbance as possible. We must not try to do more because there is nothing more worth doing, and to try would imperil the tradition that alone keeps us afloat. In a reasonably contented society, much could be said for this point of view. Adjustments are smoothly made when all parties take the main framework for granted. But Oakeshott denies that we ever can or ought to do anything else. Yet we clearly can, and on occasion might feel we ought. If our political arrangements fell very far short of ideals we set for them (no matter where these ideals came from), it might be worth working for a radical change, even at the cost of rocking the boat. Oakeshott calls such ideals 'caricatures' or 'distortions' because they stress one aspect of a tradition at the expense of the rest. But this might be precisely what one would want to do. The English revolutionaries appealed to the principle of government by consent to stress the traditional authority of Parliament, and to play down the Royal Prerogative. If anyone wished to prove that they were wrong, he would have to appeal to principles to do so.

Like Burke, Oakeshott tries to confine political discussion (if he permits it at all) within the limits of an accepted tradition, in the interests of stability. The only relevant justification for a political decision would be an analogy drawn from arrangements sanctified by custom. But the radical wants to go behind custom and precedent, to ask 'What is their point?' For Bentham, for instance, it was not enough that the unreformed House of Commons was sanctified by tradition. It did not satisfy the conditions of a truly representative assembly. And the point of representation was that it ensured that all interests would be consulted, not just a few to the exclusion of the rest. He insisted on applying criteria which he believed could be rationally justified, as conducive to the greatest happiness of the greatest number. A South African radical might agree that the Bantu Education Act is in the tradition of racial segregation; but he will insist nevertheless that men ought not to be educated differently because their skins are differently coloured; racial discrimination, he will say, is irrelevant in education. He will ask 'What is the point of the tradition of segregation?'—a question which for the traditionalist is inadmissible. He may argue that a regime authorized by such a tradition and practising politics in the light of its intimations, can have no legitimate claim—because no *rational* claim—to be obeyed. He may prefer to rock the boat, rather than keep on an even keel on that particular course.

IV. POLITICAL OBLIGATION AS MORAL OBLIGATION

(a) Social contract and consent

The central point of our criticism of traditionalism is that it removes political authority and institutions from moral criticism and assessment. Yet when we question our duty to obey established authority, and canvass a possible right or duty to overthrow it by rebellion, we are not to be answered by arguments that tell us to look to traditional standards *as such*. To speak to our condition, arguments must refer to standards that we ourselves lay down, whether traditional or not. We shall want to be satisfied, perhaps, that the established order gives a fair hearing to all classes and races; or that it allows men to criticize their government; or that it is not an obstacle to general prosperity. If, using criteria of this type, we are satisfied that present arrangements are reasonably satisfactory, we shall be ready to agree that we have an obligation to support and defend them. But this is to say that the question of obligation is ultimately a moral one. The criteria of discussion are those outlined in Chapter 2; they are not confined to answering the question 'What is customary?' We shall argue that the theory of consent is, among other things, a way of claiming that political obligation should be viewed as a moral obligation. Furthermore, it expresses an intention to examine it in the light of ends that governments ought to serve, and to judge them by their performance. In general it asserts that a duty to obey is never absolute, but depends on the use a government makes of its authority. It recognizes that the ability to govern depends on the readiness of its subjects to accept a government's lead, but it serves notice that the lead may be rejected, both in fact and as of right, if it fails to satisfy its subjects. In the various forms in which the theory has commonly been presented, it raises difficulties that we shall have to examine: nevertheless it suggests elements important for any satisfactory theory of political obligation.

The theory of consent in its modern form can be traced back to the sixteenth and seventeenth centuries, where it appears in the form of social contract theories.[21] It emerged from the religious, constitutional, intellectual, and economic upheavals of the period as a general denial that arguments from custom and scripture can be conclusive proof of political obligation. Initially, in the form common in the sixteenth century, it claims that royal authority derived from a contract of government, whereby the people collectively had undertaken to obey its ruler, so long as he governed in the general interest, and kept within the limits laid down by the contract. In the seventeenth century, the contract came to be conceived differently, and could properly be called a 'social contract'. This was envisaged as an act of the separate individuals emerging from a state of nature into civil society, whereby, for their common advantage, they undertook one with another to set up a government, to which they would give active support and submission. The association thus formed would proceed, usually by majority decision, to appoint governors, whom it empowered either by a contract of government, by a deed of trust, or by an act of delegation, to govern on its behalf, usually subject to the condition that it acted in the general interest and respected natural rights. Failure in this respect might justify disobedience and even rebellion.

If this were meant as an account of the way states have in fact originated, it would not be worth considering. Voluntary associations often do originate in this fashion, and the social contract theory is largely an attempt to construct a theory of the state on this analogy. But the only political contracts in history have been inspired by the contract theory itself, like the one made by the Pilgrim Fathers. But none of this is to the point. The contract theory is not primarily history, but a metaphor designed to illustrate the type of relation which holds between governor and governed. It is *as if* political society had been created by a contract; political authority and obligation are such as they would have been if there had been a contract, even though none has in fact been made.

The question such theories seek to answer might be put in these terms: In political societies, a few men rule many. This is not just a matter of fact, to be explained; we treat it as a matter of right, to be justified. In the common run of social dealings, we allow that all men have rights of one sort or another; but we do not admit that any man, just because he is himself, has any right to our obedience. Authority stands in need of justification. 'In nature'—i.e. political rules apart (for these are the things to be justified)—no reason could be given why one man should obey another; all men are free agents. But to be free of an obligation would appear, *prima facie*, to be preferable to being bound. Therefore, political obligation must arise from a free act of submission, i.e. from the consent of the governed. But what could induce free men to assume an obligation to obey? Suppose men living without political authority: what would they lack so urgently that they might submit voluntarily to government to get it? If we could answer these questions we might understand the ends that governments serve, as well as the limits (if any) that rational and autonomous beings would place on a self-imposed duty to submit.

i. *Hobbes: unconditional consent for the sake of peace.* For Hobbes, men fear death above everything. Government alone can guarantee their safety. In submitting to authority and undertaking to support it actively, they create the necessary conditions for peace and security. They can therefore be taken to consent to government, for if one wills an end above everything, there can be no reason for not willing the necessary means. Further, if men accept authority for the sake of order, it must be strong enough to preserve them from the violence of others. If authority were granted only upon conditions, every man would reserve the right to judge when these had been ignored, and therefore when he might refuse support of the governor. The latter could not then be depended upon to muster at all times the force needed to preserve peace. But without that guarantee there would be no point in submission—a man who cannot rely upon the governor to preserve him must take all necessary measure to preserve himself, with or without his governor's sanction. Therefore, if submission is to be reasonable, it must be unconditional.

This argument is persuasive because of the palpable need for civil peace. Whatever other ends we seek through government, if we deny it authority to maintain peace we imperil every other objective. Hobbes might conceivably have rested his case here. He would then have produced a strictly utilitarian justification for authority, like that offered later by Hume[22] and Bentham. But for Hobbes this was not enough. He had answered the question 'What purpose does government serve?' but not the question 'What is the condition for government to exercise *de jure* authority?' It might be argued that if civil disorder is the ultimate evil, and if *any* effective government is both a necessary and sufficient security against it, we have an obligation to submit, and the government a corresponding authority (i.e. a moral authority). But for Hobbes, 'authority' was not simply the correlative of such an obligation. He understood it in the narrow sense of 'an authorization': the sovereign's authority is that of an agent empowered by his principal to act on his behalf. Thus, if individuals are by nature free and equal, they must be taken to appoint their governors unconditionally as their agents. This has the merit of recognizing that political authority is nothing unless some at least of its subjects are ready to give it positive co-operation, and most of the rest, at least acquiescence.

Is the guarantee against the violence of other men a sufficient end for political authority, as Hobbes implies? Is it really beside the point what else a government does? Are we so much better off, if the price of security from our neighbours is complete surrender to the sovereign? 'What,' asked Rousseau, 'do (the despot's subjects) gain if the wars his ambition brings down upon them, his insatiable avidity... press harder on them than their own dissensions would have done?... Tranquillity is found also in dungeons; but is that enough to make them desirable places to live in?'[23] Perhaps, after all, there are better terms to be had. Hobbes denies this because for him common submission is the only (or the fundamental) social bond; if it were weakened, all else would be in jeopardy. But for Locke, men would be mainly social even without government, and to challenge it for exceeding its authority is not necessarily to dissolve society. The case for unconditional submission would then be much weaker; it might be worth the risk of civil war to get rid of a tyrant.

ii. *Locke: consent to majority rule.* For Locke, the state of nature, though already a social condition, governed by a moral or natural law, would nevertheless be precarious. Some men would break the law, and every man would be judge and executioner in his own cause. Men need an impartial authority to lay down and enforce minimum standards, and to give the rights of nature institutional guarantees. This is the principal purpose of political organization.

But again, one may ask, as the two Hebrews asked of Moses, 'Who made thee a prince and a judge over us?' For Locke, the only ultimately satisfactory answer would be: 'You did it yourselves.' No man 'can be subjected to the political power of another, without his own consent'.[24] But this cannot be taken too literally; government cannot wait for unanimity. We rightly suspect elections in which governments get 100 per cent majorities. Locke considers unanimity necessary only at the formation of society; thereafter, all contracting parties would be bound

L

by the majority principle. Though no man might be deprived of his property without his consent, for instance by a tax, he might be held to have consented to taxation if it had the consent of a majority of representatives in a legislative assembly, elected by majorities in their constituencies. Pufendorf, the seventeenth century natural lawyer, saw the majority principle as an implicit term in the social contract; for Locke, it was a law of nature, for unless corporate bodies could make collective decisions in this way, the purpose of their association would be defeated from the start (This was not obvious to Burke, who called the majority principle 'one of the most violent fictions of positive law').[25]

The consent needed to legitimize authority was therefore the consent of every individual to the constitution, majority consent to the particular government, and consent by a majority of elected representatives to legislation or taxation closely touching 'natural rights'. Individual consent is superfluous beyond the first stage. A government that misgoverns may be dismissed if the people decides that it has exceeded its authority.

Consent theory presents two major difficulties. On the one hand, if consent is a *necessary* condition for political obligation, it would deny a government any rightful authority over anyone who dissented from the basic principles of the constitution. Force used against Communists in a liberal democracy, or against liberals in a 'people's democracy', would alike be naked aggression, for the law authorizing it would not be *their* law. In this form, no one who chose to contract out could be legitimately coerced.

And is it reasonable to assume that all members of a state subscribe to its constitution? In the 1946 referendum, eight million Frenchmen voted against the constitution of the Fourth Republic, and a further eight million did not vote at all. In what sense then, did they consent to it? Some may have rejected even the majority principle. Locke argued rather lamely that to reside in a state's territory and enjoy a patrimony under its laws must be taken as consent to its form of government. But as Hume pointed out, this would be reasonable only if a man had the means to leave—and nowadays a visa too. In any case, a man might wish to belong to a society, but not on the terms laid down. This would be the Communist or Fascist position in a liberal democracy.

Locke presumed that a free agent who would never submit unconditionally to an absolute monarch would nevertheless submit absolutely to majorities. But if the objection in the one case is that he would thereby put himself defenceless in the power of another, does this not apply equally in the other case? He may at least have some idea of the sort of person the monarch is, and may be ready to trust him accordingly; but a majority is an unstable aggregate, whose members, motives, and interests will vary from day to day, and whose concern for the interests of any given individual may be no greater than the autocrat's. As Mill pointed out, self-government is government by everyone else. Is it reasonable to demand that everyone should consider himself unconditionally bound to accept without demur whatever conditions a majority of his fellow citizens put upon him? May a minority never resist a majority?

Suppose on the other hand that consent is taken as a *sufficient* condition for obligation. This would amount to saying that having agreed to the constitution, I am bound by a promise to accept its consequences thereafter. But this may commit me to results I never envisaged nor intended, and which may seem to me so thoroughly immoral that I could not possibly have a duty to submit to them. Is a democrat committed to his constitution, if it becomes the vehicle for anti-democratic revolution? But this is not the main difficulty. We may consent to a government because it suits our interest to do so, even though we know very well that its deliberate intention is to oppress minorities. Though it has majority support, it could still be said that it ought not to have it. Is it then our duty to obey, because we have made a promise; or, is that duty morally void because the promise ought never to have been made, and our duty, instead, to undo the wrong by upsetting the established arrangements at the first opportunity. (Consider in this connection the moral dilemma of the German officers who were bound by an oath to obey Hitler.) This pushes the problem of obligation a step further back. Should we not ask: 'To what political arrangements *ought* we to consent?' If it could be established that a given set of arrangements *deserved* our consent, would this not make the fact of consent irrelevant to obligation?

iii. *Rousseau: consent and the General Will*. Rousseau's General Will was an ingenious attempt to meet these difficulties. 'Men,' he says, 'are born free and are everywhere in chains . . . What can make that legitimate?'[26] Again, the problem is to justify the subjection of otherwise autonomous agents to political authority. Again, any valid obligation must be self-imposed.

Rousseau accepted, as an initial postulate, the common assumption of his day (and one that Hobbes had made before him) that men are egoists by nature. 'It is not incumbent on any will to consent to anything that is not for the good of the being who wills.'[27] Consequently, 'all, being born free and equal, alienate their liberty only for their own advantage'.[28] To what sort of authority could such a being submit? Only to one that could never will anything contrary to his interest. 'The problem is to find a form of association which will defend and protect with the whole common force the persons and goods of each associate, and in which each, while uniting himself with all, may still obey himself alone, and remain as free as before.'[29]

The first problem is to turn self-interest into moral obligation. This is accomplished by the General Will, the collective will of the corporate moral person created by the act of association. As members of this person, men have an interest in one another and in the whole, which transcends the limited personal interest that was all that had been possible before. 'The passage from the state of nature to the civil state produces a very remarkable change in man, by substituting justice for instinct in his conduct, and giving his actions the morality they had formerly lacked. Then only, when the voice of duty takes the place of physical impulses and right of appetite, does man, who so far had considered only himself, find that he is forced to act on different principles, and to consult his reason before listening to his inclinations.' Entering the society, he is no longer the slave of 'the mere impulse of appetite'; in 'obedience to a law which we prescribe to ourselves is liberty'.[30]

This law is the General Will, directed to the Common Good. As a member of the community, I must recognize the General Will as my will. If government is in accordance with the General Will, in submitting I 'obey myself alone, and remain as free as before'. I am wholly subject, yet consent to every law that binds me. I may try to indulge the mere impulse of appetite, but that is a lower non-moral will which enslaves my higher rational self.

We have referred, in Chapter 11, to some of the difficulties of General Will theory. It led Rousseau to the paradoxical conclusion that to coerce a man to conform to the General Will is to force him to comply with his own 'real' will, i.e. 'to force him to be free'. And this, whether or not he recognizes the General Will as his own. But though misleading, it makes a kind of sense in certain conditions. If in fact I see in the law the standard I ought to observe, but still wish to turn my back on it and act immorally, the restraint that prevents me makes me act as if I choose to do what is right. Yet I do so for the wrong reason, out of fear, and that is why it is misleading to say that I am free. In a sense, if I recognize the rightness of the law, I might be said to commit myself to approving my own punishment if I break it; but this sort of commitment is hardly what we usually mean by consent. But suppose I do not see the law in this light, and instead object to it on conscientious grounds? Then I could in no sense be said to impose upon myself either the law or the punishment for breaking it.

Rousseau would not allow this objection, if the law could be said to express the General Will. For then it must be directed to the Common

Good; and if I am conscientious, I too must will the Common Good. Therefore I must will the General Will, and *ex hypothesi* the law which binds me. In a purely formal sense this is true. If by the Common Good we understand 'the best for everyone concerned'; and if the General Will is what anyone would will who willed the best for everyone concerned; then in conscience I cannot reject it. Everything now turns on whether the law is the best for everyone concerned, and there can be *bona fide* differences of opinion about this. But this is what Rousseau was reluctant to admit. He envisaged a common assembly seeking to express the General Will by a vote which decides what is the best for everyone. This decision binds not only those for it but also those against it—not as a matter of convention but of necessity. For what is decided is *in fact* best; consequently the minority must rejoice at having been prevented from making a mistake which would have deprived them of what they really desired.

For Rousseau, men of good will are likely to come to the same conclusions on policy. If they do not, voting techniques establish the right answer. But this is a confusion. A vote will establish only what a majority of voters want—at best, what a majority feel to be right. It remains open to anyone to maintain a different opinion, though he too seeks the Common Good. For, as we have pointed out, 'the Common Good' is not uniquely descriptive, like 'full employment', and there can be genuine differences of opinion about what ought to be done, even among men of good will. And it is conceivable that a minority will be so outraged by a majority decision that they cannot in conscience accept it. This is the position of the conscientious pacifist in war.

Rousseau tried, but failed, to meet the difficulties of consent theory, by making universal consent follow necessarily upon any decision taken in good faith by a majority. A dissenter may be coerced into obedience because he is not really a dissenter after all. 'Consent' is thus deprived of its usual implication of free choice, and can be obligatory. Since the will to which consent is thus obligatory is by definition what it ought to be, it is both a necessary and a sufficient condition for political authority. No government would be legitimate that did not express it; any government that expressed it would be legitimate because it was doing what it ought to be doing. And there could be no genuine difference of opinion about this. But we have rejected this last proposition, and insist that there could still be moral grounds for disobedience or resistance. If the General Will be taken as a criterion of obligation, its content cannot then be settled by vote, even allowing the voters the best intentions.

The Hegelians tried to evade this criticism by re-defining the General Will as the structure of conventional rules and institutions in a given society. The General Will is thus the concrete expression of the Moral Idea, and is thus the standard by which individuals must judge. Moreover, an individual is not to be isolated from the society—the General Will is also his higher will, or Real Will. (We have quoted a passage from Bradley deprecating moral eccentricity.)* Green would countenance disobedience only if the community seemed to be acting inconsistently with its own conventional standards; any moral justification for disobedience would necessarily refer, therefore, to a socially accepted standard, not simply to one the objector sets up as his own.[31] Sir Ernest Barker[32] admits a right to resist, but only as a form of public demonstration, to draw attention to what Professor Oakeshott might call an 'incoherence' in the convention. The militant suffragettes might be justified on this basis, but not a revolutionary.

These are attempts to tame the theory of consent. They interpret it, with Rousseau, as moral agreement, and then demonstrate that moral disagreement is impossible at any fundamental level between an individual and his society. But if we admit that a political obligation is ultimately a moral obligation, each individual can ask for reasons; the question cannot be settled *for him* by reference to conventional standards as such. The communist in a capitalist society, or the liberal in a Fascist one, cannot be convinced (and *ought* not be convinced) by arguments that appeal to principles commonly held, unless he holds them too.

(b) Consent as a formal criterion for political obligation

We have suggested that at the heart of consent theory is the conviction that a political obligation must be a kind of moral obligation. We must now look more closely at what that implies. Does it necessarily involve the kind of difficulties we met with in Locke and Rousseau?

At first glance, it may seem odd to call a duty to accept authority a *moral* duty. We have insisted throughout this book that appeals to authority have no part in either morals or science. We justify moral judgments and establish moral duties by appealing to principles or rules for which there are good reasons, not by showing that someone in authority has laid them down. For that reason, in morals every man must be his own legislator and rely in the end on his own judgment. But a duty to accept authority is necessarily a duty to act on someone else's judgment, and it may commit us to courses which, left to ourselves, we should have condemned. A duty to obey can be a moral duty, then, only if it can be shown to serve a greater good or avert a greater wrong.

* See page 311.

It is therefore a conditional, not an absolute duty, and must depend on the use to which authority is put. And this implies that though we may have an obligation to *act* on someone else's judgment, we have no duty to *suspend* judgment. We are committed not to thinking what we are told, but only to doing what we are told. There is no duty to refrain from criticism, though in exceptional circumstances there might be a duty to refrain from voicing it in public.

Fundamentally, then, the theory of consent 'moralizes' political authority and obligation. When Locke said that men were free by nature, he surely meant, at the very least, that no one can deprive another of the right to form his own judgments. And this is part of what we mean when we say that a man is a moral person. In that capacity, no man can put his conscience in the permanent keeping of any authority, whether party leader, lawyer, or priest. Every man, therefore, must decide for himself whether he has a duty to accept a given authority; for no one else can decide that for him. Similarly, he can accept authority only with reservations. For he yields his freedom to act on his own moral estimate of situations, or as Locke put it, to do 'whatsoever he thought fit for the preservation of himself and the rest of mankind', only 'so far forth as the preservation of himself and that society shall require'. 'But though men when they enter into society give up the equality, liberty, and executive power they had in the state of Nature into the hands of the society, to be so far disposed of by the legislative as the good of the society shall require, yet . . . the power of the society or legislative constituted by them can never be supposed to extend farther than the common good, but is obliged to secure every one's property by providing against those . . . defects . . . that made the state of Nature so unsafe and uneasy.' If the authorities fail in this, the people 'have reserved the ultimate determination to themselves which belongs to all mankind, where there lies no appeal on earth, by a law antecedent and paramount to all positive laws of men, whether they have just cause to make their appeal to Heaven'.* In short, all men must reserve the right as moral persons to decide for themselves, when all else fails, whether their duty is to accept or challenge authority.

For Locke, as for Rousseau, the obligation to submit arises when (and only when) the authority serves the common good. But when does it? We have shown that Rousseau mistook the common good for a

---

* It is not at all clear whether Locke held that 'the people' as a whole or the individual were to be the final judges of whether authority was being rightfully used. It could be argued that his evasiveness on this point was due to his fear of the anarchic conclusions that might be drawn from his stress on the individual's obligations under natural law.

descriptive concept, instead of treating it as the most general of all moral criteria. 'Serving the common good' means, we have said, deciding impartially between all claims,* and trying to satisfy those for which the best case can be made out. The common good is not therefore a goal, but a procedure for making moral judgments. It is important, however, in the theory of consent, just because it implies that whatever goals a government sets itself, it must give due consideration to the claims of everyone. An obligation to obey an authority must ultimately be justified, then, by reference to its consequences for all interests and persons, not just for an élite, and not by appeals to prescriptive or customary rights.

Consent theory admits the legitimacy of authority, then, only when it satisfies certain moral criteria. That accounts for its historic association with natural law doctrine and intuitionist or rationalist ethics; for, like these, it insists on subjecting authority to rational criticism. It accounts too for Kant's attachment to consent theory, as an implication of the individual's moral autonomy. And it explains the association of consent theory with Protestant theology, for as one appeals to the individual conscience or 'inner light', so the other appeals to the individual reason, and both deny that an earthly authority can ever be final.

Consent theory does not insist, of course, that a man must stand on his own judgment in everything. That would be an anarchistic denial of all authority and of all political obligation. But it maintains that there must be good reasons for handing over to someone else one's right to decide. The way we accept scientific authority will serve to illustrate this. In one sense, we all have a right to our own opinions on nuclear physics; but if we are wise, we shall defer to someone who knows something about it. But before accepting anyone as an authority of that sort, we apply certain tests: his standing among scientists generally, the degrees he holds, and the journals that have accepted his published work. We apply these particular tests, rather than others which depend, say, on his religion or social, class because we can see their relevance to our purpose. Governmental authority is not mainly a matter of superior knowledge (though Plato thought it ought to be); but in this case no less than in the other, there must be good reasons for accepting it against our own judgment. And again, those reasons must be such as we can understand. Plato's dilemma was that, having assigned absolute authority to the philosopher-guardians on the strength of their esoteric knowledge of 'the good', he could give no reason for accepting that authority which any lesser mortal would appreciate. And so he fell back on myths.

* See pp. 271–3.

Of course, there are plenty of good reasons for accepting authority in general (though they may not always apply in particular). We are often in situations where it is more important to accept an umpire's judgment than to insist on our own. When little boys play cricket without an umpire, they spend more time arguing than playing cricket. Cricket is a better game if everyone agrees to accept an umpire's decision, instead of insisting on his own judgment (however impartial) every time the ball hits the batsman's pads. Again, there are plenty of good reasons for accepting leadership. An army will usually do better even with bad generals, than with no generals at all. We accept authority because most social enterprises would be hopeless without it. Nevertheless, it is the enterprise that counts; the authority is conditional on the way it promotes or preserves it.

But to say that a moral obligation to accept authority must always be conditional is not to say that a government can never exercise a rightful authority over anyone who rejects it. That, we argued, was a weakness of the contract theory, which neither Locke nor Rousseau satisfactorily remedied. But the point is not that a man must have consented before a government can properly consider him under an obligation to obey, but that he must see the point of the obligation before he can consider himself bound. The theory suggests formal criteria for legitimate authority; but people may differ on whether any particular government satisfies them. But anyone who considers that it does must treat it as legitimate for everyone else, even for those who reject it. For such a person, the objectors are simply wrong, and this is a bad reason for saying they have no obligation. Though everyone is his own moral legislator, he legislates at the same time for everyone else. Understood in these terms, there is nothing anarchical about the theory of consent.

There are good grounds, we said, for accepting authority in general. but there may be good grounds too for rejecting it in particular cases; If authority derives from a constitution, there would generally be good grounds for rejecting any exercise of it which was unconstitutional. Again, if its legitimacy depends on the way it is used, an invasion of a sphere where political authority is inappropriate might be grounds for disobedience or, in extreme cases, for resistance. We suggested in Chapter 10 that an attempt to impose religious uniformity might be such a case. Or again, a moral obligation to obey would not extend, in any ordinary case, to a positively immoral law. Germans who harboured Jews contrary to law were surely not failing in their moral duty.

The view one takes of what is a good reason for authority will tend to affect the political arrangements one recommends, and the limits one puts on authority. For Hobbes, order was a necessary and a sufficient reason; accordingly, he preferred absolute monarchy, and repudiated any system of checks and balances. The only thing beyond the sovereign's competence was to order a man to kill himself, or to submit tamely to being killed. But for Locke, order was an incomplete end; everything depended on the type of order maintained. Authority was justified only if it protected natural rights, and especially personal freedom and property. So he recommended curbing authorities by counter-authorities, and making them derive from a property-own-ing electorate. The American Constitution is a living witness to the theory of consent in this form. Rousseau, on the other hand, felt that order, personal freedom and property were no more important than the dignity of the individual as a source of claims, and the fostering of civic solidarity or fraternity. Nothing would serve, then, short of every citizen participating in a sovereign assembly. And only this will ensure that the sovereign 'neither has nor can have any interest contrary to theirs', and that it cannot hurt any in particular. But for that reason, it 'need give no guarantee to its subjects'. Its sovereignty is absolute, for it is itself the measure of moral obligation. But in this Rousseau seemed to con-fuse the necessary moral criteria for authority with the institutional arrangements designed to implement them. Though, in a very vague sense, the General Will to the common good is the highest authority, *no* institutional arrangements could ever guarantee that this will would always be expressed. Rousseau recognized the point in distinguishing the General Will from the Will of All. Even a state modelled on his *Social Contract* could be corrupt. But the basic confusion was that he supposed that there could ever be an absolute moral authority. That is a contradic-tion in terms.

The confusion of analytic truths and prescriptions for institutions is common enough in theories of consent. (We found a similar confusion in Oakeshott's traditionalism.) On the one hand, they explore the *formal criteria* necessarily implied in treating political obligation as a moral obligation; on the other, they recommend *criteria of substance* which any constitution ought to satisfy. Bentham's account of the distinction between 'free' and 'despotic' government is a fair summary of the sub-stantive criteria usually involved in theories of consent:

'The distinction turns . . . on the *manner* in which that whole mass of power, which, taken together, is supreme, is, in a free state, *distributed* among the several ranks of persons that are sharers in it: on the *source* from whence their titles to it are successively derived: on the frequent and easy *changes* of condition between governors and governed; whereby the interests of the one class are more or less indistinguishably blended with those of the other: on the *responsibility* of the governors; or the right which a subject has of having the reasons publicly assigned and canvassed of every act of power that is exerted over him: on the *liberty of the press;* or the security with which every man, be he of the one class or the other, may make known his complaints and remonstrances to the whole community: on the *liberty* of public association; or the security with which malcontents may communicate their sentiments, concert their plans, and practice every mode of opposition short of actual revolt, before the executive power can be legally justified in disturbing them.'[33]

When government conforms to this pattern, it can be properly said, though in a loose sense, to be 'government by consent'—'not because individuals ever personally agreed to accept it, but because it is sensitive to public opinion . . . and does not have to stifle opposition by force'.[34] But these institutional criteria are not deducible, in a strict sense, from the criteria for political authority and obligation enunciated by the formal theory of consent. The latter are completely general, and cannot strictly entail anything for any particular situation. We shall argue, however, in the next chapter, that any institutions which satisfy these criteria of substance are more likely than other types to satisfy the formal criteria also.

We referred early in this chapter to Margaret MacDonald's view that necessary and sufficient grounds for political obligation were not to be found. Because consent, in the institutional sense, may be very important, that is not to say that it is 'the sole criterion of political obedience, still less that having derived all political obligations from [it] . . . we can accept them all happily and go to sleep. As rational and responsible citizens we can never hope to know once and for all what our political duties are. And so we can never go to sleep.'[35] This is inescapable; but it is necessarily implied by the notion that political obligation is a kind of moral obligation; and that, we said, is implicit in the theory of consent itself. For then we can never suspend judgment; we can never put our conscience in the keeping of other men, even of a majority of them. And we can therefore never go to sleep.

CHAPTER 15

DEMOCRACY

I. THE MEANING OF 'DEMOCRACY'

(a) Prescriptive force and descriptive criteria

In 1949, UNESCO sponsored an inquiry into the conflict of ideals associated with the concept 'democracy'. A questionnaire was sent to scholars for many countries, and two points emerged clearly from their answers:

i. 'There were no replies averse to democracy. Probably for the first time in history, "democracy" is claimed as the proper ideal description of all systems of political and social organization advocated by influential proponents.'
ii. 'The idea of democracy was considered ambiguous and even those who thought that it was clear or capable of clarity were obliged to admit a certain ambiguity either in the institutions or devices employed to effect the idea or in the cultural or historical circumstances by which word, idea, and practice are conditioned.'[1]

We have observed, in dealing with 'liberty' and 'equality', that though a word may be descriptively ambiguous, it may still have the same prescriptive force in the different contexts in which it is used. The unanimity recorded in (i) indicates that 'democracy' is now a term of approval in practically every context; to call an idea, an institution, or a decision 'democratic' is implicitly to commend it. A hundred years ago, the word 'democracy' could still be used pejoratively; but its prestige was fairly generally established by the end of the First World War. The Fascists and Nazis of the 1930s did, indeed, attempt to reverse the tendency, and used 'democracy' as a term of abuse; but the victory of the self-styled 'democracies' in the Second World War seems to have made it a propaganda asset which no party can afford to surrender to its opponents.

General agreement on the prescriptive force of the word has to be paid for, however, by ambiguity or vagueness in its descriptive meaning. For surely a Communist commending the Soviet Union as a 'democracy' cannot mean quite the same thing as the liberal similarly commending the United States. (It is just possible, of course, that both employ the same descriptive criteria for the use of the word, but that one or other is mistaken in thinking that his own candidate satisfies them; or one may be deliberately trying to deceive by an outright lie.) John Plamenatz suggests that both would agree that 'democratic government' means 'government by persons freely chosen by and responsible to the governed'; but he admits that there might be difference of opinion about what constitutes 'free choice' and 'responsibility'.[2] But if definitions can be constructed that would be acceptable to everyone, that is only because the definitions can be interpreted in as many different ways as 'democracy' itself. We know what is meant by 'a government freely chosen by the governed' only when we know what particular set of institutional arrangements the speaker has in mind when he uses that phrase.

There is the further difficulty that 'democracy' is often used nowadays in an extended sense, to cover other things besides forms of government. Thus we come across phrases like 'economic democracy' and 'social democracy', which have only this in common with the political use of the word, that they suggest some sort of egalitarianism. Bryce remarked that, in America and Australia, to describe a person as 'democratic' meant that he was 'a person of simple and friendly spirit and genial manners, "a good mixer", and who, whatever his wealth or status, makes no assumption of superiority'. When a word is so far extended, it is well on the way to becoming meaningless, except as an expression of approval or disapproval. In this chapter, we shall confine ourselves to 'democracy' in its primary sense, as a political system, though we admit that there are analogous forms of organization (in industry, for instance) which might be termed 'democratic' in some extended sense.

Though 'democracy' means different things according to the political ideals favoured by the speaker, it may be possible, nevertheless, to pin down what it means in a certain type of context. We shall try to do this for 'democracy' as generally understood in political discussion in Britain among people who do not favour Communism. In this sort of context, it would be generally agreed that Britain, the United States, the Scandinavian countries, the countries of the British Commonwealth (or at least the older ones), are all governed 'democratically', whatever their specific differences; and that the Soviet Union, China, Spain and Egypt are not democracies. There may be borderline cases (among the Southern American republics, perhaps), but there always are such cases, in all classifications. The problem is to discover what characteristics can be found common to all or most of the states agreed to be 'democracies', which would warrant calling another state 'a democracy' if it too possessed all or most of them.

(b) Democracy as 'the sovereignty of the people'

Some people try to give a descriptive content to 'democracy' by saying that in every democracy the people is sovereign, and that this is what 'democracy' means. Art. 3 of the French Constitution of 1946 declared in terms which were impeccably democratic:

> 'National sovereignty belongs to the French people. No section of the people nor any individual may assume its exercise.'

This is an echo of the Declaration of the Rights of Man:

> 'The principle of all sovereignty rests essentially in the nation. No body and no individual may exercise authority unless it emanates expressly from the nation.'

It was natural, perhaps, for the men of 1789, who were accustomed to thinking of an absolute monarch as a sovereign authority, to interpret their revolution as the transfer of sovereignty from the king to the whole people.

The phrase 'popular sovereignty' will not take us far, however, towards an understanding of democracy. It is at least as vague as Plamenatz's 'government by persons freely chosen by and responsible to the governed'. This is evident from the ease with which it can be borrowed by any government which claims to have majority support. The Communist countries certainly claim that their peoples are sovereign. Yet in the sense in which we understand 'democracy', these states are not democracies. How then are we to decide whether the people is sovereign in any given case? Can we specify the criteria for 'popular sovereignty', even as used in the sort of contexts we defined above?

The ambiguity of 'sovereignty' has been indicated already, in Chapter 12. Clearly, the people is not sovereign in the same sense in which we say 'Parliament is sovereign'. For 'Parliamentary sovereignty' means that whatever laws Parliament passes must be accepted by a court as valid law, no matter what they are about, whereas in Britain at least the people has no direct part in the legal process of law-making. Dicey distinguished accordingly between a 'legal' and a 'political sovereign', defining the latter as 'that body . . . the will of which is ultimately obeyed by the citizens of the state'.[3] One might say that, in a democracy, the electorate was the 'political sovereign' because its will was ultimately obeyed, or was the dominant influence in deciding policy. 'Popular sovereignty' would not then be a legal concept; it would say who exercised political power or *de facto* authority. And many Englishmen would accept such a description as true of British government, even though we have no constitutional provision for a referendum. But what would it mean to say in this way that the 'will of the electorate' or of 'the people' was dominant, or the will which was ultimately obeyed?

If we said that a certain *person* were dominant, that would mean that his commands were usually obeyed; so far, so good. Again, a *special interest group*, like bankers or landowners, could also be called dominant, in that whenever its interests were affected, its members would be roughly agreed on what was to be done, and in a position to see that it was done. However, we should be very much surprised to find it said of a group like motorists, even if the motoring associations were always able to get their way. For motorists *as such* have no interest in important matters like food production, housing or education. It is only if a group has a wide range of common interests on most of the important matters that governments deal with, that one could say it was the dominant influence in the state. But just because an economic interest group tends to have such a wide range of common concerns, it would be quite intelligible to talk of such a group in this way. We should know very well what was meant if we were told that the landowners were the dominant influence in eighteenth century England, because *qua* landowners, they shared a common point of view on most of the important questions.

But 'the people' is only like this if we take it to mean just poor people, as Aristotle did when he described democracy as government by the poor. Marxists can equate 'the dictatorship of the proletariat' with 'democracy' because they exclude any but the workers from 'the people'. In much the same way, the Republicans of the French Revolution could deny votes to aristocrats, without prejudice to their democratic principles. But this is not what is meant by 'the people' in the contexts we have in mind. We should say that a system was just as undemocratic if it denied people votes because they were rich, as if it denied them votes because they were poor. And if hereditary seats were abolished in the House of Lords, we should expect peers to be given the same right as anyone else to vote in elections for the House of Commons. 'The people' in this sense includes everyone, rich and poor, high and low. But in that case it is not an interest group like the landowners or the bankers, or even like the proletariat, but a mass of competing interest groups. And so it could not be said to be dominant in the same sense as an interest group might be, for it is a group of quite a different sort.

We can only say that 'the people' has a will if it is organized by some sort of voting procedure, which operates to decide only questions of certain understood types. But then, whether 'the people' (or the electorate) wills to be governed by the Labour or the Conservative Party may well depend on what methods are used for voting and counting votes and on how the constituencies are drawn. The will of the people cannot be determined independently of the particular procedure employed, for it is not a natural will, nor is it a sum of similar wills of persons sharing a common interest, but the result of going through a procedure which weighs some wills against others.

(c) Democracy as 'majority rule'

The vagueness of the concept 'popular sovereignty', and the difficulties associated with 'the will of the people', have led some writers to seek a more precise meaning for 'democracy', by stressing the fact that the 'will of the people' is said to be expressed in decisions carried by a majority of votes. Bryce defines 'democracy' as 'government in which the will of the majority of qualified citizens rules'.[4] 'The will of the peoples' is now taken to mean 'the will of the majority'. But again, we must draw attention to certain difficulties and ambiguities concealed in such a concept.

In certain conditions, a majority of citizens might constitute an interest group, with definite purposes which conflict with those of other groups. The majority might then be said to have 'a will' in the sense that all its members want much the same things: and if they are in a position to get them, they might be said to be dominant, or 'to rule'. But this is not the typical situation in this country, in the USA, or in any of the countries we usually call democracies. There is no set of important issues on all of which the British people are regularly divided between a majority interest group and one or more minorities. Any individual is likely to find himself ranged with a majority of his fellow-citizens on some, and with a minority on other issues. The groups are constantly shifting.

There is, however, another sense in which people talk of 'majority sovereignty'. On a given issue, or at any given election, there will be more people in favour of one course than of another. In this case each is an aggregate, not an interest. On another issue, the various interests will divide differently, and a new majority will appear, composed, in part of the same, in part of different people. To say, in this sense, that the majority has its way in any given election or referendum, means only that a given number express a preference for one course, a smaller number for another, and that by the rules of the game the former course must be adopted. Majority and minority are not necessarily competing interests, but aggregates of individuals in a certain arithmetical relation. This relation is significant as a way of arriving at decisions only because of the rule that makes it so. To say, then, that the will of the majority of citizens rules is only another way of describing election or referendum procedure. It is not something else which this procedure brings about. It is in no way analogous, therefore, to 'the king rules' or 'the landowners rule'. From statements of the latter type it might be possible to forecast what decisions would be likely on certain types of issue; such a forecast could not necessarily be made from 'the majority rules', for what is likely to be done depends on which of many competing interests can muster the largest number of votes on polling day. Until the count is made, there may be no way of telling which interest *is* the majority, and which, therefore, will 'rule'. It is only in the special case, where there is a sectional interest which is also in a permanent majority, that one could say in advance what course is likely to be adopted. One could confidently say, for instance, that a referendum in Ireland would reject a proposal to introduce divorce, because there is a large, permanent Catholic majority. But one could not say with the same confidence what the result would be of a referendum on introducing bullfighting there, because there is no single group with an interest in the matter which has a clear majority.

(d) Democracy as the rule of groups

To describe 'democracy' as majority rule either presupposes the existence of a dominant majority interest group, which may not be the case; or it is an account of a certain sort of procedure which is part of the process of democratic government, but may equally well exist in other systems, like the Soviet Union. We shall argue later that a system where the majority rules in the first of these senses is not democratic at all.

In any case, the idea that there is always a majority opinion for a government to reflect is surely mistaken. Most political issues involve conflicts of minority claims, each interest group exerting pressure to have the matter decided in its favour. Even on issues which affect the bulk of the people, it is unusual to find as many as twenty per cent of them sufficiently concerned to form any definite opinion.* This is not surprising, for unless we have a personal or professional interest in a subject, we are not likely to know or care much about it. Why should we expect the layman to form opinions on complex social and economic questions, when we take it for granted that his views on nuclear physics will probably be worthless?

Democracy does not presuppose majority opinions on every matter, nor does it require that government should reflect them even where they exist. It requires only that governors should periodically satisfy a majority of electors in order to remain in authority. But in practice,

* An American survey of attitudes to world organization, made in 1953–5, found that between 80% and 87% of those who actually expressed opinions had done nothing to spread them, not even as much as discussing them with their friends.[5]

that usually means attending to a great variety of sectional claims, in the hope that out of the mass of individuals governed, enough will be satisfied with the treatment they have received to put the government back into power. The majority principle is important in a democracy mainly as a way of ensuring sensitivity to the widest possible range of interests. It is this sensitivity which distinguishes democracies from plebiscitary dictatorships.

On election day, the voters 'pass judgment' on a government's record, and, by choosing between political parties, settle the broad lines on which government will be conducted in the next few years. But between elections, the government must mediate between interest groups, none of which, perhaps, could claim to speak for a majority, but each of which may include people on whose support the government must rely in the next election. No government, democratic or otherwise, can ignore sectional claims altogether, for it needs as much co-operation as it can get. But a democratic government has a particularly strong inducement to attend to all sectional claims, for the way it treats anyone of them may well settle whether it is to stay in power. This would not be the case without universal, or at least a very wide suffrage. An interest may be safely disregarded if it has no votes.

But this is not the only condition necessary for democracy. For an election to do what democracy requires of it, there must be alternatives besides the officially sponsored ones. In the Polish elections of 1957, for instance, though candidates were drawn from four parties, and there were more candidates than seats to be filled, no candidate could stand who was unacceptable to the government. If the right to propose candidates is restricted, some interests may be ignored by all the officially sponsored candidates. If the electoral system is to ensure wide sensitivity, any group of electors must be free to propose its own candidates if none of the others shows any interest in it. This implies freedom to associate to sponsor candidates and canvass on their behalf. Again, choice is unreal unless electors can find out all they need to know about the possible alternatives. If the channels of publicity are reserved for official parties, or for some particular group or interest, the elector is not likely to get a very accurate impression of the choices open to him. But legal rights to speak, publish, and criticize freely are not enough; the means of mass communication must not be effectively monopolized by one group, interest, or party, and the resources of all parties must not be so unequal as to deprive any of a fair hearing.

Marxist critics of 'bourgeois democracy' complain that, despite formal equality of political rights, anti-capitalist programmes reach the electorate only in the distorted versions served up by the bourgeois press.

The poorly educated masses are all too susceptible, they say, to capitalist propaganda. So far from being sensitive to a wide range of interests, liberal democracy is a formal façade obscuring domination by an economic class. Should it ever threaten to be other than that, the mask would be dropped and the brutal features of power exposed. This, they believe, is the explanation of the collapse of liberal democracies between the wars, the rise of Fascism and Nazism, the Spanish Civil War, and the ignominious fall of France and the surrender of the Third Republic to Vichy in 1940.

These criticisms may have some force in certain conditions. In some countries democratic institutions were accepted by powerful interests only with reservations; when these were challenged they abandoned democracy. It is true that if the bulk of the electorate is ignorant, if passion and prejudice can be readily exploited by organized propaganda, if anti-semitic or nationalist excitements can deflect attention from social injustice, then politicians may not need to take account of the electors' claims, and democratic institutions lose their point. It is true, too, that economic obstacles may inhibit criticism at least as effectively as legal prohibitions. It must be admitted that the outward forms of democracy in some countries in South America, for example, carry very little conviction. But it cannot be said *a priori* that formally democratic institutions must be a sham in any country. The Labour revolution in Britain was made possible just because political rights were not regularly thwarted by economic power. Though Communists profess to despise that revolution, few Marxists of the 1930s believed that economic levelling on such a scale could ever be attempted without smashing the formal framework of democracy.

Again, while the distribution of economic power is certainly one factor affecting the operation of democratic institutions, it cannot be assumed that the influence always operates in one way only. Whatever the links between a democratic party and sectional economic interests, its political leaders have their own independent interest in power, which may force reluctant compromises upon their financial backers. The extensions of the franchise in nineteenth century Britain were carried out by parties outdoing one another in the search for votes, rather than pursuing the interests of the propertied classes which financed them. Those classes have unquestionably lost many of their former advantages as a direct result of this competition.

Nevertheless, the Marxist is right so far: legal forms of election, freedoms of speech, publication, and association may not be enough in themselves to warrant calling a state a democracy. If the idea behind these forms is frustrated by economic power, government may be sensitive only to the interests that wield it, and the state would be a disguised oligarchy.

II. CAN DEMOCRACY EXIST?

The Marxist denies the possibility of the very existence of democracy, as we understand the term. For he insists on the one hand that a government must always be committed to one particular set of interests, so long as economic conflicts remain. On the other hand, the dictatorship of the proletariat ushers in a society without conflicts, and in such a society sensitivity to *competing* claims would be meaningless. The will of the working class, according to Vishinsky, is 'the will of the entire Soviet people . . . In so far as the exploiters have been liquidated as a class in Soviet society, we can rightly speak of the *unified will* of the Soviet people, of the *popular will* in the genuine, socialist sense of the word and of Soviet rule as its genuine expression.'[6] Thus the very conditions in which alone democracy makes sense, as a way of adjusting conflicting interests, are the ones which, according to the Marxist, make it necessarily a sham. The criticism is unacceptable, however, not only because in our experience governments are not necessarily tied to any single interest, but also because the idea of a society without conflicts is itself an impossible one.* For that reason, 'the unified will of the Soviet people' is only a rhetorical flourish concealing the existence of conflicting claims, which still have to be dealt with somehow.

The possibility of democracy has been questioned, however, on quite different grounds.[7] In the first place, there are those who maintain that people in general do not want the responsibility that democracy puts on them. Thus Erich Fromm[8] interpreted the retreat from democracy since about 1930 in terms of 'a fear of freedom'. In a world of uncertainties, it is said, few men are strong enough to be free; the majority yearn for discipline, for the chance to submit blindly to authority. This is not so much a criticism of democracy as a statement of certain sociological or psychological conditions under which it cannot exist. It might well be said, for instance, that this was the state of mind of many Germans in the '20s and '30s, who were all too ready to submit to Hitler's charisma in order to escape from the responsibilities of democracy. In such conditions, democratic forms degenerate into plebiscitary dictatorships. But there is no reason to suppose that such a state of mind is common to all societies. Anglo-Saxon and Scandinavian experience suggest that ordinary men and women may adopt a truculent

* See Chapter 6 on the inevitability of conflicts wherever there is a question of 'sharing-out'.

attitude to their leaders as readily as a submissive one. It would be difficult to reconcile the defeat of Churchill's government in 1945 with a universal proneness to submit to charismatic leadership, to avoid the responsibility of choosing.

The democratic idea has also been attacked as impracticable because it asks for qualities which the ordinary man cannot possibly be expected to possess. Consequently, to try to realize it would produce a parody of democracy at best. Government, it is argued, is a highly technical business, calling for a range of specialist knowledge and skills which not even the most conscientious elector could ever hope to acquire. If electors try to impose their uninformed preferences on their governments, and censure them if they act on their own superior understanding of affairs, their governments will lose touch with reality, and will lack the nerve to cope with difficulties calling for unpopular remedies. If democracies appear to work, that is only because they are technocracies masquerading as such.

We have argued, however, that democracy does not mean a system in which governments reflect 'the people's will', or even 'the will of the majority'. The judgment of most electors on, say, the finances of a state superannuation scheme or on credit policy, is not likely to be worth much, and there is no reason why a government should be expected to defer to it. What Burke said of a member of Parliament's relations with his constituents would apply equally well to a democratic government's relations with its subjects:

'Their wishes ought to have great weight with him; their opinion, high respect; their business, unremitted attention. It is his duty to sacrifice his repose, his pleasures, his satisfactions to theirs; and above all, ever, and in all cases, to prefer their interest to his own. But his unbiased opinion, his mature judgment, his enlightened conscience, he ought not to sacrifice to you, to any man, or to any set of men living . . . Your representative owes you, not his industry only, but his judgment; and he betrays, instead of serving you, if he sacrifices it to your opinion . . . If government were a matter of will upon any side, yours, without question, ought to be superior. But government and legislation are matters of reason and judgment, and not of inclination; and what sort of reason is that, in which the determination precedes the discussion; in which one set of men deliberate, and another decide; and where those who form the conclusion are perhaps three hundred miles distant from those who hear the arguments?'[9]

There is nothing undemocratic about a government's adopting unpopular policies. It must hope that its moral authority and good reputation are enough to maintain support, and that experience will vindicate it. In practice, we do not ask only whether a policy is popular but whether it is rationally justifiable; and the Opposition usually cries 'No mandate' only when it has decided on quite other grounds that a policy is wrong.

There is a place for leadership and specialized knowledge, in democracies as in other states. The ruler's job is not to follow opinion; it is to use his authority in support of proposals put forward by people who know what they are talking about. Electors in a democracy decide what is to be done only in the sense that they choose themselves leaders whose initiatives they are prepared to accept. Where democratic institutions differ from others is that legal authority depends directly on the confidence of the electors, and elections are periodic tests to make it so. If leaders will not lead, but prefer to play for easy popularity, democratic government degenerates into mob-rule—but it is then no longer democracy but simply the rule of the majority.[10] There is no reason to suppose, however, that this is the inevitable fate of all democracies.

Though there may be relatively few electors competent to express an informed opinion on any given issue, those most nearly affected by it will usually have something important to say. In a democracy, sectional pressures are strongest on just those matters where the groups have first-hand knowledge. In pressing its view on the Minister for Agriculture, the National Farmers' Union contributes essential, if one-sided experience, which even a government of experts would be foolish to ignore. Because a democratic government *must* consult very many interests, it has a valuable pool of knowledge to draw from in solving its problems.

There are some issues, of course, which can produce massive and definite expressions of opinion, capable of inducing a government to change its minds. Question of sexual behaviour, capital punishment, and pacifism are of this sort. Differences on such matters depend less, hc w-ever, on technical conditions than on moral principles, and the views people hold are rarely related to any special interest they have in the matter. These are reasons why such issues can arouse widespread concern and move unusually large numbers of people to action. The pacifist movement of the 1930s was a moral rejection of war, and technical considerations were almost wholly irrelevant to it. Similarly, people's attitudes on capital punishment and homosexuality are frequently quite unconnected with the sort of facts marshalled by psychologists and penologists. They seem much more like absolute judgments or moral intuitions. Again, the wave of indignation in 1935 that led the British government to abandon the plan to partition Ethiopia was a protest against a cynical breach of a moral rule for reasons of expediency. In cases of this sort, the technical incompetence of the ordinary citizen is beside the point; and there is no reason to suppose that on such matters governments are less subject to passion and prejudice than anyone else. We do not say that on any issue capable of stimulating a moral protest the popular view is necessarily right; but equally, there is no reason to suppose that it is always wrong. What is important, however, is that free discussion in such cases holds out a better hope that reason will prevail than if the official, expert view were the only one expressed.

In the end, however, a government must make up its own mind, and not merely wait to be pushed into action. Yet the alternatives open to it are limited by the willingness of its subjects to accept its authority. The democratic process, even more than others, is a subtle interplay of pressure and leadership. A government that bent before every gust of opinion would earn in the long run neither gratitude nor respect. The critics of democratic government who say that the people want authority, not freedom, are right thus far, that though people clamour to get their grievances redressed and exert pressure in matters that concern them closely, they expect governments to know what they are about, to act with firmness, and to initiate policies in which they can have confidence, not to wait on opinion to push them into them. The essential skill of the expert is to suggest ways of solving problems: that of the statesman, to see which suggestions the public would turn down.

Much the same answer can be given to the so-called 'iron law of oligarchy'. Every association, it is said, is run by a few energetic and ambitious men; the rest merely respond to their proposals. Democratic forms merely obscure this fact; they do not alter it. But the 'iron law of oligarchy', in this crude form at least, is in part a necessary truth. For an association is a structure in which the bulk of the members fall in with the proposals of the few in authority. The difference between a democratic association and an oligarchic one is that in the former case the leaders owe their authority to free election and are bound to give reasons for their decisions. Naturally, they will tend to be ambitious and energetic; so will their rivals for office. But unless they use their energy in ways which satisfy the electors, their ambitions will usually be disappointed.

III. THE MORAL JUSTIFICATION OF DEMOCRACY

We suggested in Chapter 14* that the theory of consent laid down certain formal criteria for justifying political authority: government should be directed to satisfying the needs of the governed, and rulers should

* See pp. 326–31.

consider all claims impartially. But also, we said, it offered certain criteria of substance. These broadly corresponded with the conditions for democracy examined above. We claimed that though the former could not strictly entail the latter, any political system which satisfied these criteria of substance would be more likely than other types to satisfy the formal criteria also. We shall try to make good that claim in this section.

(a) The Jacobin theory of democracy

The French Republican tradition, manifest in the passages we quoted from the Declaration of the Rights of Man and the Constitution of the Fourth Republic, has been strongly influenced by Rousseau. According to this tradition the function of government is to give expression to the General Will, whose object is the Common Good. Since the people is itself both the subject and the object of the General Will, authorization by the people is a necessary and a sufficient condition for all governmental authority.

We have said enough already about the concepts 'the General Will' and 'the Common Good'; we need not repeat the analysis. It is worth pointing out, however, how the doctrine has been used to prop up plebiscitary dictatorships from Robespierre to the present day.[11] If the people's will is sovereign, opposition must be malignant, being calculated to frustrate the General Will to the Common Good. Thus the Jacobin Party (or the Communist Party of the Soviet Union), claiming to express the people's will, could suppress its opponents, and concentrate power into its own hands, in order to realize the Republic of Virtue (or the Classless Society), which was the ultimate goal of the General Will. Checks and balances were needless impediments; if the people was sovereign, whom should it fear? The more powerful and highly organized the state machine, the more efficient it would be for the people's sacred purpose.

These arguments are evidently specious, and the systems they have been used to defend would not qualify as democratic in our sense. We have seen that there is no 'will of the people' beyond an election result. There is no popular will to a determinate Common Good; there are only the wills of individuals pitted one against another in an electoral contest, which determines no moral truths and no transcendental right. Such a contest, we have said, can only establish the fact that one course, candidate, or party is more popular than another. The majority is a shifting aggregate of interests, and its only claim to prevail is that it is more numerous, not that it is more virtuous. We shall argue later that a selfish majority has no better claim to have its way than a selfish minority, except that a constitutional rule lays it down that it should. There may be good reasons for that rule; but they are quite different from the presumption that the majority will is always directed to the Common Good.

This criticism of Jacobin democracy applies, though with less force, to extreme forms of the doctrine of the 'mandate', as it arises in British politics. It is sometimes assumed that the job of a democratically elected government is to implement the electors' will, by enacting as quickly as it can the programme on which it was returned to office. But this is quite untenable. The electors' will is limited to the single question decided at the poll: Who shall govern? Nothing can be inferred beyond that. To say that a party programme has been endorsed by the electorate —or even by a majority of electors—is highly misleading, for no one can say how many voted for the party *despite* any given item, or even despite the entire programme. The mandate theory is capable of a negative application at best: one can say of any given proposal of a victorious party only that it was not so unpopular that it cost the party the election. That is scarcely an electoral authorization to proceed. But even if it were, there might still be grounds for holding back, if it could be shown that the majority of the electors demanded action that would oppress a minority.

To argue that the function of government is to implement the General Will to the Common Good does not mean anything, unless it means that a government must deal impartially between all conflicting interests. As Rousseau himself saw, that is not at all the same thing as saying that any interest ought to have its way, if it can muster a majority.

(b) The natural right theory of democracy

Jacobin theory is collectivist. A different type of democratic theory, however, associated with the ideas of natural right and social contract, grew out of the individualism of the seventeenth century. Locke himself did not believe in universal suffrage; for he claimed that the right to participate in government by voting belonged only to property-owners, since they had most to lose. Though government could be justified only by consent, that did not imply a right to choose one's governors, but only that the general political arrangements should be widely acceptable. On this interpretation, the monarchy of Elizabeth I could be said to be government by consent.

But the principle that governments derive their just powers from the governed, and that the purpose of government is to protect the natural rights of the subject, was thought by some to imply a universal right to participate in the choice of governors. 'Every man that is to live under a government,' said Colonel Rainborough in 1647, 'ought first by his own consent to put himself under that government; and . . . the poorest man in England is not at all bound in a strict sense to that government that he hath not had a voice to put himself under.' This meant that the right to vote in elections was a necessary condition for political obligation. For some it was itself a natural right, for others, a necessary safeguard for the natural rights of life, liberty and property, which government might otherwise disregard. In either case, representative government on a broad or universal franchise, and deciding by majorities, was the only insurance against tyranny.

The emphasis here is different from Rousseau's—or at any rate, from Robespierre's version of Rousseau. For Robespierre, popular election authorized a government to do whatever was necessary for the Common Good; it gave a moral sanction to whatever policies the government could father on 'the people'. For the natural right democrats, the right to vote is rather a way of restraining the abuse of authority. Governments are never to be trusted; they must be watched and checked. For Robespierre the people's government could never harm it, being a reflection of its own will. For the Levellers, like Lilburne and Rainborough, as later for Tom Paine, government was a necessary evil, to be curbed by the people, and made to respond to its needs.

The individualist approach to democracy assigns a much humbler place to governors than Jacobin theory, and for this very reason makes it easier to change them without a civil war. A Robespierre can see himself as the incarnation of the Republic and the General Will. Every objection to his policies appears as a check to the sovereign people; every challenge a threat of revolution; every opponent an enemy of the people. The corruption of absolute power works not only in the crude self-indulgence of a Nero, but in the subtler forms of megalomania. The higher the ideal the popular dictator sets himself, the greater the temptation to identify the enlargement of his own power with the realization of the ideal. Yet there will always be other energetic and ambitious men eager to replace him, and ready to work on grievances to rally support against him. In a democracy, there are accepted procedures for changing governors. In a plebiscitary dictatorship, it must be done by conspiracy and force. Moreover a democratic leader so displaced retains some sort of a status in the system; a dictator overthrown becomes at once a public enemy. Consequently, where a British Prime Minister fears for his office, a dictator fears for his life; his reactions to opposition will be correspondingly more violent.

The notion of constitutional opposition is difficult to fit comfortably into Jacobin theory. Yet it is an idea essential to democracy. Furthermore, a spell in opposition may be a recurrent necessity if political leaders are to be spared megalomania. If elections do no more than substitute Tweedledum for Tweedledee, they are still of substantial importance. Who wins an American election may make very little difference to the way the United States is governed, for there are few differences of principle dividing the Democrats and the Republicans. But the very fact that there are two parties competing constitutionally for power prevents the governors of the USA from persuading themselves that their own political survival and the safety of the state are identical objectives.

The individualist or natural right theory of democracy was worked out to meet the danger of authority and power being used tyrannically. Yet it did not meet it without raising difficulties of its own. While preventing a governing minority from attacking the natural rights of the rest, it seemed to place minorities completely at the mercy of majorities. If the majority could be relied upon to be public-spirited—i.e. tender to the rights of all citizens—all might be well. But suppose the majority is itself a sectional interest group, intent only on selfishly exploiting the minority? This was the difficulty envisaged by Madison, in the discussions which preceded the adoption of the United States Constitution.[12] His solution, embodied in the Constitution, was an elaborate system of checks and balances, which comes near at times to paralysing American government. Put in Madison's terms, the problem is insoluble; for he is seeking a form of government that will permit majorities to act when they are not attacking the natural rights of minorities, but will inhibit their action when they are. But who is to decide in each case? If the majority, any formal inhibition will be ineffective; if the minority concerned, government is impossible, for no interest would consent to legislation against its interests, whether justifiable or otherwise. The American device of a Bill of Rights, protected by judicial review of legislation, is a doubtful way out. Though the Court formally implements the Constitution, the rights in question had to be framed so broadly that it enjoys a virtually absolute discretion. As we have shown elsewhere,* the natural rights of Americans, understood in the light of Supreme Court decisions, have little of the universality, the permanence, or the objective and self-evident reality that natural right theory would lead us to suppose. It is questionable whether nine men drawn from among the most successful members of a specialized profession, and therefore from the same social class, and accountable in practice to no one but themselves, are the best judges of which of the acts of a representative assembly infringe the rights of minorities. Until recently, for

* See Chapter 4.

example, the Supreme Court was more zealous in striking down legislation which extended the rights of negroes than legislation which curtailed them.

One effect of Madisonian checks is that sectional minorities can often resist attempts to remedy any injustices which are to their advantage. The fear of a sectional majority led to built-in safeguards for sectional minorities. The Southern Whites are even now fighting a vigorous rearguard action against a very widespread sympathy for the rights of negroes. Despite the more liberal attitude of the Supreme Court since the last war, the checks and balances of a federal constitution have provided plenty of opportunity for this particular minority to thwart the general trend of American opinion towards race equality. Madison's fear of majority tyranny has resulted in entrenched minorities, which can prevent a government responding to the needs of others which compete with them.

Madison put his faith, however, not only in institutional checks, but in the sheer size and diversity of the American electorate. Where needs and interests were so various, it seemed unlikely that a sectional majority would emerge. Though there might be a permanent division between minority and majority interests on some matters, there would be so many other sectional differences splitting the latter that it would never become a homogeneous and decisive pressure group. He glimpsed, therefore, the way in which a democratic government would operate in a 'plural society', balancing and adjusting sectional interests rather than responding automatically to a majority interest.

Nevertheless, Madison's fear of a sectional majority does suggest that sometimes democratic institutions may not produce that wide sensitivity which is essential to the idea of democracy. Wherever there exists a group with a wide range of common interests, and able to outnumber any conceivable grouping of competing interests, the latter may find a formally democratic system working permanently against them. Parties aiming at electoral majorities may court the large group at whatever cost to the rest. Even if several parties share its votes between them, none of them can afford to alienate it by championing the smaller groups competing with it. If the smaller groups form parties of their own, these will tend to be disgruntled, factious and irresponsible, because they can never hope to achieve power.

Madison feared that the numerous poor would despoil the rich, and he was not altogether wrong. The redistributive revolution in Britain and elsewhere, which has been a direct consequence of universal suffrage, would certainly have seemed to Madison a robbing of the rich to subsidize the poor—a flouting of natural rights. It is significant that the parties which are generally considered sympathetic to property interests, and which are usually critical of high taxation, nevertheless approach the social services with caution and respect. Many of their devoted supporters find this attitude curiously inconsistent with their avowed principles. In bidding for the workers' votes, Conservative politicians in Britain boast of their party's share in creating the Welfare State; but many of their middle class supporters feel that in the process their own interests have been largely disregarded. Where a very large interest is in conflict with smaller ones, the latter may find few politicians to champion them.

The position of the propertied class in Britain is hardly desperate; but the situation can be a good deal more serious for a racial or cultural minority. In the United States, communal integration has gone much further in the North than in the South. In the North, many issues cut across the racial division between white and black. Negro votes are now eagerly sought by both parties. In the southern states, however, where there are few enfranchised negroes, and racial conflict is acute, no politician can afford to show much sympathy for negro aspirations. Northern Democrats try to win back, by their own enthusiasm for negro rights, some of the votes they lose in the North through the damaging attitude of Democrats in the South.

Where large homogeneous interests conflict with smaller ones, democracy is always in danger of becoming mere majority rule. It can be preserved only if there are traditions of tolerance, and if the competing groups feel sufficient solidarity and concern about one another's welfare to be ready to compromise and respond to appeals to justice. This is another way of saying that democracy will work only if enough people want it to work, and are prepared to make the necessary adjustments that the claims of others demand.[13]

From this point of view, many colonial territories are unready for democratic self-government, and must move towards it piecemeal if they want it at all. Meanwhile, the paternalism of the Colonial Governor responsible to the Colonial Office may be not only more stable and more efficient, but may hold out a better hope that competing claims among the people themselves receive impartial attention. The greatest impediment to Nigerian self-government has been the reluctance of some sections of the population, like the Hausas and the smaller tribal minorities, to submit to majority rule by the more advanced Ibo and Yoruba peoples, whom they trust even less than the colonial administrator. Many Nigerians recognize that their most urgent problem is to create a sense of national solidarity that will be stronger than tribal loyalties.

(c) *Democracy and the criteria of morality*

Madison's concern for the natural rights of minorities led him to seek institutional devices which would protect them from sectional majorities. We have suggested that when such majorities exist, and are resolved to exploit their numerical superiority, democracy breaks down and institutional devices cannot save it. Nevertheless, Madison's anxiety about this suggests the lines on which justification for democracy must proceed.

The theory of natural rights had this to recommend it: it recognized the moral principle that every person must be respected as a source of claims, and must not be treated as a mere instrument; and further, that all interests must be weighed impartially. The natural right democrats believed that only a democratic government could be expected to govern in that spirit, not because it ensured that the majority would have its way, but because it conferred on every individual the opportunity to voice a claim which no government could afford to ignore. This seems to us the most promising line for a justification of democracy. 'The rights and interests of every or any person are only secure from being disregarded,' wrote Mill, 'when the person interested is himself able, and habitually disposed, to stand up for them . . . We need not suppose that when power resides in an exclusive class, that class will knowingly and deliberately sacrifice the other classes to themselves: it suffices that, in the absence of its natural defenders, the interest of the excluded is always in danger of being overlooked; and, when looked at, is seen with very different eyes from those of the persons whom it directly concerns.'[14]

This suggests two criteria for political organization: that there should be adequate channels through which all interests can make their claims known; and that no interests should be so powerful that a government can safely attend to them alone. Conversely, no interest should be so weak that a government could afford to disregard any convincing case it might put up. If one of a government's main concerns is to stay in power, it will be very tempted to placate powerful interests at the expense of weak or inarticulate ones. The problem then is so to distribute political influence that no interest can be safely ignored.

We have seen that where 'the majority' is not an interest, but a shifting aggregate of interests, the need to secure a majority of favourable votes at an election means that a democratic government can rarely feel safe in identifying itself with one interest or group of interests, to the exclusion of the rest. It must be sensitive to all interests, for any may include voters vital to its majority. It will be bound to reconcile claims where it can, and give good reasons for disappointing those it cannot satisfy. Moreover, it cannot hope to succeed unless it takes active steps to discover the views of those affected by its policies. A paternalist government, like the 'enlightened despotisms' of the eighteenth century, may have the will to serve its subjects' interests, but it is inclined to assume that it knows what they are without doing much to find out. Everyone is bounded by the limits of his own experience; the average university teacher has little idea of what it feels like to be a dockworker, and vice versa. The merit of democracy is that in requiring the would-be legislator to court his constituents, it forces him to examine their needs at close quarters. He must consult their experience, rather than assume, on the strength of his own, that he knows either what they want, or what would be good for them. It would be rash to say that every man knows best what is best for himself; but it is wise nevertheless to ask him what he wants and why he wants it, before concluding that he is mistaken. And this is the minimum compatible with the moral criterion of respect for persons as sources of claims.

If the technique of representation works in this sort of way, it is not important, in one sense, who wins an election and who governs. All parties would be sensitive to a wide range of interests, and whoever governed would have to justify their policies by appealing to widely accepted moral criteria. Their decisions would not be influenced by any one particular sectional viewpoint, and whatever they did would have to stand up to criticism. That is not to say that all parties would adopt the same policies; of course elections make a difference to what is actually done. The point is rather that whatever was done could be rationally defended. However, though some policies are more prudent than others, there is no reason to suppose that the one preferred by the electoral majority is therefore the wisest. We do not settle such questions by counting heads. Democratic techniques like elections prevent the adoption of policies which are morally indefensible; they do not ensure that the kings will be philosophers. But then, no convincing technique has ever been found that would guarantee wise and virtuous rulers. Even Plato himself warned against the dangers of being taken in by false philosophers. Democracy is only a safeguard against the abuse of power, not a guarantee that it will be wisely used. It encourages rulers to behave *as if* they were virtuous, because it lays their decisions open to the scrutiny of rivals as competent as themselves, who have their own interest in drawing the voters' attention to partiality or corruption.

Democratic government confers on every voter a mite of political power; and that means, in Professor Leoni's significant phrase, 'the possibility for individuals of their personal choices being identified with the decisions of the groups to which they belong'.[15] The effect of this is to moralize politics, by making every individual a worthwhile object for a government's attention, and a person to whom reasons must be given when his claims are disappointed. The functions of a Member of Parliament illustrate this. On the one hand, he mediates between the governors and the governed, explaining and justifying in the hope of winning or retaining support; on the other, he interprets the needs and experience of the subject to the government, passing on grievances, pressing for redress, warning of discontent, and claiming attention for interests that are being overlooked. He is not, of course, the only channel. We have mentioned the importance of consultations between the government and organized sectional interests, which are now an essential part of the process of government in nearly all democracies. Such consultations are conducted not only by the informal methods of lobbying, but through formal institutious like the National Production Advisory Council in Britain and the Economic Council of the Fourth Republic.

An important difference between democracy and mere 'majority rule' is precisely the assumption underlying such consultations, that reasons must be given for governmental policies. This accounts too for the constitutional function of the official Opposition, which is to insist on the government justifying itself publicly. Government is not then a matter of *mere* authority or of *mere* will—even of the majority. It proceeds in an atmosphere of criticism, on the presumption that a sufficient justification cannot be given for a decision by an appeal to someone's will (whether it be the will of a minister or of a majority interest), simply because it is that person's will. And this is precisely the point we made in Chapter 5, when we said that 'I want to' cannot of itself be a sufficient justification for any decision, no matter who the 'I' happens to be. Democracy has been called 'government by discussion'. In a sense, of course, this is true of all government; for the most authoritarian of governments must have its committees to pool experience and co-ordinate departmental policies. But it is true of democracy in the special sense that the whole process presumes the give and take of criticism and justification, conducted within the framework of moral criteria.

Freedom of discussion is thus not merely a safeguard against the abuse of authority in a democracy, but a condition for democracy itself. But discussion degenerates into mere abuse unless there is a minimal respect for persons as sources of arguments. Democracy presupposes, then, a willingness to assume good faith in opponents. 'It is impossible,' said Rousseau, 'to live at peace with those we regard as damned; to love them would be to hate God who punishes them: we positively must either reclaim them or torment them.'[16] Discussion presupposes, then, a consensus on fundamentals, for where this is lacking, men will treat one another as scoundrels, and differences of opinion will be undiscussible. The lack of such consensus has been one reason for the chronic weakness of democracy in France. Since 1789, there have always been significant minorities for whom the constitution and the property structure have been open questions, and the nation has been seriously divided on religious questions. A lack of common standards has meant a lack of solidarity. Where men start from different assumptions, there are no adjustments and no compromises generally felt to be fair and reasonable. In such conditions, politics is a cynical grasping for whatever advantages temporary power combinations can secure. If those who are permanently disgruntled do not actually fight, it is not because they live in hopes of ultimately persuading the others to give them a fair deal, but because they are too weak to hope for victory. In such cases, the forms of democracy do not achieve the wide sensitivity to all claims, and the adjustment of conflicts in a spirit of impartiality; for without appropriate attitudes, and the will to conduct politics in a rational and tolerant spirit, democratic institutions work undemocratically. 'Institutions,' as Popper says, 'are like fortresses. They must be well-designed *and* manned.'[17]

(d) The democratic rights of the anti-democratic

Democracy, we have said, presupposes a readiness to consult all experience, to respect all persons as sources of claims and arguments. It assumes, therefore, the right of opposition groups to seek majority support, and the readiness of governments to yield office when defeated at the polls. So long as these assumptions are accepted by all parties, all is well; but an opposition group that uses its rights to destroy democracy creates a genuine dilemma for the democrat. If we defined democracy as 'rule by the majority', we should be committed to the view that whatever the majority decided should be loyally accepted, even if that meant acquiescing in the suicide of democratic institutions. That would mean allowing an anti-democratic party free exercise of the usual democratic rights, to build up, if it could, an anti-democratic majority, in the full knowledge that the moment of its success would spell the end of similar rights for anyone else.*

* Indeed, such parties have not always waited for electoral majorities; the Nazis in Germany in 1933 and the Communists in Czechoslovakia in 1948 had very substantial support, but never polled a majority in a free election. There is a point short of electoral victory at which such an opposition can paralyse a democratic republic and wreck it from within.

M

We have argued, however, that to treat democracy as 'rule by the majority' is to miss the point of it, namely, that it requires that every claim should be given a hearing. If it fails in this, the majority principle becomes a mere assertion of the power of numbers, and fifty-one in a hundred possess no intrinsic moral authority over the other forty-nine. Democracy involves not only decision by majority voting, but also that political rights be conceded to minorities. Deny one, and the moral case for the other largely disappears. The democrat confronted by an anti-democratic government is not necessarily bound to respect its authority just because it can claim majority support.

Does this imply, however, that a democratic majority must concede full political rights to anti-democratic minorities? *Prima facie*, it does; for those rights do not depend on a man's political beliefs, but on his importance as a source of arguments and claims. If his experience leads him to challenge the democratic order, this too is important, and the statesman who prefers to close his mind to it does so at his peril, and at the peril of the order he professes to defend. A democratic system becomes increasingly difficult to work the greater the measure of dissent on fundamentals; but if dissent is not confined to a tiny eccentric minority, but affects a group large enough to constitute a threat to the order, denying it political rights is only a recognition that the order is in peril; it is not to save it. The only hope of a permanent remedy would be to attend to the grievances out of which the challenge has developed.

Nevertheless, there is a point at which an anti-democratic party becomes dangerously large, when it employs its democratic rights to obstruct and discredit the democratic process, and when it threatens to become powerful enough to overturn it. At this stage the rights of the minority in question have to be weighed against the rights of all those who would be its victims. There is now a conflict of claims, including the claims of democracy itself. Though suppression may not provide a permanent solution to this problem in practice, it could conceivably be justified as a precaution, while other remedies were given a chance to operate. If a restriction on minority rights could be effective in preserving democracy, it would be a misguided quixotry to oppose it.

The difficulty, of course, is to determine when this point is reached. To wait too long may be to lose the opportunity for effective action. It is at least arguable that the German democrats were over-indulgent to the Nazi party in the 1920s. However, there is always a temptation to suppress opposition before the danger arises at all. There are some people in Britain who would welcome the suppression of the Communist Party, though it would be absurd to consider it a danger to our democratic institutions. American and South African experience suggests that suppression of anti-democratic action becomes too readily a convenient cloak for intolerance of any unorthodox opinions. The self-styled defenders of democracy against Communism can be as anti-democratic as the enemy they oppose.*

IV. CONCLUSION

We have taken 'democracy' to mean not merely a set of political institutions like universal suffrage, parliamentary government, and decisions by majority procedure, but also a set of principles which such institutions tend to realize. These are (to repeat Bentham's words): '*responsibility* of the governors; or the right which a subject has of having the reasons publicly assigned and canvassed of every act of power that is exerted over him . . . the *liberty of the press;* or the security with which every man . . . may make known his complaints . . . the *liberty of public association;* or the security with which malcontents may communicate their sentiments, concert their plans, and practice every mode of opposition short of actual revolt'.[18] These are intimately connected we suggest, with the same principles of impartiality and respect for persons as sources of claims and arguments, which we first enunciated in Chapter 2, and which underlie all the central political ideals, like justice, liberty and equality. The principle of universal suffrage is a way of giving practical recognition to the moral value of every man as a source of claims; it is also a way of providing that governors will attend to them. Again, the principle 'one man, one vote', however it may be varied in detail, is an expression of the *prima facie* equality which is basic to the idea of justice. And without the freedoms of discussion and association, there is no way of ensuring that a man will have the chance to state a claim, and no hope that it will receive impartial attention.

But in addition to all this, democracy is a way of coming to terms with the need for authority without accepting a duty to submit to whatever abuses it might bring in its train. The right to criticize and censure a government, and the right to exercise a vote to remove it, is a practical recognition of the principle that the duty to obey, understood as a moral duty, must always be conditional, and is never a duty to suspend judgment. It depends in the end of how authority is exercised. Democracy provides a peaceful way of getting rid of governments which fail to convince a majority of their adult subjects that they have a lively concern for the interests of the governed. It is not a denial of the need for authority, but a recognition that no authority can ever be keeper of a man's conscience.

* The question of treason is another matter; but not all Communists are spies, and a man is not less likely to be a traitor for being deprived of political rights.

APPENDIX ON INTERNATIONAL RELATIONS

This book has dealt with the normative orders, like law, custom and morals, which bind men together in society, and with the grounds of their obligations and rights as citizens of states. We shall consider briefly in this appendix whether there is any analogous system of rules binding nation-states in an international society, and whether the general principles we have examined could be applied to such a society.

I. IS THERE AN INTERNATIONAL SOCIETY?

The concept of an international society is not, on the face of it, one towards which men are attracted by strong sentiments or lasting traditions. There is no international 'image' to parallel the national 'image'. The solidarity felt by members of a nation-state with persons or groups outside its frontiers is generally far weaker than the sentiment of nationality, and can rarely compete with it effectively. The over-riding solidarity of the international proletariat, which Marx urges in the *Communist Manifesto*, has been shown in two World Wars to be still a wish, not a reality. Nevertheless, there may still be an international order, though of a weaker sort than the national orders.

(a) The meaning of an 'international society'
The first step is to call attention to ambiguities in the use of the word 'international'. When we refer to the United Nations Organization as 'an international institution', we mean that it regulates relations between nation-states. 'International' in this context means 'inter-state'. But the 'international money market' is a system of financial institutions, like banks and discount houses; states are concerned with it, but it is not primarily an organization of states. Similarly, there are 'international' bodies like the Catholic Church, or the International Political Science Association, which include people of all nations, organized for sectional purposes. Such associations are independent of governments. They might be more accurately called 'extra-national' rather than 'international' associations, since nationality is strictly irrelevant to them.

It is important not to underestimate the very considerable extra-national organization that exists in the world. International trade is organized in a highly elaborate system of rules and institutions, and similar systems exist in the fields of art, religion, science and sport. To this extent, 'international society' is meaningful.

It is a society, however, over-shadowed by nation-states, which may interfere drastically with its operations. For the world's political organization follows the pattern of the strongest loyalties. There is only a very loose association of nation-states, acknowledging only very limited obligations to one another, or to the world's society as a whole. When public men refer rhetorically to 'a duty to society', they rarely see beyond the national frontiers. Thus the idea of an 'international society' smacks of an unattainable ideal, rather than a description of a real order.

(b) What sort of order is the inter-state order?

This has not always been the case. For the men of the Middle Ages, the idea of a universal society was closely linked to the idea of the Universal Christian Church, which was co-terminous in principle, if not in practice, with all mankind. But by the end of the sixteenth century, no one could pretend that this conception had anything to do with reality. The Universal Church was split beyond repair. Geographical exploration and an expanding trade with America and the Indies had revealed a bewildering diversity of creeds, cultures and social organization. Where kings had once wrangled with Popes and bishops over the exact limits of their respective jurisdictions, they now claimed exclusive authority within their domains. Most important of all was the development of national self-consciousness. Even where Protestantism was repulsed, men came to regard the Papacy as a more or less foreign institution. The idea of the transcendent world order gave way before the greedy exclusiveness of the sovereign state.

Political and legal theorists had to devise new concepts for explaining this new situation. Hobbes, for example, denied that there could be such a thing as an inter-state order. For an order presumed rules, and there could be no rules without sovereign authority. States were in a state of nature one to another, a condition in which there could be neither legal nor moral obligation. The world of states was not an order, but an international anarchy.

The raw material for a new theory of international order, to replace the outdated mediaeval concept of a universal community, was to hand, however, in the mediaeval doctrine of natural law, and in the Roman concept of a *jus gentium*, or law of nations. For the Romans, the latter had been the common element in all positive legal systems, which could be used therefore as the basis for commercial relations between subjects of different legal orders. It was now developed, however, into a notion of a law generally agreed to be binding on *states*. Its rules derived from two sources, custom and treaty; it was thus a system which depended on recognition and agreement.

For Grotius, however, the 'Father of International Law', the law of nations was subordinate to natural law, the law of reason. For as a law constituted by agreement, the former depended for its validity on the rule of natural law that promises must be kept. Furthermore, though nations might agree to vary their obligations by treaty or custom, (by creating, for instance, the legal status of 'neutral' which, according to Grotius, did not exist in natural law), they remained answerable to God for their conduct under the law of nature.

The idea of natural law was an approximation, we have suggested,* to the concept of 'morality'. The natural law theory of international relations was thus a way of saying that states could have mutual moral obligations, even though there was no political authority competent to bind them, and no international coercive power to enforce their obligations. The point at issue between Hobbes and Grotius can be translated, therefore, into modern terms, by asking whether there can be a morality between states or whether their relations are governed only by self-interest.

II. MORAL PRINCIPLES AND INTERNATIONAL POLITICS

(a) The ambiguity of 'national interest'

The case put forward by those who are attracted by the concept of international anarchy is that national interest is either the sole or the dominant motive which operates in dealings between states. This makes them view talk of morality between states as either meaningless chatter or as a sort of façade of respectability which hides the realities of power. Machiavelli, for instance, exhorted his Prince always to appear respectable, but to use this as a cloak for doing whatever the security of the state required.[1] 'National interest', however, is an ambiguous concept. In its broad sense the term is significant rather by what it denies than by what it asserts. A state is seeking 'national interest' when it is not concerned with the interests of any groups outside its own jurisdiction, except to the extent that they may affect domestic interests. In its foreign as in its domestic policy, a government must decide between conflicting claims; to decide in 'the national interest' is to limit con-

* See Chapter 2.

sideration only to the claims of its nationals. But even within those limits, 'national interest' may not be 'in the public interest';* for the government may favour a sectional group at the expense of others. Or it may use its foreign policy to distract public attention from short-comings in its domestic policy. It may pick quarrels, for instance, in order to appear as champion of the national honour.

On the other hand, 'national interest' may be used more narrowly, to exclude policies which are not in 'the public interest' of the people of the state in question. In this sense, 'national interest' is a kind of moral criterion, for a statesman might *justify* his actions by saying that he was defending national interests. He would mean that his policy was important for all his nationals' interests, or else that it did justice to all their claims if they conflicted. According to the theory of international anarchy, such a justification would be final. The statesman could have no obligation to attend to any claims beyond the several and collective claims of his own nationals.

(b) 'My country, right or wrong' as a moral principle

Such a view would be inconsistent with our understanding of morality. Admittedly, if in our ordinary moral judgments we considered the claims only of our own countrymen, we might look for a similar limita-tion from our statesmen. But we do not do this. In our private dealings, we recognize *prima facie* moral duties to pay debts, relieve suffering, and avoid injuring others, irrespective of nationality. So far from finding the parable of the Good Samaritan unintelligible, we accept it as a moral ideal. Why then should we limit consideration to the claims of our own nation when we deal with corporate acts and interests? Should we maintain that trade unionists have no moral obligations to non-unionists, or that union leaders would be justified in *any* act, so long as it promoted the interests of their members? Or, *mutatis mutandis*, company directors, church or party leaders? Membership of an associa-tion creates special responsibilities to fellow members, and its agents have a particular duty to defend their interests; but these do not exclude all others. Why then should it be otherwise with the state?

The patriot who attends exclusively to his country's welfare—'My country, right or wrong'—sets arbitrary limits to moral consideration, i.e. limits for which no rational justification can be given. He is not saying 'I have special duties to my own country', but rather 'I do not recognize the moral status of any but my own countrymen'. Such a principle cannot satisfy the criterion of impartiality or 'equal considera-tion', essential to the notion of morality. Would it be more reasonable,

* See Chapter 12, pp. 271–3, for an analysis of 'the public interest'.

however, to maintain that *everyone* should do what is best for his own country, irrespective of the claims of others? This looks more like a universal principle; but it would have the paradoxical consequence that, for instance, an Englishman would have to approve a Russian statesman's acts if they served Russian interests, while doing everything in his power to frustrate them because they impaired British interests. Moreover, to lay down a moral principle is to prescribe for others as well as for oneself; but to teach foreigners to pursue the interests of their own countries may be to prescribe conduct contrary to the interest of one's own—which is contrary to the principle. It is a curious moral principle that can be consistently followed only by keeping it a secret.

(c) The duty of a statesman

Where, then, does the statesman's duty lie? It is often said that he stands as trustee, that he is no more entitled to look beyond national interests than to be generous with funds held in trust for another. The analogy, however, is incomplete and misleading. The trustee is bound to do his best for the trust, but subject to duties which he owes to others too. We should blame him for using trust funds in a dishonest way, even if he made nothing out of it himself. Similarly, though the statesman has a special duty to his nation, it does not rule out other duties too. But in any case, we do not accuse governments of abusing funds held in trust for the nation, when they contribute to international relief funds for victims of flood, famine, and war. Statesmen often have to defend giving aid to under-developed countries in terms of national self-interest; but they are rarely pressed for similar justifications when the cause is more obviously humanitarian.

It may be objected that a statesman is not a principal but an agent; so long as his countrymen are deaf to the appeals of a wider morality, he has no mandate to be otherwise. If his policies are selfish, the fault is theirs, not his. But this surely misrepresents the situation. A government is open to criticism; in democratic countries it is constitutionally bound to justify its stewardship, and must seek re-election from time to time. But this is quite different from saying that statesmen are delegates, with a mandate to pursue specified objectives, and entitled to act only within limits authorized by their subjects.

Admittedly, what the statesman can achieve may be governed by the support he can command. If he ignores other people's views, they may be able to thwart him, no matter how well-meaning he may be. The refusal of the United States Senate to ratify the treaty creating the League of Nations, of which President Wilson had been the principal architect, is the classic case of a statesman's high aspirations brought to nothing through lack of support. Nevertheless statesmen can lead as well as follow opinion. American opinion was led by Franklin Roosevelt from isolationism to Lend-Lease, and thereafter by Harry Truman to the Marshall Plan and Point Four Aid. Of course, these policies were represented as in the best long-term interests of the United States; but the moral appeal to help those in trouble may have been at least as important in getting them accepted as the appeal to enlightened self-interest.

Nevertheless, though moral obligation does not stop short at national frontiers, it would be naïve to use the same criteria for judging the acts of states as for those of private persons in a settled society. Where there is no authority capable of ensuring security, statesmen must put the claims of national self-preservation very high. We condemn spying on the family next door because we do not usually expect them to be plotting against us. States have no such assurance, and must safeguard themselves as best they can. But that is not to say that national security is the only proper end of statesmanship, nor even that it must always be the overriding one. If morality means anything at all in the context of international relations, there must be other principles for the conduct of states besides self-preservation.

(d) The principle of non-interference in relations between states

The principle of international law that states must not interfere in one another's domestic affairs provides a clue to the minimal requirement of international morality. This principle is reminiscent of Mill's 'self-protection' principle. which he regarded as fundamental to personal liberty. We suggested in Chapter 10 that this derived directly from the moral criterion of respect for persons, as having ends of their own. Admittedly, states are not persons in this sense, nor is their autonomy the same as the moral autonomy of individuals. The analogy may nevertheless be suggestive. We said in Chapter 13 that there was a strong *prima facie* case for leaving people free to associate for their own purposes, and that the state must have good reasons for interfering. Now nation-states are themselves associations of individuals with their own common interests and aspirations, expressed within a common tradition. Within its own jurisdiction, a state has a claim to interfere with other associations as umpire, providing it does so impartially. But in international affairs, states are very rarely impartial, and their own interests are bound to weigh heavily in shaping their policies. When one state meddles in another's affairs, the nationals of the victim are rarely considered on the same footing as those of the interfering state. The latter treats them rather as means for its own ends.

But even if that were not the case, it is doubtful how far any state would be justified in deciding what was best for other peoples, just because it is so difficult to know the needs and attitudes of the people one aspires to help. And where their traditions are very different from one's own, it is very difficult indeed to predict what will come of the arrangements one imposes on them. The missionaries and traders who brought civilization to Africa gave little thought to the disrupting effects of western ideas and industry on the traditional tribal communities and religious beliefs. Even those who were well disposed towards the native inhabitants had no way of telling whether the order they were imposing would benefit or harm them. There may, of course, have been a case for colonization on other grounds. Sidgwick, for instance, denied that any particular community had an exclusive and unqualified right to 'the utilities derived from any portion of the earth's surface'.

If the case for interfering with primitive peoples for their own good is a doubtful one, the case for crusading among civilized ones is even more so. Men can learn something from the experience of other nations, if they can absorb it into their own experience; but for outsiders to impose solutions to other people's problems, in the name of 'liberty' or 'social justice', is to meddle with matters they can neither understand nor control. Again, when a state decides to interfere in the internal affairs of another, it has no way of consulting the people themselves, on whose behalf it claims to act. For intervention of this sort rarely happens except when a nation is split. At such a time, 'the people's will' has no meaning, and there is no way of telling what the general response will be to intervention on either side. To say, for instance, that British intervention in Jordan in 1958 saved the state from subversion by the United Arab Republic, is to ignore the fact that many of its inhabitants would have preferred the success of the subversion, and believed that their highest interests would have been served by Union with the Republic. Intervention of this sort can never be impartial as between a government and its dissident subjects. And once a clear answer can be given to what a people wants, it is already well on the way to settling its own problems for itself.

There might be other duties, of course, which in exceptional cases would be more important than the duty not to interfere. Intervention might be justified, for instance, in defence of a minority, like the Jews in Nazi Germany, which was being treated so abominably that no conceivable argument could justify it. In the end, moral duties are owed to men; they are owed to states only in so far as they are organizations which serve men. The duty of non-interference rests on the assumption that the claims of a state's members will generally be better served if they are left to work out their own salvation. But this could not possibly have been the case for the German Jews, who were not accorded even the minimum of respect due to a person as a source of claims.

Even in such a case, however, there might be weighty reasons for not interfering, given the precariousness of the international order. Unless intervention had the support of nearly all other states, it could become a pretext for counter-intervention; and the repercussions of any disturbance of the balance of power are unpredictable. States can live in peace together only by respecting one another's independence, and by strictly observing what generally accept rules there are, even when they work out unhappily.

III. INTERNATIONAL LAW—ITS SCOPE AND LIMITATIONS[2]

The suggestion of established rules for dealings between states introduces naturally the second main issue raised by the classical theorists —especially Grotius, that of the possibility of international law.

International law, of course, has grown considerably since Grotius. There have been the spectacular instances of international lawlessness, like the invasion of Belgium in 1914, in defiance of treaty obligations; but in the routine of international intercourse there has developed a body of rules, admittedly not always well-defined, which states generally find it convenient to observe, and expect one another to observe. Moreover, during the nineteenth century, it became common for states to agree to settle minor disputes by arbitration. The Hague Conventions of 1899 and 1907 produced the Permanent Court of Arbitration. After the First World War, the Court of International Justice was established, replaced in 1945 by the present International Court of Justice. Arbitrators and judges have created a considerable body of case law, and international conventions, adopted by very many nations, have pronounced formally on what is agreed custom in many spheres. There is thus unquestionably a body of rules governing the conduct of states, and providing criteria for determining disputes between them. Moreover, as Brierly points out, violations, though often sensational when they occur, are nonetheless rare, and largely confined to the law of war: 'the laws of peace and the great majority of treaties are on the whole regularly observed in the daily intercourse of states'.[3] And this is so because it suits states to maintain them. The International Telegraphic Union, the Universal Postal Union, and similar arrangements for international collaboration work in a regular and orderly fashion, and no state has any interest in disrupting them.

But international law does not ask much of states. For instance, no state need submit to arbitration or adjudication unless it chooses, or has agreed to do so in advance; and in accepting the jurisdiction of the International Court, states have been careful to exclude any matter which might affect their vital interests. International law is effective within its limits, but the very narrowness of these shows how far the society of states falls short of a community. Because the law can so rarely be enforced, it would be imprudent for jurists to oblige states to do things which they would not normally be willing to do without compulsion. Frequent conflicts of interest and duty would only bring the law into disrepute.

A further limitation on international law is the lack of any but the most rudimentary arrangements for changing it. There is no international legislature, and no other authority competent to vary existing rights, except with the agreement of all affected parties. It is true that because international law is in part customary, its tribunals take account of generally accepted changes in practice. Also innovations are sometimes introduced by conventions whose ostensible purpose is to define existing practice. If such innovations are supported by a large number of states, including the Great Powers, they will usually be accepted as law. Beyond that, however, changes in legal rights and duties depend on treaty, i.e. on the consent of all concerned. The law therefore tends to preserve the *status quo*, for it can be altered only by general agreement or by war. This defect is the more serious because the explosive questions are usually those which seek quite openly to change legal relations, despite the objections of interested parties.

(a) Is international law 'law'?

Because international legal institutions are so rudimentary, and because there is nothing like an international police power, some jurists have doubted whether international law is rightly 'law' at all. Austin, for instance, defined 'law' in terms of a command from a superior to an inferior, supported by effective sanctions*; he was thus led to classify international law as 'positive morality', i.e. customary rules supported by general opinion, but not 'law properly so-called'. But this is misleading. For at any given time the conduct of states is judged by reference to a variety of standards; yet it would be odd to term all such standards rules of international law. In the nineteenth century, for instance, wars to liberate oppressed nationalities, or to unite groups of common nationality into one state, were fairly widely approved, even when they were waged in defiance of the legal rule forbidding interference in the domestic affairs of other states; but a government has

* See Chapter 3, Section III, for a discussion of the command theory of law.

never been under an international legal obligation to grant independence to any portion of its subjects who dislike its rule, if they belong to a different nationality from the rest.[4] Again, the Universal Declaration of Human Rights might be said to be a statement of positive moral principles, but it was explicitly pointed out when it was adopted that it was not a statement of law or of legal obligations.[5] If international law is not 'law', we need another term to distinguish the rules which are the business of international lawyers from those of 'positive international morality'.

Many international jurists have felt that to deny the dignity of the term 'law' to the lawyers' rules would weaken respect for them. They have been trenchant critics, therefore, of the command theory, arguing that rules could be 'law' by agreement, as well as by being imposed by authority. Some, like Kelsen, agree with Austin that law necessarily implies sanctions, but they consider reprisals and war to be the sanctions of international law. Where there is no authority capable of enforcing the law, every state must do it for itself; if one state is injured by another it is empowered by international law to take reprisals. For Kelsen, the criterion of a rule of law is not that the sanction is effective, but only that the rule authorizes a sanction. Consequently by treating reprisals as sanctions he can bring international law within the terms of his definition of 'law', even though weak states may be incapable of effective reprisals against strong ones.

The argument is largely about how the word 'law' is to be used; it is to that extent unprofitable. But it is not purely a verbal matter, for it draws attention to some crucial differences between the international and national (or, as lawyers say, 'municipal') legal systems. If reprisals and war are 'sanctions', they are a good deal less reliable than the sanctions of municipal law: reprisals by the Republic of Liberia against the United States are practically impossible, and would certainly have no effect. Moreover, a system in which every state can choose whether to submit to an independent tribunal or remain judge in its own cause is very different from the systems of municipal law in civilized states, though parallels might be found among some primitive tribal laws. Whether the term 'law' should be refused to such a system on these grounds matters little, once the relevant distinctions are grasped.

(a) Sovereignty and the validity of international law

Austin denied that the system was 'law properly so-called' because there was no sovereign to validate it. International lawyers who adopt a positivist approach maintain, however, that what validates international law is the consent of sovereign states. To call a state 'sovereign' might be understood to mean that it was a self-subsistent legal order, and that its basic norm was neither deivative from nor subordinate to any other system. It would follow that to be valid, international law must be received, or adopted, as part of a state system, by a process of 'auto-limitation', i.e. the state would be bound or limited by law only because it bound itself.[6] Looked at from the point of view of the municipal courts, this is certainly how it must appear. An English judge admits international law as validated by the Common Law of England—but like the rest of the Common Law it can be overridden by statute. And the same is true, with appropriate modification for the courts of any other state.[7] But this is not how it looks from the standpoint of an international court. From that standpoint, to enforce a statute in conflict with international law would be an international delict. International law is a self-subsistent legal order, on the same logical footing as the legal orders of states. Consequently, from the standpoint of the international lawyer, there can be no question of demonstrating its legal validity, any more than for the English lawyer there can be any question of demonstrating that of English law, considered as a whole. The basic norm of *any* legal system, is, to use Kelsen's phrase, 'a legal postulate', without which legal argument would be infinitely regressive.

The 'auto-limitation' theory has been developed to explain how a state can be both sovereign and bound by law. The problem arises, however, only because 'sovereignty' is ambiguous. It comes from treating the word as if it meant the same thing both in the context of municipal and of international law. In the first context, it means that the state system is self-subsistent, i.e. that the basic norm or criterion of validity applied by its courts is within the system, not outside it. But in the second context, it means that a state is self-governing in respect of other states (as distinct, for example, from a colony subject to the municipal law of a parent state); but this does not mean that it is not a partial order in relation to international law. In the international context, 'sovereign state' is a term denoting a particular sort of legal personality, analogous to 'corporation' in municipal law. That does not entail that it is bound by law only because it so chooses. Again, when 'sovereignty' is used in connection with a state's legislature, it suggests an unlimited competence; when it is used of a state *vis-à-vis* other associations in its territory, it suggests supremacy or overriding authority. But these suggestions are out of place in the context of international law. It is surely a contradiction to say that a state can be at once a subject of law and also sovereign, in the sense that it has unlimited competence to decide what norms shall govern its conduct.

The legal rights of sovereign states in international law lend a certain colour, however, to the 'auto-limitation' theory. For instance, a state enjoys the right of freedom from interference by others in its domestic jurisdiction which is said to be implied in the principle of 'equality of sovereign states'. Again, in the absence of an international legislature, new obligations cannot be placed on a state without its agreement. But these are principles of *international law*; to quote them is implicitly to say that international law *accords* these rights to states, that states have rights deriving from the law, not that the law as a whole derives from the choice of the states. Similarly, custom and treaty are the principal sources of international law; but it does not therefore follow that states are bound by law because they choose to consider themselves so, but rather that the law lays down criteria of validity that make custom and treaty binding. Consent is a criterion of validity of rules within international law; it is not a principle which could meaningfully be said to validate the system as a whole.

Nevertheless, the idea for which 'sovereignty' stands in international law is clearly important, though one that is difficult to define precisely. Given that the freedom of action of a sovereign state can be limited by treaty, how much can it limit that freedom without ceasing to be sovereign? In setting up the United States of America, did the thirteen states make a treaty, as the Confederate States later alleged, limiting their freedom of action by mutual agreement but retaining their several sovereignties, and therefore, a right to secede? Or did they form a new state, extinguishing their independent sovereignties? When the six countries of Western Europe agreed to form the European Coal and Steel Community, they undertook to implement its decisions in their domestic policies and to receive its rules as valid parts of their national legal orders; but did they cease to be sovereign states? Again, a state may bind itself by treaty to relinquish control of its foreign relations to another, to accept military occupation, and to accept the status of 'protection'; does it yet remain sovereign, because it has imposed these limitations upon itself? Is a colony not sovereign, though as self-governing as a protected state in its domestic affairs, and as subject to an imperial power in defence and foreign affairs, just because these arrangements have had a different origin? At what stage did the British Dominions attain sovereignty? Was it only with the Statute of Westminster of 1931? Yet they were signatories of the Peace Treaties and full members of the League of Nations from the very beginning; they entered into full diplomatic relations with other states and behaved generally as independent members of the society of nations.

The distinction between self-governing and non-self-governing states is not, apparently, absolute, but a matter of degree. The critical question for international law must surely be whether a state's legal status gives it the freedom of action necessary to fulfil its legal obligations, or whether, like a colony or a member-state of a federation, it might be prevented from fulfilling them by the rules of the greater legal whole of which it forms a part. Since such dependence of one state on another is recognized in international law, the dependent one could be regarded rather like a minor in English law: responsibility for its actions would rest with the parent order, and it would have no independent competence to incur obligations of its own. But what precise qualifications are laid down by international law for sovereign status, and what rights attach to it, can be known only by examining the substance of the law, not by *a priori* deductions from the concept 'sovereignty' in general.

This is a further demonstration of the point that international law cannot be said to derive its validity from the agreement of sovereign states. For to know what states are sovereign, we must first look at the law, whereas the 'auto-limitation' view would have us look first to the states. But without the law, how should we know which states to look at?

IV. THE CONCEPT OF A WORLD STATE

If it is accepted that the concept of international law is not an absurd one, it seems obvious enough to press the analogy between international law and municipal law, and to argue that there must eventually be a political order or world-state co-extensive with the international legal order and providing the sanctions which it so manifestly lacks at the moment. And, of course, there are many who have put forward this sort of thesis. How might such a world-state look?

(a) The hegemony of a dominant state

One possibility is a political order imposed by a nation-state powerful enough to force the rest to submit to it. This was the way Rome ruled the Ancient World from the Atlantic to the borders of Russia and the Persian Gulf. Hitler dreamed of a vastly greater empire that would rule the world. There is nothing logically absurd about the idea of a world empire. But it is doubtful whether the conditions necessary for the maintenance of such an order exist. A state must be preserved, not just by armies, but by a sense of solidarity, which is stronger than that which binds men to any lesser associations that might conflict with it. So long as the concept of nationality remains powerful, it seems unlikely that nations would submit tamely to the domination of one of their number.

(b) A world-state as a state of states

What is more usually envisaged is a world-state formed by a union of national states, which would retain their separate identities, but submit to some higher authority created by agreement. This would be a practical example in the international sphere of Social Contract creating a civil society out of states in a state of nature. The model for such a 'state of states' already exists in federal states like the United States of America and Australia. It is one peculiarly fitted to societies where there is a desire to retain the autonomy of constituent groups in their domestic affairs, while enabling them to organize collectively for matters of common concern. If such a union is to be really a state, however, it must have a monopoly of armed forces in the association. The constituent states do not remain 'states', therefore, in the full sense of the word.*

Two World Wars and the menace of a third have made such an organization attractive to very many people. But the very conditions that make it so desirable make it impracticable. For international society lacks the solidarity without which an effective political order is unthinkable. There is no wide consensus on moral standards for the settlement of claims. Whatever minor concessions states might make for the sake of international order, each has its vital interests for which it would rather fight than surrender. The stronger the state, the more inflexible its view of what is 'vital'. No great power is disposed to put these interests at the mercy of a federal assembly of states, each with its own axe to grind. Hobbes has often been taken to task for suggesting that men could ever have contracted out of the natural state of war, if they had distrusted one another as much as he supposed. This is precisely the problem of the world-state under present conditions.

V. THE UNITED NATIONS AND POWER POLITICS

Any practical plan for international organization must take account of these facts. The United Nations Organization has been much criticized: it is paralysed by the great power veto in the Security Council: voting in the Assembly merely registers the relative weight of competing pressures; almost no attempt is made to deal with issues on their merits; every dispute is viewed as part of the struggle between rival blocs. But how could it be otherwise?

The primary aim of UNO is to facilitate the peaceful settlement of disputes. Enforcement of its decisions is possible only against a small state which no great power is prepared to protect. Against a great power it is impossible, for this would mean embarking on a major war, which

* See Chapter 12.

it is the very purpose of the organization to avoid. The great power veto in the Security Council is simply a realistic admission of the fact. Unenforceable resolutions would only bring the organization into disrepute. If the great powers were ever disposed to make war on one of their own number, the organization would be virtually killed, and a resolution of the Council would only celebrate the funeral rites.

The machinery of international order can be effective, then, only to the extent that great powers would rather sacrifice their interests than fight about them. The immediate need is for a system which can settle a dispute by exploring the balance of interests and powers, to find a solution which the powerful states are prepared to back. It will not necessarily be a just solution. If one of the great powers has an interest in a state's friendship, that state will fare better than another which is of interest to none of them. Under present conditions, international organization can aim at conciliation; failing that, it can seek to contain a dispute, to prevent it spreading into a major war; it can seek to end minor hostilities once they have begun. But it can hardly aspire to justice, where every member of the jury is an interested party, and does not hestitate to behave like one. There are some tribes where disputes are settled according to the number of kinsmen each of the litigants can muster to testify under oath on his behalf. That system shares with the United Nations Organization the virtue that it gives peacefully the decision for which the stronger party might otherwise be ready to fight. What is important in both cases is not that the system often works unjustly, but that it works at all. For the alternative in each case might be war.

Is there any chance that out of this, something more stable might emerge? Two conditions might favour such a development. Firstly, there is a greater reluctance than ever before to risk a major war. Great powers can no longer contemplate war as a rational way of satisfying their own aspirations, nor is it even a rational way of preventing others from satisfying theirs. Secondly, the United Nations, for all its weakness, provides machinery for seeking acceptable compromises. Furthermore, the group of smaller states uncommitted to the rival blocs have an interest in the principle of non-interference; and because they are worth courting, the greater powers must show an interest in it too. Admittedly, power often counts for more than justice in settling disputes, especially since the criteria of justice are themselves in dispute. Nevertheless, states have to give reasons and answer criticisms; and because they have to justify themselves in a public forum, there is likely to be a search for generally acceptable criteria in terms of which a case can be made out.

International controversies, like industrial disputes, are now regularly conducted by appeals to moral principles. No doubt the discussion is often a decent veil disguising a preoccupation with interest and power. Often, indeed, it is not discussion at all, but the mere exchange of abuse. But the fact that it occurs, and that it uses the forms of moral argument, is a tribute to a growing world opinion which applies moral tests to international politics, and is no longer prepared to accept national interest as a final justification.

NOTES

NOTES TO CHAPTER I

1. For discussion of this and related points about social wholes and the methods of the social sciences see K. R. Popper, *The Poverty of Historicism* (1957).

2. For a fuller treatment of the distinction between nature and convention see K. R. Popper, *The Open Society and Its Enemies*, Vol. 1, Ch. 5 (1957).

3. For elaboration of the point that the concept of 'action' involves the notion of standards and cannot, therefore be analysed in terms of mere movements, responses to stimuli, and so on, see R. S. Peters, *The Concept of Motivation* (1958), passim—especially Ch. 1.

4. There is a great deal more to be said about the concept of 'authority' which is not strictly relevant to the theme presented in this chapter. See R. S. Peters, *Authority*, in symposium on the subject in Proc. Aristotelian Soc., Supp. Vol. XXXII, (1958).

5. T. Hobbes, *Leviathan* (Ed. Oakeshott), pp. 105–6.

6. B. de Jouvenel, *Sovereignty* (1957), pp. 29–31.

7. M. Weber, *Theory of Economic and Social Organization* (tr. Talcott Parsons, 1947). pp. 300–1.

8. Op. cit., p. 301.

9. T. D. Weldon, *The Vocabulary of Politics* (1953), p. 56.

10. See B. de Jouvenel, op. cit., Chs. 2 and 3.

11. Students requiring a fuller consideration of the major social codes should consult a text-book like R. M. MacIver and C. Page, *Society* (1949), Bk. 11, Part 1.

12. For stimulating sketches on this back-ground see R. H. Tawney, *Religion and the Rise of Capitalism* (1926), Ch. I, Sec. 1, and Ch. IV, Sec. 1, and E. Fromm, *The Fear of Freedom* (1942), Ch. III.

13. See R. S. Peters, *Hobbes* (1956), Ch. VIII.

14. One of the earliest classical discussions of this is in Bks. 1 and 2 of Plato's *Republic*.

15. For fuller treatment of the concept of the 'law of nature' at this period see G. H. Sabine, *History of Political Theory* (1951), Ch. VIII.

16. A. D'Entreves, *Natural Law* (1951), should be consulted for an account of the development of natural law.

17. See L. T. Hobhouse, *Morals in Evolution* (7th ed. M. Ginsberg, 1951), Chs. VI, VII.

NOTES TO CHAPTER 2

1. See J. Piaget, *The Moral Judgment of the Child* (1932).

2. See G. H. Sabine, *History of Political Theory* (1937), Ch. VIII.

3. See G. H. Sabine, op. cit., Ch. XXI.

4. See G. H. Sabine, op. cit., Ch. XXVI.

5. For the use to which Hobbes put the concept of the law of nature see R. Peters, *Hobbes* (1956), Ch. VIII.

6. H. Sidgwick's *The Methods of Ethics* (1874), Bk. III, distinguishes these different types of intuitionism and is probably the most careful and competent exposition of the intuitionist and utilitatian approaches to ethics.

7. D. Hume, *Treatise on Human Nature*, Part III.

8. For the classical refutation of this type of theory see G. E. Moore, *Ethics* (1912), Chs. III, IV.

9. J. Butler, *Sermons on Human Nature*, I, II, III, and XI.

10. I. Kant, *Groundwork of the Metaphysic of Morals* (Ed. Paton, *The Moral Law* [1948]).

11. For a brief discussion of Kant's categorical imperative see S. Korner, *Kant* (1955), Ch. VI. For fuller treatment see H. Paton, *The Categorical Imperative* (1946), R. Hare, *Universalizability*, Proc. Aris. Soc., Vol. LIV, 1954–5, and J. Harrison, *Kant's Examples of the First Formulation of the Categorical Imperative*, Philosophical Quarterly, Vol. 7, No. 26, Jan. 1957.

12. H. Sidgwick, *The Methods of Ethics*, Bk. III, Chs. 5 and 13.

13. For fuller discussion of this see A. P. Griffiths, *Justifying Moral Principles*, Proc. Aris. Soc. LVIII, 1957–8.

14. See R. Hare, *The Language of Morals* (1952), Chs. VII and VIII, and P. Nowell-Smith, *Ethics* (1954), Chs. V, VII, VIII.

15. See S. E. Toulmin, *The Place of Reason in Ethics* (1950), Part III, to which the view of ethics here put forward owes much, and also R. Peters, *Nature and Convention in Morality*. Proc. Arist. Soc., 1950–51 where some of the views here developed were even more crudely adumbrated.

16. See J. O. Urmson's most important article on 'The Interpretation of the Moral Philosophy of J. S. Mill'. *Philosophical Quarterly*, Vol. 3 No. 10. January, 1953.

NOTES TO CHAPTER 3

1. *English Law and the Moral Law* (1953), p. 19.

2. Ibid., pp. 27–28.

3. Ibid., pp. 28–37.

4. *Principles of Social and Political Theory* (1951).

5. *Lectures on the Principles of Political Obligation*, esp. Sec. G; 'Will, not Force, is the basis of the State'.

6. A. Hägerström: *Inquiries into the Nature of Law and Morals* (ed. by Karl Olivecrona, trans. by C. D. Broad, 1953), p. 65 (quoted by Goodhart, op. cit., pp. 23–24, with approval).

7. Cf. Hägerström, loc. cit.: 'When a person's own interests are not involved the conviction of law brings about directly a reaction against the infringer . . . the pressure which fear of this reaction exerts on the individual . . . together with (his) own conviction of law, also has the effect that within certain limits the thought of the possibility of acting against what one takes to be the positive law simply does not arise.'

8. Goodhart: op. cit., pp. 26 ff.

9. Op. cit. The argument is summarized in Bk. V., Sec. 5.

10. Cf. H. L. A. Hart: *The Ascription of Responsibility and Rights*, Aristotelian Society, Proceedings, 1948–9, p. 171, also in A. Flew (ed.): *Logic and Language*, Vol. I, 1951, and O. C. Jensen: *The Nature of Legal Argument* (1957), Pt. I.

11. Cf. the title of the seventeenth century pamphlet advocating tyrannicide, 'Killing Noe Murder' (Edward Saxby, 1655).

12. J. L. Montrose: *Legal Theory for Politicians and Sociologists*, Political Studies, Vol. III, 1955, p. 214n.

13. See J. C. Rees: *The Limitations of Political Theory*, Political Studies, Vol. II, 1954, pp. 242–57; T. D. Weldon: *The Vocabulary of Politics* (1953), p. 57, and pp. 61–62; Margaret Macdonald: 'The Language of Political Theory' (read as a paper to the Aristotelian Society 1940–41), reprinted in A. G. N. Flew (ed.): *Logic and Language* (1951).

14. Cf. Roscoe Pound's account of the way in which legal theory has developed throughout the centuries, in response to the different conditions in which the legal process has operated, in *Introduction to the Philosophy of Law* (rev. ed., 1954).

15. *The Province of Jurisprudence Determined* (ed. H. L. A. Hart, 1954), p. 2.

16. Ibid., p. 14.

17. Ibid., p. 24.

18. Ibid., p. 194.

19. Cf. R. Wollheim, op. cit., and H. L. A. Hart's introduction to Austin, op. cit.

20. For Austin's own rather complicated answer to this objection, see op. cit., pp. 245f. Its weakness is precisely that dealt with above in the paragraph following, namely, that the sovereign is determinate only in legal terms.

21. Ibid., p. 147.

22. Cf. G. Marshall: *What is Parliament? The Changing Concept of Parliamentary Sovereignty*, Political Studies, Vol. II, 1954, pp. 193–209. Also, S. I. Benn: *The Uses of 'Sovereignty'*, Political Studies, Vol. III, 1955, pp. 109–22.

23. H. Kelsen: *General Theory of Law and State* (1945), p. 124. For short expositions of Kelsen's doctrines, see his *The Pure Theory of Law*, 50 L.Q.R , p. 474, and 51 L.Q.R., p. 517. Also H. Lauterpacht, *Kelsen's Pure Science of Law*, in W. I. Jennings (ed.): *Modern Theories of Law* (1933), p. 105.

24. Kelsen, op. cit., p. 114.

25. Cf. A. L. Goodhart, op. cit., p. 16: 'It does not attempt to explain the existence of the basic norm on which the whole legal system is founded . . . But without an adequate foundation no legal system can stand . . . so that a theory of law which merely takes this foundation for granted can be of little value.' But that depends on what it is setting out to do; whether it is of value will depend on the reader's interests.

26. Kelsen, op. cit., p. 116.

27. Ibid., p. 120.

28. Cf. R. Wollheim, op. cit., p. 135 n.4.

29. Kelsen, op. cit., p. 363 and p. 375.

30. Ibid., p. 135 'Statutes and customary laws are, so to speak, only semi-manufactured products which are finished only through the judicial decision and its execution. The process through which law constantly creates itself anew goes from the general and abstract to the individual and concrete. It is a process of steadily increasing individualization and concretization.'

31. Cf. H. L. A. Hart's Introduction to Austin, op. cit., pp. xiii–xiv.

32. 'The prophecies of what the courts will do in fact, and nothing more pretentious are what I mean by law.' O. W. Holmes: *Path of the Law* (1897), 10 Harv. L. Rev. 457, reprinted in *Collected Papers* (1920), 167. It is significant, however, that Holmes was addressing himself in this passage to an audience who

viewed the law mainly from the standpoint of the legal adviser, not from that of the judge.

33. See B. Cardozo: *Nature of the Judicial Process* (1921).

34. *Law and the Modern Mind* (1930). The English edition of 1949 has a preface in which Frank reviews his position and answers critics. See also K. N. Llewellyn: *Some Realism about Realism* (1931), 44 Harv. L. Rev. 1222.

35. E. H. Levi: *An Introduction to Legal Reasoning* (1949), p. 2.

36. J. Frank, op. cit., pp. ixf. distinguishes the 'rule skeptics', who attribute the uncertainties of law merely to the considerations noted above, and 'fact-skeptics' (including himself), who are even more impressed by the uncertainty of what facts judge or jury will 'find' on the evidence. Not only is there doubt about the scope of the major premise, the rule, there is doubt about the minor, the particular fact to which the rule is said to apply. He rightly points out that findings of fact and law cannot be separated in this way. (See also H. L. A. Hart, *The Ascription of Responsibility and Rights*, loc. cit., on this point.)

37. H. J. Laski: *Grammar of Politics* (5th ed., 1948), p. vi: 'Granted its postulates, I believe the pure theory of law to be unanswerable, but I believe also that its substance is an exercise in logic and not in life . . . a jurisprudence of formal concepts now satisfies few save the veterans of an earlier age.' Professor H. Lauterpacht, loc. cit., criticizes Kelsen for not recognizing the part of natural law in judicial interpretation; Professor Goodhart, op. cit., pp. 17–18, for not showing what makes law 'obligatory'.

38. J. Stone: *Province and Function of Law* (1950), p. 110.

39. Cf. Kelsen's reply to Ehrlich's objection, that since individuals comply with law from other motives, coercion cannot be an essential element in law: 'This doctrine does not refer to the actual motives of the behaviour of the individuals subjected to the legal order, but to its content, to the specific means used by the legal order to bring about a certain behaviour of the individuals, to the specific technique of this social order . . . to the fact that the legal order provides for sanctions and that by this very fact . . . is it distinguished from other social orders.' Kelsen, op. cit., p. 25.

40. Cf. ibid., p. 31: 'A command is binding . . . because the individual commanding . . . is "authorized" or "empowered" to issue commands of a binding nature. And he is so "authorized" or "empowered" only if a normative order, which is presupposed to be binding, confers on him this capacity, the competence to issue binding commands.' The 'because' is misleading; Kelsen is not offering a *reason* why a command is binding, of the sort that Professor Goodhart is seeking; he is elucidating what it means to say that a command is binding.

41. See Note 39, supra. This would have been less misleading had Kelsen said that what characterizes a legal order is not the 'specific means used . . . to bring about a certain behaviour', but 'the logical form of its rules, such that a sanction is consequent upon a delict'. Note that Kelsen defines the sanction as a 'reaction of the legal order against the delict' (op. cit., p. 20); this rather suggests that the sanction is always effective. Elsewhere, however, he denies that *every* norm need be effective: effectiveness is required only of the system generally (ibid., p. 42). For the effectiveness of the sanction is not really in question; it is important only as a formal characteristic of a 'complete' legal rule. Kelsen uses a stipulative definition of 'legal order' that limits it to effective orders; it follows therefore that *most* of the sanctions of a 'legal order' in this sense would have to be effective. There is a certain perverseness in Professor Goodhart's comment on this point (op. cit., p. 16).

NOTES TO CHAPTER 4

1. Max Radin: *A Restatement of Hohfeld*, 51 Harvard Law Review, p. 1141 (quoted by G. B. J. Hughes: *Jurisprudence:* p. 351).

2. *Tractatus Politicus:* II. 4 and III. 2.

3. Cf. H. Warrender: *The Political Philosophy of Hobbes* (1957), especially Chs. VIII and XI.

4. *Province of Jurisprudence Determined* ('Library of Ideas' ed. with intro. by H. L. A. Hart, 1954), p. 285n.

5. H. L. A. Hart: *Definition and Theory in Jurisprudence*, Law Q. Rev., Vol. 70 (1954), p. 43.

6. A. Hägerström: *Inquiries into the Nature of Law and Morals* (tr. by C. D. Broad, 1953), p. 1.

7. Ibid., p. 16.

8. Cf. W. D. Lamont, in Symposium on *Rights* (with J. Plamenatz and H. B. Acton) in Aristotelian Soc. Sup. Vol. XXIV (1950).

9. 'What you have a right to have me made to do (understand a political right) is that which I am liable, according to law, upon a requisit n made on your behalf, to be *punished* for not doing. I say *punished*; for withou the notion of punishment . . . no notion can we have of either *right or duty*.' *F gment on Government* (1776), in Blackwell ed. by W. Harrison, 1948, p. 106, note 1, paras 2 and 3. Bentham recognizes other types of duty, besides political duty, in this section (i.e. 'moral', in the sense of conventional, and 'religious' duties), but, like Austin, he makes them depend on sanctions of appropriate types. If these duties give rise to rights, the latter would also have to be defined in terms of sanctions. Nevertheless, in the *Constitutional Code* (Wks. Vol. IX, p. 19), he is prepared to speak of 'original or primary right which has place antecedently to the formation of government . . . no man, as yet, being under any obligation to abstain from making use of anything, every man has, as yet, a right to make every use of everything'. This is equivalent to Hobbes' natural right. His attitude to natural rights in Locke's sense, however, is quite clear: 'Right . . . is the child of law: from real laws come real rights; but from imaginary laws, from laws of nature, fancied and invented by poets, rhetoricians, and dealers in moral and intellectual poisons, come imaginary rights, a bastard brood of monsters, . . . Natural rights is simple nonsense: natural and imprescriptable rights, rhetorical nonsense—nonsense upon stilts. But this rhetorical nonsense ends in the old strain of mischievous nonsense: for immediately a list of the pretended natural rights is given, and those are so expressed as to present to view legal rights.' *Anarchical Fallacies*, Wks. Vol. II, pp. 501–2, 523.

10. A. P. D'Entreves: *Natural Law* (1951), p. 59.

11. *Second Treatise*, Ch. VI, 61.

12. This is the substance of Burke's criticism: 'The moment you abate anything from the full rights of men, each to govern himself, and suffer any artificial, positive limitation upon those rights, from that moment the whole organization of government becomes a consideration of convenience.' *Reflections on the Revolution in France*, Wks. Vol. II (Bohn), p. 333. 'The pretended rights of these theorists (i.e. natural rights) are all extremes: in proportion as they are metaphysically true, they are morally and politically false. The rights of men are in a sort of *middle*, incapable of definition, but not impossible to be discerned. The rights of men in governments are their advantages; and these are often in balance between differences of good; in compromises sometimes between good and evil, and sometimes between evil and evil. Political reason is a

computing principle; adding, subtracting, multiplying and dividing, morally and not metaphysically, or mathematically, true moral denominations.' Ibid., p. 335.

13. *Lectures on Political Obligation*, para 144. Cf. B. Bosanquet *Philosophical Theory of the State*, Ch. VIII, 6.

14. *Grammar of Politics* (5th ed., 1948), p. 94.

15. Ibid., p. 95.

16. See *Human Rights*, a symposium prepared by UNESCO, 1949. The Declaration appears as an appendix.

17. H. L. A. Hart: *The Ascription of Responsibility and Rights*, in Aristotelian Society Proceedings 1948–9, p. 189 [reprinted in A. Flew (ed.): *Logic and Language*, Vol. I, 1951].

18. Benedetto Croce questioned the wisdom and utility of producing any declaration that could command assent from men of all opinions. In replying to the UNESCO Committee of Experts he wrote: 'A working organization . . . in which representatives of all currents, especially the two most directly opposed, will participate . . . cannot possibly proclaim in the form of a declaration of rights, a declaration of common political action, an agreement which has no existence . . . Nor do I even see how it would be possible to formulate any half-way or compromise declaration which would not prove either empty or arbitrary . . .' He warned against 'the danger of causing readers to smile at the ingenuousness of men who have conceived and formulated such a declaration'. *Human Rights*, p. 94.

19. Cf. Field J. in Butcher's Union Co. v. Crescent City Co. (1883), 111 U.S. 756: 'As in our intercourse with our fellow men certain principles of morality are assumed to exist without which society would be impossible, so certain inherent rights lie at the foundation of all action, and upon a recognition of them alone can free institutions be maintained' [Quoted by J. Stone: *Province and Function of Law* (1950), p. 252].

20. In the Adkins Case, the Supreme Court of the U.S. declared unconstitutional a minimum wage act for women employees in the District of Columbia. Mr Justice Sutherland, delivering judgment, admitted there could be no absolute liberty of contract; nevertheless, 'freedom of contract is . . . the general rule and restraint the exception, and the exercise of legislative authority to abridge it can be justified only by the existence of exceptional circumstances' (1922). 261 U.S. 545 (Quoted by J. Stone, op. cit., pp. 253–4).

21. Cf. R. Pound: *Liberty of Contract* (1909), 18 Yale L. Jo. 454 (cited by J. Stone, op. cit., p. 253).

NOTES TO CHAPTER 5

1. *Second Treatise of Civil Government*, Chap. II (Everyman edn. pp. 118–19).

2. L. T. Hobhouse: *Elements of Social Justice* (1922), p. 95.

3. Ibid., p. 109.

4. See Chapter 6, below, for a fuller discussion of 'needs'.

5. Cf. E. F. Carritt: *Ethical and Political Thinking* (1947), p. 156: 'Equality of consideration is the only thing to the whole of which men have a right.' And p. 157: 'It is just to treat men as equal until some reason, other than preference, such as need, capacity, or desert, has been shown to the contrary.'

6. See Chapter 3, sec. III, above, for a discussion of moral maxims and

formulae of a high order of generality, and of the procedures adopted in moral discussion.

7. See the Putney Debates, in A. S. P. Woodhouse (ed.), *Puritanism and Liberty* (1938), e.g. pp. 55–59, and passim.

8. But see D. Daiches Raphael: *Justice and Liberty*, Aristotelian Society, Proceedings, 1950–51, pp. 167–97, for another view. Mr Raphael considers that 'equality' can constitute a positive ground of claim, and that claims based on special needs are directed to making equal what nature has made unequal. 'Need' as a criterion of distinction is discussed below, in the next chapter. See also a symposium on *Equality*, by R. Wollheim and I. Berlin, in Aristotelian Society, Proceedings, 1955–6. I. Berlin believes that the 'ideal limit or idealized model at the heart of all egalitarian thought' is a society in which not only will everyone be treated alike, but in which natural differences will have been ironed out; but that 'when the pursuit of equality comes into conflict with other human aims . . . it is only the most fanatical egalitarian that will demand that such conflicts invariably be decided in favour of equality alone, with relative disregard of the other "values" concerned' (pp. 315 and 319). Such fanatics may exist; but in our view, the important egalitarian movements have not thought in this way. It has not been a question of compromising with a total egalitarianism for the sake of other values, but of attacking existing inequalities on a much narrower front. The two positions are theoretically reconcilable; but we believe that a negative interpretation corresponds more closely to the pattern of actual egalitarian thinking.

9. We treat these questions more fully in Chapters 6 and 7.

10. Cf. *Towards Equality—Labour's Policy for Social Justice* (submitted to the Annual Conference of the Labour Party, 1956): 'A classless society and our present pattern of education cannot be reconciled.' Of public schools: 'The broad effect is to heighten social barriers, to stimulate class consciousness, and to foster social snobbery.'

11. *Principles of Social and Political Theory* (1951), Bk. IV, Sec. 3.

12. H. Kelsen: *General Theory of Law and State* (1945), p. 93.

13. L. T. Hobhouse, op. cit., p. 104.

14. See Chapter VIII, below, for a fuller discussion of the criteria for punishment.

15. L. T. Hobhouse, op. cit., p. 103.

16. Ibid., pp. 102–3.

17. Cf. B. Cardozo: *The Nature of the Judicial Process* (1921). For case studies illustrating the evolution of legal categories through judicial interpretation, see E. H. Levi: *An Introduction to Legal Reasoning* (1949). See also Chapter 3, Secs. III (b) and IV (a), above.

18. A. V. Dicey: *Law of the Constitution* (9th edn. by E. C. S. Wade, 1941), pp. 202–3. See also Intro. Sec. 3 and App. I. Cf. W. I. Jennings, *The Law and the Constitution* (4th edn., 1952). Ch. VI, Sec. 2, and App. II, for a detailed criticism of Dicey's views. See also C. J. Hamson: *Executive Discretion and Judicial Control* (1954), for a comparative treatment of English and French administrative justice.

19. See Aristotle's *Politics*, Bk. III, passim.

20. The Home Secretary, however, enjoys an absolute discretion in exercising the prerogative of mercy, and in dealing with the naturalization of aliens. Whatever criteria he employs are entirely his own concern.

21. Cf. Aristotle: 'Laws, when good, should be supreme; and . . . the magis-

trates should regulate those matters only on which the laws are unable to speak with precision owing to the difficulty of any general principle embracing all the particulars.' *Politics*, III, 11.

22. See *Report of the Committee on Ministers' Powers*, 1932 (Cmd. 4060), pp. 75–80.

23. Ibid., pp. 73–75, and elsewhere. On the matters discussed in this section, see *Report of the Committee on Administrative Tribunals and Enquiries* (Cmnd. 218), 1957; W. I. Jennings, op. cit.; and W. Robson, *Justice and Administrative Law* (3rd. edn., 1951), and E. C. S. Wade and G. G. Phillips: *Constitutional Law* (5th edn., 1955), Pt. VII.

24. The problem is illustrated by the Stanley-Belcher case; see *Report of the Tribunal appointed to inquire into Allegations reflecting on the Official Conduct of Ministers of the Crown and other Public Servants* (Lynskey Tribunal), 1949 (Cmd. 7616). See also *Report of the Committee on Intermediaries*, 1950 (Cmd. 7904), dealing with the general issues to which the case drew attention, and especially pp. 34–39.

25. See, for example, H. J. Laski: *Parliamentary Government in England* (1938), Ch. VII.

NOTES TO CHAPTER 6

1. The application of ethical criteria to wage fixing is not a peculiarity of the twentieth century. Mediaeval ideas on economics were regularly couched in moral terms; and Professor R. H. Tawney's classic, *Religion and the Rise of Capitalism* (1926), is largely concerned with the evolution of moral attitudes to economic questions during the early capitalist period.

2. A study of the leader and correspondence columns of *The Times* during the strike of locomotive engineers, of June, 1955, will provide ample illustration. Some writers assert categorically 'that a skilled man is worth more to the community than an unskilled man . . .' that every person's earnings beyond an essential minimum 'shall depend on the skill and the value of the work done' (Letter from Mr St John Ervine, June 7, 1955). Still more categorical, 'Senior firemen . . . should not take home less than £7 for a full week's work' (Mr Frank Jacques, June 6, 1955).

3. Cf. Mr St. John Ervine, loc. cit.: 'No one ought to have the folly to say that an engine-driver, on whose skill and courage and general ability the lives of many passengers depend, is not of far greater worth to the rest of us than a man whose chief ability is to carry suitcases.'

4. Cf. H. J. Laski: *Grammar of Politics* (5th ed.), pp. 190–4.

5. Cf. B. de Jouvenel: *Ethics of Redistribution* (1952), p. 56 n.: 'in the case of surpluses', over income necessary to maintain function, 'it is plausible to argue that more "surplus" is called for in the case of the most distasteful labours'.

6. The point is made by Thorstein Veblen: *The Theory of the Leisure Class* (1925) Ch. V. and is given practical application in R. Lewis and A. Maude, *The English Middle Classes* (1949).

7. 'In a higher phase of communist society, after the enslaving subordination of individuals under division of labour, and therewith also the antithesis between mental and physical labour, has vanished, after labour has become not merely a means to live but has become itself the primary necessity of life, after the productive forces have also increased with the all-round development of the individual, and all the springs of co-operative wealth flow more abundantly—only then can the narrow horizon of bourgeois right be fully left behind and society in-

scribe on its banners: from each according to his ability, to each according to his needs'. Karl Marx: *Critique of the Gotha Programme* (Selected Works Vol. 2 [1942], p. 566). By 'bourgeois right', he meant: 'The right of the producers is *proportional* to the labour they supply; the equality consists in the fact that measurement is made with an *equal standard*, labour . . . This *equal* right is an unequal right for unequal labour . . . it tacitly recognizes unequal individual endowment and thus productive capacity as natural privileges' (p. 564). Marx seems to be saying that while in an imperfect society 'desert' criteria are relevant to income distribution, they will not be so in the perfect society of the future, when the only relevant criteria will be 'needs'. Cf. V. I. Lenin: *State and Revolution* (*Essentials of Lenin*, Vol. 2, p. 207) ' . . . when people have become so accustomed to observing the fundamental rules of social intercourse and when their labour is so productive that they will voluntarily work *according to their ability* . . . "The narrow horizon of bourgeois right" . . . will then be left behind. There will then be no need for society to regulate the quantity of products to be distributed to each; each will take freely "according to his needs".' The hypothesis rests on the doubtful assumption that the demand for all commodities at zero price is finite.

8. For fuller analysis of concept of 'need' see R. S. Peters, *The Concept of Motivation* (1958), pp. 17–18, 104–6.

9. March 24, 1953.

10. Op. cit., p. 54.

11. e.g. Barbara Wootton's comment on *The Times* view (*Social Foundations of Wage Policy* [1955], p. 129): 'Justice, it seems, must be rich as well as blind: travel by bus would threaten her—but not by Rolls-Royce.'

12. Barbara Wootton notes (op. cit., pp. 130–1) only one case in which the criterion was challenged by the employers' side. On that occasion, it was argued that the tribunal had no concern with living standards as such; their job was to assess 'the remuneration appropriate to services rendered'. What constituted a 'proper standard of life' was a matter of 'national concern and can be, and is being, achieved without interference with the principles upon which employment and remuneration are based'. See also P. Ford, *The Economics of Collective Bargaining* (1958), esp. pp. 85–106, for a very useful discussion of these problems.

13. Cmd. 9084 (1954). See also Report of Court of Inquiry into the engineering dispute of 1957 (Cmnd. 59), Secs. 39–60.

14. Op. cit., p. 120, and in a letter to *The Times*, June 4, 1955.

NOTES TO CHAPTER 7

1. The Fifth Amendment to the U.S. Constitution declares 'No person shall be . . . deprived of life, liberty, or property, without due process of law; nor shall private property be taken for public use, without just compensation.' Art. 17 of the Declaration of the Rights of Man of 1789 declares: 'The right to property being inviolable and sacred, no-one ought to be deprived of it, except in cases of evident public necessity, legally ascertained, and on condition of a previous just indemnity.'

2. See UNESCO symposium *Human Rights*, 1949, p. 269.

3. R. H. Tawney: *The Acquisitive Society* (1921). Chapter V.

4. Cf. Quintin Hogg: *The Case for Conservatism* (1947): 'No man is fully free unless possessing some rights of property in something, since property is the means whereby he develops his personality by impressing it upon his external surroundings without dependence on the will of others. No degree of security, no ration scale however generous, no organized hostelry with furniture

and services all provided, no uniform clothing however lavish or becoming is a substitute for property. Property is in itself a good and a legitimate aspiration for human striving.' Few since Plato have challenged this argument, as applied to personal goods. The harnessing of the argument to property in general, however, is a failure to see an obvious distinction.

Most of the arguments mentioned above occur in Chap. 18 of Mr Hogg's book, and are used in this way.

5. Cf. Martin Buber: *Paths in Utopia* (1949), p. 70. ' . . . it is readily understandable from the facts that a champion of the Consumer Co-operative Societies should call the Producer Co-operatives which work for the open market "thoroughly unsocialistic in spirit and essence", because "producers, set up by and for themselves, always and in all circumstances have separatist, individualist or cliquish interests".' Chap. VII of Professor Buber's book demonstrates the sad tendency of experiments in industrial organization to fall away from the altruistic purpose of their founders.

6. This is a recurrent theme in the writings of the Socialist pioneers, e.g. Charles Fourier: 'Every person engaged in an industry is at war with the mass, and malevolent toward it from personal interest. A physician wishes his fellow citizens good, genuine cases of fevers, and an attorney good lawsuits in every family. An architect has need of a good conflagration which would reduce a quarter of the city to ashes, and a glazier desires a good hailstorm which should break all the panes of glass' (quoted by Sir Alexander Gray *The Socialist Tradition* [1947], p. 177). Robert Owen: 'From this principle of individual interest have arisen all the divisions of mankind . . . creating the angry and malevolent passions, and all the crimes and misery with which the human race have been hitherto afflicted' ('Report to Lanark' (Everyman ed.), p. 269— quoted by Alexander Gray, op. cit., p. 210) V. Considerant: 'Nous vivons dans un monde où les hommes se spolient à peu près sur tous les points où ils se touchant' (*Destinée Sociale*—quoted in Paul Louis: *Cent Cinquante Ans de Pensée Socialiste* (1947)].

7. Professor R. H. Tawney summarizes the ideal thus: 'What the working class movement stands for is obviously the ideal of social justice and solidarity, as a corrective to the exaggerated emphasis on individual advancement through the acquisition of wealth. It is a faith in the possibility of a society in which a higher value will be set on human beings, and a lower value on money and economic power' (*Equality* [rev. ed., 1951], p. 28). B. de Jouvenel, no friend to socialism, recognizes the moral force of the ideal, which he calls 'a joyful acceptance of . . . interdependence; it is that men, called to serve one another ever increasingly by economic progress and division of labour, should do so 'in newness of spirit', not as the 'old' man did who grudgingly 'measured his service against his reward', but as a 'new' man who finds his delight in the welfare of his brethren' (*Ethics of Redistribution* [1952], p. 8). Both Professor Tawney and M. de Jouvenel recognize that the movement sometimes falls away from the ideal; the former writes: 'When it does so, what it is apt to desire is not a social order of a different kind, in which money and economic power will no longer be the criterion of achievement, but a social order of the same kind, in which money and economic power will be somewhat differently distributed' (op. cit., p. 28). It is redistribution of this type, rather than the idealism of the pioneers, that is the target of M. de Jouvenel's criticism.

8. Every monastic community, says M. de Jouvenel, is 'based not upon economic independence but upon a fraternal partaking of the common produce,

and inspired by the deep-seated feeling that its members are of one family'. Its ideal differs from the Socialists', however, in that 'material goods are shared without question *because* they are spurned. The members of the community are not anxious to increase their individual well-being at the expense of one another, but then they are not very anxious to increase it *at all*. Their appetites are not addressed to scarce material commodities, and thus competitive; they are addressed to God, who is infinite. "Socialism" . . . seeks to restore sharing as amongst brothers without contempt for worldly goods . . . (yet) if "more goods" are the goal to which society's efforts are to be addressed, why should "more goods" be a disreputable objective for the individual?' (op. cit., pp. 11–12).

9. See R. H. Tawney: *Religion and the Rise of Capitalism* (1926), on the transition from mediaeval to modern views of 'usury'.

10. Cf. A. Cairncross: *Introduction to Economics* (1944), p. 257: '(Interest) is paid to some people rather than to others, because some people own capital while others do not. If we wish to justify interest *payments*, therefore, we must first justify these differences in ownership . . . (which) are an integral part of the capitalist system. Until we have considered the merits of capitalism, therefore, it is difficult to decide on the merits of one of its chief by-products—inequality. For we may judge that inequality is not too high a price to pay for the advantages listed by the apologists for capitalism . . .'

11. Cf. James Harrington's proposal in *Oceana* (1659) to restrict inheritance, to guard against the social and political instability produced by the accumulation of huge fortunes.

12. Op. cit., pp. 71–72. 'An innovator as bold today as he was in his day would not get by the boards of control which administer public funds. Nor is this scandalous: it is not the business of those who administer the common chest to subsidize bold ideas. These have to be offered on the market for ideas by convinced venturers.'

13. Cf. R. H. Tawney *Equality* (rev. ed. 1951), p. 39: 'Equality of provision is not identity of provision. It is to be achieved, not by treating different needs in the same way, but by devoting equal care to ensuring that they are met in the different ways most appropriate to them . . . The more anxiously, indeed, a society endeavours to secure equality of consideration for its members, the greater will be the differentiation of treatment which, when once these common human needs have been met, it accords to the special needs of different groups and individuals among them.'

NOTES TO CHAPTER 8

1. A. Flew 'The Justification of Punishment', in *Philosophy*, Vol. XXIX, 1954, pp. 291–307.

2. *Introduction to the Principles of Morals and Legislation* (ed., W. Harrison, 1948), Ch. XIII, Sec. I, 2, p. 281.

3. Ibid., loc. cit., n. 1.

4. Quoted by F. H. Bradley: *Ethical Studies* (2nd edn., 1927), p. 28 n.l. (and see also p. 57 n.l.), from I. Kant *Die Metaphysik der Sitten*.

5. See *Philosophy of Right* (trans. by T. M. Knox, 1942). Secs. 97 and 99, and Addition No. 61. A. M. Quinton in his 'On Punishment', in *Philosophy, Politics, and Society* (ed. P. Laslett, 1956), p. 84 comments: 'The doctrine of "annulment" . . . is clearly utilitarian in principle. For it holds that the function of punishment is to bring about a state of affairs in which it is as if the wrongful act had never happened. This is to justify punishment by its effects, by the

desirable future consequences which it brings about.' See also the discussion
in A. C. Ewing: *The Morality of Punishment* (1929), pp. 24–25.

6. Cmd. 8932, Sec. 53 (1953).

7. Thus Sir Ernest Barker, in *Principles of Social and Political Theory*
(1951), p. 182: 'the mental rule of law which pays back a violation of itself by a
violent return, much as the natural rules of health pay back a violation of themselves by a violent return'. The persuasive pun on 'violation' and 'violence' is
misleading—the relation is one of sound, not of sense.

8. J. D. Mabbott makes a point rather like this when he asserts ('Punishment'
in *Mind*, Vol. 48, 1939, p. 161) that any particular act of punishment must be
justified retributively, and that 'punishment is a corollary not of law but of law-
breaking. Legislators do not *choose* to punish. They hope no punishment will be
needed . . . The criminal makes the essential choice; he "brings it on himself".' But considerations of utility come in on two quite different issues. Should
there be laws, and what laws should there be? . . . The choice which is the
essential *prius* of punishment is the choice that there should be laws.' And in
Mabbott's view a characteristic difference between laws and attempts to stand-
ardize conduct by advice or requests is that the former threaten punishment. (See
also J. D. Mabbott: 'Freewill and Punishment' in *Contemporary British Philosophy*, 3rd Series [ed. H. D. Lewis, 1956], p. 303.)

9. B. Bosanquet: *The Philosophical Theory of the State* (1923 edn.), p. 211.
Cf. Hegel, op. cit., Sec. 100: 'The injury which falls on the criminal is not merely
implicitly just—as just, it is *eo ipso* his implicit will, an embodiment of his freedom, his right . . .' 'Punishment is regarded as containing the criminal's right and
hence by being punished he is honoured as a rational being. He does not receive
this due honour unless the concept and measure of his punishment are derived
from his own act. Still less does he receive it if he is treated either as a harmful
animal who has to be made harmless, or with a view to deterring and reforming
him.' And see Sec. 220.

10. Cf. Bosanquet, op. cit., pp. 209–210: 'If a man is told that the way he
works his factory . . . is rendering him liable to fine or imprisonment, then, if he
is an ordinary, careless, but respectable citizen, he will feel something of a shock,
and recognize that he was getting too neglectful of the rights of others, and that, in
being pulled up, he is brought back to himself.' This is plainly a utilitarian argument.

11. This criticism is prompted by Bentham's assertion: 'It is the idea only
of the punishment (or, in other words, the *apparent* punishment) that really acts
upon the mind . . . It is the apparent punishment, therefore, that does all the
service, I mean in the way of example, which is the principal object' (Op. cit.,
Ch. XV, 9, p. 303). Some 'indirect utilitarians' have maintained that rules must
be observed, and punishments inflicted, even when the immediate effects are
not on balance beneficial, in order that the over-all advantage of respect for
law shall be preserved. J. D. Mabbott contends that this argument could always
be met by the injunction to 'keep the exception dark' (*Punishment*, pp. 155–7).

12. Cf. A. Quinton, op. cit.

13. *Ethical Studies* [2nd edn., 1927], pp. 26–27.

14. Op. cit., p. 86.

15. Cf. C. W. K. Mundle: *Punishment and Desert*, in Philosophical Quarterly,
Vol. 4, 1954: 'the retributive theory implies that punishment of a person by the
State is morally justifiable, if and only if he has done something which is both a
legal and a moral offence, and only if the penalty is proportionate to the moral
gravity of his offence' (p. 227).

16. Cf. Hume, in App. III to *Enquiry concerning the Principles of Morals.*

17. Op. cit.

18. Op. cit., p. 162.

19. Op. cit., Ch. XV, 11–12, pp. 303–4.

20. Cf. the discussion of the relative guilt of accomplices in Capital Punishment Report, Sec. 118.

21. Ibid., Secs. 289–295.

22. See H. L. A. Hart, 'Murder and the Principles of Punishment: England and the United States' in *Northwestern University Law Review*, Vol. 52, 1957, pp. 433–61.

NOTES TO CHAPTER 9

1. For fuller treatment see M. Cranston, *Freedom: A New Analysis* (1953), Part I.

2. See P. H. Nowell-Smith, *Ethics* (1954), Chs. 19, 20.

3. See 'Every Event has a Cause' by G. J. Warnock. Reprinted in *Logic and Language*, Vol. II (ed. Flew, 1953).

4. For further discussion see *Causal Laws in Psychology*, Proc. Aris. Soc. Supp., Vol. XXIII, 1949.

5. For fuller development of these points see R. Peters, *The Concept of Motivation* (1958), Chs. I, III.

6. See A. MacIntyre, *Determinism*, Mind LXVI, Jan., 1957.

7. See C. L. Stevenson, *Ethics and Language* (1944), Ch. 14.

8. See R. Peters, *Hobbes* (1956), Ch. 7, Part 5.

9. F. H. Bradley, *Ethical Studies* (2nd ed., 1927), Ch. 1.

10. H. L. Hart, 'The Ascription of Responsibility and Rights' (reprinted from the Proceedings of the Aristotelian Society in *Logic and Language*, Vol. I [ed. Flew, 1951].

11. See J. Bowlby, *Child Care and the Growth of Love* (1953).

12 *See Note 9 to Chapter 8.*

NOTES TO CHAPTER 10

1. *Lectures on the Principles of Political Obligation:* 'On the Different Senses of "Freedom" '—Sec. 2.

2. Cf. *Personal Freedom—Labour's Policy for the Individual and Society*, Labour Party (1956). 'To us freedom means something quite different from a mere absence of restraint', p. 6.

3. In the Preface to the Second Edition of *The Grammar of Politics* (1930), H. J. Laski wrote: 'In 1925 I thought that liberty could most usefully be regarded as more than a negative thing. I am now convinced that this was a mistake, and that the old view of it as an absence of restraint can alone safeguard the personality of the citizen.'

4. *Second Treatise of Civil Government*, Sec. 57.

5. *Spirit of the Laws*, Bk. XI, ch. III.

6. *Social Contract*, Bk. I chap VII (Everyman edn. by G. D. H. Cole, 1913), p. 17.

7. See J. Towster: *Political Power in the U.S.S.R.*, 1917-1947 (1948), pp. 184-6.

8. J. S. Mill, *On Liberty* (Everyman edn.), pp. 67–8.

9. Mill, op. cit., p. 68.

10. Ibid., pp. 150–1.

11. Ibid., pp. 72–73.

12. Ibid., p. 74.

13. *The State and the Citizen* (1948), p. 62.

14. J. Fitzjames Stephen: *Liberty, Equality, Fraternity* (1873), p. 163.

15. *A Letter Concerning Toleration* (ed. Gough, 1956), p. 152.

NOTES TO CHAPTER 11

1. *Reflections on the Revolution in France*, Wks. Vol. II (Bohn edition, 1855), p. 368.

2. For an amplification of this distinction, see S. F. Nadel: *The Foundations of Social Anthropology* (1951), Chap. V, Sec. 5.

3. See S. F. Nadel, op. cit., Chaps. VI and VII.

4. *Leviathan* (ed. M. Oakeshott), p. 107.

5. Cf. D. Emmet: *Function, Purpose and Powers* (1958), particularly Chaps. IV and V.

6. One of the best treatments of the different senses of 'function' is to be found in R. K. Merton: *Social Theory and Social Structure* (1949), Chap. I on 'Manifest and Latent Functions'. See also A. Radcliffe-Brown: *Structure and Function in Primitive Society* (1952).

7. B. Bosanquet: *The Philosophical Theory of the State* (4th edn., 1923), pp. 275 ff.

8. Cf. R. K. Merton, op. cit., Chap. VII, on 'The Self-Fulfilling Prophecy'.

9. Cf. R. M. MacIver and C. H. Page: *Society* (1949), Chaps. 1 and 10–21, for a general treatment of types of association and community. See also F. Tönnies: *Community and Association* (trans. C. P. Loomis) (1955).

10. See J. Folsom: *The Family and Democratic Society* (1948), for further treatment of the family.

11. See, for instance, A. Kardiner: *Psychological Frontiers of Society* (1945), and A. Kardiner and R. Linton: *The Individual and his Society* (1939); also the works of Margaret Mead, such as *Growing Up in New Guinea* (1930), *Coming of Age in Samoa* (1928), and G. Gorer, such as *The American People* (1948).

12. See F. Hertz: *Nationality in History and Politics* (1944); also A. Kolnai: *The War against the West* (1938).

13. For the early development of German nationalist ideas, see H. S. Reiss (ed.): *The Political Thought of the German Romantics, 1793–1815* (1955), also R. Aris: *History of Political Thought in Germany, 1789–1815* (1936), G. P. Gooch: *Germany and the French Revolution* (1920), and E. N. Anderson: *Nationalism and the Cultural Crisis in Prussia, 1806–1815* (1939).

14. See G. F. Hegel: *Philosophy of Right* (trans. T. M. Knox, 1942), Sec. 349, pp. 218–19.

15. H. Kelsen: *General Theory of Law and State* (1945), pp. 181 ff.

16. See, for instance, A. D. Lindsay: *The Modern Democratic State* (1943), p. 245; Sir Ernest Barker: *Principles of Social and Political Theory* (1951), Bk. II, passim.

NOTES TO CHAPTER 12

1. See Otto Gierke: *Political Theories of the Middle Age* (trans. F. W. Maitland) (1900), for a valuable discussion of the relations of 'State' and 'Law' in mediaeval political thought. See also R. Peters: *Hobbes* (1956), Chap. IX for further remarks on changes in the concept of 'law'.

2. For a detailed treatment of the ambiguities of 'sovereignty', see S. I. Benn: *The Uses of 'Sovereignty'*, in Pol. Studies III (1955), and W. J. Rees: *The Theory of Sovereignty Restated*, in P. Laslett (ed.): *Philosophy, Politics and Society* (1956).

3. See G. Marshall: *Parliamentary Sovereignty and the Commonwealth* (1957), for a valuable discussion of 'sovereignty' as a constitutional concept, and see Chap. XI in particular for the problems of sovereignty in South Africa.

4. Essay *Of the First Principles of Government.*

5. H. Kelsen: *General Theory of Law and State* (1945), p. 100.

6. Ibid., p. 191.

7. H. Finer: *Theory and Practice of Modern Government* (Rev. ed., 1949), p. 10.

8. *Politics*, I, 1.

9. *Social Contract*, IV. 1.

10. Ibid., II. 3.

11. Ibid., II. 3.

12. Quoted in J. M. Thompson: *French Revolution Documents*, 1789–94 (1933), p. 83 (our translation).

13. Quoted in L. G. Wickham Legg: *Select Documents of the French Revolution*, Vol. II (1905), pp. 148–9 (our translation).

14. *Leviathan*, Chap. XXIX.

15. *Philosophy of Right* (trans. T. M. Knox, 1945), Sec. 288, p. 189.

NOTES TO CHAPTER 13

1. K. Hopper: *The Poverty of Historicism* (1957), pp. 89, 90.

2. A. de Tocqueville: *Democracy in America* (ed. H. S. Commager, 1946); see especially Chapters XXV and XXXIV.

3. J. N. Figgis: *Churches in the Modern State* (1914), p. 224.

4. Court of Appeal (1954). 2. W.L.R. 691. See also House of Lords (1955). 3 W.L.R. 788.

5. For further studies in 'political pluralism' see F. W. Maitland: *Collected Papers*, Vol. III (1911) and his Introduction to O. Gierke: *Political Theories of the Middle Age* (1900). See also Leicester C. Webb (ed.): *Legal Personality and Political Pluralism* (1958).

6. A. de Tocqueville, op. cit., pp. 579–80.

7. See J. S. Mill: *On Liberty* (Everyman edn. by A. D. Lindsay), p. 164 and *passim.*

8. For further discussion see E. Westermarck, *The Future of Marriage in Western Civilization* (1936), J. Folsom, *The Family and Democratic Society* (1948), and O. MacGregor, *Divorce in England* (1957).

NOTES TO CHAPTER 14

1. T. D. Weldon: *Vocabulary of Politics* (1953), pp. 56–57.

2. See Margaret Macdonald: 'The Language of Political Theory', in *Logic and Language: First Series* (ed. A. Flew, 1951); and J. C. Rees: *The Limitations of Political Theory*, in Political Studies, Vol. II, 1954, pp. 242–57.

3. M. Macdonald, op. cit., p. 186.

4. See B. de Jouvenel: *Sovereignty* (1957), for a suggestive discussion of the relation between the attributes of leadership and the notion of Divine appointment.

5. J. W. Allen: *A History of Political Thought in the Sixteenth Century* (1941), pp. 122 and 123.

6. M. Weber: *Theory of Social and Economic Organization* (ed. Talcott Parsons, 1947), p. 301.

7. Constitution of the U.S.S.R., 1936, Art. 126.

8. See K. R. Popper: *The Poverty of Historicism* (1957).

9. Op. cit., Chapter 2.

10. Joseph de Maistre: *Etude sur la Souveraineté*, I. XII; quoted in *Une Politique Experimentale* (ed. B. de Vaulx, 1940), pp. 149–50 (Our translation).

11. Ibid., I. XIII, pp. 151–2.

12. For an account of the religious basis of Burke's political theory, see C. Parkin, *The Moral Basis of Burke's Political Thought* (1956).

13. E. Burke: *Appeal from the New to the Old Whigs*. Wks. (Bohn edn.) III, p. 111.

14. Ibid., p. 106.

15. E. Burke: *Speech on Conciliation with America*. Wks. I., p. 479.

16. E. Burke: *Reflections on the Revolution in France*. Wks. II, p. 359.

17. J. Locke: *Second Treatise of Civil Government* (Everyman ed.), pp. 230–1.

18. E. Burke: *Letter to C. J. Fox, October 8, 1777*. Wks. V., p. 453.

19. *Ethical Studies* (1927), p. 200.

20. The quotations from Professor M. Oakeshott are all from 'Political Education' in *Philosophy, Politics and Society* (ed. P. Laslett, 1956), pp. 1–21.

21. For a fuller treatment of social contract theories, see J. Gough: *The Social Contract* (2nd edn., 1957).

22. See D. Hume's Essay: *Of the Original Contract*, where he criticizes a contractual theory of obligation as superfluous.

23. *Social Contract*, I, 4.

24. *Second Treatise*, Sec. 95.

25. *Appeal from the New to the Old Whigs*. Wks. III., p. 83.

26. *Social Contract*, I, 1.

27. Ibid., II. 1.

28. Ibid., I. 2.

29. Ibid., I. 6.

30. Ibid., I. 8.

31. T. H. Green: *Lectures on the Principles of Political Obligation*. Secs. 137–47.

32. Sir Ernest Barker: *Principles of Social and Political Theory* (1951), V. 6.

33. J. Bentham: *A Fragment on Government* (ed. W. Harrison, 1948), pp. 94–5.

34. J. Gough: *John Locke's Political Philosophy* (1950), p. 72.

35. M. Macdonald, op. cit., p. 186.

NOTES TO CHAPTER 15

1. *Democracy in a World of Tensions*, UNESCO, Paris, 1951. App. III, p. 527. For an exhaustive semantic analysis of the replies to the questionnaires, see A. Naess, J. A. Christophersen, and K. Kvalø, *Democracy, Ideology and Objectivity* (1956).

2. In *Democracy in a World of Tensions*, p. 304.

3. A. V. Dicey: *Introduction to the Study of the Law of the Constitution* (ed. and rev. E. C. S. Wade, 1948), p. 73.

4. Lord Bryce: *Modern Democracies* (1921), Vol. I, p. 26.

5. See R. A. Dahl: *A Preface to Democratic Theory* (1956), pp. 130–1.

6. Quoted by J. Towster: *Political Power in the U.S.S.R.*, 1917–1947 (1948), p. 48.

7. See D. Spitz: *Patterns of Anti-Democratic Thought* (1949), for a fuller study of the critics of democracy.

8. E. Fromm: *The Fear of Freedom* (1942).

N*

9. E. Burke: *Speech to the Electors of Bristol, November* 3, 1774. Wks. (Bohn edn.). I. pp. 446–7.

10. See W. Lippman: *The Public Philosophy* (1955), for a view of the dangers of democratic institutions without courageous leadership.

11. See J. L. Talmon: *The Origins of Totalitarian Democracy* (1952), for a fuller account of Jacobin theory.

12. See A. Hamilton, J. Madison, and J. Jay: *The Federalist,* esp. No. 10 (ed. Max Beloff, 1948). Cf. also Madison's letter to Jefferson on October 17, 1788: 'Wherever the real power in a Government lies there is a danger of oppression. In our government the real power lies in the majority of the community and the invasion of private rights is *chiefly* to be apprehended not from acts of Government contrary to the sense of its constituents, but from acts in which the Government is the mere instrument of the major number of the constituents.' Quoted by Beloff, p. 478. For a criticism of Madisonian democratic theory, see R. A. Dahl, op. cit.

13. Cf. J. S. Mill: *Representative Government,* Chapter I.

14. Ibid. (Everyman edn.), pp. 208–9.

15. B. Leoni: *The Meaning of 'Political' in Political Decisions* in Political Studies, Vol. V, 1957, p. 238.

16. *Social Contract,* IV 8.

17. K. R. Popper: *The Open Society and its Enemies* (1957), Vol. I, p. 126.

18. J. Bentham: *A Fragment on Government* (ed. W. Harrison, 1948), pp. 94–5.

NOTES TO APPENDIX ON INTERNATIONAL RELATIONS

1. *The Prince,* Ch. XVIII.

2. For an introduction to the principles of International Law, see J. L. Brierly, *The Law of Nations* (5th edn., 1955).

3. Ibid., p. 72.

4. Cp. H. Sidgwick: *Elements of Politics* (2nd edn., 1897), p. 287.

5. Cp. the statement by Mrs Roosevelt, the Chairman of the Commission on Human Rights, quoted by G. Schwarzenberger: *Power Politics* (1951), p. 636.

6. See H. E. Cohen: *Recent Theories of Sovereignty* (1937), on Jellinek.

7. See A. Ross: *A Textbook of International Law* (1947)—especially his discussion of the Spanish Constitution of 1931, pp. 63–64.

INDEX

REFERENCES TO NOTES. The letters fn. following a page reference (e.g. 192fn.) indicate a note at the foot of that page.
The letter n. followed by a figure after the page number (e.g. 91n.4) refers the reader from that page of the text to the Notes to Chapters (pp. 372–388).

LIBRARY